Text and Context

Contrapuntal Readings of the Bible in World Christianity

Series Editors: K. K. Yeo, Melanie Baffes

Just as God knows no boundaries and incarnation happens in shared space, truth does not respect borders and its expression in various contexts is kaleidoscopic. As God's church is birthed forth from local cultures, it is called into a catholic community—namely world Christianity. This series values the twofold identity of biblical interpretations that seek to engage in contextual theology and, at the same time, become part of a global and "many-voiced" conversation for the sake of mutual understanding. By promoting contrapuntal readings that hold contextual and global biblical hermeneutics in tension, this series celebrates interpretations in three movements: (1) those based on the biblical text that honor multiple and interacting worldviews (reading the world biblically/theologically); (2) those that work at the translatability of the biblical text to uphold various dynamic vernaculars and faithful hermeneutics for the world (reading the Bible/theology contextually); and (3) those that respect the cross-cultural and shifting contexts in which faithful communities are embedded, and embody, real-life issues.

International Advisory Board

Walter Brueggemann, William Marcellus McPheeters Professor Emeritus of Old Testament at Columbia Theological Seminary (U.S.)

Adela Yarbro Collins, Buckingham Professor of New Testament Criticism and Interpretation, Yale Divinity School (U.S.)

Kathy Ehrensperger, Research Professor of New Testament in Jewish Perspective, University of Potsdam (Germany)

Justo L. González, Emeritus Professor of Historical Theology, Candler School of Theology, Emory University (U.S.)

Richard A. Horsley, Distinguished Professor of Liberal Arts and the Study of Religion Emeritus, University of Massachusetts—Boston (U.S.)

Robert Jewett, Emeritus Professor of New Testament at Heidelberg University (Germany)

Peter Lampe, Professor of New Testament Theology, Heidelberg University (Germany)

Tremper Longman III, Robert H. Gundry Professor Emeritus of Biblical Studies, Westmont College (U.S.)

Daniel Patte, Professor Emeritus of Religious Studies, New Testament, and Christianity, Vanderbilt University (U.S.)

Volumes in the Series (2018–2019)

Volume 1: *Text and Context: Vernacular Approaches to the Bible in Global Christianity*, edited by Melanie Baffes

Volume 2: *What Has Jerusalem to Do with Beijing? Biblical Interpretation from a Chinese Perspective* (Twentieth Anniversary Edition), K. K. Yeo

Volume 3: *Chinese Biblical Anthropology: Persons and Ideas in the Old Testament and in Modern Chinese Literature*, Cao Jian

Volume 4: *Cross-textual Reading of Ecclesiastes with Analects: In Search of Political Wisdom in a Disordered World*, Elaine Wei-Fun Goh

Text and Context

Vernacular Approaches to the Bible
in Global Christianity

Edited by
Melanie Baffes

PICKWICK *Publications* · Eugene, Oregon

TEXT AND CONTEXT
Vernacular Approaches to the Bible in Global Christianity

Contrapuntal Readings of the Bible in World Christianity 1

Copyright © 2018 Wipf and Stock Publishers. All rights reserved. Except for brief quotations in critical publications or reviews, no part of this book may be reproduced in any manner without prior written permission from the publisher. Write: Permissions, Wipf and Stock Publishers, 199 W. 8th Ave., Suite 3, Eugene, OR 97401.

Pickwick Publications
An Imprint of Wipf and Stock Publishers
199 W. 8th Ave., Suite 3
Eugene, OR 97401

www.wipfandstock.com

PAPERBACK ISBN: 978-1-5326-4340-8
HARDCOVER ISBN: 978-1-5326-4341-5
EBOOK ISBN: 978-1-5326-4342-2

Cataloguing-in-Publication Data

Names: Baffes, Melanie, editor.

Title: Text and context : vernacular approaches to the Bible in global Christianity / edited by Melanie Baffes.

Description: Eugene, OR: Pickwick Publications, 2018. | Contrapuntal Readings of the Bible in World Christianity 1. | Includes bibliographical material and index.

Identifiers: ISBN 978-1-5326-4340-8 (paperback). | ISBN: 978-1-5326-4341-5 (hardback). | ISBN: 978-1-5326-4342-2 (ebook).

Subjects: Bible—Hermeneutics. | Bible—Criticism, interpretation, etc. | Christianity and culture. | Christianity—Developing countries.

Classification: BS476 T41 2018 (print). | BS476 (ebook).

Scripture quotations in chapter 1 taken from the New Jerusalem Bible, copyright © 1985 by Darton, Longman and Todd, Ltd. and Les Editions du Cerf. Used by permission.

Scripture quotations in chapters 4, 7, 9, 10, and 11 taken from New Revised Standard Version Bible, copyright © 1989 National Council of the Churches of Christ in the United States of America. Used by permission. All rights reserved worldwide.

Scripture quotations in chapter 5 taken from the Holy Bible, NEW INTERNATIONAL VERSION®, NIV® Copyright © 1973, 1978, 1984, 2011 by Biblica, Inc.® Used by permission. All rights reserved worldwide.

Scripture quotations in chapters 8 and 12 taken from the New King James Version®. Copyright © 1982 by Thomas Nelson. Used by permission. All rights reserved.

Manufactured in the U.S.A.   10/19/18

Contents

List of Contributors | vii

Acknowledgments | xi

Introduction | 1

Part I: Reading the Bible Contextually

1 Defining a Pentecostal Hermeneutic for Africa | 11
—Marius Nel

2 Resisting Definitive Interpretation: Seeing the Story of the Exodus through Caribbean(ite) Eyes | 31
—Anna Kasafi Perkins

3 Anabaptist Hermeneutics and Theological Education | 48
—Antonio González Fernández

4 Less is More—Revisiting Classical Christian Texts in a "De-Churched" Society: The Case of Philippians | 70
—Eva van Urk and Peter-Ben Smit

5 Apostolic Hermeneutics and an Evangelical Doctrine of Scripture: Moving Beyond a Modernist Impasse | 86
—Peter Enns

Part II: Reading the World Biblically

6 "Text of Life" and "Text for Life": The Bible as the Living and Life-Giving Word of God for the Dalits | 121
—Peniel Jesudason Rufus Rajkumar

7 The Pilgrim Motif in Hebrews: A Biblical Response to the Refugee Problem in Kenya | 130
—Emily J. Choge-Kerama

8 Compelling Replication: Genesis 1:26, John 3:16, and Biblical Politics in Fiji | 149
   —Matt Tomlinson

9 The Samurai Christians: Uchimura, Ebina, and Their Bible | 172
   —Murayama Yumi

10 Homeless Voices: Self and Other | 188
   —David Nixon

11 Offending, Restoration, and the Law-Abiding Community: Restorative Justice in the New Testament and in the New Zealand Experience | 200
   —Christopher D. Marshall

12 "Discover Your Destiny": Sensation, Time, and Bible Reading among Nigerian Pentecostals | 226
   —Jesse Davie-Kessler

Subject Index | 249
Name Index | 253
Scripture Index | 259

Contributors

Emily J. Choge-Kerama is Associate Professor at Moi University, Eldoret, Kenya. She has published many articles; among them are the entry on "Social Ethics" in *The Global Dictionary of Theology* and "Hospitality in Africa" in the *Africa Bible Commentary*. She is the author of *An Ethic for Refugees: Pilgrim Motif in Hebrews and Refugee Problem in Kenya* (forthcoming 2019).

Jesse Davie-Kessler is a researcher for an education technology company. She completed a PhD in anthropology at Stanford University, where her study focused on the process through which Nigerian born-again Christians learn to experience feelings of God. Her current research centers on the interface between ethnography, teaching, and learning. She is the author of *Knowing the Cosmos, Growing the Person: Faith in a Nigerian Pentecostal Church* (2014).

Peter Enns is Abram S. Clemens Professor of Biblical Studies at Eastern University in St. Davids, Pennsylvania. His publications include *The Sin of Certainty: Why God Desires Our Trust More than Our "Correct Beliefs"* (2016), *Inspiration and Incarnation: Evangelicals and the Problem of the Old Testament* (2015), *The Bible Tells Me So: Why Defending Scripture Has Made Us Unable to Read It* (2014), and *The Evolution of Adam: What the Bible Does and Doesn't Say about Human Origins* (2012).

Antonio González Fernández is Director of Research and Publications at Fundación Xavier Zubiri in Madrid. His publications include *Surgimiento: Hacia una Ontología de la Praxis* (2014), *El Evangelio de la Paz y el Reinado de Dios* (2008), *Philosophie de la Religion et Théologie chez Xavier Zubiri* (2006), and *The Gospel of Faith and Justice* (2005).

Christopher D. Marshall holds the Diana Unwin Chair in Restorative Justice in the School of Government at Victoria University of Wellington, New Zealand. His recent publications include *All Things Reconciled: Essays* on *Restorative Justice, Religious Violence and the Interpretation of Scripture* (2018) and *Compassionate Justice: An Interdisciplinary Dialogue with Two Gospel Parables on Law, Crime, and Restorative Justice* (2012).

Murayama Yumi is a Research Fellow at the Nanzan Institute for Religion and Culture in Nagoya, Japan. She completed her PhD at the University of St. Andrews, where her dissertation addressed the role of the Bible in Imperial Japan. Her current research focuses on women and religion in modern Japan.

Marius Nel is Research Professor and Chair of Ecumenism, Pentecostalism and Neo-Pentecostalism in the Unit for Reformed Theology at North-West University in South Africa. His publications include *"He Changes Times and Seasons": Narratological-historical Investigation of Daniel 1 and 2* (2017) and *Aspects of Pentecostal Theology: Recent Developments in Africa* (2015), as well as a co-edited volume, *The New Testament in the Graeco-Roman World* (2015).

David Nixon is an Honorary Research Fellow at the University of Exeter and Dean of Studies at South West Ministry Training Course. His research interests center on the theological and sociological perspectives of marginalization. He is the author of *Stories from the Street: A Theology of Homelessness* (2016).

Anna Kasafi Perkins is Senior Programme Officer in Quality Assurance at University of the West Indies in Mona, Jamaica and Adjunct Faculty at St. Michael's Theological College in Kingston. She is the author of *Quality in Higher Education in the Caribbean* (2015), *Is Moral (Dis)ease Making Jamaica Ill?: Reengaging the Conversation on Morality* (2013), and co-editor of *Justice and Peace in a Renewed Caribbean: Contemporary Catholic Reflections* (2016).

Peniel Jesudason Rufus Rajkumar is Programme Executive for Interreligious Dialogue and Cooperation and Professor at the Ecumenical Institute, Château de Bossey, of the World Council of Churches in Geneva, Switzerland. He is author of *Dalit Theology and Dalit Liberation: Problems, Paradigms, and Possibilities* (2016) and *Asian Theology on the Way: Christianity, Culture and Context* (2015), as well as co-editor of *Many Yet One?: Multiple Religious Belonging* (2015).

Peter-Ben Smit is Professor of Contextual Biblical Interpretation in the Dom Hélder Câmara Chair at Vrije Universiteit Amsterdam, Professor by special appointment at Utrecht University, Research Associate in the Faculty of Theology at University of Pretoria (South Africa), and Dean of the Diocese of Haarlem and Assistant Pastor in the Old Catholic parish of Amsterdam. He is the author of *Masculinity and the Bible: Survey, Models, and Perspectives* (2017) and *Paradigms of Being in Christ: A Study of the Epistle to the Philippians* (2013).

Matt Tomlinson is Associate Professor of Anthropology at Australia National University's College of Asia and the Pacific in Canberra. He is the author of *Ritual Textuality: Pattern and Motion in Performance* (2014), *In God's Image: The Metaculture of Fijian Christianity* (2009), and co-editor of *The Monologic Imagination* (2017), *New Mana: Transformations of a Classic Concept in Pacific Languages and Cultures* (2016), and *Christian Politics in Oceania* (2013).

Eva van Urk is currently completing a PhD project in theology and biblical studies at the Vrije Universiteit Amsterdam. The title of her dissertation is "Religion as Ecological Resource in the Anthropocene: The *Imago Dei* in a Time of Mass Extinction."

Acknowledgments

"Resisting Definitive Interpretation: Seeing The Story of The Exodus Through Caribbean(ite) Eyes" by Anna Kasafi Perkins appeared originally in *Caribbean Quarterly* 51.2 (June 2005) 53–66. Copyright © University of the West Indies. Reprinted by permission of Taylor & Francis, Ltd, http://www.tandfonline.com on behalf of University of the West Indies.

"Anabaptist Hermeneutics and Theological Education" by Antonio González appeared originally in *Mennonite Quarterly Review* 84 (April 2010) 207–28. Copyright © *Mennonite Quarterly Review*. Reprinted by permission.

"Apostolic Hermeneutics and an Evangelical Doctrine of Scripture: Moving Beyond a Modernist Impasse" by Peter Enns appeared originally in *Westminster Theological Journal* 65 (2003) 263–87. Copyright © *Westminster Theological Journal*. Reprinted by permission.

"'Text of Life' and 'Text for Life': The Bible as the Living and Life-Giving Word of God for the Dalits" by Peniel J. Rufus Rajkumar appeared originally in *Bible in Mission*, Regnum Edinburgh Centenary Series 18, edited by Pauline Hoggarth, Fergus Macdonald, Knud Jørgensen, and Bill Mitchell, 178–84 (Oxford: Regnum Books International, 2013), ISBN: 1-9083-5542-3. Copyright © Regnum Books International. Reprinted by permission.

"Compelling Replication: Genesis 1:26, John 3:16, and Biblical Politics in Fiji" by Matt Tomlinson appeared originally in the *Journal of the Royal Anthropological Institute* 16 (2010) 743–60. Copyright © John Wiley & Sons, Inc. Reprinted by permission.

"The Samurai Christians: Uchimuro, Ebina, and Their Bible" by Murayama Yumi appeared originally as "The Samurai Bible: Ebina Danjō and Uchimura Kanzō" in *Japan Mission Journal* 70.1 (2016) 43–61. Copyright

© *Japan Mission Journal*/Oriens Institute for Religious Research. Reprinted by permission.

"Offending, Restoration, and the Law-Abiding Community: Restorative Justice in the New Testament and in the New Zealand Experience" by Christopher D. Marshall appeared originally in the *Journal of the Society of Christian Ethics* 27.2 (2007) 3–30. Copyright © The Society of Christian Ethics. Reprinted by permission.

"'Discover Your Destiny': Sensation, Time, and Bible Reading among Nigerian Pentecostals" by Jesse Davie-Kessler appeared originally in *Anthropologica* 58.1 (2016) 1–14. Copyright © 2016 Canadian Anthropology Society. Reprinted with permission from University of Toronto Press (www.utpjournals.com), DOI: https://doi.org/10.3138/anth.581.A07.

Introduction

Vernacular Hermeneutics

NEARLY TWO DECADES AGO, R. S. Sugirtharajah published a collection of essays called *Vernacular Hermeneutics*, offering interpretations of the biblical text informed by readers' identity, heritage, and experience. By calling scholars' attention to a hermeneutics that privileged indigenous culture, native characteristics, and everyday experience as legitimate sources for the construction of biblical theology, Sugirtharajah was the first to recognize the importance of "context-sensitive vernacular texts."[1] His intent was to dislodge mainstream Western theories as dominant in biblical criticism and lift up voices that had been lost among more prominent movements, including more recent developments such as Latin American Liberation Theology.

In the years since that volume first appeared, postcolonial biblical interpretation, one of the most significant movements in biblical criticism of the late twentieth century, has continued to evolve from its beginnings in liberation hermeneutics with its focus on colonization and economic exploitation to a broader emphasis on contextual hermeneutics and attention to the cultural significance of diverse communities in a globalized world. Over this same period, biblical hermeneutics has moved increasingly toward the inclusion of vernacular approaches to the text, which Sugirtharajah defines in this way:

> Vernacular interpretation seeks to overcome the remoteness and strangeness of these biblical texts by trying to make links across the cultural divides, by employing the reader's own cultural resources and social experiences to illuminate the biblical narratives . . . In opening up the biblical narratives, vernacular reading draws on three-dimensional aspects of a culture—ideational (world view, values, and rules), performational (rituals

1. Sugirtharajah, *Vernacular Hermeneutics*, 12.

and roles), and material (language, symbols, food, clothing) . . . What, in effect, such readings have done is to make culture an important site for hermeneutics.[2]

As Sugirtharajah makes clear, however, defining vernacular hermeneutics was something to be celebrated when local cultures were remote and isolated from one another. Now, in a world increasingly ordered by globalization and the intermingling of cultures, this construct is less meaningful. He warns against holding too tightly to the contrast between vernacular and metropolitan, pointing instead to the increasing need to connect the local and the global: "a hermeneutics which is capable of distinguishing between local and non-local and yet achieves continuity and unity between vernacular and metropolitan, is one that is worth upholding and promoting."[3]

More recently, Alissa Jones Nelson has fine-tuned the definition of vernacular readings as those that are "experience-primary," based on the interpreter's experience—as opposed to "idea-primary," readings grounded in an "objective" academic idea. Nelson rightly points out that, although vernacular approaches to the Bible have finally found a place in biblical scholarship, academic approaches are still prioritized over vernacular approaches in the academy: "their marginality has been firmly maintained by people in both circles" and, if "certain types of voices and certain perspectives are excluded from this conversation by the very nature of its parameters, one has to ask whether that makes for very good scholarship."[4] Nelson points to the ethical issue inherent in the field of biblical scholarship which, while acknowledging readings from diverse interpretative communities, continues to segregate them from mainstream Western criticism.[5]

Contrapuntal Readings

Both Sugirtharajah's and Nelson's work is grounded in Edward Said's concept of contrapuntal reading, which they have adapted to the field of biblical hermeneutics—specifically Said's idea that text interpretations must integrate both the dominant (colonizer) voices *and* the marginalized (colonized) voices. Said's use of the musical term "contrapuntal" signifies the bringing together of different interpretive voices without trying to harmonize or

---

2. Sugirtharajah, *Bible and the Third World*, 182.
3. Ibid., 198.
4. Nelson, *Power and Responsibility*, 1, 3–4.
5. Ibid., 1.

blend them; instead, contrapuntal readings lift up the uniqueness of each voice so, together, they create a polyphonic conversation.[6]

The *Contrapuntal Readings of the Bible in World Christianity* series celebrates biblical interpretations that engage in contextual theology while taking part in the polyphonic conversation that is global Christianity. As the first book in the series, this volume highlights reading methods and text interpretations that hold contextual and global hermeneutics in tension. They are "local" in the sense that culture (and, in some cases, faith tradition) is the site of interpretation, and "they address issues close to home"[7]; at the same time, they take their rightful place in a global, "many-voiced" conversation.

The essays in this volume also bridge the gap between vernacular/experience-primary *and* scholarly/idea-primary readings. They are vernacular in that they give readers a glimpse of how diverse communities of faith around the world read the Bible through the lens of their own contextual realities, and they reveal how these distinct contexts inform believers' understanding of the biblical texts. In addition, these essays emphasize human experience, addressing the ways in which people on the ground are living, thinking about, and experiencing the Bible.

But the essays in this volume also can be categorized as scholarly or idea-primary readings, because they employ critical interpretive approaches and ask thoughtful questions that are relevant to their communities of faith and to biblical scholars alike. The questions inherent in any interpretation of the biblical text is determined by the methods of criticism we employ; these authors ask questions that emerge directly from their contexts, choosing interpretive approaches that allow them to explore vernacular concerns and the lived experience of their faith communities.

Transforming Texts

The essays in this volume also embody another two-fold dimension of biblical texts: what Anthony Thiselton calls "transforming texts." On one hand, *interpreters can transform the meaning of texts* by bringing to bear their own experiences and cultural understandings in reading the Bible. On the other hand, those same readers and reading communities *can themselves be transformed and shaped by reading* and appropriating the messages inherent in those texts.[8] The essays in Part I of this volume, "Reading the Bible

---

6. Said, *Culture and Imperialism*, 51.
7. Sugirtharajah, *Vernacular Hermeneutics*, 12.
8. Thiselton, *New Horizons*, 31–32.

Contextually," offer glimpses of the ways in which the biblical text is being understood in various Christian communities, demonstrating *how culture is read into the biblical text*. Part II, "Reading the World Biblically," focuses on *how the Bible is read back into the culture*, illustrating how biblical narratives shape readers' understanding of themselves, others, the world, and God. These aspects of transforming texts are, of course, two sides of the same coin and many of the essays in this volume explore both dimensions.

In chapter 1, Marius Nel seeks to identify a distinctive biblical hermeneutic for African Pentecostal believers by exploring the central role of the Holy Spirit and the primacy of personal experience in the Pentecostal religious consciousness. Nel's analysis examines not only how the community's belief in an animating and empowering Holy Spirit informs Pentecostals' interpretation of the biblical narratives but also how the text in turn shapes their understanding of themselves, their faith, their ministry, and their witness.

Anna Kasafi Perkins, in chapter 2, offers an alternative perspective on the biblical story of the exodus—which too often is received by Caribbean believers as a model for interpreting their own experiences of enslavement, emancipation and the struggle for self-determination and freedom. Perkins seeks to challenge readings of Exodus, specifically those that are not liberating or life-giving, with her own reflections and with other interpretations from the margins in order to lead readers to a greater awareness of the limited and ambiguous nature of the prevailing triumphalist interpretations.

Chapter 3 examines the Anabaptist perspective, which prioritizes in its theology and hermeneutics the *following of Jesus* and the *community of the Spirit* that comes together around the act of following. Antonio González Fernández explores the crucial role of community in the act of interpreting the biblical text—an act that includes asking real-life questions and seeking intimate knowledge about how to follow Jesus—and the implications of the Anabaptist hermeneutical process for theological education today.

In chapter 4, Eva van Urk and Peter-Ben Smit explore the issue of marginality/marginalization among Dutch churches to determine whether it offers a fresh perspective for interpreting forgotten or ignored aspects of the biblical text. With marginality as their hermeneutical lens, the authors read the epistle of Paul to the Philippians, identifying the ways in which this biblical text was written *by* a marginalized author (Paul) *for* a marginalized community (the Philippians), exploring how the situation of marginality is negotiated in the letter, and relating it to the marginalization/decline experienced by churches in the Netherlands.

Peters Enns, in chapter 5, considers the apostles' "doctrine of Scripture"—specifically their interpretations of the Old Testament in the

Second-Temple period—in an effort to discern what is and what is not appropriate for the post-apostolic setting. Reclaiming the hermeneutical trajectory set by the apostles, Enns explores its usefulness for the church to engage as it continues to work out its own understanding of Scripture, and he asks whether an apostolic hermeneutic may move the church beyond the impasse imposed by modernist assumptions.

In chapter 6, Peniel Jesudason Rufus Rajkumar illustrates the two-fold role of the Bible in Dalit communities of India. On one hand, the biblical text serves as a "text *of* life" for readers by reflecting their everyday concerns and struggles; on the other hand, it is a "text *for* life" in that it offers guidance for Dalits in resisting oppression, reaffirming identity, and recovering possibilities for the flourishing of life. Rajkumar shows how, in Dalit readings of the Bible, "there is a mutual embrace of the world of the Bible and the world of the Dalits."

Chapter 7 examines the "pilgrim" or "exile" motif in the book of Hebrews as a paradigm for radical faith and hope in the face of adverse circumstances. Emily J. Choge-Kerama argues that this kind of hope should characterize the body of Christ anywhere in the world, but more specifically in Africa where wars, famine, and disease have caused huge displacements of peoples who live scattered in various lands as refugees, aliens, and strangers. In this essay, the author makes an urgent call to Christians everywhere to claim our true identity as "pilgrims and strangers" and reflect on how this will change the way we live and view the world.

Matt Tomlinson investigates in chapter 8 the dissemination and replication of biblical passages and the purpose these texts serve in markedly political contexts. By delving into the use of Gen 1:26 among indigenous Fijians in Kadavu Island, the author demonstrates the ways in which this text resonates with popular discourse about the decline and loss of a world moving farther away from the divine model, highlights the gap between divine plans and humanity's present situation, and motivates believers' attempts at personal and collective transformation.

Chapter 9 explores the impact of the Christian Bible when it was handed down to Japanese intellectuals from Western missionaries. By focusing on the theological frameworks of two prominent Japanese figures—both from samurai families—author Murayama Yumi is able to trace the influence of the biblical narratives on theological and political opinion, positions on Japanese church and society, a model for the true samurai, and the understanding of Japanese imperialism.

In chapter 10, David Nixon relates his experience conducting Contextual Bible Study with homeless individuals, a process that pays special attention to where the Bible is read and with whom. By juxtaposing biblical narratives with the perspectives of study-group participants, Nixon reveals how the text shapes these individuals' perceptions of themselves, of others, and of Jesus and God. Participants' understanding of the biblical text from a liminal, insider-outsider standpoint allows them to "subvert established discourses, providing flashes of imagery which might be deemed prophetic."

Christopher D. Marshall, in chapter 11, argues that justice in the biblical text involves proper ordering of the universe, conducting our lives as God intended us to do, and restoration of harmony when things go wrong. Based on this assumption—and on his reading of the Parable of the Prodigal Son—the author proposes a model of restorative justice as an alternative to the more common retributive and rehabilitative models found in the New Zealand system. Marshall advocates for a justice system that more closely resembles the mechanisms used by indigenous societies to address wrongdoing, healing, and well-being.

Chapter 12 considers the perspective of members of the Redeemed Christian Church of God (Pentecostal) in Nigeria, who view the Bible as both a means of immediate felt contact with God and a guide for self-improvement and moral purity. Author Jesse Davie-Kessler shows how Redeemers approach their reading of the Bible as a sensual event that involves bodily reception of the Holy Spirit in visions, voices, and feelings, as well as a temporal experience that helps them connect the present to the future as they seek to uncover their God-given destinies.

Text and Context: Vernacular Approaches to the Bible in Global Christianity builds on the important work begun by Sugirtharajah and others by exploring a broader spectrum of critical readings from around the world—and by bridging the categories of local and global, vernacular and academic, experience-primary and idea-primary. At the same time, they highlight the two-fold nature of the Bible as a transforming text: the ability to be transformed and to transform. By celebrating the dynamic faith and concrete realities of Christian believers around the world, these writings make an important contribution to the ongoing global and "many-voiced" conversation of biblical interpretation.

Bibliography

Nelson, Alissa Jones. *Power and Responsibility in Biblical Interpretation: Reading the Book of Job with Edward Said*. Bible World. Sheffield: Equinox, 2012.

Said, Edward W. *Culture and Imperialism*. New York: Knopf, 1993.

Sugirtharajah, R. S. *The Bible and the Third World: Precolonial, Colonial and Postcolonial Encounters*. Cambridge: Cambridge University Press, 2001.

———, ed. *Vernacular Hermeneutics*. The Bible in Postcolonialism 2. Sheffield: Sheffield Academic, 1999.

Thiselton, Anthony C. *New Horizons in Hermeneutics: The Theory and Practice of Transforming Biblical Reading*. Grand Rapids: Zondervan, 1992.

Part I

Reading the Bible Contextually

1

Defining a Pentecostal Hermeneutic for Africa

Marius Nel

Introduction

UNDERLYING EACH DIFFERENT THEOLOGICAL tradition is a specific way of reading and interpreting the Bible (hermeneutics), serving as a rationale for traditions distinguishing themselves from others in the broader Christian family. Conversely, these different traditions also have been shaped by their specific ways of reading and interpreting the Bible, because the interpretation of biblical texts leads to "sense-making with existential consequences,"[1] resulting in different theologies informing the different denominations.

Hermeneutics is the unavoidable activity of interpretation, an intellectual quest to discover meaning that is driven by a governing question: "What does the process of interpretation involve, and can it even uncover a conclusive meaning?"[2] The term *hermeneuein* was deployed by the Greeks to refer to three basic activities: a) to express aloud in words or vocalize; b) to explain; and c) to translate. Palmer argues that in all three cases, something foreign, strange, and separated in time, space, or experience is made familiar and comprehensible.[3] It is interpreted and explained in such a way that the unfamiliar becomes familiar.[4]

---

1. Lategan, "New Testament Hermeneutics," 13.
2. Kennedy, *Modern Introduction*, 164.
3. Palmer, *Hermeneutics*, 14.
4. Kaiser and Silva, *Introduction*, 37.

Hermeneutical Problem

A wide variety of theoretical approaches characterize the modern hermeneutical debate,[5] summarized by Thiselton as: the hermeneutics of understanding; the hermeneutics of self-involvement; the hermeneutics of metacriticism and the foundations of knowledge; the hermeneutics of suspicion and retrieval; the hermeneutics of socio-critical theory; the hermeneutics of liberation theologies and feminist theologies; the hermeneutics of reading in the context of literary theory; and the hermeneutics of reading in reader-response theories of literary meaning.[6] In discussing a Pentecostal hermeneutic, it is best classified in Thiselton's terms as a hermeneutics of metacriticism, where the foundations of knowledge, the basis of understanding the biblical text, and modern readers' possible relationship to the text's message are addressed.[7]

A Pentecostal hermeneutic emphasizes three elements: the interrelationship between the *Holy Spirit* as the One animating *Scripture* and empowering the *believing community*[8] for the purpose of equipping members for ministry and witness in culturally appropriate ways.[9] In the rest of this article, these three elements—the Holy Spirit, Scripture, and the believing community—will be explored to identify the way in which Pentecostals interpret the Bible.

The hermeneutical challenge can be described in this way. While the *Aufklärung* (Enlightenment) demanded that understanding be objective and proposed that truth could be found through rigorous methodical exercises, modern consensus holds that all understanding is necessarily based on preconceptions or presuppositions determined by prior understanding that emerges from engagement with the matter involved.[10] Readers' prior experiences and presuppositions are part of the horizon within which they will interpret what they read, with the latter influencing the present horizon. Lategan calls this the reader's "personal backpack," which comprises an individual's past experiences, preconceived ideas, an understanding of how the world works, personal prejudices, fears, and expectations.[11] It is important to know the role played by pre-understanding, although it is not necessary (or possible) to rid oneself of one's past experiences or prejudices

---

5. Cf. Ibid., 275–93.
6. Thiselton, *New Horizons*; cf. Kaiser and Silva, *Introduction*, 34.
7. Gräbe, "Hermeneutical Reflections," 14.
8. Cf. Archer, *Pentecostal Hermeneutic*.
9. Rance, "Fulfilling the Apostolic Mandate," 8.
10. Gadamer, *Warheit und Methode*, 278.
11. Lategan, "New Testament Hermeneutics," 81.

before one can participate in the act of understanding. What is necessary is rather to take the prejudices into account and place them in balance, leading to the conscious act of a fusion of horizons.[12] To understand is, according to Gadamer, to confront the text with the conscious awareness of one's pre-understandings or one's own "horizon of expectation"[13] in order to validate or correct one's pre-understandings through the text.[14] "The ongoing cyclic process of pre-understanding—challenge—rejection or acceptance—adjustment—new self-understanding—new pre-understanding is what is understood as the 'hermeneutical circle.'"[15]

A precondition to understanding is the consciousness of one's participation in the effective histories of the text—where the different variations of historical criticism (text criticism, source criticism, form criticism, tradition criticism, and later variations such as redaction criticism) can help to explain the origins of phenomena and plot their development.[16] Bultmann already emphasized that understanding implies a living relationship between the interpreter and the text based on "fore-understanding,"[17] because it is presupposed already and not attained through the process of understanding. When reading the Bible, the Christian believer utilizes necessarily a Christian existential fore-understanding,[18] because the New Testament originated within and was specifically intended for the Christian community.[19]

The Bible cannot be understood adequately in terms of an individual's self-understanding only, based on his or her participation in the world, but also must be understood from faith's self-understanding, determined by the fact that faith is a gracious act of God that happens to the one who has faith.[20] Faith is a pneumatological reality[21] and, from a Pentecostal perspective, the Bible is interpreted as the product of an experience with the Spirit that the Bible describes in phenomenological language,[22] and leading to the

12. Gadamer, *Warheit und Methode*, 289.
13. Thiselton, *New Horizons*, 61.
14. Cf. Gräbe, "Hermeneutical Reflections," 17.
15. Lategan, "New Testament Hermeneutics," 81.
16. Jeanrond, "Biblical Interpretations," 4; Lategan, "New Testament Hermeneutics," 83.
17. Gadamer, *Truth and Method*, 295; Lategan, "New Testament Hermeneutics," 35.
18. Gadamer, *Truth and Method*, 296.
19. Kasper, "Prolegomena zur Erneuerung," 523.
20. Gadamer, *Philosophical Hermeneutics*, 54.
21. Schütz, *Einführung in die Pneumatologie*, 3–4.
22. Ervin, "Hermeneutics: A Pentecostal Option," 33.

expectation by modern-day Pentecostals that the Spirit would apply biblical truth and promises to their everyday experiences and circumstances. "The experience of the presence and involvement of the Spirit in the believer's life enables one to come to terms with the apostolic witness in a truly existential manner,"[23] leading to a continuity with the original faith community for whom the epistle or gospel was intended, as well as the modern-day community.

The results of a Pentecostal encounter with the Bible are: a) a deepening respect for the witness of the Scriptures and especially the apostolic witnesses concerning Jesus contained in it;[24] b) a denial that all passages should be read and interpreted literally as though the truths contained in the passage is transferred in a mechanistic or automatic way; and c) interpretation of the biblical text within the pneumatic continuity of the faith community through all ages.[25] The community is defined in terms of being Spirit-driven, Spirit-led, and Spirit-empowered to accomplish God's purposes for and through the community, a community that is to be Spirit-governed, Spirit-supported, and Spirit-propagated.[26]

If understanding is defined as the fusion of horizons conditioned by effective historical criticism, the important question remains: how does one validate one's experience with the text? Ricoeur was concerned about text comprehension and showed that the relationship between interpreter and text should be approached methodically in a critically accountable way.[27] The interpretive process is dialectical, progressing from an initial naive understanding to an explanation of the text, and a deeper understanding of the text and a methodological validation of the results of the first or naive understanding.[28]

True understanding always includes the act of application.[29] The text that is understood historically always is forced to abandon its claim that it is uttering something true, argues Gadamer, and the acknowledgment of the otherness of the other involves the fundamental suspension of its claim to truth, leading to the dilemma of theology when the biblical text is applied in an edifying way in Christian preaching.[30] Here, understanding involves

---

23. Gräbe, "Hermeneutical Reflections," 19.
24. Gee, *Pentecost*, 8.
25. Gräbe, "Hermeneutical Reflections," 19.
26. Rance, "Fulfilling the Apostolic Mandate," 9.
27. Jeanrond, *Text und Interpretation*, 27.
28. Jeanrond, "Biblical Interpretation," 5; *Text und Interpretation*, 42.
29. Gadamer, *Truth and Method*, 270.
30. Kaiser and Silva, *Introduction*, 329.

the application of the text to be understood to the present situation of the interpreter.[31]

The relationship between interpreter and text consists in "understanding"; the methodological activity taking place between interpreter and text leads to "explanation"; a last element consists in "assessment," consisting of the reader's personal responsibility toward the meaning of the text that opens up before them.[32] Assessment of biblical texts consists of discovering the claim(s) made by the text and making a personal response to it.

By way of concluding, faith does not render scientific, methodologically-controlled interpretation of biblical texts impossible but forms a framework that makes the enterprise meaningful.[33] However, the ceaseless movement of biblical interpretation begins and ends in the risk of a response, which is not exhausted by commentary.[34] Faith forms the necessary and unique from which basis believers orient themselves in all their choices. Hermeneutics reminds us that biblical faith cannot be separated from the movement of interpretation, which elevates it into language.[35] Faith is interpreted from a Pentecostal perspective as a transforming and empowering encounter with the divine, as described in Acts, leading to a Christian community eager to bear witness to the power and love of God that they experienced[36] and a consciousness of the real presence and power of the Spirit.

The Pentecostal movement believes that the Spirit has manifest itself again with glossolalia, prophecy, miracles of healing, and other signs happening in contemporary times. Pentecostals now read the Bible in order to understand themselves,[37] a mode of subjectivity that responds and corresponds to the power of the New Testament to display its own world radiated by the living Lord and present among his people, the community of faith, through the Holy Spirit. And they also expect these same signs and wonders to occur in their ministry; they prioritize spectacular displays of celestial power, such as healing and deliverance from sinful habits and Satanic bondage, to authenticate the preaching of the Word and leading to faith in the Word.[38]

31. Gadamer, *Truth and Method*, 274; Kaiser and Silva, *Introduction*, 328.
32. Jeanrond, *Text und Interpretation*, 70, 125.
33. Stuhlmacher, *Vom Verstehen*, 204.
34. Ricoeur, "Philosophical Hermeneutics," 31.
35. Kaiser and Silva, *Introduction*, 56; Gräbe, "Hermeneutical Reflections," 23.
36. Schnackenburg, *Belief in the New Testament*, 81–82.
37. Ricoeur, "Philosophical Hermeneutics," 30.
38. Anderson, "Towards a Pentecostal Ecclesiology," 5.

The Centrality of the Holy Spirit

At the heart of classical Pentecostalism stands the Bible as the inspired Word of God, affirming that the (whole) Bible is a reliable revelation of God, and that it states the exact truths that the Holy Spirit intends to convey.[39] The starting point and foundation for Pentecostal faith and praxis is the biblical text; the distinctive nature and function of Scripture in the faith community only can be realized in terms of the role of the Spirit.[40] The three main elements of a Pentecostal hermeneutic can thus be described as: the interrelationship between the *Holy Spirit* as the One animating *Scripture* and empowering the *believing community* in order to realize the Christ-event in the present, with the purpose of equipping members for ministry and witness in culturally appropriate ways. These three elements are now explored in order to demonstrate how Pentecostals interpret what they read in the Bible.

Holy Spirit as the One Who Realizes the Christ-event in the Present

The accusation has been leveled at Pentecostals that they emphasize the work of the Spirit at the cost of the christocentric gospel.[41] However, Pentecostals teach that the experience of an encounter with Christ is the result of the Spirit revelation that never leaves a person neutral.[42] The center of the Christian message is Jesus Christ, Pentecostals confess; what is critical for them is the personal awareness of and experiencing of the indwelling of the Spirit who sets Jesus present in the daily life of the believer.[43] The Spirit facilitates the encounter with Christ.

The doctrine is upheld that the Holy Spirit dwells in some sense, and to some extent, in every believer, but there is another gift that Pentecostals expect and wait for, entirely distinct and separate from conversion and acceptance of the forgiveness of sins. Christians need this gift in order to be empowered for service.[44] Möller describes this experience as a gift of grace based on the promise of Acts 1:5, 8—that God would reveal himself in a personal, immediate, intimate, and lasting way to believers by bringing

---

39. Arrington, "Use of the Bible," 101.
40. Ibid., 107.
41. Möller, "Christ and Pentecostalism," 140.
42. Ma, "Full Circle Mission," 8.
43. Williams, "Pentecostal Reality," 1.
44. Daniels, *Moody*, 396–403 (quoting Moody); Harper, "Waves Keep Coming," 105.

humans under the control and fullness of his Spirit, leading to their sensitized consciousness of the risen and glorified Christ in their lives, resulting in being more effective witnesses for Christ and worshipping him in a fuller dimension.[45] While Protestants emphasize orthodoxy (correctness of doctrine and confession as derived from Scripture), Pentecostals stress orthopraxy. They do not deny the importance of doctrine being founded on the Bible, but they seek validation of doctrinal truth in the dynamic activity of the Spirit. In their preaching, they do not primarily aim to communicate doctrinal truths but to minister to the spiritual, physical, psychological, and social needs of the people assembled to meet the Word, Jesus Christ.[46] The liturgical implication is that many worship services in Pentecostal churches allow for prayers for and ministry to people in need, changing the worship service into an experiential event for attendees.

The emphasis on experience of an encounter with Christ can be linked to postmodern thought. Pentecostalism stands over against modernism's philosophical presupposition, shared by (cessationist) fundamentalists, that only what can be proven to be historically and objectively true is meaningful.[47] Central to the Pentecostal worldview is the confession that God speaks and acts today as he did as recorded in the Bible, leading to a high valuation of experience and non-rational forms of knowing and a resultant unfortunate scepticism toward learning and higher education, as almost opposed to the (S)spirit.[48] Stronstad's analysis of a Pentecostal hermeneutic consists of three elements; that it is *experiential*, at both levels of presupposition and verification; *rational*, by incorporating historical-grammatical principles of exegesis; and *pneumatic*, as it recognizes the Spirit as illuminator and inspirer of Scripture.[49] However, his analysis is positivistic and limited to a segment of a diverse Pentecostal movement, where a majority (conservative) devalues (with some justice) the second element consisting of rational forms of knowing.

Pentecostals emphasize re-experiencing the biblical text through preaching an immediate meaning for Scripture, sometimes with little significance placed on the original context, and accompanied by the giving of testimonies that God is still working miracles in the present as found in biblical narratives.[50] Klaus speaks of believers' participating in Christ's

---

45. Möller, *Die Diskussie van die Charismata*, 43–4.
46. Clark and Lederle, *What Is Distinctive?*, 64–5.
47. Cargal, "Beyond the Fundamentalist-Modernist Controversy," 168.
48. Turnage, "Early Church," 9.
49. Stronstad, "Pentecostal Experience," 25.
50. Fogarty, "Toward a Pentecostal Hermeneutic," 5.

continuing redemptive ministry, empowered by the Spirit before Christ's return.[51]

The risen Christ is a reality that believers experience on a continual basis through the working of the Spirit. The Spirit empowers the believing community by introducing them to Christ and by enriching them with his gifts and fruit; the Spirit also bridges the gap between encounters that early disciples had with Jesus and believers' present encounters with him,[52] leading them in all truth (John 16:13). The Spirit is the power through which the exalted Lord is present in the history of the cosmos as principle of a new history and a new world.[53] "The baptism into the Holy Spirit is not an encounter with the Spirit but with Christ, the baptizer. This means total surrender and absolute commitment to Jesus. Without this, he cannot baptize a believer in the Spirit."[54]

Pentecostals interpret Ezek 37 as the work of the Spirit in the age of the new covenant to revive the dry bones, and Isa 44 as bringing seemingly dead people to new life and vitality.[55] As the rain brings the promise of new life and vitality, the outpouring of the Spirit promised in Joel 2 and 3 is interpreted as leading to a new dispensation related to the Spirit.[56] Lochman describes the "new" element in terms of *Vergegenwärtigung* (making present of) and *Teilhabe* (gaining part of);[57] the Spirit is the power through which God is made present in the Christ event, allowing God to be involved and partake directly in the life of the present-day church. Christians live in the "relevant presence of God,"[58] changing their perspective on reality dramatically.

Not only does the Spirit in the daily lives of believers introduce God, but also the Spirit allows believers to partake in the divine. People are not only the object of God's interest, but also, they are addressed in their subjectiveness. The crucified and resurrected Lord is present in the midst of his people; to understand in what way, it is necessary to know what the New Testament teaches about the Spirit, explaining Pentecostal interest in the subject.[59] For Pentecostal people, the apostolic witness is crucial, as can be seen

---

51. Klaus, "Pentecostalism and Mission," 8.
52. Veenhof, "Holy Spirit," 115.
53. Gräbe, "Hermeneutical Reflections," 14.
54. Du Plessis, *Spirit Bade Me Go*, 71.
55. Schafroth, "An Exegetical Exploration," 62–63.
56. Lochman, *Das Glaubensbekenntnis*, 149.
57. Ibid., 150.
58. Gräbe, "Hermeneutical Reflections," 16.
59. De Beer, *Valence of Spirit Manifestation*, 380.

in their preference for the term to be incorporated in the early Pentecostal movement. For example, the Azusa Street Mission, where the Pentecostal movement originated, was called "Apostolic Faith Mission,"[60] and the earliest magazine published by the mission was called "The Apostolic Faith."[61] The apostles were the direct witnesses of Jesus's life and ministry, and their message is seen as one of primary importance. The New Testament as the result of their preaching sees an essential identity and continuity between Jesus of Galilee and the Lord who promises to be with them always—to the end of time (Matt 28:20).

Holy Spirit as the One Who Quickens and Animates Scripture

Archer comments on Pentecostals' life with the Bible:

> Pentecostals love their Bible. Biblical themes, stories and significant biblical numbers (3, 7, 12, 40) permeate Pentecostal literature. More importantly, these things saturate Pentecostal oral testimonies. In their narrated testimonies, one can clearly hear echoes of biblical stories, themes and phrases. Pentecostals assimilated scriptural stories, verses and concepts into their interpretation of reality.[62]

The Bible speaks about God and claims to be his Word, a claim that results in Pentecostals' acknowledgement of the homiletical value of the Bible and the necessity of the Spirit's guidance in interpreting it. However, it is not doctrine or tradition that makes Pentecostalism what it is; it is the presence of God in and among his people "in a manner which is readily evident to participator and bystander alike."[63] Pentecostal experience of the Spirit is in Pentecostal hermeneutics the legitimate presupposition of biblical interpretation.[64] For this reason, the goal of studying Scripture is "knowledge of (not simply about) God."[65] Understanding Scripture serves the larger aim of knowing God. Pentecostals emphasize that the authority of the Spirit comes before the authority of Scripture.

---

60. Burger and Nel, *Fire Falls in Africa*, 18.
61. McClung, *Azusa Street and Beyond*, 22.
62. Archer, *Pentecostal Hermeneutic*, 161.
63. Clark and Lederle, *What Is Distinctive?*, 65.
64. Stronstad, "Pentecostal Experience," 18.
65. Autry, "Dimensions of Hermeneutics," 42.

The same God who spoke and acted in salvation-history events and in the inspiration of Scripture speaks and acts today, and Pentecostals read the Bible in order to find the hermeneutical implications of God's present activity in the faith community.[66] The Bible does not present itself as the Word of God per se, but what we read in the Bible is mentioning of or references to the Word of God.[67] Although God inspires the Bible, not everything in the Bible is from divine origins or a report of God's words and acts. Biblical writers utilized information available to their contemporaries and at times reported what they heard. The words of sinful and uninspired people also are written down. That the Bible is inspired implies that what is written down in the Bible is what God wanted to present to people and what is necessary for sinful man to know about God and to live in correct relationship with him.[68] The Bible is called the Word of God when it contains something that Jesus revealed about God (John 14:24; 17:14, 17), as a reference to the message of the gospel (Rev 1:2, 9), or what God revealed to the prophets and other individuals (Isa 2:3; Dan 9:2; Hos 1:1; 1 Thess 4:15).[69]

The Word is God, but the Bible is not God. The Bible is the written witness about the Word of God, a road sign indicating the way to God and containing everything needed by humans about God and his will.[70] As a result, Scripture is viewed as the primal point of reference for encounter with God, because "(t)o encounter the Scriptures is to encounter God."[71] Reading Scripture should lead to affective transformation to be effective, although it does not exclude intellectual understanding as necessary in the Pentecostal understanding of truth based on Scripture. McQueen argues that a distinctive Pentecostal experiential pre-understanding determines how Pentecostals read the Bible, and experience plays a dialogical role in opening up the biblical text.[72] Although he adds that the communal nature of a Pentecostal hermeneutic demands that conclusions reached be viewed as one member's voice among those of other members of the Christian community, he uses his Pentecostal experience to interpret Joel in an invalid way.[73] He bases his reading of the Bible on Moore's[74] suggestion that an implosion of "utter

66. McQueen, *Joel and the Spirit*, 3–4.
67. Möller, *Words of Light and Life*, 91.
68. Nelson and Wawire, *Bible Doctrines*, 14.
69. Möller, *Words of Light and Life*, 91.
70. Ibid., 93.
71. Johns, *Pentecostal Formation*, 14.
72. McQueen, *Joel and the Spirit*, 5.
73. Ibid., 6, 106–7.
74. Moore, "Deuteronomy and the Fire of God," 23.

confession and utter criticism" occurs at the core of the Pentecostal experience. In those moments of intense encounter and communion of the believer with the Spirit, known in and expected by the Pentecostal community, confession is evoked by the claim of the Spirit. The believer is so claimed by the Spirit as "to be disclaimed, to be seized, taken captive and dispossessed of everything previously claimed," that these moments become critical. And even though it occurs outside the dialectic of text and reader, it opens up a different reading of reality and a different reading of the text.[75]

To be a Pentecostal interpreter of Scripture, one's confession about the text must agree with the previously evoked confession about the Spirit. The claim of the Spirit will be in agreement with the claim of the text, and one comes to know the claim of the text in light of the claim of the Spirit.[76] This is where the danger of subjectivism looms, as McQueen illustrates when he describes his experience of "a glorious encounter with the Spirit who filled me with rejoicing . . . Groans were replaced with glossolalia, and I was filled with a new sense of emotional and intellectual integration."[77] In this way, his conclusions in reading Joel were illuminated by Pentecostal experience. His experience allowed him to look "with new eyes intuitively focused" on the biblical book, and three "confessions" arose out of the encounter: That the book of Joel enjoys literary and theological unity; that the theme of judgment in the book should not be subsumed under the theme of salvation, as happens in many commentaries, but should form a separate and third theme; and that the transitions between the three movements of the book of Joel are found in the interaction of human cry and divine response.[78] However, these conclusions are based on a rational reading of the book and to claim a pneumatological precedent for attaching authority to one's understanding of the biblical book is rather subjectivist and far-fetched. "Pentecostals do not found their understanding of the authority of Scripture on a bedrock of doctrine, but that, in fact, their doctrine is itself resting on something more fundamental, dynamic and resilient; their experience of encountering a living God, directly and personally."[79]

Möller distinguishes between *fides humana* and *fides divina* at the hand of 1 Cor 2:4–5's reference to Paul's proclamation that was not "meant to convince by philosophical argument, but to demonstrate the convincing power of the Spirit, so that your faith should depend not on human wisdom

---

75. Ibid.
76. McQueen, *Joel and the Spirit*, 106.
77. Ibid., 107.
78. Ibid., 107–8.
79. Ellington, "Pentecostalism and the Authority of Scripture," 17.

but on the power of God."[80] Pentecostal *hermeneusis* allows that a passage in Scripture may address an individual in certain circumstances while, at a later stage in different circumstances, the passage does not address the same person;[81] the Spirit convinces the reader that the specific encounter with the Bible passage contains a unique revelation of God for them.[82] This, however, does not imply that the study of the Bible should not try to determine what the biblical writer intended as a message for the original listeners or readers (hermeneutics).

Pentecostals believe that the Bible contains not only the Word of God for human beings but also a specific word for their situation. A result of reading the Bible prayerfully in the belief that the Spirit will reveal Christ (or the Word) to them is that they apply promises from the Bible as though it is given to them when they experience that the Spirit highlights a specific passage for them. In this way, they read the Bible from a promise-fulfilment scheme, applying certain passages to their daily situation.[83] This may lead to the situation where the Bible is read a-historically, as though the text has no history or an underlying theology or ideology, allowing them to find an uncomplicated message directed to their present-day circumstances, a kind of *lectio divina* borrowed from mystical theology. The working of the Spirit (subjectively evaluated) is then supposed to guarantee that the Word becomes the truth of God for them in today's world. Pentecostals agree with Karl Barth who described Scripture as becoming the Word of God to the reader or hearer through the action and participation of the Spirit.[84] The danger is evident, that the reader hears in the Bible what they wish to hear. It may happen when Pentecostals allow for a directly inspired word from God functioning outside the narrow borders of the Bible, called "prophecy," where one person feels inspired by the Spirit to speak a personal and individualised word to another or to the assembly as they perceive it to be a word from God.

How can dangerous subjectivizing tendencies in a Pentecostal hermeneutic be avoided? Thomas suggests a holistic Pentecostal hermeneutic that incorporates both Spirit and experience and he deduces his paradigm from Acts 15, where Spirit and community play an important role in the

---

80. Möller, *Words of Light and Life*, 97. All biblical citations are from the New Jerusalem Bible (NJB).

81. Van der Walt and Jordaan, "Die Kontekstualisering," 508.

82. Althouse, "Towards a Pentecostal Ecclesiology," 8.

83. Rance, "Fulfilling the Apostolic Mandate," 17.

84. Clark, *Investigation*, 57; Fogarty, "Toward a Pentecostal Hermeneutic," 7.

interpretive approach regarding the issue of Gentile Christians.[85] He observes that the interpretive process moves from the believing community's context to the biblical text. This reverses the order of exegetical processes that normally start from the text and then move to the context. The Spirit enables the community that depends upon the Spirit to enlighten them in the interpretive process. This dependence goes far beyond evangelical claims to "illumination by the Spirit." The Spirit actually guides the community into a new understanding of God's will. The three primary components in the hermeneutic are the community, the activity of the Spirit, and Scripture. These components are not static but are in dialogue with each other. The community testifies to the experiences attributed to the Spirit and then engages Scripture to validate or repudiate the experience or issue, necessitating a dynamic balance between individual, Spirit, Scripture, and faith community.[86] In this way, Scripture becomes authoritative and central to the rule and conduct of the church. Pinnock explains that the community needs the controlled liberty of the Spirit, where the Spirit takes what the inspired authors intended to say and discloses its significance for the contemporary community.[87] The original meaning is determinate and does not change, but God's Spirit in his working out of salvation history uses this witness in new ways in ever new settings, creating significance for readers and hearers. "The Spirit is active in the life of the whole church to interpret the biblical message in the languages of today. He actualises the word of God by helping us to restate the message in contemporary terminology and apply it to fresh situations. The result is that salvation history continues to take effect in us."[88]

In his quantitative research, Huckle finds that prophecy influences the contemporary American Pentecostal church to a large extent, that prophecy is understood in terms of personal and communal enlightenment and encouragement, and that nearly 95 percent of fellowships surveyed used Scripture to judge prophecies, as doctrinal statements of these denominations require.[89] However, most respondents did not bring prophecy into relation with explication of Scripture. Prophecy did help some to apply the Bible to a specific situation or emphasize the blessings of God as expounded in Scripture, but they realized that they should not be viewed as additions to

---

85. Thomas, "Women, Pentecostals and the Bible," 43.
86. Ellington, "Pentecostalism and the Authority of Scripture," 28.
87. Pinnock, "Work of the Holy Spirit," 4.
88. Ibid.
89. Huckle, "Contemporary Use of the Gift," 84.

the written Bible. Where they have been equated with Scripture, the dangers of heretical doctrine became very real.

Holy Spirit as Present among the People, the Community of Faith

What distinguishes Pentecostal Bible reading from other traditions is not a different interpretive method but a distinct meta-narrative that leads to a coherent and cohesive interpretive manner in which the Spirit plays the most important role, and the community of faith and its story forms the influential hermeneutical filter as pre-understanding forming the condition for understanding.

The use of any method is not objectively free from the social and cultural location of the person utilising it; both method and person-in-community have been historically conditioned.[90] Comprehension is both discovery and creation of meaningful understanding.[91] McQueen also emphasizes that methodology can never be value-free. There must be a correspondence between method and content, between formal and substantive matters.[92] He concludes that a hermeneutic that embraces the critical claim of the Spirit simply cannot be fitted into a methodology that allows reason to be the final arbiter of truth, no matter how critical or creative the results.

Although the Pentecostal community is part of the larger Christian community, it is different from the rest of the Christian world due to its distinct narrative tradition. The Pentecostal community is bound together by a shared Pentecostal experience of baptism with the Spirit, leading to a shared story based on the meta-narrative of the general Christian story about the meaning of creation and God's role in creation, as derived from the general narrative found in the Bible.[93] However, Pentecostals concentrate specifically on the narratives found in the New Testament relating to encounters of early Christians with the Holy Spirit leading to an emphasis on the synoptic gospels (with a predilection for Luke[94]—and especially Acts of the Apostles).[95] Because the Pentecostal community understands itself to be a restorationist movement, it argues in many instances also that it is the best representation of Christianity as an authentic continuation of

---

90. Archer, *Pentecostal Hermeneutic*, 129.
91. Lategan, "Hermeneutics," 153–54.
92. McQueen, *Joel and the Spirit*, 109.
93. Cf. Fackre, *Christian Story*, 8–9; Nelson and Wawire, *Bible Doctrines*, 14.
94. Mittelstadt, *Reading Luke-Acts*, 2–3.
95. Hollenweger, *Pentecostals*, 336; Mittelstadt, *Spirit and Suffering*, 2.

the New-Testament church.[96] However, its conservative nature also allows for operating legalistically when it succumbs to over-literal interpretations of Scripture, leading it to become socially unhelpful—for instance, in the age of the earth debates, the role of women in the church and society, and the uncritical acceptance of the authority of governments.[97] Rather, Clark argues, the Bible should be used to provide direction and boundaries to proclamation and experience, with "text" and "Spirit" proving balanced emphases.

Pentecostals regard their narrative tradition as synonymous with the New-Testament narratives of experiences with baptism in the Spirit, and this narrative tradition provides the context for their search for meaning when they read the Bible. Penney says that the experience of the day of Pentecost in Acts 2 becomes a "normative paradigm for every Christian to preach the gospel," and that Luke's "primary and pervasive interest is the working of the Holy Spirit in initiating, empowering and directing the church in its eschatological worldwide mission."[98] In this way, an experiential narrative forms the hermeneutical framework for interpreting Scripture, as well as for experiencing reality. Their narrative tradition allows for God's involvement in restoring the Spirit and its gifts to the Christian community, and God's dramatic involvement in their reality and biblical events are interpreted to allow for the same miracles and interventions from the "other side" to happen in their world. They desire to live as the eschatological people of God as part of the final drama of God's redemptive action, during the last of the last days.

All reading is a transaction between the biblical text and the community, which results in the finding of meaning approximated by the reader.[99] Between the biblical text and the community, there is a dialectical encounter made possible by a working plot within the biblical story that is recreated in the community. Hawk explains that a plot functions on the surface level of a tale as the framework of the story and as the arrangement of incidents and patterns as they relate to each other in a story, but the abstract notion of plot also operates within the mind of the reader who organizes and makes connections between events and relates present-day experiences to the plot in the tale.[100]

---

96. Archer, *Pentecostal Hermeneutic*, 133.
97. Clark, "Pentecostalism and Philosophy of Religion," 3.
98. In Anderson, "Towards a Pentecostal Missiology," 3.
99. Hart, *Faith Thinking*, 107.
100. Hawk, *Every Promise Fulfilled*, 19; Hart, *Faith Thinking*, 27.

The Pentecostal community reads Scripture in order to develop a praxis where biblical tales are placed into the cohesive Pentecostal narrative tradition that interprets Pentecostal existence in terms of the outpouring of the Spirit. Biblical tales challenge and reshape the Pentecostal tradition and provide language to describe their praxis. In this way, the encounter between biblical text and community is dialogical as well as dialectical, and the search for and approximation of meaning takes place primarily within the community.[101] Pentecostal interpretation of the Bible includes an act of obedient response to Scripture's meaning,[102] as perceived by the Pentecostal community.

Stronstad challenges two standard evangelical principles of hermeneutics, using textual evidence: first, he challenges evangelicals' hermeneutical principle to use Paul to color all discussions of the Holy Spirit; he argues that Luke's and Paul's pneumatological lenses were different, with Paul using primarily salvation-initiation language and Luke using subsequent-empowerment language. He suggests that Luke should be left to speak for himself and that it would demonstrate the uniqueness of Luke. The second principle he challenges is that the didactic genre of Scripture should be used exclusively to define doctrine, while the narrative genre should be used to reconstruct the history. Stronstad demonstrates the legitimacy of the narrative genre to carry theological intent, recognizing the legitimacy of the Pentecostal nexus that shapes Pentecostal mission and mission strategy.[103]

Two important differences between Pentecostals and many evangelicals flow from Pentecostals' emphasis on the Spirit's involvement in explicating Scripture: They emphasize an immediate and experiential meaning for Scripture that does not necessarily exactly equate with a historical-critical or grammatical-historical analysis of the text, and they believe that the Spirit can say more than Scripture, although never in contradiction to Scripture.[104] A hermeneutic that focuses only on what the original author meant (if it is possible to determine it) does not satisfy Pentecostal sentiments, which assert that the spiritual and extraordinary supernatural experiences of biblical characters are to be duplicated for contemporary believers. A Pentecostal hermeneutic will always take into account the role of the Spirit and the impact of personal experience.

---

101. Fish, *Is There a Text in this Class?*, 34.

102. Archer, *Pentecostal Hermeneutic*, 136.

103. Stronstad, *Charismatic Theology*, 49; cf. Menzies, *Development of Early Christian Pneumatology*; Penney, *Missionary Emphasis*, 84.

104. Fogarty, "Toward a Pentecostal Hermeneutic," 5–6.

Conclusion

Why do Pentecostal people reach different conclusions when they read the Bible compared to believers in other Christian traditions? And how does their hermeneutic inform their practice? It has been argued that a Pentecostal hermeneutic emphasizes three elements: the interrelationship between the *Holy Spirit* as the One animating *Scripture* and empowering the *believing community*. For them, the experience of an encounter with God through his Spirit is imperative, and interpretation of the information contained in the Bible is determined by their praxis.

Bibliography

Althouse, Peter. "Towards a Pentecostal Ecclesiology: Participation in the Missional Life of the Triune God." Paper presented at the Society for Pentecostal Studies, 38th Annual Meeting, Eugene, OR., March 27, 2009.

Anderson, Allan. "Towards a Pentecostal Missiology for the Majority World." Paper presented at the International Symposium on Pentecostal Missiology, Asia-Pacific Theological Seminary, Baguio City, Philippines, January 29–30, 2003.

Archer, Kenneth J. *A Pentecostal Hermeneutic: Spirit, Scripture and Community*. Cleveland: CPT, 2009.

Arrington, F. L. "The Use of the Bible by Pentecostals." *PNEUMA: The Journal of the Society for Pentecostal Studies* 16.1 (1996) 101–7.

Autry, Arden C. "Dimensions of Hermeneutics in Pentecostal Focus." *Journal of Pentecostal Theology* 1.3 (1993) 29–50.

Burger, Isak, and Marius Nel. *The Fire Falls in Africa: A History of the Apostolic Faith Mission of South Africa*. Vereeniging: Christian Art, 2008.

Cargal, T. B. "Beyond the Fundamentalist-Modernist Controversy: Pentecostals and Hermeneutics in a Postmodern age." *PNEUMA: The Journal of the Society for Pentecostal Studies* 15 (1993) 163–87.

Clark, Mathew. "An Investigation into the Nature of a Viable Pentecostal Hermeneutic." ThD diss., University of South Africa, 1997.

———. "Pentecostalism and Philosophy of Religion." Paper presented at the Philosophy and Religious Practices Workshop, University of Wales, Cardiff, UK, May 2013. https://philosophyreligion.wordpress.com/2013/05.

Clark, M. S., and Lederle, H.I. *What Is Distinctive about Pentecostal Theology?* Miscellanea Specialia 1, Unisa. Pretoria: University of South Africa, 1989.

Daniels, W. H., ed. *Moody: His Words, Works, and Workers*. New York: Nelson & Phillips, 1877.

De Beer, F. J. "The Valence of Spirit Manifestation, and Its Influence on the Transformation of the Mind and Redemption of the Body and Flesh according to Romans 8 and 12 and Its Application in a Secular Society." DLitt et Phil diss., University of Johannesburg, 2014.

Du Plessis, David. *The Spirit Bade Me Go: The Astounding Move of God in the Denominational Churches*. Gainesville, FL: Bridge-Logos, 2004.

Ellington, Scott A. "Pentecostalism and the Authority of Scripture." *Journal of Pentecostal Theology* 9 (1996) 16–38.

Ervin, Howard M. "Hermeneutics: A Pentecostal Option." In *Essays on Apostolic Themes: Studies in Honour of Howard M. Ervin*, edited by Paul Elbert, 23–35. Eugene, OR: Wipf & Stock, 2007.

Fackre, Gabriel J. *The Christian Story: A Narrative Interpretation of Basic Christian Doctrine*. 3rd ed. Grand Rapids: Eerdmans, 1996.

Fish, Stanley. *Is There a Text in this Class? The Authority of Interpretive Communities*. Cambridge: Harvard University Press, 1980.

Fogarty, Stephen. "Toward a Pentecostal Hermeneutic." Webjournals.ac.edu.au. http://webjournals.ac.edu.au/ojs/index.php/PCBC/article/view/8912/8909.

Gadamer, Hans-Georg. *Wahrheit und Methode: Grundzüge einer philosophischen Hermeneutik*. 2. Aufl. Tübingen: Mohr, 1965.

———. *Philosophical Hermeneutics*. Translated by David E. Linge. Berkeley: University of California Press, 1976.

———. *Truth and Method*. Translated by William Glen-Doepel. London: Sheed & Ward, 1979.

Gee, Donald. *Pentecost*. Springfield, MO: Gospel, 1932.

Gräbe, P. J. "Hermeneutical Reflections on the Interpretation of the New Testament with Special Reference to the Holy Spirit and Faith." In *The Reality of the Holy Spirit in the Church: In Honour of F. P. Möller*, edited by P. J. Gräbe and W. J. Hattingh, 14–26. Pretoria: van Schaik, 1997.

Harper, Michael. "The Waves Keep Coming In." *Journal of the European Pentecostal Theological Association* 28.2 (2008) 102–16.

Hart, Trevor A. *Faith Thinking: The Dynamics of Christian Theology*. London: SPCK, 1995.

Hawk, L. Daniel. *Every Promise Fulfilled: Contesting Plots in Joshua*. Louisville: Westminster John Knox, 1991.

Hollenweger, Walter J. *The Pentecostals*. London: SCM, 1988.

Huckle, John S. "The Contemporary Use of the Gift of Prophecy in Gatherings of Christians in Comparison with their Use in the 20th Century." *Journal of the European Pentecostal Theological Association* 29.1 (2009) 73–86.

Jeanrond, W. G. "Biblical Interpretation as Appropriation of Texts: The Need for a Closer Cooperation between Biblical Exegetes and Systematic Theologians." *Proceedings of the Irish Biblical Association* 6 (1982) 1–18.

———. *Text und Interpretation als Kategorien Theologischen Denkens*. Hermeneutische Untersuchungen zur Theologie 23. Tübingen: Mohr/Siebeck, 1986.

Johns, Cheryl Bridges. *Pentecostal Formation: A Pedagogy among the Suppressed*. Journal of Pentecostal Theology Supplement 2. Sheffield: Sheffield Academic, 1993.

Kaiser, Walter C., Jr., and Moisés Silva. *Introduction to Biblical Hermeneutics: The Search for Meaning*. Rev. ed. Grand Rapids: Zondervan, 1994.

Kasper, W. "Prolegomena zur Erneuerung der Geistlichen Schriftauslegung." In *Vom Urchristentum zu Jesus: Für Joachim Gnilka*, edited by Hubert Frankemöller, and Karl Kertelge, 508–52. Freiburg: Herder, 1989.

Kennedy, Philip. *A Modern Introduction to Theology: New Questions for Old Beliefs*. London: IB Tauris, 2006.

Klaus, B. D. "Pentecostalism and Mission." Paper presented at the American Society of Missiology, Assemblies of God Theological Seminary, Springfield, MO, June 17, 2006.

Lategan, B. C. "Hermeneutics." In *Anchor Bible Dictionary*, edited by David Noel Freedman, 3:153–4. 6 vols. New York: Doubleday, 1992.

———. "New Testament Hermeneutics (Part I): Defining Moments in the Development of Biblical Hermeneutics." In *Focusing on the Message: New Testament Hermeneutics, Exegesis and Methods*, edited by Andreas B. Du Toit, 13–63. Pretoria: Protea, 2009.

———. "New Testament Hermeneutics (Part II): Mapping the Biblical Hermeneutics." In *Focusing on the Message: New Testament Hermeneutics, Exegesis and Methods*, edited by Andreas B. Du Toit, 65–105. Pretoria: Protea, 2009.

Lochmann, Jan Milič. *Das Glaubensbekenntnis: Grundriss der Dogmatik im Anschluss an das Credo*. Gütersloh: Gütersloher, 1982.

Ma, Wonsuk. "Full Circle Mission: A Possibility of Pentecostal Missiology." *Asian Journal of Pentecostal Studies* 8.1 (2005) 5–27.

McClung, L. Grant, ed. *Azusa Street and Beyond: Pentecostal Missions and Church Growth in the Twentieth Century*. South Plainfield, NJ: Bridge, 1986.

McQueen, Larry R. *Joel and the Spirit: The Cry of a Prophetic Hermeneutic*. Cleveland: CPT, 2009.

Menzies, Robert. *The Development of Early Christian Pneumatology with Special Reference to Luke-Acts*. JSNT Supplements 54. Sheffield: JSOT, 1991.

Mittelstadt, Martin W. *Reading Luke-Acts in the Pentecostal Tradition*. Cleveland: CPT, 2010.

———. *The Spirit and Suffering in Luke-Acts: Implications for a Pentecostal Theology*. Journal of Pentecostal Theology Supplements 26. New York: T. & T. Clark, 2004.

Möller, François Petrus. "Christ and Pentecostalism." In *The Reality of the Holy Spirit in the Church: In Honour of FP Möller*, edited by P. J. Gräbe and W. J. Hattingh, 140–4. Pretoria: Van Schaik, 1997.

———. *Die Diskussie van die Charismata Soos wat dit in die Pinksterbeweging Geleer en Beoefen Word*. Braamfontein: Evangelie, 1975.

———. *Words of Light and Life: Part 1*. Westdene: AGS, 1991.

Moore, Richie D. "Deuteronomy and the Fire of God: A Critical Charismatic Interpretation." *Journal of Pentecostal Theology* 3.7 (1995) 11–33.

Nelson, P. C., and Pius Wawire. *Bible Doctrines*. Africa's Hope Discovery Series. Springfield: Gospel, 2004.

Palmer, Richard E. *Hermeneutics: Interpretation Theory in Schleiermacher, Dilthey, Heidegger, and Gadamer*. Northwestern University Studies in Phenomenology & Existential Philosophy. Evanston: Northwestern University Press, 1969.

Penney, John Michael. *The Missionary Emphasis of Lukan Pneumatology*. Sheffield: Sheffield Academic, 1997.

Pinnock, Clark H. "The Work of the Holy Spirit in Hermeneutics." *Journal of Pentecostal Theology* 1.2 (1993) 3–23.

Rance, DeLonn L. "Fulfilling the Apostolic Mandate in Apostolic Power: Seeking a Spirit Driven Missiology and Praxis." Paper presented at the Society for Pentecostal Studies, 38th Annual Meeting, Eugene, OR., March 27, 2009.

Ricoeur, Paul. "Philosophical Hermeneutics and Theological Hermeneutics." *Studies in Religion/Sciences Religieuses* 5 (1975) 14–33.

Schafroth, V. "An Exegetical Exploration of 'Spirit' References in Ezekiel 36 and 37." *Journal of the European Theological Association* 29.2 (2009) 61–77.

Schnackenburg, Rudolf. *Belief in the New Testament*. Translated by Jeremy Moiser. Deus Books. New York: Paulist, 1974.

Schütz, Christian. *Einführung in die Pneumatologie*. Theologie. Darmstadt: Wissenschaftliche Buchgesellschaft, 1985.

Stronstad, Roger. *The Charismatic Theology of St. Luke*. Peabody, MA: Hendrickson, 1984.

———. "Pentecostal Experience and Hermeneutics." *Paraclete* 26.1 (1992) 14–30.

Stuhlmacher, Peter. *Vom Verstehen des Neuen Testaments: Eine Hermeneutik*. Grundrisse zum Neuen Testament, NTD Ergänzungsreihe 6. Göttingen: Vandenhoeck & Ruprecht, 1979.

Thiselton, Anthony C. *New Horizons in Hermeneutics: The Theory and Practice of Transforming Biblical Reading*. Grand Rapids: Zondervan, 1992.

Thomas, John Christopher. "Women, Pentecostals and the Bible: An Experiment in Pentecostal Hermeneutics." *Journal of Pentecostal Studies* 5 (1994) 41–56.

Turnage, Marc. "The Early Church and the Axis of History and Pentecostalism: Facing the 21st Century: Some Reflections." *Journal of the European Pentecostal Theological Association* 23 (2003) 4–29.

Van der Walt, S. P., and G. J. C. Jordaan. "Die Kontekstualisering van die Nuwe Testament binne 'n Postmodernistiese Paradigma: Die skep van Betekenis of die Toepas van betekenis." *In die Skriflig* 38.4 (2004) 495–517.

Veenhof, Jan. "The Holy Spirit and Hermeneutics." *Scottish Bulletin of Evangelical Theology* 5 (1987) 105–22.

Williams, J. Rodman. "The Pentecostal Reality." The Christian Broadcasting Network. http://www.cbn.com/spirituallife/biblestudyandtheology/drwilliams/bk_pentecostal.aspx?mobile=false&u=1.

2

Resisting Definitive Interpretation
Seeing the Story of the Exodus through Caribbean(ite) Eyes

Anna Kasafi Perkins

To understand concrete reality, human beings require examples. Some examples are better than others, and exemplary written examples are called "classics." When examined from a hermeneutical perspective, such classics can be seen to bear an excess and permanence of meaning while resisting definitive interpretation.[1] Classics originate within a unique cultural context yet possess the paradoxical capacity to be universal in their effect and appeal. In their continued reception, another paradox also is evident: their capacity to function as classics is culturally dependent upon the instability of the receiving culture's shifting canon of classics.[2] In any particular period, some classics will disappear from the canon while others that may have previously been forgotten or even suppressed may reappear.

Perhaps the best-known classical text in the Christian West is the Bible, which has assisted in the founding and shaping of Western culture. Similarly, the Bible has an important place in the canon of classics for the Caribbean region, especially as its moral vision finds deep resonance within the context of Caribbean history. According to Grenadian scholar of Caribbean religion Leslie R. James:

> From the turn of the fifteenth century to the present, Caribbean people have struggled to become the subjects of their own history. Their struggle has been fundamentally for justice and human rights. This struggle has made the Bible a valid text and a rich source of metaphors, images, and symbols for interpreting Caribbean history and articulating the vision of an alternative

1. Tracy, *Plurality and Ambiguity*, 12.
2. Ibid.

Caribbean future. Consequently, biblical terms such as "exodus," "pharaoh," "wilderness," "promised land," "Babylon," and others have had, and continue to have, deep resonances in Caribbean historical consciousness and search for authentic cultural identity.[3]

The biblical story of the exodus[4] has been, and continues to be, received by Caribbean peoples as a religious classic, a paradigm for interpreting our experiences of suffering, enslavement, emancipation, struggling for self-determination and true freedom in a modern world ruled by new masters. Often-times this exodus motif is conflated and interwoven with the exile, or the second exodus. This theme finds expression in our music. Bob Marley's "Exodus" is a key example; it tells the story of Jamaican people ("Jah People"), using the motifs of both exodus and exile ("Babylon"). Marley treats both events as if they were the same and brings them into the current time by calling on Jamaicans to "open [their] eyes and look within." Such soul-searching leads to dissatisfaction with the status quo and a desire to move out of the circumstances that oppress. The call is to then move to "the Father land" (Africa).[5]

It also appears in our literature:

> Out of the milieu of constitutional advancement, a new type of society and a new type of leader emerged—a leader with a sort of Moses complex, who appeared to regard the local masses as oppressed Israelites, the local Government and Colonial Office in England being the bad-minded Pharaohs. This "let-my-people-go" approach to politics provided the political leader with an indispensable reservoir of profitable emotionalism, and it encouraged the masses to put vague, charismatic considerations above intelligence, solid achievement and even integrity, in estimating the worth of some of their political leaders. . . . The charisma of a Moses placed him above censure for petty moral lapses.[6]

And it is expressed in our theology as well:

> For the [Caribbean] Christian, the concept of liberation is derived from the biblical record of the emancipation of the people of Israel from Egyptian bondage. Exodus is not merely the name

---

3. James, "Text and the Rhetoric of Change," 162.

4. The term "Exodus" appears in upper case when referring to the biblical text; it appears in lower case when alluding to the exodus event.

5. Marley, "Exodus," lines 1, 13–18.

6. Thomas, 1977: 1.

of one of the books of the Bible. In the exodus, God is the liberator and Moses the human instrument. The slavery in Egypt is the context in which the need for liberation is felt, the wilderness the context in which the process evolves, and the possession of Canaan the goal of the liberated people.[7]

No text is purely autonomous, however. The book of Exodus comes bearing with it the history of all its former receptions, and these receptions influence us and the way we read the text. Caribbean people therefore cannot honestly avoid the need to face, alongside the reality of the plurality of its receptions, the ambiguity of the reception of a classic text like the book of Exodus in our history as well as in the history of Western Civilization. The plurality of receptions and the accompanying ambiguities are clear in the various historical events in which the exodus was formative for interpreting self, in-group, and the Other—thus serving to ground action. These events clearly paralleled the Exodus account of God's empowering of the wandering band of escaped slaves to form a new nation in a land they obtained by murdering its Canaanite inhabitants.

In England, Oliver Cromwell struggled bravely for religious freedom while unleashing a terrible fate upon the Irish Catholics who fell into his self-righteous path. The "noble experiment" of the New England Puritans led to the near-destruction of the native inhabitants of America. Europeans in their courageous search for "new" lands encountered the Taino and Carib populations, which they decimated through disease, cruelty, and overwork. Africans were forcibly taken from their homeland and communities, transported via the inhuman Middle Passage to be used cruelly like beasts on plantations. Exodus inspired the Boers on their long trek to "the Promised Land" that originally belonged to the Bantu peoples from whom they stole, and whom they murdered and dehumanized. Even the contemporary struggles for progress by richer countries, which engender the impoverishment and starvation of others in the process, bear the stamp of an Exodus mentality. Exodus is not an innocent text!

In this essay, I attempt to heed theologian David Tracy's call for theology to pay greater attention in all its interpretations to the pluralistic and ambiguous reception of its classic texts, including the book of Exodus.[8] I will present a reflection from the margins, i.e., the perspective of a woman, a descendant of enslaved Africans from the English-speaking Caribbean—a Caribbean(ite) perspective. "Caribbean(ite)" is a deliberately constructed polyvalent term (echoes of Caribbean and Canaanite), part of the impor-

7. Smith, *Real Roots*, 19–20.
8. Tracy, "Exodus," 118.

tant task of naming myself and my reality. I seek to present a perspective that challenges interpretations of the exodus that disregard or do not deal effectively with those aspects of the Scriptures that make us uncomfortable or which we cannot in all honesty name as "liberating" or even inspired. I, therefore, hope to question any elitist, privileged, and definitive readings of Exodus. In so doing, I locate myself in a space that often has been at the receiving end of triumphalist interpretations of the exodus. An example of the arrogance of the Christian conquerors is found in the words of one Catholic priest who argued with impunity that, "The King of Spain might very justly send men to require those idolatrous Indians to hand over their land to him for it was given him by the Pope. If the Indians would not do this, he might justly wage war against them, kill them and enslave those captured in war, *precisely as Joshua treated the inhabitants of the land of Canaan.*"[9]

Ironically, this also is the space in which Exodus is often read and interpreted somewhat naively, selectively, and uncritically. As the previous quote from Ashley Smith demonstrates, few Caribbean or liberation theologians for that matter seem really alert to the ambiguities of Exodus or its plural uses. As a result, such uncritical readings from the margins have prevented us from seriously wrestling with this religious classic in a manner that would enrich our Caribbean theology and ethics. So, while Exodus resists definitive interpretation, a critical reading of this classic from the margins, from the perspective of its victims, may lead to a greater awareness of the limited and ambiguous nature of our own interpretations and lead us to tread lightly in the presence of those whom it might lead us to victimize.

A Caribbean(ite) perspective highlights also the importance and value of doing theological reflection from the location of the Anglo-Caribbean. Too often, the Caribbean perspective is subsumed under the liberation theologies of Latin America and is not given a chance to speak out of its own uniqueness. The reflection is informed by and in dialogue with the feminist critique of Caribbean Theology issued by Jamaican theologian Theresa Lowe-Ching, as well as other interpretations from the margins, including representatives of the Native American, Womanist, and South African voices.

Canaanites, Cowboys, and Indians—
a Native American Appropriation

Of course, talk about the plurality and ambiguity of interpretations and receptions of the Exodus classic should not ignore the fact that these arise

9. Murrell, "Dangerous Memories," 12 (emphasis added).

from within the narrative itself. The conquest is the dark side of the Bible's central liberative event, the exodus. The truth is that there is no exodus in the Bible without the conquest. Israel is liberated from bonded labor in Egypt, and made YHWH's people in Sinai, in order to possess "the land" (Exod 6:8).

Native American theologian Robert Warrior argues passionately that the story of the exodus is an inappropriate way for Native Americans to think about liberation.[10] The liberationist picture of YHWH that many find so liberating is, in his eyes, an incomplete one. YHWH the deliverer goes before the Israelites to give them the land he promised them. He wields the same power he used against the Egyptian slave masters to defeat the innocent indigenous inhabitants of Canaan. YHWH commands the merciless annihilation of the indigenous population. YHWH the deliverer becomes YHWH the conqueror! Native Americans identify with and read the story of the exodus with Canaanite eyes (as do Palestinians and South Africans). Caribbean people too often identify themselves with the Israelites!

Warrior does not ignore scholarly research, which has made a strong case that the actual events were much different from those presented in the narrative. The usual scholarly consensus is that the Canaanites were not systematically annihilated, nor were they driven from the land. Rather, the Israelites may have settled among them peacefully, and they came to make up, to a large extent, the people of the new nation of Israel. But plausible historical reconstructions do not change the status of the indigenes in the narrative nor the theology and politics that emerge from it. People read the narratives as they are, not as the experts and scholars would like them to be read and interpreted. This fact poses an additional challenge to theologies of liberation, which emphasize empowering the poor to read and interpret the biblical text in light of their experience, while making narratives like the exodus central for theology and political action. The danger is that the narratives will be read without attention to the history behind them. The text cannot be altered by interpretation to fit how its reception may be altered. Whatever dangers are identified in the text and the god represented there will remain as long as the text remains. Claiming Exodus as part of Christian heritage is an honor, but it as much a source of discomfort.

Further, in the Native-American experience, the Exodus narratives also tell another story—the story of what happens when indigenous people put their hope and faith in ideas and gods that are foreign to their culture. The Canaanites trusted in the god of outsiders, and their story of oppression and exploitation was lost (this essay and the work of people like Warrior are

---

10. Warrior, "Canaanites, Cowboys and Indians," 262.

part of the attempt at "re-membering" such stories). Inter-religious praxis became betrayal, and the surviving narrative tells us nothing about it.[11]

Rastafarians, Babylon, and Black Israelites— a Jamaican Appropriation

Nathaniel Samuel Murrell, in discussing current Anglican Bishop of Barbados John Holder's "Land Acquisition Solution Model" of biblical hermeneutics for the Caribbean, describes Holder as wanting to present Caribbean people with a Torah in one hand and a land title in the other. Holder's model rests on the dire need for land acquisition as the solution to the colonial legacy of Caribbean impoverishment, underdevelopment, landlessness, identity crisis, and cultural negation.[12] Holder wants to keep Caribbean people focussed on the memory of their exodus experience of liberation from Egypt (slavery and colonialism) on the one hand, and, on the other hand, hold a title deed to a piece of land or property from the other side of the Jordan (independent Caribbean countries). Holder advocates remembering a special relationship with God and the land. Like the Israelites, we too are to cherish and share the land and respect our neighbor's possession as a gift from YHWH.

Murrell highlights the problem of bringing Holder's dream into reality. Giving the people the Torah is easy; the people already have their Torah, their classic, the Bible. But the people must first have land for which they can be grateful to YHWH and use it to engender hope and memory of the goodness of God.[13] The land must come from somewhere, but there are no free crown lands in the Caribbean. YHWH no longer owns the lands, as Holder implies. Murrell continues by making the important yet oft-forgotten connection with the text: the ancient Israelites "hijacked" the land by slaughtering and driving out the earlier inhabitants under the guise that YHWH commanded them to conduct a form of "God-blessed invasion."[14] He then poses an important question: Did YHWH really give Israel the land, or did they take it in his name? Has God really done all the evil things to the people and their lands that the biblical writers ascribe to God? "Getting the people's land by taking it from someone else in the name of God creates the kind of travesty of justice and barbarism the world witnessed in the last few decades on the West bank of Gaza with the resettlement of

11. Ibid., 263.
12. Murrell, "Dangerous Memories," 26.
13. Ibid.
14. Ibid., 27.

landless Jews on Palestinian lands."[15] Murrell, therefore, cautions us against solving our economic problems in the Caribbean by "robbing Peter to pay Paul" and discourages us from the uprooting of families and destruction of communities in the name of religion and land settlement. Murrell then goes on to suggest that we should look to the ideas of the Rastafarians for a workable solution to Holder's model.

Rastafarian theology is as basically geographical as was that of their ancient forbears, the Hebrews. The promised land, the land of exile, the deportation, and the return are conceptions that work powerfully within the Rastafarian symbol system. They sustain and animate the brethren and allow them to survive in Jamaica, land of listless and oppressive exile, while awaiting repatriation to the kingdom of Zion.

Rastafarian religion took shape in the 1920s in Jamaica's backward colonial society. It arose in response to a number of factors, the most salient of which was perhaps the continuing and increasing poverty of the black masses. Poverty was clearly underlined in terms of color, with the Jamaicans of African descent decidedly regulated to the base of society. Despite the advances that had been made with Emancipation (1838), the fundamental social relations in the country had stubbornly remained the same. This could be seen most sharply in the continued denigration of the African presence in Jamaica, and, by extension, the wider Caribbean. Two examples of this denigration are the patterns of language-use in Jamaica, which saw the ability to speak and write British English as a passport to success. This served to render as limited and low in status the Jamaican language, which had been creatively crafted by the ancestors of black Jamaicans in the face of attempts to strip them of cultural identity and connection to their African homeland. Creole was and continues to be the heart language of the majority of the population, the same masses that were enmeshed in poverty.

Similarly, ideas of beauty and acceptability resided in possessing European features, and the denigration of African-ness was given expression in curse terms in the Creole such as "Yuh black like sin!" Patterns of kinship, which were both matrifocal and extended, rendered the masses born out of wedlock non-persons, unable to inherit property and constantly needing to declare their identity for the simplest of transactions in their own country. Rastas would describe the situation in these terms: "If you black, stand back. If you brown, stick around. If you white, you all right."

Rastafarians responded by re-valuing of the African presence in Jamaican society and launching a prophetic critique on all aspects of Jamaica society, and the Western system of which it was a part, that denigrates and

15. Ibid.

impoverishes the black man. They found within the Bible itself valuable and powerful tools of critical analysis not only of the unjust social system but also of the established religion and the way in which it served the system/ "shitstem."

At the same time, Rastafarians are radically suspicious of the use of the Bible because:

> . . . the unscrupulous have consistently taken this great book and used it for the most unworthy ends: to enslave people, to make money, to glorify themselves at the expense of others; it is forever being used by business men who hypnotise the black man into accepting the religion of white men. It is not enough for the whites to enslave the bodies of the black slaves; their minds also had to be enchained. This is done through the white Bible and the white religion associated with it.[16]

They, therefore, contend that the Bible, because of its unfortunate history in recent centuries, requires careful analysis. They consider very few men to have the inspiration and intuitive sense that are required to interpret the Bible correctly. They point out many confusing and contradictory passages in the Bible, and some parts that they know must be totally discounted—although not the exodus or exile. One Rasta, in recounting the process of his conversion, told Fr. Owens how the Bible must be read: "We would have to read it with a little more understanding and read between the lines, not understanding it as how King James would want the English people to understand it, but by trying to understand it as how black people should understand it."[17]

Therefore, the Rastaman never approaches the Bible passively! He always has an inner core of wisdom and knowledge, which interacts with what he learns from the Bible to yield an even higher truth. He reinterprets the Bible in terms of the black man's experience and need (clearly a contextual theology). To understand further the enthusiasm and the seriousness with which the Rastafarians read the biblical text, it is necessary to consider the identity, which they *know* exists, between themselves and the ancient Israelites. They regard black Africans as the sole representatives of that "chosen people" whose history is recounted in the Bible.[18] They offer numerous proof-texts to prove that the chosen people were dark-skinned, notably Lam 4:8; 5:10; Joel 2:8; Hab 2:10; Job 30:30; Ps 119:83; Jer 14:2, and Rev 1:14. These texts are not offered in isolation; more important by far is their own

16. Owens, *Dread*, 33.
17. Ibid.
18. Ibid., 39.

inner experience of the identity between their history and that recounted in the Bible. The fate of the black man in recent centuries, his having been scattered by force to all corners of the earth, relates him closely to the slavery, the exile, and the diaspora of the ancient Jews.

Rastafarians present a unique and very Caribbean appropriation of the biblical story of the exodus. From their meditation on Scripture and their black experience, Rastafarians have come to view Great Britain as especially guilty of the crime of shuffling human beings around like livestock, and Jamaica gives ample witness to these forced migrations. After helping wipe out the Native Amerindian population, the British proceeded to carry in thousands of Africans as slaves. When slavery finally proved unprofitable, the British went in search of Chinese, Indians, Syrians, and whoever else was willing to sell years of their lives for a slim hope of improvement.[19] Jamaica, with its majority of people of African descent and minorities of other races, is evidence of the extravagant means the British have taken to enrich themselves. The Rastas declare that the arrogance of the British in taking Jamaica from the Amerindians and then importing countless souls from other races as laborers will lead inevitably to their downfall. The West, including Jamaica, and in contrast to Africa, is a land of enslavement and damnation. "When one Rasta exclaimed, "Leave Jamaica!"—another agreed, "Because the greatest thing in the world is to be free." The West is a comfortless region for the Rastafarians. They dwell as pilgrims in a strange land; they sit mournful by the rivers of Babylon. They hope for peace but see it only in universal repatriation: "That is the only peace that can be upon earth: if I-n-I go back to Africa."[20]

Repatriation, or "the great exodus" for the Rastafarian, means first and foremost of course, a physical return to their long-lost homeland, but it means much more besides. Repatriation signifies a return to their culture, liberation from the alienation of the West. It will deliver their destiny back into their own hands and allow them to live at peace instead of engaging in constant war against or on behalf of the whites. Repatriation is the earthly redemption, which the Israelites have long sought in vain. Speaking for twenty generations of enslaved and exiled ancestors, one of the brethren stated what return to Africa will mean to him: "I, personally, as one who has been stole [sic] from the continent of Africa nearly 500 years ago, know that our salvation does not lie in Jamaica but in our return to a liberated Africa."[21]

19. Ibid., 234.
20. Ibid., 232.
21. Owens, *Dread*, 232.

A Question for Caribbean Theologians

Caribbean theologians have attempted to be sensitive to and engage in dialogue with the message of Rastafarianism. Rastafarian theology has presented a striking critique of the "traditional" ways of doing theology in the Caribbean. Strangely enough, their unique appropriation of the Exodus narratives has rarely alerted Caribbean theologians to the ambiguities of the exodus story, to the non-liberating aspects of the story. Why?

African-American Womanist theologian Delores S. Williams may provide some insights here. According to Williams, it is possible to identify two traditions of African-American biblical appropriation that were useful for a construction of black theology in North America.[22] One of these traditions of biblical appropriation emphasized liberation of the oppressed and showed God relating to *men* in liberation struggles. Many African-American spirituals, slave narratives, and sermons refer to biblical stories and personalities who were involved in liberation struggle—Moses, Jesus, Paul, and Silas. These have formed the major sources of reflection for black male theologians.

> Their validating biblical paradigm in the Hebrew Testament was the exodus event when God delivered the oppressed Hebrew slaves from their oppressors in Egypt. Their Christian testament paradigm was Luke 4, when Jesus described his mission and ministry in terms of liberation. Their normative claim for biblical interpretation was "God the liberator of the poor and oppressed."[23]

Williams calls this appropriation "the liberation tradition of African-American biblical appropriation." A similar tradition of biblical appropriation can be seen to be at work in the articulation of Caribbean theology and other theologies of liberation (even Rastafarianism!).

Williams discovered a second exciting tradition of African-American biblical appropriation which has emphasised *female* activity and de-emphasised male authority. It is lifted from the biblical account of Hagar, the female slave of African descent who was forced to be a surrogate mother, reproducing a child by her slave master because the slave master's wife was barren. Williams claims that, for more than 100 years, Hagar has appeared in the deposits of African-American culture. Sculptors, writers, poets, scholars, preachers, and ordinary folk have passed along the biblical figure of Hagar from generation to generation of black people.

---

22. Williams, *Sisters in the Wilderness*, 2.
23. Ibid.

She found striking similarities in the Hagar story and the story of African-American women (similarities that have echoes in the lives of Caribbean women). Hagar's heritage was as African as African-American women's (and as Caribbean as Caribbean women's). Hagar was a slave. Black women have emerged from a slave heritage and still lived in light of it. Hagar was brutalized by her slave owner, the Hebrew woman Sarah. The slave narratives of African-American women and some of the narratives of contemporary days-workers tell of the brutal or cruel treatment black women have received from the wives of slave masters and from contemporary white female employers (the experiences of many modern Jamaican days-workers and helpers is no different, sadly). Hagar had no control over her body. It belonged to her slave owner, whose husband Abraham, ravished Hagar. A child, Ishmael, was born; mother and child were eventually cast out of Abraham's and Sarah's home without resources for survival. The bodies of African-American slave women were owned by their masters. Time after time they were raped by their owners and bore children whom the master seldom claimed, children who were slaves. Slave-master fathers often cast out these children and their mothers by selling them to other slave-holders. Hagar resisted the brutality of slavery by running away. Black American women have a long "herstory" of resistance that includes running away from slavery in the antebellum era. Like Hagar and her child Ishmael, African-American women slaves and their children were expelled from the homes of many slave-holders after slavery and given no resources for survival. Hagar, like many women throughout African-American women "herstory," was a single parent. But Hagar had serious personal and salvific encounters with God—encounters that helped her in the survival struggle for herself and her son. Over and over again, black women in the churches have testified about serious personal and salvific encounters with God that helped them, and their families, survive.

A superficial reading of Gen 16:1–16 and 21:9–21 in the Hebrew Bible revealed that Hagar's predicament involved slavery, poverty, ethnicity, sexual and economic exploitation, surrogacy, rape, domestic violence, homelessness, motherhood, single-parenting, and radical encounters with God. Another aspect of Hagar's predicament was made clear in the Christian testament when Paul (Gal 4:21—5:21) relegated her and her progeny to a position outside of and antagonistic to the great promise Paul says Christ brought to humankind. Thus, in Paul's text, Hagar bears only negative relations to the new creation Christ represents. In the Christian context of Paul, then, Hagar and her descendants represent the outsider position par excellence. Therefore, alienation also is part of the predicament of Hagar and her progeny.[24] The existence of Hagar and her progeny in the position of outsider has important resonances with some modern appropriations of the exodus story.

One such appropriation is that of Jewish political scientist Michael Walzer. Walzer attempts in his book, *Exodus and Revolution*, to trace a political way of reading the story of the exodus, as has been done in the writings of religious groups like the Jewish rabbis and the Puritans, as well as its survival in the Western understanding of political change. He presents exodus politics as a valid way of describing political change although it is subject to certain temptations (Messianism and Zionism). He maintains further that modern political readings of the exodus are done with an intentional forward motion and that any aspect of the story can be emphasized over the others.[25] So, for example, my own suggestion elsewhere is that a reading of the exodus story in Anglo-Caribbean politics emphasizes the role of a leader-like-Moses (the messianic leader).[26] Walzer does not dwell on those aspects of the story where there is the need to "purge counterrevolutionaries"—the killing of the worshippers of the golden calf. He brushes aside God's demand that the inhabitants of the land be exterminated by a claim that the Canaanites were outside of the moral concern of the Israelites (so that allowed them to be killed?).[27]

Walzer's analysis is certainly suspect for what he glosses over or leaves out. Palestinian social theorist Edward Said levels the same critique against Walzer that can be leveled against Caribbean theologians: Walzer reads the story in a way that does not heed the ambiguities and terror in the text. Said questions Walzer's use of "us" and "in the West" in his discussion. This usage highlights the first error that interpreters of the exodus often make. They assume that their interpretation is privileged and universally binding or relevant. Said further accuses Walzer of avoidance. The great avoidance, significantly, is of history itself—the history of the text he comments on, the history of the Jews, the history of the various people who have used Exodus, as well as those who have not, the history of models, texts, paradigms, utopias, in their relationship to actual events, the history of such things as covenants and founding texts.[28]

Said will not let Walzer get away with his refusal to meet head on the fact that the extermination of whole peoples can be seen to be sanctioned

---

24. Ibid., 4–5.
25. Walzer, *Exodus and Revolution*.
26. Perkins, "Some Theological Reflections," 70.
27. Walzer and Said, "An Exchange."
28. Said, "Michael Walzer's Exodus," 91.

by YHWH in the sacred literature. He, like many others, continues to forget the very existence of this part of the text.[29]

Warrior's analysis reminds us of the valuable contribution made to the formation of the Jewish nation by the indigenous people of Canaan. But where is that acknowledged? Walzer also is eager to disconnect from, and yet connect with, the essential parts of Exodus that he too misses, the opportunity to allow the ambiguity of the material to challenge his present context. What really happens when we place someone on the margins, when we make them an outsider? This is where there is a direct connection with Williams's identification of Hagar as an outsider. Walzer dismisses the Canaanites as being outside the world of moral concern of the Israelites, and history has shown us the results of such a reading.[30]

Williams makes the startling claim that God's response to Hagar's predicament is not liberation for, on one occasion, he instructs her to return to the home of her oppressor Sarah, that is, return to bondage. Williams interprets God's action here as an act on behalf of the survival of Hagar and her child. Perhaps neither Hagar nor her child would survive the ordeal of birth in the wilderness. When Hagar and her child were finally cast out into the wilderness without proper resources to survive, God gave her new vision to see survival resources where she had seen none before. "Liberation in the Hagar stories is not given by God; it finds its source in human initiative."[31] God's response to Hagar's situation is survival and involvement in her development of an appropriate quality of life, that is, appropriate to her situation and heritage. Williams concluded that the female-centered tradition of African-American biblical appropriation could be named the "survival/quality of life tradition of African-American biblical appropriation." This naming is consistent with the African-American community's way of appropriating the Bible so that emphasis is put upon God's response to black people's situation rather than upon what would appear to be hopeless aspects of African-American people's existence in North America. In black consciousness, God's response of survival and quality of life to Hagar is God's response of survival and quality of life to African-American women and mothers of slave descent struggling to sustain their families with God's help.

Williams's analysis reasserts a fundamental principle of contextual theology, namely, that who you are influences how you read the biblical text

---

29. Ibid.

30. Warrior, "Canaanites, Cowboys and Indians"; Walzer and Said, "An Exchange"; Williams, *Sisters in the Wilderness*.

31. Williams, *Sisters in the Wilderness*, 5.

and practice theology. This is perhaps why Caribbean theologians—both Rasta and non-Rasta—have so readily identified with the liberative themes in Exodus.

Until very recently, male theologians articulated most official theology in the region. Theresa Lowe-Ching laments the total lack of references to the experience of women and women's contribution to Caribbean theological reflection. She calls attention to the dearth of women theologians in the region also.[32] This is certainly clear in the Rastafarian appropriations of the liberation themes in the text. They are blind to their own partial and limited appropriations of the Bible and do not see who they make victims in their interpretations. They do not see the effects of their interpretation and appropriation as silencing as important a group as women, their queens, their "dawtas." As Williams demonstrates, women's lives are so much like those of the victims of Scripture that focusing solely on the liberative themes often is to disregard their experiences, experiences that often are of survival and care in a context of oppression rather than liberation. Perhaps by "befriending the dragon," as Lowe-Ching refers to the excluded female experience and creativity, Caribbean theology may be provided with a distinctly creative approach that would eventually contribute significantly to not only the theological enterprise itself but also to the immediate goal of transforming persons and society.[33]

The Word of God and the Hermeneutic of Struggle

Itumeleng Mosala of South Africa offers a radical perspective on the use of Scripture/a biblical hermeneutic of Scripture that provides further insights for a Caribbean(ite) reading. Like the Rastafarians, he warns against the failure to recognize the Bible as an ideological product. Mosala critiques black theology's idea that the Bible is simply the Word of God because it leads, as we have witnessed, to a false notion that the Bible is non-ideological.[34] Such a false or idealist notion can cause oppressed people to become politically "paralyzed" in their reading. It also runs the risk of leaving the political interpretation of the Bible to the hegemonic sectors of society, whether they be white, male, educated, or a combination. Such hegemonic interpretations often do not have to strain after an explicitly political reading, since the texts of the Bible are themselves already cast in this form. Thus, black/Caribbean/

---

32. Lowe-Ching, "Method in Caribbean Theology," 29.
33. Ibid.
34. Mosala, *Biblical Hermeneutics*, 6.

liberation theology, by colluding with a dominant epistemological view of the Bible, has helped to reproduce the status quo, contrary to its own goals.

Mosala contends further that the category of "Word of God" does not help bring out the liberating message of the Bible, because it presumes that liberation exists everywhere and unproblematically in the Bible. This category is oblivious, even within biblical communities themselves, to the history of ruling-class control and co-option of the discourses and stories of the ancient Israelite people. For example, the appropriation of the exodus story by the exile community in Babylon to express its yearnings for freedom to return to Zion and rebuild the Davidic dynasty conceals—with devastating ideological effects—the class and political differences between the first exodus and this second exodus. This kind of reuse of the exodus story goes against the invectives of the prophets and their view of Jerusalem and Zion: "Listen to me, you rulers of Israel, you that hate justice and turn right into wrong. You are building God's city, Jerusalem, on a foundation of murder and injustice" (Mic 3.9–10). The ethos of the original exodus theology is incompatible with the ideology and culture implied in the struggle for the reconstruction of Zion and Jerusalem.[35] Mosala argues that the category of "struggle" provides the lens for reading the text in a liberating fashion as well as the codes for unlocking the possibilities and limitations of the biblical texts.

The category of struggle also has value as a tool for reading black history and culture, in that such an approach leads to the important understanding that not all black historical and cultural readings of the Bible are liberating. Armed with this insight, we can clearly see a biblical hermeneutics of liberation for black theology as liberating neither because it is black nor on the grounds simply that it is biblical. Rather, it is a tool of struggle in the ongoing human project of liberation.[36]

Reading with Caribbean(ite) Eyes

How are we to respond to a Bible that contains such ambiguities? A number of responses are possible. We could ignore them or "escape into the transient pleasures of irony, or a flight into despair and cynicism or more history-as-usual."[37] We must wrestle with the ambiguity of the text and allow it to move us to hope. What we are taught as we maintain the tension between the liberating and non-liberating texts is that:

35. Ibid., 20.
36. Ibid., 9.
37. Tracy, "Exodus," 122.

Whoever fights for hope, fights on behalf of us all, whoever acts on that hope in concrete historical and political struggle acts in a manner worthy of a human being. And whoever so acts, acts in a manner faintly suggestive of the reality and power of that God in whose image human beings were formed to resist, to think, and to act.[38]

Taking seriously the plurality and ambiguity of such classical texts like the Exodus with its concomitant conquest presents Caribbean theological reflection with a number of challenges. Clearly, self-conscious and self-critical reflections are important elements in the interpretive equation. Theological reflection and biblical interpretation must pay special attention to the interpreter as a key feature of contextual understandings. The Bible and theological reflection must help make sense of the people's experience, not vice versa. Paying attention to the social location of the theologian will strip away any veneer of detached, disinterested objectivism from academic discourse to reveal the complex web of presuppositions, commitments, and constituencies that shape the process of reading. This requires a vulnerability that renders interpreters accountable for their readings and makes the Bible accountable to the world for its lack of innocence.

Bibliography

James, Leslie R. "Text and the Rhetoric of Change: Bible and Decolonization in Post-World-War II Caribbean Political Discourse." In *Religion, Culture and Tradition in the Caribbean*, edited by Hemchand Gossai and Nathaniel Samuel Murrell, 143–66. New York: St. Martin's, 2000.

Lowe-Ching, Theresa. "Method in Caribbean Theology." In *Caribbean Theology: Preparing for the Challenges Ahead*, edited by Howard Gregory, 23–33. Kingston, Jamaica: Canoe, 1995.

Marley, Bob, and Ernest Gold. "Exodus: Movement of Jah People." LP/Album: *Exodus*. New York: Island Records, 1977. https://www.azlyrics.com/lyrics/bobmarley/exodus.html.

Mosala, Itumeleng J. *Biblical Hermeneutics and Black Theology in South Africa*. Grand Rapids: Eerdmans, 1989.

Murrell, Nathaniel Samuel. "Dangerous Memories, Underdevelopment, and the Bible in Colonial Caribbean Experience." In *Religion, Culture, and Tradition in the Caribbean*, edited by Hemchand Gossai and Nathaniel Samuel Murrell, 9–36. New York: St. Martin's, 2000.

Owens, Joseph. *Dread: The Rastafarians of Jamaica*. London: Heinemann, 1976.

Perkins, Anna Kasafi. "Some Theological Reflections on Exodus Politics and Messianic Leadership in the Pre-independence English-speaking Caribbean." In *In Celebra-*

---

38. Ibid.

tion of Black History: GYRO Colloquium Papers Volume VI, 64–77. Boston: Boston College, 2001.

Said, Edward. "Michael Walzer's Exodus and Revolution: A Canaanite Reading." *Grand Street* 5/2 (1986) 86–106.

Smith, Ashley. *Real Roots and Potted Plants: Reflections on the Caribbean Church.* Williamsfield, Jamaica: Mandeville, 1984.

Thomas, G. C. H. *Ruler in Hiroona: A West Indian Novel.* Trinidad: Columbus, 1972.

Tracy, David. *Plurality and Ambiguity: Hermeneutics, Religion, Hope.* Chicago: University of Chicago Press, 1987.

———. "Exodus: Theological Reflection." *Concilium* 189 (1987) 118–24.

———. "Reading the Bible: A Plurality of Readers and a Possibility of a Shared Vision." In *On Naming the Present: Reflections on God, Hermeneutics and the Church*, edited by David Tracy, 120–30. Concilium Series. Maryknoll, NY: Orbis, 1994.

Walzer, Michael. *Exodus and Revolution.* New York: Basic Books, 1985.

Walzer, Michael, and Edward Said. "An Exchange: 'Exodus and Revolution.'" *Grand Street* 5/4 (1986) 246–59.

Warrior, Robert Allan. "Canaanites, Cowboys and Indians: Deliverance, Conquest, and Liberation Theology Today." *Christianity and Crisis* 49.12 (September 11, 1989) 261–65.

Williams, Delores S. *Sisters in the Wilderness: The Challenge of Womanist God-Talk.* Maryknoll, NY: Orbis, 1993.

Anabaptist Hermeneutics and Theological Education[1]

Antonio González Fernández

The word "hermeneutics" in Spanish means the "art of interpreting texts, especially sacred texts."[2] Etymologically, the expression derives from the Greek word ἑρμηνευτής, meaning "interpreter" or "translator." Hermeneutics may have been associated originally with the god Hermes, the messenger of the gods, dispenser of literary genius, patron of orators, god of travelers, and protector of those who cross borders.

These origins of hermeneutics reveal to us a certain specialized character it possesses. Not everybody is able to translate. The translator is someone who has a more than ordinary knowledge of another language, a knowledge that allows him to serve as interpreter between his own people and a foreign group. Normally, the interpreter is not a volunteer, but someone who earns his living by means of his translations. Of course, such professional specialization of the interpreter does not in principle indicate any originality. The interpreter or translator is not the bearer of his own message, but rather transmits the message of others, in the same way that the god Hermes transmitted the messages of the gods. Nevertheless, the translator may also always be a traitor ("*traduttore traditore*" is the Italian phrase), someone who distorts the message in the service of other interests. For that reason, the god Hermes was not only the patron of merchants and poets, but also the inspirer of thieves and liars.

---

1. This work originated as a conference given in Asunción, Paraguay, in July 2009, during a consultation on theological education in the CEMTA, on the occasion of the World Mennonite Conference. I am grateful to Professor Rogelio Duarte and the other participants for all their comments, which have been of much help to me in editing this final text.

2. This is the second definition of "hermenéutica" in the dictionary of the Real Academia.

Theological hermeneutics may sometimes bear a certain resemblance to these origins of ancient hermeneutics. The theologian or the exegete might be understood as someone out of the ordinary, a person who possesses the special ability to understand the divine messages written in the sacred books and to transmit them to people who do not possess the same kinds of knowledge. In such a perspective, theological education may be understood as a process of religious initiation that trains certain persons to become authorized, professional interpreters of the sacred books. Theological education would thus most definitely require a sort of separation of the future hermeneutist from the believing community. In the course of that separation, during his stay in a center that specializes in theological studies, he would acquire certain sacred characteristics which would enable him to transmit to the faithful the correct interpretation of the biblical texts. It is no wonder that Hermes, the messenger of the gods, was also a god.

We are well aware that, even today, such an understanding of theological education is current in many seminaries and theological faculties. We are also quite conscious of how dangerous it can be. The sanctified interpreter, separated from his community, is a "pastor" or "priest" who has his own personal, professional, and corporate interests to consider. His "translation" of sacred texts for the people of God may also be a sort of "treason," in which the true interests of the Christian community are betrayed. At the same time, the specialization and the professionalization that the interpreter undergoes may result in a language alien to that of his community and difficult for them to understand. Let us not forget that the god Hermes was associated not only with hermeneutics, but also with "hermetics," a term used to designate obscure and esoteric doctrines that were suitable only for a select group of initiates.[3] And all of us, of course, have heard at one time another sermons that are truly "hermetic" (= impenetrable, in Spanish).

The Anabaptist Perspective

It would be very easy at this point to give ourselves over to a certain anti-intellectualism, claiming simply that for sixteenth-century Anabaptists, the true subject of biblical interpretation was the Christian community, without any need of priests or professional theologians. As soon as we go deeper into this question, however, we become aware that things are not that simple. On the one hand, we may suspect that a lack of theological training could have occasioned some of the exaggerations into which certain Anabaptist

---

3. The term originally designated a complex of beliefs based on writings attributed to Hermes Trismegistus, a sage or alchemist associated with the god Hermes.

groups fell. Think, for example, of those sixteenth-century Anabaptists who, to become like children (Matt 18:3), used to crawl about on the ground and babble like babies.[4] Other problems, such as the tendency toward legalism or the mutual excommunications among later Anabaptists, may have had as a backdrop, *among other factors*, a certain naiveté in how the Bible was read. On the other hand, we also place great value on the writings of those sixteenth-century Anabaptists who, because they had a sturdier theological culture, have bequeathed to us profound reflections that continue to be relevant for our own time. Thanks to them we can understand better what the originary meaning of Anabaptism was and what its contribution to twenty-first-century Christianity might be. If our desire is to present the Christian message to a culturally complex world and to dialogue with Christians of different traditions, then it seems that we cannot do that without theological training. But then how are we to understand theological training from an Anabaptist perspective, a perspective that gives priority to the Christian community in interpreting the Bible?

Let us begin by saying that, for Anabaptists, the Christian community was understood as a *community of the Spirit*. Like the other reformers, the Anabaptists began by emphasizing the protagonism of the Holy Spirit in biblical interpretation. For them, authentic interpretation of the Scriptures was a spiritual happening, which made it possible for them to be understood from the viewpoint of their divine author; the faithful could thus better understand both what the original meaning of the biblical text was and how they were to be applied to the present. Obviously, this emphasis on the role of the Holy Spirit in biblical interpretation does not fully explain why Anabaptists came to understand biblical interpretation as a community process, in contrast to other sixteenth-century movements that also insisted on the guidance of the Holy Spirit. Nor were the Anabaptists the only reformers who held the idea of the universal priesthood of all Christians, or the resulting idea that every believer, guided by the Holy Spirit, could understand biblical texts directly, given the clarity and universal accessibility (*perspicuitas*) that the texts possessed. These same principles did not lead other Protestant reformers to a systematic development of the process of community biblical interpretation, although the idea crossed the minds of some of them.[5] In practice, the movements coming out of the Reformation oscillated between the magisterial interpretations of the church-designated

---

4. Cf. Williams, *La Reforma Radical*, 915. Williams points out that serious exegetes such as Hubmeier, Marpeck, or Menno Simons did well in warning the first Anabaptists concerning the dangers of eccentric literalism.

5. The idea of communitarian interpretation appeared in Zwingli before it did among the Anabaptists, but only the Anabaptists put it into practice.

theologians and the individualism of private interpretations. By contrast, in the sixteenth-century Anabaptist context, not only did the figure of the professional pastor disappear, but also preaching included the participation of the whole body of the faithful as interpreters of the word of God, with the result that the monologue of the priest or the pastor was replaced by a true dialogue among all believers.[6]

The theological backdrop of this involvement of the whole community in interpreting the Bible is to be found in a characteristic that is proper to Anabaptist christocentrism. Again, we should remember that christocentrism was clearly an emphasis characterizing the larger sixteenth-century reformation, not only Anabaptism. All the reformers stressed the centrality of Jesus as the only mediator, in order to counter the role given to Mary and the other saints in medieval piety. For the sixteenth-century reformers, it was essential to insist that salvation came directly and gratuitously from God by means of his Son Jesus Christ. Jesus was thus seen primarily as the one who paid for our sins by dying on the cross, and therefore also as the one to whom our faith is directed, by which faith we obtain justification. For the reformers, this faith also was a hermeneutical principle, precisely because the history of sin and of redemption though Jesus Christ became for them the key for understanding the Scriptures as a whole. Justification by faith in Jesus Christ became the principle that structured the reading of the Bible and gave it its unity.

The Anabaptists in no way denied the exclusive redeeming role of Jesus Christ or the gratuitous nature of salvation. Nevertheless, their christocentrism had a different accent. In the Anabaptist perspective, the magisterial reformers, even though they stressed the centrality of Jesus, in practice tended to ignore his message; rather, they replaced it with teachings taken from the Old Testament, as happened paradigmatically in the question of the use of violence and in the creation of state churches. For the Anabaptists, it was important to stress that Jesus was not just a general religious principle, but a concrete person and, therefore, could be really known only through direct and effective contact with him. That meant that for the Anabaptists *the following of Jesus* took on a central role in their spirituality, their theology, and their hermeneutics. We all know the famous phrase of Hans Denk: Christ can be known only by being followed in life.[7] The magisterial reformers often misunderstood the Anabaptist appeals to the following of Jesus, thinking it was a way of backtracking into the works of the medieval

---

6. Cf. "Interrogación de Ambrosius Spitelmaier," 94–95.

7. Cf. Denk, "De lo que se Pretende que Digan las Escrituras," 206–29 (specifically 224).

church. For Anabaptists, however, the following of Jesus was not a way of getting to heaven by one's own efforts, but a grateful response made possible by the work of the Holy Spirit in us. For that reason, they insisted on the need for a new birth, without which it was impossible to follow Jesus, and therefore to know him. Thus, it becomes possible to understand what we might call the "hermeneutical circle" of Hans Denk, who claimed not only that Jesus cannot be known unless he is followed, but also that he cannot be followed unless he is first known.[8] And this "first knowledge" is that which comes about when the believer is born again by the Holy Spirit.

The Essential Difference

All the foregoing shows us something very important for understanding the Anabaptist contribution to biblical hermeneutics. The community of the Spirit, from the Anabaptist perspective, is not only a charismatic community in which the gifts of the Holy Spirit are made patent. The Christian community also is a community of following, precisely because the work of the Spirit consists in making us capable of following Jesus. The fact of following Jesus is precisely what makes the church different from the world because it is clear that not everybody follows Jesus or even wants to follow him freely. Yet it is the following of Jesus that creates the community that unites around him. The community of the Spirit is therefore a community of followers who walk with Jesus: Jesus is the one who walks in the lead, both *making* the way and *being* the way by which his disciples follow him. Such a stance is charged with hermeneutical consequences that differentiate the Anabaptists in significant ways from Protestantism in general.

Protestants descended from the magisterial Reformation normally have great difficulty in understanding what is specific to Anabaptist hermeneutics. More conservative Protestants frequently perceive Anabaptists as persons who do not take the Scriptures very seriously. In fact, the most frequent accusation that authors like Calvin made against the Anabaptists was of this nature. The Anabaptists were seen as spiritualists or fanatics who slighted the letter for the sake of the Spirit.[9] Similarly, in more recent epochs, more liberal Protestants often accuse the Anabaptists of being "biblicists," or even as being responsible for fundamentalism. Nevertheless, the historical data are quite patent: the principal representatives of modern fundamentalism have had (and in large measure still have) a Calvinist theological background, while most Anabaptists have remained on the

---

8. Cf. Ibid.
9. Cf. Calvin, *Institutes of the Christian Religion* I, chapter 9.

sidelines of the arguments between liberals and fundamentalists, such as those occurring over the last century. Normally, when a church of Anabaptist origin becomes fundamentalist or liberal, it experiences a significant distancing from its roots. The fact is, Anabaptism cannot be understood within the narrow categories of liberals and fundamentalists, even though, unfortunately, these two simple, general coordinates continue to determine the way most Protestants of all theological tendencies identify themselves nowadays.

To help us understand the impossibility of inserting the Anabaptists into these coordinates that are foreign to them, it may be useful to describe the approach to Scripture we find in Calvin. This theologian begins his *Institutes of Christian Religion* by stating that the height of wisdom is knowledge of God and of ourselves. These two kinds of knowledge are linked with one another, because in knowing God we know our own misery and, in knowing our own misery, we acknowledge the greatness of God. For Calvin, knowledge of God consists not only in acknowledging his existence but also in realizing to what extent that knowledge is beneficial for us. In principle, knowledge of God is implanted naturally in the human mind, although sin corrupts that knowledge and makes way for every form of superstition and idolatry. Furthermore, every human being has access to knowledge of God in the simple contemplation of creation and the divine providence that watches over the world. Nevertheless, sin separates us from this knowledge and from all the benefits deriving from it. Now, according to Calvin, God has established another means for knowing him, one that makes possible a knowledge of God that leads us to salvation, and God bestows this knowledge on those whom he has decided to lead into a closer and more intimate relation with himself. This other means is nothing else but the Scriptures, which are therefore necessary in order to know the true characteristics of God as Creator and Redeemer, over against the collection of false gods that human beings have created for themselves. And what is needed to endow the biblical text with its full authority is the internal testimony of the Holy Spirit, which confers validity on the Scriptures in their own right, without the Catholic Church having to vouch for their credibility.[10]

There are two elements in this argument of Calvin that immediately attract our attention. First, the function of the Scriptures seems to consist primarily in providing us with knowledge: it is a kind of knowledge we are not able to acquire by ourselves, and it is knowledge that is decisive, because it leads to salvation. Second, the whole argument of Calvin may be pursued without any reference at all to a hermeneutical community. In

---

10. Cf. Ibid., chapters 1–7.

fact, all reference to community is rejected since it is associated with claims that the authority of Scripture is derived from ecclesiastical authority. Given these premises, it becomes understandable how both fundamentalism and liberalism among Protestants have deep roots in the ecclesiastical currents deriving from these conceptions so characteristic of the magisterial Reformation. Modern liberalism can emphasize that contemporary science, both human and social, provides us with knowledge about ourselves and the world which, on the one hand, contradicts certain biblical statements, but on the other suffices to produce for us the human fulfilment to which we aspire. From the liberal viewpoint, any pretension of salvation that can be found in the biblical text would have to be reduced to the various ways in which the secular sciences tell us it is possible to achieve human plenitude. For its part, fundamentalism reacts by defending the permanent validity of the information provided by Scripture about human beings, society, and nature, and it also insists on the necessity of such knowledge to obtain salvation. Now, in both cases, the Scriptures are considered primarily as a source of information: more or less antiquated for one side, more or less infallible for the other.

The Anabaptist perspective is radically different from this primarily cognitive and doctrinal use of Scripture. For the Anabaptists of the sixteenth century, the Scriptures were not primarily a source of information about God, the world, or human beings. For them, the Scriptures were above all a means *for following Jesus and, in this way, knowing him personally*. It was not a question of gaining knowledge about the structure of our salvation, but of entering into a personal bond with the Messiah. For that very reason, what was decisive was Jesus himself; the Scriptures were simply signposts indicating the way to follow him. According to the famous expression of Ulrich Stadler, the Scriptures could be understood in the same way as a sign indicating that in a certain inn there was wine.[11] The sign is essential, because it indicates the way to the wine, but the sign is not the wine. Jesus, as the Word of God par excellence, is the goal of the hermeneutical process, and the Scriptures are an instrument for moving toward him. This does not mean ignoring the human need for salvation or our own fragility due to sin. To the contrary, the possibility of understanding the sign, and of desiring and receiving the wine, is without doubt the work of the Spirit that brings about in us a new birth. And that Spirit is none other than the Spirit of Jesus, who, instead of leading us down a solitary road, places us on a path being trod also by others who are following him. Precisely because of our smallness (including that of exegetes and theologians), our fellow believers

---

11. Cf. Stadler "La Palabra Viviente y Escrita," 112–16 (esp. 112).

are an indispensable aid. By insisting on the need for a communitarian hermeneutical process, the Anabaptists, in contrast to Protestants, implicitly acknowledged that the Scriptures were susceptible to different interpretations, some of which did not necessary lead to following Jesus. For that reason, the initial clarity of the biblical text yielded to a process that went beyond any individual reading, including that of a specialist.

When some "sign" is subject to different interpretations, the presence of other persons, all impelled by the same Spirit and desiring to follow the same Lord, helps to prevent individuals from ignoring one another and following their own separate paths. It also thwarts attempts to impose one person's interpretation on everybody else. If we are all led by the same Spirit, and if we all desire to follow the same Lord—and so break with the criteria of the world—then it is worth our while to call a halt in our way and, among everybody, try to discern what direction we should follow. All of these—the activity of one and the same Spirit, the desire to follow one and the same Lord, and the rupture with the world expressed in baptism—are precisely what guarantee that the arduous attainment of unanimity in our prayerful search for the will of God will allow us to walk in the desired direction. Even today, the search for unanimity continues to characterize the decision-making processes in Anabaptist circles. In such cases, it is not a matter of being content with minimal levels of agreement, imposing the will of the majority, or following the indications of the most influential personality. Rather, the aim is to seek out collectively what is indicated by the same Spirit that impels everyone to follow Jesus. The very existence of these difficult processes of communal seeking of God's will is what best guarantees that the "community" is not simply a cover for tyrannical domination by certain individuals or groups. In contrast to both Catholic institutional mediation and Protestant individualism, the Anabaptists understood that there existed a third possibility, one characterized precisely by the fact that the following of Jesus is a communitarian process, one in which a fraternal group, to which one belongs freely, relates itself to the Lord collectively and directly.[12]

We find an example of the essential difference between Anabaptist and Protestant hermeneutics in the way the Anabaptists treated the biblical canon. For the magisterial reformers, the delimitation of the authentic canon of the Scriptures was a central question, since it also meant the delimitation of the doctrines revealed by God. Thus, for example, the exclusion of the so-called "apocryphal writings" of the Old Testament helped to exclude the doctrine of purgatory, which the Catholics found in those texts.[13] Luther

---

12. Cf. Friedmann, *Teología del Anabautismo*, 62.
13. Cf. 2 Macc 12:38.

kept those "apocryphal" or "deutero-canonical" texts in his own edition of the Bible, even though he denied their inspired character and recommended them simply as texts that were beneficial to read. He also questioned the epistle of James since he thought it laid too much stress on works. The criterion used by Luther was no doubt christocentric (*"was Christus treibt"*), but his christocentrism did not simply refer to the person or the message of Jesus in general terms. In fact, the epistle of James contains many echoes of the teaching of Jesus in the Sermon on the Mount. For Luther, however, what was decisive was Jesus as the object of the faith that justifies us, apart from the works of the law. For his part, Calvin simply suppressed the deutero-canonical books, keeping only the texts that he considered truly inspired, and this is the option that most evangelicals have followed up to the present day. Nonetheless, it is important to observe that we are not dealing simply with questions of the past or with discussions of interest only to conservative groups. In our days also, there has appeared in liberal Protestant contexts the idea of a "canon within the canon."[14] What is at issue is precisely a distinction that allows for a *doctrinal* difference to be established between the central message of the Scriptures (for example, justification by faith or some more modern equivalent) and all the other elements that might be found in biblical texts that are derived from or secondary to this message, or even opposed to it. Thus, for example, a distinction is made between the pure, primitive *kerygma* as proclaimed in the authentic letters of Paul and the "proto-Catholicism" that appears in the other epistles.

The Anabaptist perspective, centered on the following of Jesus, places the emphasis elsewhere. For one thing, the Anabaptists were much freer than the Protestants (and the Catholics after Trent) with regard to the canon of Scripture, for they used both the shorter and the longer canons of the Old Testament, without being unduly concerned about certain doctrines presumably founded on them. Even the deutero-canonical book of Tobias constituted a common reading in Anabaptist weddings. The Anabaptists never issued official decisions about the canon. Such freedom was possible for them because Old-Testament texts were interpreted in terms of the following of Jesus, and not merely as sources of doctrinal information. On the other hand, the Anabaptists were more radical than the Protestants in regard to the appropriation and application of those texts having to do with the following of Jesus. They read such texts "without gloss" (to use the expression of Francis of Assisi);[15] that is, they tried to comply fully with

---

14. Cf. Lønning, *Kanon im Kanon*.

15. Francis of Assisi, in his *Testament*, exhorts the monks to live the Franciscan rule *simpliciter et sine glossa*. In the case of the Anabaptists, the reference is the message of Jesus directly.

Jesus's instructions concerning the common ownership of possessions, non-violence, love of enemies, swearing oaths, the state, etc. Jesus was seen not simply as the key to the vault of a general theory of salvation or as a gnostic master of higher knowledge. What was decisive for them was following Jesus in their lives, and by virtue of that following they could be "deliberately naïve," practicing with regard to the biblical texts what Paul Ricoeur has called a "second naiveté."[16]

It is important to have a good understanding of this second, deliberate type of naiveté. For those who practice such "second" or "deliberate" naiveté, radical obedience to the message of Jesus does not derive from a determined conception of biblical inspiration, as is the case in the "first" or "spontaneous" naiveté of the fundamentalists. The second, deliberate type of naiveté is based, not on doctrinal consideration of the value of the biblical text or on a theory about inspiration and inerrancy, but on the desire to follow Jesus. From the Anabaptist perspective, what is decisive is not the way God inspired each word of the biblical text. Rather, what is decisive is that those words, as mediated as they may be by the editorial processes of the New Testament, are the most precious indication that we have today for following Jesus in our lives. And it is precisely the desire to follow Jesus radically that joins the more educated readers together with the less educated ones in a single way of life with a single purpose. While in Protestantism, the more educated believers and the less educated ones normally end up belonging to different churches, in Anabaptism theologians and peasant farmers have been joined together from the very beginning. From the Anabaptist perspective, it is the following of Jesus and not doctrine that gives primary shape to the community and determines the different ministries within it.

Contemporary Hermeneutics and the Following of Jesus

The hermeneutical insights of Anabaptism coincide with some important developments in contemporary hermeneutics.[17] In contrast to the traditional idea of hermeneutics as simply a stock of methods that the specialized interpreter can use to find the true meaning of a text, contemporary philosophy understands hermeneutics to be a universal process in which we are all involved by the sheer fact of being human. Interpretation takes place even in our most modest perceptions, since any meaning we attribute to

---

16. Cf. Ricoeur, *Le Conflit des Interprétations*, 294. On the "deliberate" character of the naiveté of the first Anabaptists, see Driver, *Contra Corriente*, 1–15.

17. A perspective on post-modern hermeneutics can be found in de Wit, *En la Dispersión el Texto es Patria*.

things already involves some interpretation. But such interpretation is not done through the use of the static, universal categories that every subject possesses *qua* subject. Rather, we actually are constituted as human by our being inserted into a cultural, historical horizon, from which horizon we receive the basic categories with which we understand one another and the world that surrounds us. In this way, the horizon of modern subjectivity yields collective processes, in which our identity emerges and the inevitably social character of all our interpretations, from the most modest to the most elaborate, is made manifest.[18]

On the other hand, some tendencies of contemporary hermeneutics have realized that our insertion into the interpretative horizon is not something that happens simply in the world of ideas or in the sphere of linguistic meanings. The meaning of words is linked to their usage, and this usage occurs according to the rules proper to a "linguistic game." Now, contrary to what is usually believed, linguistic games are not just about language: they are primarily games, that is, activities. Every linguistic game is part of a way of life, of a praxis,[19] and this praxis involves not just language, but also persons and activities. This is very important, because it shows us not only that our interpretations have a collective character, but also that they acquire their meaning in the context of a determined praxis. Frequently, hermeneutics has paid more attention to the linguistic character of interpretations than to the way the interpretations are embedded in the concrete activity of a group. This is a matter of great relevance, for it shows that, besides considering the linguistic horizon of a hermeneutic community, we also must refer that linguistic horizon to a praxis. To put it in theological terms, the community of the Spirit also is a community of followers, and the following of Jesus is the praxis of which the community's collective hermeneutical activity is part.

Contemporary hermeneutics often is understood as synonymous with post-modern relativism. Nevertheless, a few observations are in order. First, the post-modern trend is merely the superficial aspect of something much more profound, something of greater intellectual relevance. Post-modernism as a cultural theme began in the 1980s, but intellectual transformations signaling the overcoming of the modern "metaphysics of subjectivity" have been present at least since the end of the nineteenth century. Those transformations have evolved not only into more or less superficial types of relativism, but also into new ways of intellectually treating the question of the absolute. Actually, every form of relativism *relativizes,* insofar as it

---

18. Cf. Gadamer, *Wahrheit und Methode*, 270–312; Vattimo, *Más allá del Sujeto*.
19. Cf. Wittgenstein, *Philosophische Untersuchungen*, §§23, 241.

establishes a *relation* with a term different from itself. And that to which the relative becomes related becomes not a relativized principle, but a principle on the basis of which the relative is understood. Modern epistemology relativized what is known by referring it back to the knowing subject, which thus became a referential absolute. The theory of relativity refers all measurements back to the observer's state of movement, with respect to which they are therefore relative. In this perspective, it is necessary to begin by saying that the existence of a multiplicity of interpretations refers back in principle to a multiplicity of hermeneutical communities, and this latter multiplicity refers back in turn to a multiplicity of ways of life, and these simply give expression to the multiplicity of contemporary humanity. Of course, such multiplicity expresses not only the richness of those diverse ways of life, but also the profound economic, social, and cultural divisions that divide humankind and are directly linked with the oppression and the exclusion of those who are weakest.

From an Anabaptist perspective, the existence of a multiplicity of hermeneutical communities is a basic fact; the multiplicity is clearly presupposed in the decision of the Anabaptists to establish themselves as a fraternity that does not identify itself with society as a whole. No one is obligated to form part of one's own hermeneutical community. The very existence as voluntary community presupposes as a basic, elementary fact the existence of other groups different from one's own. It is therefore no wonder that the Anabaptists were the first to defend freedom of conscience for all religious groups, including not only Christians, but also Muslims and Jews.[20] This was something quite different from, and much earlier than, the religious "tolerance" that was reluctantly granted much later by Protestant governments when pluralism became inevitable.

Now, the existence of a multiplicity of hermeneutical communities did not mean that the Anabaptists considered their own perspective just as true (or, as the case may be, just as false) as any other perspective. The Anabaptists were quite convinced of the truth of their position, to the point of being willing to risk their own lives for that truth. And here we meet up with a characteristic that is proper to the hermeneutics of following. Contemporary hermeneutics speaks of a "fusion of horizons" (*Horizontverschmelzung*)[21] to refer to the unity that is produced in the hermeneutical process between the cultural horizon of the person interpreting a text and the horizon of the interpreted text. This dialogue is no doubt quite important, but in following

---

20. Cf. Hubmeier, "Sobre los Herejes y los que los Queman"; Denk, "Comentario sobre Miqueas," 253.

21. Cf. Gadamer, *Wahrheit und Methode*, 311–12.

Jesus we have something more, something that modern-day hermeneutics longs for.[22] In the hermeneutics of following, we are referred not to a mere text, but to a person. Following a person means leaving one's house, one's valley, one's horizon, in order to enter into unknown territories. In this following, our own interpretative horizon keeps shifting according to the person we are following. As a result, that horizon is not an absolute to which the person we are following has to adapt. It is not even an "absolute" that is "relative" to the pluralism of the multiple hermeneutical communities. Rather, the follower's linguistic and practical horizon is perceived as something secondary with respect to a reality that is neither cultural nor linguistic, but personal: the reality of Jesus. Contrary to what is usually thought in theology, the following of Jesus does not pertain primarily to the language of ethics, but to the language of love, as is so beautifully expressed in the Song of Songs.[23] For that very reason, in the following of Jesus, one's own person, one's own horizon, and even one's own life become relativized with respect to the person we are following. The relativism of this following is a dialogue that is not static, but rather dynamic. Truth does not become relative to my presumptions; rather, my presumptions become relative to a person, who may thus be understood as "Truth," with a capital "T."

From this perspective, it is no wonder that the sixteenth-century Anabaptists defended a high Christology and that most of them had no difficulty accepting the classical creeds of Christianity. Contrary to what is ordinarily thought, this high Christology was not just a relic of the past. If it had been a relic of the past, then there would never have appeared the unilaterally and lopsidedly high Christologies, such as the doctrine of Christ's celestial flesh.[24] As is well known, the Anabaptists, including Menno Simons, defended the thesis that the flesh of Jesus had been created expressly for him and therefore did not come from his mother. Fortunately, this doctrine did not gain historical longevity in Anabaptism since it clashed with the characteristic Anabaptist emphasis on the humanity of Jesus. In fact, without the historical humanity of Jesus there could be no following of him, either in the past or in the present. All the same, a hermeneutics of following is inevitably accompanied by a high Christology, one that affirms the absolute character of Jesus. People don't put their lives on the line for half-truths or half-lies. A person who follows Jesus does so because she thinks that she has found

---

22. Jacques Derrida is referring to something beyond deconstruction when he says that all deconstructive analysis "is done in the name of something, of something positively un-deconstructable"; cf. Caputo, *Deconstruction in a Nutshell*, 128.

23. Cf. Song of Songs 3:1–5.

24. This is the theology we find in Clement Ziegler and Melchor Hoffmann and that appears also in Menno Simons; cf. Williams, *La Reforma Radical*, 362–73.

a pearl that has value, not because she values it, or her community thinks it is important, but because the pearl is valuable in itself. The pearl does not become relativized to her private or her community interests; rather, all the interests of the community of followers become relativized in function of the pearl, to the point of selling everything in order to obtain it (Matt 13:46). In an Anabaptist context, which is not doctrinal, the abandoning of such "high" statements about Jesus normally indicates that the following of Jesus has lost its absolute point of reference.

And this has still a further implication. In the following of Jesus, there is mounting interest, one never satisfied, in knowing the person who is being followed. What is sought is not primarily doctrinal knowledge about salvation, but rather intimate knowledge of a person. The faith that impels us to follow Jesus needs to be constantly confirmed in the personal and inexhaustible knowledge of the one we are following. Precisely because we follow him, we can come to know him more, and precisely because we desire to know him more, we continue to follow him. It is often and rightly said that the sixteenth-century Anabaptists had no great theologians, none who bequeathed to us works comparable to those of Calvin or Melanchthon, but it is no less true that the Anabaptists held theological education in high esteem. Their "theological education," however, was a community happening, as is shown by the fact that the Anabaptist communities quickly achieved full literacy of their members. Following Jesus in community did not require only that members of the Anabaptist groups be born again and freely decide to follow Jesus; all the members of the community, both young and old, women and men, also had to be capable of taking an active part in the hermeneutical process. Instead of forming specialized pastors for the illiterate masses, the Anabaptists preferred to foster an educated community, one made up of members who were able to discern the signs of the Spirit and to interpret the Scriptures collectively, even if they could not produce great theological tomes. And this brings us back to the topic of theological education.

Relevance for Theological Education

Throughout the history of the Christian church, theological education has basically been organized according to four great models: the catechetical model of the ancient church, the monastic and the scholastic models of the Middle Ages, and the seminary model of modern times.[25] Among Anabaptists, theological training has traditionally borne some resemblance to the

25. Cf. Rooy, "Modelos Históricos," 43–58.

catechetical models of the ancient church, although starting in the twentieth century, Anabaptist churches began to create seminaries and biblical institutes similar to those of the Protestant denominations. These seminaries often had the objective of training professional pastors, as demand for these rose in Anabaptist churches during the twentieth century. It would be fair to say that the seminaries conform in large measure to patterns proper to modernity. An effort has been made in them to provide the future pastor with both theological learning and religious and moral formation. After receiving adequate training, which involved separation from the world, the pastors were supposed to be ready for their roles of instructing their congregations about the doctrines proper to their denomination, maintaining a style of life in accord with their religious function, and watching over the discipline of their flock.

Our point here is not to romanticize past models simply because they are from the past. Neither are we interested in rejecting the valuable contributions made by seminaries in the modern era or in declaring their demise. Nevertheless, it is still necessary to ask ourselves about the possibility of using the unique hermeneutical insights of the Anabaptists to help structure theological education in the twenty-first century. In this regard, we must begin by underlining that the priority of theological education, seen from the Anabaptist perspective, lies in the theological training of the people of God, and not primarily in the training of leaders. All the institutions and programs, from the most basic to the most sophisticated, should have as their objective fostering the theological formation of all believers. If all the faithful are empowered by the Holy Spirit to participate in community discernment about the proper ways to follow Jesus, that means that theological training is a necessity for the people of God as a whole, and also for each person individually. What is at issue here is whether the entire community of the Spirit is to be fully empowered—not only spiritually and morally, but also theologically—to seek out collectively the will of God in a concrete situation.

This means that the usual conceptions about theological education will have to change. In a sense, all theological education of leaders has some repercussion on the theological education of the people of God. However, that repercussion usually has the structure of a mediation: first the specialist (theologian, pastor) is trained, and then that specialist becomes responsible for the education of the faithful. The Anabaptist conception changes the emphasis, insisting that the believing people are not a final or collateral objective of theological training, but the first objective. Furthermore, it must be said that, in the Anabaptist perspective, the believing people are not just the object, but also the first agent of theological education. It is possible to wax rhetorical on this matter, but there are at least two elements that help concretize this statement. First, the conception of the people of God as hermeneutical community means that it is absolutely essential that the questions guiding the process theological training be questions that come directly from the people of God, from their needs and their concerns. Theological training cannot consist of answers to questions that nobody asks. Even the most sophisticated theological questions derive, or should derive, from the crucial questions with which the faithful are confronted in their day-to-day activity. Second, theological education does not take place in the context of a people who might be considered "lay" or "untrained" due to their ignorance of theology. The believing people possess a spontaneous theological wisdom that they have steadily built up by their experience of following Jesus, by their spiritual dealing with God, and by their reading of Scripture. This wisdom may be a limited in many ways, but it is an inescapable starting point.

Ignorance of, contempt for, or denial of the theological wisdom of the believing community frustrate the hermeneutical experience, for *they undermine its very starting point*, which is the hermeneutical horizon of those who are interpreting. Without that starting point, educated individuals will experience something like a "brainwashing," which obliges them to situate themselves in a different intellectual horizon, one in which their categories stop functioning. In such a case, what is new finds no fertile soil in which to be sown, and normally it fails to grow. It matters little whether the categories by which the brainwashing takes place are conservative or progressive, fundamentalist or liberal. It can only result in some people imposing their ideas on others and in "lay people" being trained as intellectual clones of the theologians. The root problem here is one of authority. From the Anabaptist viewpoint, hermeneutical authority does not reside in a priest or a pastor who is commissioned by some ecclesiastical institution or by some high authority to watch out for the true doctrine in a determined territory. Neither is it the case that authority resides simply in the hermeneutical community. Properly speaking, the authority resides in the risen and living Lord, whom the community desires to follow. What happens in the Anabaptist perspective is that Jesus exercises his lordship *directly* over the believing community and over each of its members. And it is precisely that structure of authority that prevents the establishment of mediators. As a result, theological specialists are not understood as mediators of divine authority, but rather as servants of a hermeneutical community whose theological wisdom is the inescapable starting point for every educational process. And this brings us to the question about the proper role of specialists in theological education.

The Role of the Specialist

In Matthew's gospel, we find the disconcerting command that we call no one rabbi or teacher; the reason given is that there is only one teacher, and all the members of God's people are brothers and sisters (Matt 23:7–10). There is a literal, and perhaps naïve, way of understanding this teaching, which simply replaces the words used by Jesus with others. Instead of teacher, for example, we might say doctor, reverend, professor, or instructor, in which case the meaning of the command would not change significantly. We might also pay little heed to the teaching, taking it to be an example of Semitic hyperbole, one of many we find in the gospels. However, we could also go to the crux of the question, which is none other than how Jesus understood the reign of God and its deep roots in biblical history. And here we meet up with a curious delegitimizing structure in the Bible. When the Scriptures present God as assuming roles of domination, that means that those same roles have no place among the people of God: they are excluded or delegitimized for human beings. If God is king, then there is no need of other kings. If God is master, then there is no need of other masters. If God is father, then there is no need of other fathers. Thus, the commands of Jesus mentioned above remind us of the basic brother- and sisterhood of the people of God, and they culminate with a call to humility (Matt 23:11–12).

Of course, this call to true fraternity does not mean that in the people of God there will not be persons especially gifted for study and teaching, as there are also for the exercise of leadership functions. Obviously, in a truly fraternal people, the limits on acquiring theological training should have nothing to do with economic means; rather, they should consider mainly intellectual talent and vocational inclination. Certainly not everyone has those talents and inclinations. Now the question is: what is the function in the people of God of those who have such talents and inclinations? Certainly, the earliest writings of Christianity reveal that, from the very beginning, there were certain persons who exercised teaching functions. There is something very interesting to observe here, however. The role of those who were teaching was not necessarily united to other gifts, such as those more associated with leadership or with care of souls, that is, the gifts of presbyters, pastors, deacons, etc. The unification of the diverse gifts of teaching, leadership, and care of souls into a single ministry represents an enormous oversimplification of the church's history. No doubt such gifts may be justifiably combined in certain persons, but it is also perfectly normal for those gifts to be found in different persons.[26] No doubt the institutional unification of different roles in a single person has historically favored the view that the

---

26. Cf. Yoder, *El Ministerio de Todos*.

ministry of teaching should act as an authority that mediates between the Christian people and the divine authority or between the Christian people and the correct denominational interpretation of the Scriptures.

To counter such tendencies, it is important to emphasize that the theological specialist is a member of the people of God. This statement may seem a truism, but it takes on meaning when we express it in hermeneutical terms. Specifically, we are speaking of the insertion of the specialist in the way of life and the style of language of the people of God. While "conservatives" are scandalized because society as a whole does not take part in the church's way of life and style of language, and while "liberals" are scandalized because the church does not take part in the way of life and style of language of the society as a whole, what is truly scandalous, in the Anabaptist perspective, is not the existence of a multiplicity of forms of life or styles of language, but rather the fact that the churches can be led by persons who do not share the linguistic praxis of their own communities. A theological specialist will certainly be able to master many linguistic registers, but the decisive question is whether his primary reference is the way of life and the language of his people, as opposed to the way of life and the language of the clergy, or the theologians, or the elite groups of his society. Because, even if one understands many linguistic registers, there is only one that is basic and essential, namely, the one by which one's own life is structured and one's crucial decisions are made. When such is the case, then even the most highly specialized theologian can still be a member of the hermeneutical community, as a true "organic intellectual," vitally joined with the people of God.

As a member of the hermeneutical community, the specialist or the theologian is a servant. The ways appeals are made to service to disguise domination is no doubt a very hackneyed topic in the history of the Christian church, but that does not mean that there do not exist criteria for evaluating whether we are dealing with true service. When the hermeneutical horizon of the believing community is negated, when its wisdom is despised, when its way of life is ignored, and its experience is ridiculed, then we have all the elements for suspecting that we are not dealing with service but with domination, or at least an attempt to dominate. That does not mean, of course, that the way of life or the concrete wisdom of the community is an absolute. If the community is following in the way of the Messiah, it will be ready and willing to have its own hermeneutical horizon undergo transformations as it moves into new territories. The labor of the specialist is not to trace a path apart from the hermeneutical community, but to walk along with the community and place his resources and talents at the service of that walking together. To return to the metaphors with which we began this reflection:

Hermes was the Greek god of travelers and those who cross borders. When the onetime devotee of Hermes is called to the following of Jesus, his specialization as a hermeneutist does not make him, like Hermes, a mediator between the community and the gods. Rather, it is now Jesus who guides the whole community directly by means of the Spirit who, through his gifts, becomes present in the midst of the community. The specialized interpreter is simply another member of the community, one who places his translating ability at the service of the community's experience, which is the experience of the people as they follow along the way. And that interpreting service does not consist in translating divine messages by himself, thus arrogating to himself the role of messenger of the gods; rather, it consists precisely in teaching the whole people to translate—and in learning oneself, along with the people, to translate ever more effectively.

In a New Century

Our new century provides us with important opportunities and challenges precisely in this direction. For one thing, globalizing of human relationships points toward the establishment of a sort of worldwide society in which all the members of humankind will engage in interactions that have a planetary character. The dynamisms that are impelling this globalization of human relationships are basically economic, although they also involve the establishment of other global ties, such those of an ecological nature. Now, the process of globalization has been made possible by the establishment of wide-reaching information networks, especially the Internet, and these networks are in turn driven by the globalizing process. In fact, our globalized world may fairly be described as an information society, a society that functions through institutions that are structured in the form of networks. In a network, there is no one center; rather, there are many centers that take the form of nodes linked with one another through reciprocal transmission of information. With networks there is not one transmitter and a whole bunch of receivers; rather, there is a multiplicity of both transmitters and receivers. As a result, networks allow more flexibility and adaptability in the way we work, thus fomenting a culture of endless deconstruction and construction, a politics that immediately processes new values and opinions, and a social organization that seeks to be independent of space and time. Such developments can be observed in formal and informal economies, in cultural and religious movements, and even in illegal armed organizations.

It would be naïve to think these processes are the same as democratization. Global power still is highly concentrated in gigantic multinational corporations, which function in the economic network as nodes around which small and medium-size businesses group themselves. In these networks, capital flows escape control of individuals, and power takes on an anonymous character; it appears as a sort of "faceless collective capitalism," which is nevertheless decisive for the lives of millions of people. For individuals, the economic and financial networks seem to be in disorder; they appear as forces that are incomprehensible, out of control, and threatening to their identity. And that question of identity has become a decisive one in our world today. The fact is that the great "network society" is unable to provide people with any more identity than that which derives from the worship of technology, the adoration of the power of capital and information flows, and the veneration of the logic of the markets. As a result of all this, identities are now formed outside the institutions of civil society, by means of an alternative social logic, one independent of the principles prevailing in society as a whole. For that reason, the alternative powers engaging in conflict with the dominant logic in today's information society are being articulated precisely by those particular identities (national, religious, sexual, ethnic, etc.). The classic conflict between capital and labor thus assumes the form of the conflict between anonymous flows of capital and the cultural values of people's daily experience. Of course, that does not mean that these resistance identities do not also have to organize themselves in the form of networks.[27]

In this context, the Anabaptist conception of church acquires a new relevance, unsuspected in recent centuries. The Christian church does not necessarily have to be a centralized organization, but it can be a fraternal network of communities gathered around Jesus. The believing community, as a reality distinct from the world, is the domain in which a new identity is constituted, over against a society so reduced to material production that it is barely able to provide its members any identity at all. Nevertheless, the Christian identity is not a national, ethnic, or tribal identity; rather, it is a global identity, one that gives rise to a fraternal people spread throughout the world. This identity expresses not only a rejection of the structures currently dominant on the planet, but also a hope for all humankind. It is an eschatological hope, one that is able to discern, in the individual and collective transformations that are taking place in the people of God, the first fruits of God's project for all peoples, who are therefore not condemned to oppression, despair, and meaninglessness, but are welcomed into a radical renewal of all of creation, until God is all in all.

---

27. Cf. Castells, *La Era de la Información*.

These brief observations also may be relevant for an Anabaptist conception of theological education in the new century. The current social and cultural situation of our world perhaps opens up to us the possibility of setting forth on new paths. Information technologies offer new possibilities for transcending the traditional frameworks of classroom education and nationally organized institutions. Of course, it is not enough just to opt for new technologies will not be enough, for these require economic resources and types of linguistic and technical knowledge that are not within the reach of all. The Internet makes it possible for certain people who are able to gain access to information to place themselves at the service of broader constituencies, in the form of groups organized for the purpose of theological training and reflection in the different communities. Such a procedure can be quite relevant for theological education in certain linguistic realms, for example, Spanish. In Latin America, there are a few Anabaptist seminaries, but they can hardly satisfy the needs of all the churches on the continent. In Spain, there is no specifically Anabaptist seminary. In such a context, would it not make sense to develop a true network for Anabaptist theological education in Spanish, one which uses as its nodes the various educational institutions that already exist, and which places itself in service of theological education geared to local churches? Creating such a network would be a way of bringing about, in a horizontal, fraternal manner, a renewal of the hermeneutical community for the needs of the twenty-first century.

Bibliography

Calvin, John. *Institutes of the Christian Religion*. Christian Classics Ethereal Library. http://www.ccel.org/ccel/calvin/institutes/.

Caputo, John D., ed. *Deconstruction in a Nutshell: A Conversation with Jacques Derrida*. New York: Fordham University Press, 1997.

Castells, Manuel. *La Era de la Información: Economía, Sociedad y Cultura*. 3 vols. Mexico City: Siglo Veintiuno, 1999.

Denk, H. "Comentario sobre Miqueas" (1527). In *Selecciones Teológicas Anabautistas*, edited by W. Klaassen. Scottdale, PA: Herald, 1985.

———. "De lo que se Pretende que Digan las Escrituras." In *Textos Escogidos de la Reforma Radical*, edited by John Howard Yoder, 206–29. Buenos Aires: Ediciones La Aurora, 1976.

de Wit, Hans. *En la Dispersión el Texto es Patria: Introducción a la Hermenéutica Clásica, Moderna y Posmoderna*. San José: Universidad Biblica Latinoamericana, 2002.

Driver, John. *Contra Corriente: Ensayo de Eclesiología Radical*. 3rd ed. Guatemala City: Semilla, 1998.

Friedmann, Robert. *Teología del Anabautismo: Una Interpretación*. Bogotá: Clara, 1998.

Gadamer, Hans-Georg. *Wahrheit und Methode: Grundzüge einer Philosphischen Hermeneutik*. Tübingen: Mohr/Siebeck, 1990.

Hubmaier, Balthasar. "Sobre los herejes y los que los queman" ("Concerning Heretics and Those Who Burn Them; January 1, 1524). Georgetown University, Berkley Center for Religion, Peace, and World Affairs. https://berkleycenter.georgetown. edu/quotes/balthasar-hubmaier-concerning-heretics-and-those-who-burn-them-on-dealing-with-the-godless.

"Interrogación de Ambrosius Spitelmaier" (1527). In *Selecciones Teológicas Anabautistas*, edited by W. Klaassen. Scottdale, PA: Herald, 1985.

Lønning, Inge. *Kanon im Kanon: Zum Dogmatischen Grundlagenproblem des Neutestamentlichen Kanons*. Forschungen zur Geschichte und Lehre des Protestantismus 10/43. Munich: Kaiser, 1972.

Ricoeur, Paul. *Le Conflit des Interpretations: Essais d'Hermeneutique*. Paris: Seuil, 1969.

Rooy, Sidney. "Modelos Históricos de la Educación Teológica." In *Nuevas Alternativas de Educación Teológica*, edited by C. René Padilla, 43–58. Buenos Aires: Creación, 1986.

Stadler, Ulrich. "La Palabra Viviente y Escrita" (1527). In *Selecciones Teológicas Anabautistas*, edited by W. Klaassen. Scottdale, PA: Herald, 1985.

Vattimo, Gianni. *Más allá del Sujeto: Nietzsche, Heidegger y la Hermenéutica*. Barcelona: Paídos, 1989.

Williams, George Huntston. *La Reforma Radical*. Mexico City: Fondo de Cultura Económica, 1983.

Wittgenstein, Ludwig. *Philosophische Untersuchungen*. Frankfurt: Suhrkamp 1984.

Yoder, John Howard. *The Fullness of Christ: Paul's Revolutionary Vision of Universal Ministry*. Elgin, IL: Brethren Press, 1987.

———. *El Ministerio de Todos: Creciendo Hacia la Plenitud de Cristo*. Bogotá: CLARA, 1995.

4

Less is More—Revisiting Classical Christian Texts in a "De-Churched" Society

The Case of Philippians

Eva van Urk and Peter-Ben Smit

Introduction[1]

THIS PAPER PRESENTS AN experimental case study in contextual hermeneutics. It explores the hermeneutical and heuristic potential of taking seriously the contemporary experience of marginalization of churches in the Netherlands as a context from which to approach the biblical text—with an eye toward gaining a stronger sensitivity for and awareness of marginality and marginalization. The focus on these particular religious communities and these particular texts is incidental, but since there is much material available concerning them, they provide a good starting point. In principle, this study also could have been conducted with Muslim communities, with the Qur'an as a starting point, for instance. An overarching concern of the experiment at stake here is to show that contextually based hermeneutics can indeed contribute fresh insight into texts, insights that are of historical relevance as well.

In order to answer the question of whether exploring the biblical text from the perspective of marginalization can be hermeneutically fruitful, we

---

1. Versions of this paper were presented to the Netherlands Missionary Council (Nederlandse Zendingsraad) on 8 December 2017 (Amersfoort, The Netherlands), in a workshop on the study conference "Hartsverlangen" organized by "Op Goed Gerucht" on 26 January 2018 (Driebergen, The Netherlands) and to an audience of religious practitioners in a seminar on 24 February 2018 (Inspiratiedag Contextuele Bijbelinterpretatie, "Lezen met Passie," Ermelo, the Netherlands).

study it from several perspectives. First, we survey the current situation of churches in the Netherlands, using recent research from the field to establish the numerical decline and sense of marginalization they experience. At the same time, we explore the Bible in Dutch society, also drawing our findings from recent empirical research. Second, we approach a section of the biblical text, specifically Paul's Letter to the Philippians, with the context of marginality and marginalization in mind. We take a fresh look at three sections of the letter: Paul's introduction of himself in chapter 1; the Christ "hymn" in chapter 2; and aspects of Paul's instructions to the community in Philippi in chapter 3. At the conclusion of this study, we will have demonstrated that taking seriously the experiences of marginality (and marginalization) as currently experienced by Dutch churches indeed does offer new insight into the biblical text, making visible (again) aspects of the text that have been forgotten, in part because of their status as canonical texts.

Churches in the Dutch Religious Landscape: Survey and Trends

In the twentieth century, the Netherlands underwent a drastic change regarding the religious affiliation of the population. From a society that was once "pillarized"—organized into pillars or "parallel societies" based on religion or ideology, a process undertaken with a very high level of involvement and commitment of the people—Dutch society since the 1950s has developed at an increasingly rapid speed, resulting in more than half of the population now being "unaffiliated." Given current demographic trends,[2] it is likely that this number will continue to increase. Recent research also shows that not only is the number of people affiliating themselves with a religious tradition declining, but also those who do remain believe less firmly in doctrines.[3] Although such studies always can be questioned, and these trends may not necessarily persist,[4] it is nonetheless the case that Dutch churches have decreased significantly. In addition, another trend also can be observed: whereas, until the 1950s, the church typically was respected and enjoyed a relatively positive image, this has shifted substantially, with (institutionalized) religion having a very negative image in the Dutch media and public discourse at large.[5] Despite the efforts of smaller churches and movements within churches that have attempted to counter the trend (e.g.,

2. Cf. Schmeets, *De religieuze kaart*.
3. Cf. the research report by Bernts and Berghuijs, *God in Nederland 1966–2015*.
4. Cf., with an eye to the Dutch context, Paul, *Secularisatie*.
5. Cf. e.g., the essay by Mikkers, *Religiestress*.

new-church plants or the adoption of the Anglican "Fresh Expressions" approach by the Protestant Church in the Netherlands) and the fact that there are strong regional differences (e.g., the Dutch "Bible belt"),[6] the fact is that churches must reorganize, downsize, close and sell off buildings, and prepare themselves for further decline. One important result of this trend is that churches have begun to see themselves as being marginal in Dutch society, certainly in those areas of the country that are politically, culturally, and economically dominant—such as the Randstad area, which includes large cities such as Amsterdam, Rotterdam and Utrecht. This is true despite the fact that churches continue to have considerable resources (and societal privileges) at their disposal. The expectation of continuing decline tends to dominate discussions; in church reports and statements by church representatives, for example, the assumption that the decline will continue is evident in statements such as "in the village of so and so, people are *still* going to church on a regular basis."[7] Churches are only beginning to come to terms with this traumatic experience and with the realization that attempts to counter the tide, so far at least, have not worked.[8] The resulting situation for churches can be described as one of uncertainty in a "de-churched" society. A "secularized society" may not be the best way to describe it, as religion continues to play a major role in Dutch *politics* (currently two out of four parties in the ruling coalition are explicitly Christian; Islam is a major political topic even if only five percent of the population is Muslim), in Dutch *culture* (much is invested in the restoration and renovation of historical churches, for instance), and in Dutch *media* (much attention continues to be given to religious groups, positively or not). At the same time, however, religion seems to be in the process of transforming itself.

The Bible in Dutch Society

One of the institutions quite preoccupied with changes in the Dutch religious landscape is the Netherlands Bible Society (Nederlands Bijbelgenootschap). On a regular basis, this society commissions or conducts research into the use of the Bible in the Netherlands. Such research usually is conducted in both public and private partnerships, ensuring both its scholarly quality and its relevance to the purposes of the Netherlands Bible

---

6. On which, see Snel, "Waarom daar?"

7. This issue is noted and (partially) addressed by the Protestant Church in the Netherlands in its business plan; Plaisier, *Kerk 2025*, 9.

8. Cf., e.g., from the Dutch setting, the outline and proposal of missiologist Paas, *Vreemdelingen en priesters*.

Society—purposes not primarily academic in nature. The last survey was conducted in 2017,[9] the results of which are relevant to the current study. First, the survey showed that a substantial segment of the population—as high as 20 percent—continues to read the Bible. This is surprising, given the trends described above. Probably not incidentally, the Bible was voted to be the single most important book of the Netherlands a few months prior to this research project.[10] These findings may be indicative of two things: the continuing commitment to the Christian tradition of a substantial part of the population *and* a shared recognition in society of the enduring cultural and intellectual value of the Bible.[11] Furthermore, the way in which the Bible was approached by survey participants appeared to relate to biographical factors more than to denominational factors—suggesting that the "pillarization" of Dutch society also has lost its hold on approaches to the Bible.[12]

Particularly noteworthy, as perceived from the Dutch context of marginalized churches and declining religious affiliation, was that several participants from divergent traditions (both from the more liberal and the more orthodox ends of the spectrum) indicated that they experienced the Bible as something "tangible" that has the potential to positively unite people and create a sense of community. Many reported a desire to participate in some sort of reading group and to share their positive experiences with such a group. The idea of people reading the Bible together, particularly with a shared sense of its importance and/or spiritual value, seemed to represent something to rely on in the midst of life's insecurities and societal changes. It could thus very well be that an awareness of being "marginalized" as a religious believer—in a society in which church attendance and church life is less and less firmly structured and taken for granted—might come together with a need to find or hold fast to common religious grounds like "a shared Bible," however variously perceived. Thus, it is perhaps not only aspects of

---

9. The official research report has been published on the website of the Netherlands Bible Society; see "NBG-Onderzoek Bijbelgebruik."

10. Cf. the announcement by the organization of the competition, a coalition of publishers and other stakeholders (most of which are secular or at least not affiliated with a church), "De Bijbel gekozen."

11. At the same time, however, just like churches and (institutionalized) religion may suffer from a poor image, reading or possessing a Bible is frequently seen as something strange and utterly surprising. One participant in the qualitative survey on Bible use (commissioned by the Netherlands Bible Society, "NBG-Onderzoek Bijbelgebruik Nederland") reported that he—as a "non-believer" and someone who is intellectually interested in the Bible—hears from his friends that they, as a matter of course, stay far away from it.

12. On the concept of pillarization (and a critique of it), see the contributions in van Dam, Kennedy and Wielenga, *Achter de zuilen*.

individual biblical texts—like Philippians—that can be rediscovered from within a "de-churched" society, but also the significance of the biblical corpus as a whole as it is still present in the hearts and minds of people.

Moreover, participants in both the qualitative and quantitative survey of the research project indicated that they would appreciate a variety of reading helps for understanding the Bible. However, the kind of "tools" they requested varied—from more historical background, to information about the cultural value of the Bible, to help for connecting the Bible to everyday life. Yet, what this research project did not (and did not aim to) investigate, is what kind of hermeneutics the current religious climate in the Netherlands produces, or which opportunities it offers for rediscovering aspects of the biblical texts that have previously been ignored or underrepresented in biblical interpretation (scholarly or "popular"). Taking into account both the current situation of churches in the Netherlands and the recent survey of Bible use, this study asks whether the declining numbers and social status of churches—and the resulting trauma and sense of marginalization—offers a hermeneutical vantage point for rediscovering forgotten (or ignored) aspects of biblical texts.

The Marginal in Biblical Interpretation

In biblical interpretation—and New Testament studies in particular—the "marginal" plays a role in two ways. On one hand, most exegetes are aware of the fact that all New Testament texts were written with small communities in mind.[13] On the other hand, a substantial number of scholars also would argue that the New Testament texts have a preference for people at the margins of society; they might express this a "preferential option for the poor," now frequently incorporated as part of "empire criticism."[14] In other words, the biblical texts often are interpreted as speaking primarily to the situation of the marginalized. Yet, these two understandings of the marginal in the New Testament frequently emerge from different scholarly discourses, and in neither case is the historical question asked about what it means for a text to be produced and received within a marginal (or minority) situation. Rather, what happens all too often is the fact that a text is produced by a marginal author (e.g., Paul) and read by a marginal community

---

13. Cf., e.g., the description of Pauline Christianity in Meeks, *First Urban Christians*, and the statistics in Stark, *Rise of Christianity* and Bryant, "Sociology of Early Christianity," 311–39.

14. Cf. e.g., with a focus on poverty, Sandford, *Poverty, Wealth, and Empire*; Armitage, *Theories of Poverty*.

(e.g., small groups of Christians somewhere in Greece), but this often is not taken into account in understanding the texts themselves. The same applies to liberation-theology-inspired hermeneutics: the fact that the texts themselves stem from a marginal setting frequently does not play an in-depth role in their interpretation.[15] For this hermeneutical tendency, an explanation is readily available: it takes a considerable effort to imagine a text that, for all practical purposes, functions as one of the world's foremost "classics" as having functioned in quite a marginal setting. Rather, the texts of the New Testament are read in relation to questions and concerns that emerged when the Christian *ekklesia* was no longer a marginal phenomenon, but a major player in society. Contemporary exegetes, of whichever variety, primarily speak to a large audience—even an average college classroom or a small-to-medium parish is probably larger than the Pauline congregation in, say, Philippi. In both settings, there is a strong awareness of either teaching a classic of a dominant world religion or of being part of such a religion. This influences our appreciation of a text, both historically and when it comes to the kind of questions we are inclined to ask about it. The fact that the texts themselves are marginal as well is, apparently, forgotten.

A Case Study: Paul's Letter to the Philippians

In this case study, we approach the letter of Paul to the Philippians with the context of marginalization in mind. We ask several questions: *In what way is Paul's situation marginal? In what way is the Philippians' situation marginal? How is the situation of marginality negotiated in the letter? Does this "marginal" approach, made possible by the sense of marginalization of Dutch churches, lead to new (historical) insight into the text?* In order to explore these questions, we consider both Paul's situation and that of the Philippians at large, as well as a number of key texts from the letter—in each instance asking to what extent marginalization plays a role and, if so, the ways in which it is negotiated.[16]

---

15. A notable exception and an attempt to do things differently—and by doing so revealing a trend in earlier scholarship—is Carr and Conway, *Introduction to the Bible*. An example of the trend would be Clements, *Mothers on the Margin?*, who does note the topic of marginality, but does not relate it to Matthew's negotiation of his own place in the Greco-Roman world.

16. In this context, it should be stressed that here no distinction is made between "perceived" and "real" marginalization or persecution; for self-perception and strategies of negotiation, this hardly matters for Paul or for the Philippians. Cf. on the construction of precariousness as an identity marker of religious groups, e.g. Beekers, "*Precarious Piety.*" On negotiation in relation to Pauline epistles, see also: Harrison,

Paul and the Philippians: Multiple Marginalization

In exploring the marginal situation of Paul and of the Philippian community, there are several considerations. First, Paul and the Philippians are part of a minority within a minority: the Jewish community within the Roman Empire. Pauline Christianity should be seen as a variant of this larger group, a marginal phenomenon in terms of number of members as well as political and cultural status. Within this group, the early "Christ devotees"—those who recognized the Messiah or savior in Jesus—represented an even smaller minority that was at odds with "mainstream" Judaism. They were a sect within a sect—in the sociological sense of the word.[17] This may not have led to outright persecution, but it certainly led to tensions.

Furthermore, as is apparent from Paul's letter, he himself is in prison, which indicates further marginalization (even if it is unclear why or where he is in prison). The Philippians are under some sort of external pressure as well and, even though the source of this pressure is not clear, it does contribute to anxiety in the community and needs to be negotiated. In his letter, Paul proposes a connection between his own marginal situation and that of the Philippians, by stating, in one of the first sections of his letter:

> Only, live your life in a manner worthy of the gospel of Christ, so that, whether I come and see you or am absent and hear about you, I will know that you are standing firm in one spirit, striving side by side with one mind for the faith of the gospel, and are in no way intimidated by your opponents. For them this is evidence of their destruction, but of your salvation. And this is God's doing. For he has graciously granted you the privilege not only of believing in Christ, but of suffering for him as well— since you are having the same struggle that you saw I had and now hear that I still have. (Phil 1:27–30)[18]

In addition, it should be noted that the community of Christ devotees in Philippi is likely small; estimates run from 40 to about 100 members.[19] Even

---

"Paul and Empire," 165–84.

17. Cf. Elliott, "Jewish Messianic Movement," 75–95.

18. All biblical citations are from the New Revised Standard Version (NRSV).

19. Cf., e.g., the estimations in the following commentaries. Hawthorn and Martin, *Philippians*, xxxiv–xxxix, do acknowledge the minority status of the Philippians, but make little use of this insight in the course of their exegesis of the letter. The same applies to the (plagiarizing, but nonetheless useful) commentary by O'Brien, *Epistle to the Philippians*. Reumann, *Philippians*, 3–6, does not pay attention to the question of the size of the community. These commentaries also pay scant attention to the marginal situation of both Paul and the Philippians and the negotiation of this situation. Although interested in marginalization as such, this applies to Agosto, "Letter to the Philippians,"

by the modest standards of an ancient city, this is not a large group of people, especially as it was most certainly not only made up of upper-class members.

All of this is well known in scholarly literature, but it does establish a vantage point for further interrogating the letter of Paul to the Philippians. Although it has been read and continues to be read as a religious classic with a readership of billions, for all practical purposes, the letter originated as a semi-private piece of correspondence for a readership of fewer than a hundred people, authored by an obscure man in prison in an unknown place. Is this situation of marginalization addressed in a particular way or even negotiated in Philippians? In order to answer this question, we consider Paul's own situation, as he presents it—as well as aspects of the situation of the Philippians—by focusing on three texts from Phil 1, 2 and 3.

Philippians 1: Paul in Prison

Paul's imprisonment is an obvious place to begin when it comes to exploring experiences of marginalization (the location of Paul's imprisonment—in Rome, Ephesus, Caesarea or yet somewhere else—is, for the purposes of this essay, of secondary importance). Imprisonment is always a form of marginalization; being excluded from society with restricted freedom of movement was in antiquity an even greater hardship than it is today. In addition, imprisonment usually meant that someone was awaiting trial; punishments usually took the form of physical punishment, banishment, fines, or a combination of all three. Prisoners typically had to provide for themselves while imprisoned and were, as a result, dependent on others for their survival.[20]

When considering Paul's remarks about his own imprisonment and marginal status, it would seem that his strategy is to turn the tables on those holding him prisoner and seeking to marginalize him—possibly even in a rather definite fashion (cf. 1:20–24; capital punishment may have been on the horizon, even if only as a possibility),[21] which turns him into a credible and honorable leader figure again.[22] This is the case, because from the

---

281–93. This also applies to Harrison, "Paul and Empire." For a good overview of all kinds of power relations in and around Philippians, see: Marchal, *Philippians*. Works such as Holloway, *Consolation in Philippians*, as well as Holloway's 2017 commentary (*Philippians*), do pay attention to the marginal nature of the situations of both Paul and the Philippians, yet the terminology of "consolation" may obscure the agency and creativity claimed and exercised by Paul.

20. On which, see: Wansink, *Chained in Christ*, 27–95.

21. Paul is not suicidal, though, cf. Smit, "War Paulus suizidal?," 113–18.

22. Cf. Shaner, *Enslaved Leadership*, on power play in the *ekklesia* in relation to Paul's imprisonment.

very first line of the letter onwards, Paul uses dishonorable language about himself (and Timothy) and interprets the meaning of this language in the light of the Christ event (as described in Phil 2:5–11). This is to say: he introduces himself and Timothy as follows: Παῦλος καὶ Τιμόθεος δοῦλοι Χριστοῦ Ἰησοῦ ("Paul and Timothy, servants of Christ Jesus," Phil 1:1). Except for someone familiar with the language of the LXX, in which devotees of YHWH are referred to as slaves of YHWH,[23] this would be a surprising introduction, which, as a matter of fact, only occurs in a Pauline introduction here. To be a slave was not desirable, to be the slave of someone who was himself a slave, i.e. Christ (cf. Phil 2:7), even less so. Yet, as in Phil 2, it is precisely the *obedience* (not the disobedience, as one might expect) of Christ, the voluntary slave, that is the reason for his hyper-exaltation. Being the slave of Christ, the voluntary and now-exalted slave, is, in fact, a verbal badge of honor, in a way, a *nom de guerre*, as it were.[24] Paul continues this strategy in the remainder of chapter 1, describing his own imprisonment, which, as he underlines, is "for Christ" (ἐν Χριστῷ, v. 13) in terms that turn it into an effective tool for evangelization, rather than allowing it to marginalize him. In a way, Paul reverses the center and margin of the (physical) and social space, in which he finds himself; pressed into the margins, he presents the margins as the center, from which the good news penetrates the world around it:

> I want you to know, beloved, that what has happened to me has actually helped to spread the gospel, so that it has become known throughout the whole imperial guard and to everyone else that my imprisonment is for Christ; and most of the brothers and sisters, having been made confident in the Lord by my imprisonment, dare to speak the word with greater boldness and without fear. Some proclaim Christ from envy and rivalry, but others from goodwill. These proclaim Christ out of love, knowing that I have been put here for the defense of the gospel; the others proclaim Christ out of selfish ambition, not sincerely but intending to increase my suffering in my imprisonment. What does it matter? Just this, that Christ is proclaimed in every way, whether out of false motives or true; and in that I rejoice. (Phil 1:12–18)

Although imprisoned, Paul claims agency for himself, and uses the politically connoted (yet at this stage also already "Christianized") term εὐαγγέλιον ("gospel," v. 12) as an expression to describe the message that

---

23. Cf., e.g., the overview of references and brief discussion in Thompson and Longenecker, *Philippians and Philemon*, 22 (and the literature mentioned there).
24. A term that, coincidentally, also derives from Dutch history.

penetrates the "imperial guard" (ἐν ὅλῳ τῷ πραιτωρίῳ, "throughout the whole imperial guard," v. 13; the expression also can connote a building),[25] the place from which the (imperial) εὐαγγέλιον would be likely to come forth, as such an εὐαγγέλιον would typically have feats of the imperial army or the emperor as its contents.

In a next step, Paul also addresses the various options for his future, which seem to come down to either death or liberty, in which case, he will return to the Philippians. In the face of all this, Paul positions himself in a detached manner, that reminds us of (and probably is intended as an expression of) *autarkeia*, i.e., self-sufficiency, not allowing oneself to be determined by the circumstances of life (cf. also: 4:11–12). For Paul, however, Christ's glorification as his ultimate point of orientation and the perspective from which he evaluates things, rather than cynicism, is what enables this attitude. As Christ's glorification can be furthered both by Paul's living body and or by the death of his body (provided he remains steadfast and is not be put to shame, cf. 1:20), both are equally valid options:

> . . . for I know that through your prayers and the help of the Spirit of Jesus Christ this will turn out for my deliverance. It is my eager expectation and hope that I will not be put to shame in any way, but that by my speaking with all boldness, Christ will be exalted now as always in my body, whether by life or by death. For to me, living is Christ and dying is gain. If I am to live in the flesh, that means fruitful labor for me; and I do not know which I prefer. I am hard pressed between the two: my desire is to depart and be with Christ, for that is far better; but to remain in the flesh is more necessary for you. (Phil 1:19–24)

Ultimately, this also allows Paul to turn himself into an example for the Philippians,[26] given that he establishes himself to such an extent as a paradigmatic figure (at least when seen within the frame of reference that Paul presupposes, i.e. that of the *cursus honorum* of Christ, as presented in chapter 2 and of the glorification of Christ as the central measuring rod for what is and is not valuable). At the very end of what is now chapter 1 of Philippians and which also constitutes the conclusion of Paul's introductory remarks and his sharing of news about himself from an epistolary and rhetorical point of view, he is even able to state the following:

> For he has graciously granted you the privilege not only of believing in Christ, but of suffering for him as well—since you are

25. Cf. on the possible meanings of *praetorium*, e.g., Becker, "Polemik und Autobiographie," 233–54, 240–41.

26. On which, see Smit, *Paradigms of Being in Christ*.

having the same struggle that you saw I had and now hear that I still have. (Phil 1:29–30)

Thus, within the scope of thirty verses, Paul has moved from being a pitiable, marginalized prisoner, who, as he may hint at in v. 4 and as will become a major topic in the course of the letter (cf. especially 4:10–20), depends on support from the Philippians, to being a model Christ devotee, in charge of even his circumstances in prison, unafraid of what may happen to him and focused on that what matters to him: the glorification of Christ, either by dying or by living. This, indeed, represents a certain strategy of negotiating marginalization, and Paul accomplishes this by introducing a different frame of reference, that of Christ and his devotion to Christ, and evaluating his circumstances from that perspective. With that, he also is able to (re)claim agency for himself and try to exhort the Philippians to follow in his footsteps. Paul negotiates marginalization by introducing different standards for determining what marginal is; he seems to consider his prison cell not a place of dishonor and exclusion from society but rather the center of the world, from which the good news emanates and from which he sends advice to communities elsewhere.

Philippians 2: Christ Crucified

Paul's dependence on a very particular frame of reference, i.e. the Christ event and his total dedication to Christ as Lord, invites further consideration, especially as Paul introduces this frame of reference explicitly in chapter 2, the famous "hymn" that he quotes there. The tradition-historical background of the text in vv. 5–11 do not need to concern us here, but its relation to a marginalized existence does.[27] In a manner akin to Paul's *modus operandi* in chapter 1, here the crucifixion itself—as a ritualized form of execution and the "best" way to marginalize someone totally and ensure his complete exclusion from any form of human society, even from a recognizable existence as a human being—is denied all marginalizing power. As Christ empties himself and takes on human form voluntarily, acting the role of a slave on purpose and dying on the cross out of obedience, the entire logic of the crucifixion—a penalty meant for those subverting social order, for instance by running away as a slave—is thereby subverted. Instead of a gateway to dishonor for disobedient slaves, it becomes a gateway to the highest honor imaginable due to Christ's obedience (cf. v. 9). This notwithstanding the fact that the shape of Christ's obedience to God was simultaneously the shape

---

27. For this and the following also see Smit, "Cruci*fiction*?," 12–24.

of his disobedience vis-à-vis the powers of this world, notably of those in a position to inflict crucifixion, i.e. Roman imperial authorities. A radical reinterpretation is an expression of reclaiming agency, given that the Christ devotees themselves who created the text determine what the true meaning of the cross is, thereby also negotiating both their marginal position and the seemingly marginal position of the crucified Christ, whom they claim received glory rather than shame by being crucified. The "repositioning" of Christ from the margin (cross) to the center (the name above all names, receiving cosmic worship, cf. 2:9–11) also means repositioning the community of Christ devotees, who may seem to be in the margins, but, viewed from this interpretation of the cross, are actually connected to the center of the order of things. By renegotiating the position of Christ in the order of things, by means of the "hymn," those who produced the hymn and now Paul,[28] who employs it in a new context, also renegotiate their own apparent marginal position. A side-effect of this is, of course, also that the societally dominant frame of reference is unmasked as precisely that: a frame of reference, not as the "natural order" of things. By voicing a "countercultural" view of the world, the early Christian perspective will have served to reveal that the dominant culture was precisely that: culture, not nature.

Philippians 3: Reevaluating Values

Part of the result of this renegotiation of the marginality of Paul, in terms of his imprisonment, and the community, in terms of the oppression it is encountering and its marginal position in society, can be found in chapter 3 of Philippians. One of the more controversial chapters of the letter, especially in view of the possible anti-Jewish rhetoric contained in it, here, the focus is on the way in which Paul seeks to argue for a view of the Philippian Christ devotees' place in society that may differ from the view they would be inclined to take or that others, Paul fears, may inculcate into them. Such anxiety is clearly palpable in v. 2, with its exclamation about watching out for the dogs; Paul's counterproposal starts out in v. 3, with his reference to the Philippian community (and he) being "circumcision," i.e. the people of God, as they worship God in the Spirit and find their honor in Christ, without relying on themselves. In a subsequent *paradeigma*,[29] Paul substantiates finding one's honor in Christ, with obvious echoes from the Christ "hymn"

---

28. Cf. Smit, *Paradigms of Being*; the fact that Paul uses the text as an *exemplum* suggests that it was known to the Philippians and hence, at the very least, not composed for this occasion. It is likely that Paul had received it as tradition as well.

29. Cf. ibid.

in chapter 2 that allow for seeing an analogy between Paul's "career" here and Christ's "career" in the preceding chapter, which gives Paul's example of himself here additional authority.[30] The example lasts until v. 14, after which Paul calls upon the Philippians to be of the same mind (compare the terminology in 2:5 and here), which means that the Philippians ought to follow Paul's example (explicitly so in v. 17). This is contrasted with having one's belly for god ("their god is the belly," v. 19), having one's glory in one's shame, and focusing on earthly things, which, even if it also may refer to the issue of circumcision in particular, probably also refers to a more general societal order of things. This is contrasted by Paul's orientation, which is the heavenly Christ, who (voluntarily and obediently) endured crucifixion and is now glorified and belongs to the heavenly realm. Therefore, Paul claims that for the Philippians, living in a city in which (Roman) citizenship played an important role,[31] their true source of worth and honor is located elsewhere than in the "given" order of things:

> But our citizenship is in heaven, and it is from there that we are expecting a Savior, the Lord Jesus Christ. He will transform the body of our humiliation that it may be conformed to the body of his glory, by the power that also enables him to make all things subject to himself. (Phil 3:20-21)

In doing so, Paul may be seen as equipping the Philippian community of Christ devotees for their own renegotiation of their position in society; rather than conforming to the ordinary view of what honor is, where it stems from and how it can be perceived, he urges them to view things from the perspective of Christ's "career": if Christ is the one in whom they place their trust, then they should also entrust themselves to a "Christlike career," one without hope for earthly glory but with all the more hope for eschatological honor. In the meantime, precisely this view of things serves to give them self-esteem and endurance to persist faithfully as a marginalized and challenged community.

Reading from a Minority Perspective: Concluding Observations

When considering the above and comparing it to contemporary mainstream research on Philippians, it becomes apparent that reading with an increased

---

30. Paul's use of himself as an example does not need to have been problematic to an ancient audience, cf. Smit, "Paul, Plutarch," 341–59.

31. On which, see Schinkel, *Die himmlische Bürgerschaft*.

awareness of and sensitivity to marginality and its negotiation does indeed highlight aspects of Philippians that are otherwise not as visible. This pertains in particular to the following aspects.

First, it has become apparent that consistent attention for the marginal character of Paul and the Philippians makes instances of negotiating a marginal existence, be it that of Paul in prison or that of the Philippians in their community under pressure, visible to begin with. This is an important gain.

Second, reading from the perspective or marginality also increases awareness that Paul's letters, read for nearly two millennia as texts with self-explanatory authority, are not primarily involved in "explaining" what the true "cruciform" order of things is, but rather engaged in crafting and negotiating an alternative order of things. What Paul states is not a piece of self-explanatory handbook theology; it is, if anything, theology in the making and, in making this theology, Paul also creates a new space for himself to exist in and for the community he addresses. Paul's letters are performative in this respect, even if they seem to be "merely" descriptive.

Third, reading Philippians in this way helps us remain aware of the direct societal connection of texts that seems to be dealing with matters Christological (the Christ hymn), moral (the instructions in chapter 3), or personal (the account in chapter 1) at first sight. All of these are always more than "just" personal, moral, or Christological; they all serve the purpose of crafting a space, both mental and intellectual, for the early Christian community (and Paul) to inhabit in an honorable way.

Fourth, this approach to Philippians also makes us aware that the process of canonizing this letter and reading it as a canonical text subsequently has induced readers to a certain kind of forgetfulness when it comes to marginality, at least in those places where the main centers of exegetical research are currently the situation. Now that these centers, to the extent that they are located in (Western) Europe, are confronted with a social reality in which churches are beginning to experience themselves as marginal again, there is an opportunity to overcome this forgetfulness and to give the marginal character of these texts, and the manner in which this marginality is negotiated in them, their due. It ought, therefore, to be stressed that remembering always involves more forgetting that remembering, strictly speaking; canonizing a text and inscribing it formally into the communal memory of a group also invites a particular kind of forgetting, namely of a text's origins, in particular if these origins were far humbler than the exalted status of a canonical text would suggest.[32]

---

32. Following Assmann, *Formen des Vergessens*.

Bibliography

Agosto, Efraín. "The Letter to the Philippians." In *A Postcolonial Commentary on the New Testament Writings*, edited by Fernando F. Segovia and R. S. Sugirtharajah, 281–93. Bible and Postcolonialism 13. London: Bloomsbury, 2007.

Armitage, David J. *Theories of Poverty in the World of the New Testament*. Wissenschaftliche Untersuchungen zum Neuen Testament 2/423. Tübingen: Mohr/Siebeck, 2016.

Assmann, Aleida. *Formen des Vergessens*. Historische Geisteswissenschaften 9. Göttingen: Wallstein, 2016.

Becker, Eve-Marie. "Polemik und Autobiographie: Ein Vorschlag zur Deutung von Phil 3,2–4a." In *Polemik in der frühchristlichen Literatur: Texte und Kontexte*, edited by Oda Wischmeyer and Lorenzo Scornaienchi, 233–54. Beihefte zur Zeitschrift für die neutestamentliche Wissenschaft und die Kunde der älteren Kirche 170. Berlin: de Gruyter, 2011.

Beekers, Daan. "Precarious Piety: Pursuits of Faith among Young Muslims and Christians in the Netherlands." PhD diss., Vrije Universiteit Amsterdam, 2015.

Bernts, A. P. J., and Joantine Berghuijs. *God in Nederland 1966–2015*. Utrecht: Ten Have, 2016.

Bryant, Joseph M. "The Sociology of Early Christianity: From History to Theory and Back Again." In *The New Blackwell Companion to the Sociology of Religion*, edited by Bryan S. Turner, 311–39. Blackwell Companions to Sociology. Malden, MA: Wiley-Blackwell, 2010.

Carr, David M., and Colleen M. Conway. *An Introduction to the Bible: Sacred Texts and Imperial Contexts*. Malden, MA: Wiley-Blackwell, 2010.

Clements, E. Anne. *Mothers on the Margin? The Significance of the Women in Matthew's Genealogy*. Eugene, OR: Pickwick, 2014.

Dam, Peter van, James Kennedy, and Friso Wielenga. *Achter de zuilen: Op zoek naar religie in naoorlogs Nederland*. Amsterdam: Amsterdam University Press, 2014.

"De Bijbel gekozen tot het belangrijkste boek" ("The Bible Chosen the Most Important Book"). 2016 Year of the Book. September 23, 2016. http://www.b2016jaarvanhetboek.nl/2016/09/23/de-bijbel-gekozen-tot-het-belangrijkste-boek/.

Elliott, John H. "The Jewish Messianic Movement: From Faction to Sect." In *Modelling Early Christianity: Social-scientific Studies of the New Testament in Its Context*, edited by Philip F. Esler, 75–95. London: Routledge, 1995.

Harrison, James R. "Paul and Empire 2: Negotiating the Seduction of Imperial 'Peace and Security' in Galatians, Thessalonians, and Philippians." In *An Introduction to Empire in the New Testament*, edited by Adam Winn, 165–84. Resources for Biblical Study 84. Atlanta: SBL, 2016.

Hawthorn, Gerald F., and Ralph P. Martin. *Philippians*. Word Biblical Commentary 43. Waco: Word, 2004 (1983).

Holloway, Paul A. *Consolation in Philippians: Philosophical Sources and Rhetorical Strategy*. Society for New Testament Studies Monograph Series 112. Cambridge: Cambridge University Press, 2001.

———. *Philippians: A Commentary*. Hermeneia. Minneapolis: Fortress, 2017.

Marchal, Joseph A. *Philippians: Historical Problems, Hierarchical Visions, Hysterical Anxieties.* Phoenix Guides to the New Testament 11. Sheffield: Sheffield Phoenix, 2014.

Meeks, Wayne A. *The First Urban Christians: The Social World of the Apostle Paul.* New Haven: Yale University Press, 2003 (1983).

Mikkers, Tom. *Religiestress: Hoe je te bevrijden van deze eigentijdse kwelgeest.* Zoetermeer: Boekencentrum, 2012.

Netherlands Bible Society. "NBG-Onderzoek Bijbelgebruik Nederland" (Bible Use in the Netherlands). https://www.bijbelgenootschap.nl/wp-content/uploads/2017/09/NBG-rapport-onderzoek-V3_def.compressed.pdf.

O'Brien, Peter T. *The Epistle to the Philippians.* New International Greek Testament Commentary Series. Grand Rapids: Eerdmans, 1991.

Paas, Stefan. *Vreemdelingen en priesters: Christelijke missie in een postchristelijke omgeving.* Zoetermeer: Boekencentrum, 2015.

Paul, Herman. *Secularisatie: een kleine geschiedenis van een groot verhaal.* Amsterdam: Amsterdam University Press, 2017.

Plaisier, Arjan. *Kerk 2025: Waar een Woord is, is een weg (Church 2025: Where a Word Is, Is a Way).* Utrecht: Protestant Church in the Netherlands, 2016.

Reumann, John. *Philippians: A New Translation with Introduction and Commentary.* Anchor Yale Bible 33B. New Haven: Yale University Press, 2008.

Sandford, Michael J. *Poverty, Wealth, and Empire: Jesus and Postcolonial Criticism.* New Testament Monograph 35. Sheffield: Sheffield Phoenix, 2014.

Schinkel, Dirk. *Die himmlische Bürgerschaft: Untersuchungen zu einem urchristlichen Sprachmotiv im Spannungsfeld von religiöser Integration und Abgrenzung im 1. und 2. Jahrhundert.* Forschungen zur Religion und Literatur des Alten und Neuen Testaments 220. Göttingen: Vandenhoeck & Ruprecht, 2007.

Schmeets, Hans. *De religieuze kaart van Nederland, 2010–2015.* The Hague: CBS Centraal Bureau voor de Statistiek, 2016.

Shaner, Katherine A. *Enslaved Leadership in Early Christianity.* Oxford: Oxford University Press, 2018.

Smit, Peter-Ben. "Crucifiction? Crucifixion as a Failed Ritual in Phil. 2." *Biblical Theology Bulletin* 46 (2016) 12–24.

———. *Paradigms of Being in Christ: A Study of the Epistle to the Philippians.* Library of New Testament Studies 476. London: Bloomsbury, 2013.

———. "Paul, Plutarch and the Problematic Practice of Self-Praise (περιαυτολογία): The Case of Phil 3.2–21." *New Testament Studies* 60 (2014) 341–59.

———. "War Paulus suizidal? Eine psychiatrisch-exegetische Notiz." *Biblische Notizen* 158 (2013) 113–18.

Snel, Jan Dirk. "Waarom daar? De Refoband of Refogordel als onderdeel van de Protestantenband." In *Refogeschiedenis in perspectief: Opstellen over de bevindelijke traditie,* edited by Fred Van Lieburg, 51–91. Heerenveen: Groen, 2007.

Stark, Rodney. *The Rise of Christianity: A Sociologist Reconsiders History.* Princeton: Princeton University Press, 1996.

Thompson, James W., and Bruce W. Longenecker. *Philippians and Philemon.* Paideia: Commentaries on the New Testament Series. Grand Rapids: Baker, 2016.

Wansink, Craig S. *Chained in Christ: The Experience and Rhetoric of Paul's Imprisonments.* JSNT Supplements 130. Sheffield: Sheffield Academic, 1996.

5

Apostolic Hermeneutics and an Evangelical Doctrine of Scripture

Moving beyond a Modernist Impasse

Peter Enns

Introduction

THE PURPOSE OF THIS essay is to explore the role that apostolic hermeneutics (i.e., the manner in which Christ and the NT authors used the OT) could have on an evangelical doctrine of Scripture. To put the matter this way is to imply that apostolic hermeneutics has not had the influence it should. As I see it, a cause of this state of affairs is, ironically, the influence of Enlightenment thinking on evangelical theology, specifically assumptions concerning standards of "proper interpretation." In what follows, I hope to approach the matter of apostolic hermeneutics not as a problem to be solved, as is too often the case in evangelical theology, but as a window into the apostles' "doctrine of Scripture" (however anachronistic such a concept might be). It is my opinion that the church should engage this phenomenon very directly as it continues to work out its own understanding of Scripture.

In this essay, I use the word "evangelical" to mean, very broadly, conservative, traditional Christianity as it has been practiced at least in America, particularly as it has been a response to the influence of "modernism" in the nineteenth and twentieth centuries. The words "modernist," "modernism," and "Enlightenment" are restricted in their use to refer to the higher-critical biblical scholarship (largely a- or anti-supernaturalistic) of that same period.[1] Despite the fact that evangelicals and modernists

---

1. By defining my terms in this manner, I do not wish to create the false impression that this historical period can be so easily captured by the use of such labels.

are on opposite sides of the divide on many things, it is striking the extent to which they have shared similar assumptions, particularly as they affect biblical interpretation.[2] By way of introduction, below are two examples of where such influence can be seen.

The assumption that an historical account is true only to the extent that it describes "what actually happened"[3] mutes the varied witness of Scripture to a number of historical events. This varied witness can be seen in the so-called "synoptic problem" (Chronicles and Samuel/Kings; Gospels). The modernist assumption that varied accounts of one event constitute faulty information (error) in at least one of the accounts provides the impulse to harmonize synoptic portions of Scripture, which has been a common practice in evangelicalism.[4] The practice of harmonization, although at times legitimate, owes more to modernist assumptions of the nature of what historical accounts should look like than to allowing the varied witness of Scripture to speak.

Assumptions concerning the necessarily unique quality of divine revelation (somewhat understandable in view of critical scholarship's consistent attack on any positive role of revelation) have muted the proper role that extrabiblical evidence should take in shaping our own ideas of the nature of Scripture. But the last 150 years have introduced to the discipline of biblical scholarship a wealth of archaeological, textual, and scientific information. In my view, the evangelical response has largely been restricted to the mere observation that the OT fits in the general Ancient-Near-East context or to the general relevance of science, particularly when it confirms generally accepted views. But when the topic turns to the doctrinal implications of such observations, particularly when they challenge accepted positions, a defensive posture becomes the norm. It is not often asked how these ancient

---

Moreover, I do not wish to suggest that developments in biblical interpretation during this period are necessarily negative. The benefits of "modern" biblical scholarship, such as developments in textual criticism and broader historical/cultural issues pertaining to the ANE and Greco-Roman periods, are felt by students of Scripture across the ideological spectrum.

2. For an example of this phenomenon, see Enns, "William Henry Green," 385–403.

3. The ideal of a historian's objectivity is a standard that many consider to have been set in place by the German historian Leopold von Ranke (1795–1886) in his famous dictum *"wie es eigentlich gewesen"* (as it actually happened). See Krieger, *Ranke*.

4. More recently, harmonization of synoptic accounts can no longer be considered to be the consensus evangelical position. See Dillard, *2 Chronicles*; Dillard, "Harmonization," 151–64; Long, *Art of Biblical History*, 76–87. This development in evangelical biblical scholarship reflects the broader scholarly acknowledgement that all attempts to reconstruct history have a local dimension.

Near Eastern parallels or scientific observations concerning the opening chapters of Genesis *positively* contribute to our doctrine of revelation.[5]

What I see at work in these two examples are preconceived notions concerning: 1) the nature of historiography; and 2) the relationship between general and special revelation. And when such assumptions are adopted, handling the biblical evidence becomes problematic. We have the all-too-familiar situation where the evidence is made to fit the theory rather than the other way around. What can be said for these two examples can be said all the more concerning apostolic hermeneutics. An articulation of how the apostles handled the OT and its implications for a Christian understanding of Scripture also has been hindered by certain assumptions of what constitutes "proper hermeneutics." Without wishing to overstate the case, how the apostles handled their Scripture has run the risk of being misunderstood in evangelicalism wherever modernist assumptions of proper hermeneutics have been considered supremely normative. More specifically, the implications of understanding apostolic hermeneutics for what it is, a Second-Temple phenomenon, has been in direct conflict with an evangelical doctrine of Scripture, which includes among other things the notion that proper interpretation must be consistent with the author's intention.[6]

By expecting the apostles to conform to modern assumptions, we run the danger of missing the theological and kerygmatic richness of the apostles' use of the OT. In an effort to better understand the NT's use of the OT, I outline below the phenomenon of apostolic hermeneutics as a function of the apostles' cultural and eschatological moment. The cultural moment to which I refer is the hermeneutical milieu of the Second-Temple period.[7] The eschatological moment is the apostolic message that Christ

---

5. Young, *Biblical Flood*; Young, "Antiquity," 380–96. On the role of science and theology, a very succinct summary can be found in Van Till, "Fully Gifted Creation," 173–8.

6. It is of interest to note that such a problem is mainly confined to evangelicalism in that evangelicals have stood to lose more by locating the apostles' hermeneutical practices in the Second-Temple period. The way the lines have been drawn in evangelicalism, the following observation by Crawford Howell Toy would no doubt be perceived as inadequate: "We must accept the local setting of [the apostles'] teaching as part of their human shape; and be content to take spiritual essence of their thought, undisturbed by the peculiar forms which it received from the times. Here we are dealing with them only as interpreters of the Old Testament; and the only question to be answered is, how far they have given the sense of the passages they cite" (*Quotations*, xxv; emphasis added).

7. Of course, there are other dimensions to the culture of first-century Palestine, but in keeping with the purpose of this essay, I limit myself to the phenomenon of Second-Temple biblical interpretation. I do acknowledge, however, a degree of artificiality in separating this hermeneutical phenomenon from the myriad of other factors at

has come to fulfill one chapter of the history of God's people and to begin another chapter to be completed at the consummation of all things. I hope that such a description of apostolic hermeneutics also will contribute to a discussion of how the church today thinks of and uses its Scripture. I take it as foundational that the church's understanding of how to handle its own Scripture must interact on a fundamental level with the hermeneutical trajectories already in evidence in Scripture. By reclaiming the hermeneutical trajectory set by the apostles, the church may be able to move beyond the impasse imposed by modernist assumptions.

I want to clarify, however, that I am not advocating a superficial biblicism with respect to hermeneutics, that is, "watch what the apostles do and then do the same thing." What I intend to outline in the concluding section of this article is that apostolic hermeneutics sets a trajectory for the church, a trajectory that sets the church on a very definite path but does not define every stage of the journey. Moreover, coming to grips with the phenomenon of apostolic exegesis involves a delicate interplay of historical, doctrinal, hermeneutical, philosophical, and theological factors. To be sure, this complexity virtually guarantees that the discussion will be ongoing and that a consensus will not likely be reached. This is of very little concern to me. Variety in interpretation has been a constant companion of the church throughout its history, the Lord has seen fit to honor it, and my intention here is not to bring this hermeneutical adventure to an end. The church today is not an interpretive island. It is, rather, to shift metaphors, one stage in a stream of interpretive tradition, which has its source within the pages of the OT itself (inner-biblical exegesis) and which I believe has been guided by the spirit of Christ.

Apostolic Hermeneutics as a Cultural Phenomenon

Even casual readers of the NT will notice that the OT is cited a large number of times. According to one count, there are 275 direct quotations of the OT in the NT.[8] The rather obvious point to be made is that the NT writers, and Jesus himself, understood the gospel message to be connected in some vital way to Israel's Scripture.

---

work in Second-Temple Judaism, be they political, sociological, cultural, etc.

8. McCalman Turpie, *Old Testament in the New*, 267–69. Others come up with a different count. For example, the third edition of the Greek New Testament published by the United Bible Societies lists 251 OT passages that appear in the NT. And, since some passages are used more than once, there are 317 NT passages that quote an OT text.

The sheer number of OT references is easy enough to see in most modern English translations of the NT. But along with this is a second factor that begins to address the nature of the problem at hand: the manner in which the apostles handled the OT seems unexpected, strange, even improper by modern conventions. The apostles do things with the OT that, if any of us were to do likewise, would be criticized as deviations from "normal" hermeneutical standards. And thus, in a nutshell, we have the problem. As Christians with a high view of Scripture, we are dependent on "the whole counsel of God," the entire Bible, both OT and NT, for directing us in all matters of faith and practice. And we are encouraged in this by observing that the apostles themselves, by virtue of their recurring referencing of the OT, clearly set the church in this hermeneutical trajectory. But when we look more closely at how specifically the apostles actually handle the OT—what they say about particular passages or events and how they arrive at their conclusions—we become aware of the hermeneutical distance between ancient and modern interpreters.

Some of the problems with the NT's use of the OT are purely textual in nature.[9] These types of problems may well be explained either by appealing to the fluidity of text types in first-century Palestine, or perhaps more simply to the biblical writer's memory. Such matters are worthy of detailed discussion but are not of concern here. Rather, there is another problem that proves to be more problematic, and that I feel can be stated quite plainly, despite recurring protestations to the contrary: NT writers attribute meaning to OT texts that clearly differ from the intention of the OT author.[10] This problem can be fleshed out more precisely: The content of the NT authors' interpretive conclusions on the OT is directly tied to two early documented

---

9. For example, Matt 2:23 and John 7:23 have no corresponding OT referent, nor do references to the resurrection "according to the Scriptures" in Mark 8:31; Luke 24:46; and 1 Cor 15:3. Some appear to be conflations of OT texts: Rom 9:33 (Isa 8:14 and 28:16); Matt 27:9–10 (Zech 11:12–13 and Jer 32:6–9[?]). At times, the NT citation agrees with the LXX over against the MT; at other times, the reverse is true. Still other times, the NT citation conforms to no known LXX or MT text. Many scholars present the various statistics in a variety of ways, but all illustrate the textual problems of the NT's use of the OT. See Ellis, *Paul's Use of the Old Testament*, 150–187; Ellis, *Old Testament in Early Christianity*, 51–74; Silva, "Old Testament in Paul," 630–34. For a specific example, see Silva, "New Testament Use of the Old Testament," 147–65.

10. This is not a private observation. Klyne Snodgrass puts it well, "The main problem for modern readers in the New Testament use of the Old Testament is the tendency of New Testament writers to use Old Testament texts in ways different from their original audience"; "Use of the Old Testament in the New." (This essay is reprinted in Beale, *Right Doctrine*, a valuable resource for many major articles on apostolic hermeneutics. In subsequent references to articles reprinted there, I will cite the original bibliographical information followed by *Right Doctrine* and the page number in that volume.)

phenomena: 1) the interpretive methods they employ; and 2) the interpretive traditions they transmit, both of which locate the apostles squarely in the Second-Temple world.

Interpretive Methods

There can be no serious doubt that the exegetical methods employed by the apostles bear similarities to the well-documented methods of the Second-Temple period.[11] To put it another way, if one knew nothing of the NT but were well acquainted with the literature of Second-Temple Judaism and then read the NT for the first time, one would easily understand the NT as a Second-Temple interpretive text. Any contemporary investigation of apostolic hermeneutics that does not treat the NT in the context of its hermeneutical environment will at best tell only part of the story, and at worst misrepresent the issue. There is no question that this continues to raise certain doctrinal issues concerning the role of the apostles in defining "proper hermeneutics," but these concerns cannot drive the discussion. The New Testament authors

---

11. The central importance of understanding the NT's use of the OT in its Second Temple context is hardly necessary of defense. "As a Christian, I am, of course, vitally interested in the exegetical phenomena of the New Testament. But as an historian, I am concerned to have an accurate understanding of both Jewish and Christian hermeneutics during the period under study, believing that each must be seen in relation to the other" (Longenecker, *Biblical Exegesis in the Apostolic Period*, 3); ". . . it is obvious that the earliest Christians employed many of the exegetical presuppositions and practices that were common within various branches of Judaism in their day, and that they did so quite unconsciously" (ibid., 187); "The influence of Paul's general cultural milieu, and in some particulars his rabbinic training, on his style and dialectical methods is quite apparent" (Ellis, *Paul's Use*, 54); "In order to understand how the Old Testament functions in the New, we must immerse ourselves in the writings of the time" (Moyise, *Old Testament in the New*, 7); "Biblical interpretation in the New Testament church shows in a remarkable way the Jewishness of earliest Christianity. It followed exegetical methods common to Judaism and drew its perspective and pre-suppositions from Jewish backgrounds" (Ellis, *Old Testament in Early Christianity*, 121); "The very fact . . . that so many New Testament scholars have turned to the evidence of the Jewish religion and literature contemporary with the New Testament writers is, or should be, a solid indication that more is required for an understanding of the New Testament than the New Testament text alone, with the Old Testament as background" (McNamara, *Palestinian Judaism*, 37). John Lightfoot was of the same opinion nearly 350 years ago: ". . . when all the books of the New Testament were written by Jews, and among Jews, and unto them; and when all the discourses made there, were made in like manner by Jews, and to Jews, and among them; I was always fully persuaded, as of a thing past all doubting, that the New Testament could not but everywhere taste of and retain the Jews' style, idiom, form, and rule of speaking" (*Commentary on the New Testament*, 3). The fact that Lightfoot was restricted in his comparative work to the Talmud should not cloud the significance of the observation made.

give us ample opportunity to observe their hermeneutical behavior, and it is upon these facts—the facts of Scripture understood in their historical context—that doctrine ultimately must be based, particularly if what one is after is the articulation of a doctrine of Scripture.

I would like to draw an analogy with grammatical-historical exegesis. Grammatical-historical exegesis insists that the interpretation of texts must begin with the words in front of us understood in the context in which these words were written. Even with the caveats that pure objectivity is an illusion and that the author's intention is essentially unrecoverable (or better, recoverable only on the basis of the words in front of us, which places the modern interpreter in a hermeneutical circle), it is nevertheless a fundamental notion that meaning must be "anchored" somehow in something beyond the mere will of the interpreter. Any writer (including this one) who wishes to be understood will have a deep-rooted sympathy for such a hermeneutical principle.

A problem arises, however, when we observe how the apostles handled the OT. Despite protestations to the contrary, grammatical-historical hermeneutics does not account for the New Testament's use of the Old. However self-evident grammatical-historical hermeneutics may be to us, and whatever very important contributions it has made and continues to make to the field of biblical studies, it must be stated clearly that the apostles did not seem overly concerned to put this principle into practice.[12] Of course, it is equally clear that at times NT writers interpret the OT somewhat literalistically, and I have no desire to dispute this.[13] But when the smoke clears, the overall picture remains: apostolic hermeneutics, apart from the expenditure of significant mental energy and denial of plain fact, cannot be categorized as being "essentially" grammatical-historical.[14] A proper under-

---

12. For example, "... the conviction that the grammatical-historical meaning is the entire and exclusive meaning of the text seems to stem more from post-Enlightenment rationalistic presuppositions than from an analysis of the Bible's understanding and interpretation of itself" (McCartney, "New Testament's Use," 103).

13. For example, Paul's use of Deut 25:4 in 1 Cor 9:9 and 1 Tim 5:18. Many correctly address this issue of the variety of ways in which Second-Temple authors in general and the NT authors specifically use the OT; for example, literalism, typology, analogy, promise-fulfillment, contrast. See Greidanus, *Preaching Christ*, 69–277; Longenecker, *Biblical Exegesis*, esp. chapters 1 and 4; Nicole, "New Testament Use," 135–51/ Beale, *Right Doctrine*, 13–51; Marshall, "Assessment of Recent Developments," 1–21/ Beale, *Right Doctrine*, 195–216; Moo, "Problem of Sensus Plenior," 187–91, 209–10; Ellis, *Old Testament in Early Christianity*, 79–101.

14. Although it is certainly true that the strangeness of apostolic hermeneutics often is acknowledged in evangelical literature, there is nevertheless a significant line of argumentation that tries vigorously to maintain the "essential" grammatical-historical foundation of the apostles, i.e., that the apostles' interpretation of the OT must remain

standing, therefore, of apostolic hermeneutics must begin elsewhere, and that starting point is to engage very directly—with all its attendant doctrinal implications—the "hermeneutical-historical" context of the New Testament authors. So, to complete the analogy: in the same way that grammatical-historical exegesis is vital for our understanding the words of the biblical authors, a hermeneutical-historical approach is vital for our understanding of the hermeneutics of biblical authors. In other words, we must extend what is implied in grammatical-historical exegesis, the principle that original context matters, to the world of apostolic hermeneutics.

Returning, then, to interpretive methods, we see again and again that the apostles approached the Old Testament in ways that are averse to grammatical-historical exegesis but are firmly at home in the Second-Temple world. What else can be said, for example, of Jesus's argument with the Sadducees over the resurrection of the dead (Luke 20:27–40; Matt 22:23–33; Mark 12:18–27)?[15] To understand Exod 3:6 as demonstrating that "the dead rise" (Luke 20:37), as Jesus does, violates our hermeneutical sensibilities, and we should not pretend otherwise. And it will not do to soften the blow by suggesting that Jesus is merely "applying" Exod 3:6, a point made clear in his retort to the Sadducees: "You are in error because you do not know the Scriptures or the power of God" (Matt 22:29).[16] Knowing the

---

related in some direct way to the intention of the OT author. "[Typological exegesis] does not read into the text a different or higher sense, but draws out from it a different or higher application of the same text" (Beale, "Did Jesus and His Followers?," 89–96/ Beale, *Right Doctrine*, 395); "[The Apostles] stay within the conceptual bounds of the Old Testament contextual meaning, so that what results often is an extended reference to or application of a principle which is inherent to the Old Testament text" (ibid.; *Right Doctrine*, 397); "God could have multiple referents in mind, even if the prophet may not have known all the constituent details. This concept is not a bad one, provided it is clear what the human author said and whatever more God says through him are related in sense" (Bock, "Use of the Old Testament," 104–5). See also Moo, "Sensus Plenior," 204, 211. Such a stance will never be able to account for the very radical way in which the NT authors re-interpret the OT. Ellis is much subtler in his understanding of Paul's exegesis of the OT as "grammatical-historical plus" (*Paul's Use*, 147–48). McCartney, however, points out that the "plus" is precisely what makes apostolic hermeneutics not grammatical-historical ("New Testament's Use," 102). It is probably best to say, along with McCartney, that grammatical-historical exegesis is compatible with apostolic hermeneutics, but no more (ibid., 111).

15. This is not the place to multiply and catalogue the "odd" uses of the OT by the NT authors. I am assuming that the reader is sufficiently familiar with the nature of the problem, either first-hand or by virtue of the fact that the presence of the problem continues to generate scholarly attention. For a recent treatment see Moyise, *Old Testament in the New*. Ellis includes helpful bibliographic information on scholarly works on apostolic hermeneutics from 1950 to 1990 (*Old Testament in Early Christianity*, 63–66).

16. All biblical citations are from New International Version (NIV).

Scriptures and the power of God entails reading Exod 3:6 the way Jesus did, and whatever we might think of the persuasiveness of the argument, the point is that the crowd listening was quite impressed: "Some of the teachers of the law responded, 'Well said, teacher!' And no one dared ask him any more questions" (Luke 20:39–40; see also Matt 22:33).[17] In isolation, one can certainly find creative ways of "handling" this and other problematic passages in conventional ways, but the weight of accumulated evidence, both from the NT and its surrounding world, would quickly render such arguments unconvincing.[18] The interpretive methods of Christ and the NT writers were quite at home in the Second-Temple world.

Interpretive Traditions

What can be said about the interpretive methods of the NT authors also can be said of the interpretive traditions that find their way into their writings. Not only did the apostles handle the OT in ways consistent with other Second-Temple interpreters, but also they transmitted existing interpretive

---

17. It is a recurring line of argumentation among evangelicals that the NT writers would have needed to engage the OT in something approximating grammatical-historical exegesis if their purpose was to convince their contemporaries. This is especially true for Matthew's Gospel, which was written for a Jewish audience. Concerning Matthew, Walter Kaiser Jr., writes, "The gospel was more than a catechetical handbook or even a liturgical guide—it was a tract written to move tough-minded resisters to conclude that Jesus was the promised Messiah from God. If that were so, then all such embellishment would be recognized for what it is: worthless as an evangelistic or apologetic tool and singularly unconvincing" (Kaiser, *Uses of the Old Testament*, 44; see also 229). But in fact, the opposite is the case. It is precisely the employment of Second-Temple hermeneutical standards that gave their arguments the proper hearing. Charles R. Taber, whom Kaiser cites disapprovingly, has it correct in my view: "the New Testament writers used a hermeneutic in relation to many Old Testament citations which was derived from rabbinic interpretation but was at the opposite pole from what we would consider legitimate today. In our terms, some of the Old Testament passages cited are clearly taken out of context. But the fact of the matter is that what they considered proper hermeneutics was part and parcel of their cultural heritage" ("Is There One Way?"; cited in Kaiser, *Uses of the Old Testament*, 234). My only correction to Taber's observation is to replace "rabbinic" with "Second Temple." See also Moo, "Sensus Plenior," 203: ". . . we must be careful not to think that methods of proof not convincing to us would necessarily have been equally unconvincing to first-century Jews."

18. If this were an isolated case, one could make the argument that Jesus here does not mean what he says but is only adopting the illegitimate hermeneutical practices of his opponents. Besides the fact that there is absolutely no indication of this in Jesus' own words, if we are willing to make that argument here, we would need to be willing to make it everywhere. Moreover, one would only think of making such a case if one assumed at the outset that Jesus would not have handled Scripture in this way. It is precisely such an assumption that this essay is addressing.

traditions. In my opinion, evangelical scholarship has focused almost entirely on the question of the exegetical methods the apostles shared with other Second-Temple interpreters. But investigating Second-Temple interpretive traditions that find their way into the NT gives us added and valuable information of another sort, namely, how NT authors understood a number of OT stories and passages. The fact that New-Testament writers sometimes say things about the Old Testament that are not found there but are found in other interpretive texts of the Second-Temple period should not be marginalized as we think through the apostles' doctrine of Scripture.

This phenomenon, reflected in the NT as well as throughout much of Second-Temple literature, often is referred to as the "retold" or "rewritten" Bible.[19] Some prominent and lengthy examples include: Jubilees (second-century BCE, retelling of creation to Sinai), Book of Biblical Antiquities (first-century CE, retelling of creation to David), Genesis Apocryphon (first-century BCE, what survives is largely a first-person re-telling of the Abraham story), 1 Esdras (second-century BCE, retelling of Josiah to Nehemiah). In addition, and more relevant to the topic at hand, shorter retellings are reflected in many other Second-Temple texts: Wis 10:1—11:4 (first-century CE, Adam to wilderness), Sir 44:16—49:11 (second-century BCE, Enoch to Zerubbabel). The significant examples from the NT are Acts 7:2-53 (Abraham to Solomon) and Heb 11:3-31 (creation to Rahab). Although these are all distinct literary works written for distinct purposes, what they have in common is that their retelling of the biblical stories incorporated existing interpretive traditions, that is, notions about what certain biblical texts meant that were already matters of common knowledge (at least within particular communities).

The "retold Bible" is not merely an ancient phenomenon. Rather, it is a phenomenon that has accompanied biblical interpretation throughout its history, including our own day. If we reflect on our own situation, we see that we also bring into the interpretive act our own preconceived notions about what the Bible says. For instance, several years ago I heard a sermon on Moses's raised hands (Exod 17:11). The preacher mentioned, somewhat casually, that Moses's hands were raised in prayer. This may or may not be the case, but the point is that Exod 17 does not say this. The preacher, however, gave no indication that he was offering an interpretation of what Moses's raised hands meant. As far as he was concerned, this is what the Bible "says."

---

19. See Kugel, *Traditions of the Bible*, 23. Kugel attributes the term to Vermes, *Scripture and Tradition*, 67–126.

Of course, this is only one example, but many more could be adduced. And it should be self-evident that, for various portions of Scripture, we have in our minds pre-existing interpretations of the Bible that reflect what we have come to think the Bible contains. So, when one is asked to talk about the battle with the Amalekites in Exod 17, one may very likely "retell" that story and include in that retelling interpretive traditions that arose at a much earlier time[20] but that have come to be included as "part" of the biblical text, not as a conscious alteration of the biblical text but as an unconscious addendum to it. These views are sometimes held so deeply (and unwittingly) that it is only through considerable argumentation that someone can be shown that what they may consider part of the Bible really is not.[21]

New Testament authors also bear witness to their participation in the phenomenon of the "retold Bible," not only in the longer examples cited above (Acts 7, Heb 11) but by reproducing interpretive snippets that add very little if anything to the argument being made. They simply represent, by virtue of their Second-Temple setting, the biblical author's own understanding of what the OT says. Some examples are the following:

1. According to Gal 3:19, Acts 7:53 (and very likely Heb 2:2), the law was mediated through angels. This has no direct support in the OT but is reflected in the general notion that angels were present with God on Mt. Sinai in such places as Jub. 1:27–29. There the Angel of the Presence is instructed to write down for Moses the history of Israel from creation to the building of the sanctuary. In fact, the entire contents of Jubilees (which spans from creation to Sinai) is purported to have been spoken to Moses on Mt. Sinai by the Angel (Jub. 2:1).[22]

---

20. The "Moses raised his hands in prayer" tradition goes back at least to Targum Pseudo-Jonathan, an early medieval Targum but whose traditions may go back much earlier, perhaps even to the pre-Christian era.

21. Another common example is the tradition that there were three wise men. Just what constitutes an interpretive tradition will likely depend on the interpretive community of which one is a part. From personal experience, I can say that I stumbled a bit when several years ago I was challenged to show where in the early chapters of Genesis I saw a "fall" or "Satan." Of course, as Christians, we make such determinations in the context of the whole of Scripture, which includes the NT. The point, however, remains the same; my understanding of the garden narrative is very much informed by the interpretive tradition (in this case the NT) of which I am a part.

22. To be clear, I am not suggesting that the NT authors read Jubilees and derived their theology from it directly, but that the notion of angels mediating the law is not in the OT but reflects Second-Temple interpretive activity. One could derive a teaching that angels are associated with Sinai on the basis of Deut 33:2–3, particularly in the translation of this passage in LXX, but this is hardly a "plain reading" of the text.

2. In 2 Tim 3:8, Paul refers to the magicians of Pharaoh's court as "Jannes" and "Jambres." These names do not come to us from the OT but from the Second-Temple interpretive world of which Paul was a part. The name "Jannes" is found in CD 5.17–19. Both names are found in Tg. Ps.-J to Exod 1:15.

3. Peter refers to Noah as a "preacher of righteousness" in 2 Pet 2:5. No such activity is attributed to Noah in the OT, but a similar depiction of Noah as one who attempted to persuade his contemporaries to repent is found in Jos., *Ant.* 1.74; Sib. Or. 1:125–95;[23] and b. Sanh. 108a.

4. The dispute over Moses's body, mentioned nowhere in the OT, is mentioned somewhat matter-of-factly in Jude 9. The original source of this story remains a debated topic. We do know, however, that Clement of Alexandria attributed this episode to the Assumption (also, Ascension) of Moses.[24] What is not debated, however, is the extracanonical origin of Jude's comment.

5. Jude cites a portion of prophecy supposedly uttered by Enoch (vv. 14–15), which is found in 1 En 1:9 but not in the OT.[25]

6. Acts 7:22 refers to Moses's Egyptian education, which, although perhaps implied in Exodus (Moses was raised in Pharaoh's house), is not at all explicit. It is mentioned explicitly in Philo's *Mos.* 1.21–24 and Ezekiel the Tragedian's *Exagoge* 36–38 (second-century BCE).

7. In 1 Cor 10:4, Paul is participating in a well-documented interpretive tradition that has a rock, or "well" of water, follow the Israelites through the desert. See for example Ps-Philo's *LA.B.* 10:7; 11:15; t. Sukk. 3:11; Tg. Onq. to Num 21:16–20.[26]

These interpretive traditions did not derive from a grammatical-historical reading of the OT. Moreover, it is certain that they did not even

23. The Sibylline Oracles are actually a diverse collection of writings of Jewish origin with extensive Christian reworking. Book one is considered to be of Jewish origin dating to the second century BCE. For a summary of the arguments, see Collins, "Sibylline Oracles," 331–32.

24. For succinct discussions of the issue, including the complex relationship between the Testament of Moses and the Assumption of Moses, see Neyrey, *2 Peter, Jude*, 65–7; Bauckham, *Jude–2 Peter*, 47–48; 65–76. See also Kugel, *Traditions of the Bible*, 886.

25. To my knowledge, the attribution of Jude 9 to 1 En 1:9 is universally accepted.

26. Enns, "'Moveable Well,'" 23–38. See also Ellis, "Note on First Corinthians 10:4," 53–6 (reprinted in Ellis, *Paul's Use*, 66–70); Fee, *First Epistle to the Corinthians*, 448 n. 34; Strack and Billerbeck, *Kommentar zum Neuen Testament aus Talmud und Midrash*, 3:406–8.

originate with the New-Testament authors. Not only are they too brief to have any meaning apart from a larger interpretive climate in which these traditions would have been well known, but also several of these traditions are found in texts older than their New-Testament counterparts. Further, some interpretive traditions in the NT also are found in more developed versions in later, rabbinic texts. Eliminating the most unlikely possibility that later rabbis read earlier, abbreviated forms of these traditions in the New Testament and decided to "follow the Christian lead" and expand them, we can safely conclude that both the rabbinic and New-Testament versions of some of these traditions point to interpretive conclusions reached before either. At the very least, we must conclude that any direction of influence would be most difficult to pin down. It is perhaps best to think of Second-Temple interpretive traditions not in terms of a discernible linear progression but as a net of mutual influence.[27]

The matter will no doubt continue to be debated among evangelicals, but I take it as beyond any reasonable doubt that the Second-Temple interpretive environment is the proper starting point for understanding what the NT authors said about the OT. My impression as to why the debate over Second-Temple influence on the NT authors continues is not because the facts are in serious question (although they should always continue to be thought through), but because these facts cause difficulties for a doctrine of Scripture that modern evangelicalism has constructed for itself. What must become a significant point of discussion in the evangelical dialogue concerning doctrine of Scripture is the implications of the fact that apostolic hermeneutics is a Second-Temple phenomenon. To be sure, it is more than merely a Second-Temple phenomenon, but it is certainly a Second-Temple

---

27. See also my arguments for a similar phenomenon in the Wisdom of Solomon (Enns, *Exodus Retold*, 135–54). Rabbinic evidence always runs the risk of being applied too quickly to the question of apostolic hermeneutics. It must always be kept in mind that the earliest rabbinic literature post-dates the NT by several generations at least. This is not to say, however, that the evidence should play no role. Although it would be injudicious at best to appeal to later rabbinic practices to "explain" a NT writer's hermeneutic, it is nonetheless the case that there are deep similarities that rabbinic writers share with Second-Temple interpreters. As Donald Juel puts it, ". . . formal questions are not the sole considerations in the study of postbiblical scriptural interpretation. The rabbinic midrashim still share both an approach to the scriptural text and specific interpretive traditions with Qumran commentaries, targumic literature, and the NT. It is this world of stored approach and interpretive traditions that is of greatest interest to us" (*Messianic Exegesis*, 37–38; emphasis added). Post-NT midrashic literature, therefore, is still relevant to our discussion if one understands "midrash" not simply as a genre of literature but an interpretive attitude. See also the classic essays by Bloch, "Midrash,"; reprinted in Green, *Approaches to Ancient Judaism*, 1:29–50; Bloch, "Note méthodologique," 194–227; reprinted in Green, *Approaches to Ancient Judaism*, 1:51–75.

phenomenon in that no understanding of apostolic exegesis can proceed without giving full attention to its historical context.

It will not do to argue, as has been done, apparently in an effort to safeguard the hermeneutical integrity of the apostles, that the apostles were not really "interpreting" the Old Testament but "applying" it.[28] It would need to be demonstrated that such a distinction would have been recognizable to Second-Temple authors. But such a position seems motivated more by a desire to protect a particular doctrine of Scripture than it is by a direct assessment of the evidence. The same can be said for the related and well-known distinction between meaning and significance,[29] that is, that the apostles did not assign new meaning to the OT but only explained its significance for the church. Such a distinction, it is thought, safeguards a high view of Scripture. There is no question that this distinction is a welcome corrective to flights of fancy in some contemporary literary theories, but it should be questioned whether this distinction can be applied without further ado to all literature, and particularly to the Bible. For one thing, the Bible is a religious text. However much we value the distinction between what the author meant and how those words can be applied by others, the Bible has a dimension that the meaning/significance dichotomy is not set up to handle: the divine author. God, by whose will Scripture exists, is not an author who sees only the part but the whole, and so his intention is not to be equated merely with that of the human author.

Of course, I realize it is still a debated point whether the meaning/significance distinction holds for the Bible, or to what extent it does, and I do not intend here to dismiss that debate as trivial. But I wish to make a more historically verifiable, and I hope therefore less conjectural, observation, namely, that however much the meaning/significance distinction may or may not hold for contemporary literature, it is clearly not a distinction that Second-Temple interpreters were intent to maintain. Therefore, it is wholly anachronistic to appeal to a modern theory of proper interpretive practice to explain an ancient phenomenon, particularly if the evidence for ancient hermeneutical practice is so well documented. An understanding of the hermeneutical practices of the apostles must be undertaken first and foremost by studying this evidence. This will lead, I hope, to an articulation of a doctrine of Scripture that Scripture is better prepared to support, rather than one that drives us to explain away what is in fact the case. A doctrine of Scripture that can account for the historical-hermeneutical setting of the

---

28. See Kaiser, *Uses of the Old Testament*, 226: "The only change that we have detected in the NT use of the Old is in application—not in meaning."

29. This distinction is clearly articulated in Hirsch, *Validity in Interpretation*.

apostles, indeed, a doctrine of Scripture for which apostolic hermeneutics is a central component, will need to move beyond conventional modes of explanation.

Apostolic Hermeneutics in Context: Eschatology

Second-Temple interpreters had an "axe to grind."[30] This is to say that they did not interpret their Scripture out of idle curiosity or in an attempt to gain objective or academic clarity. Rather, Scripture was called upon in service of some larger goal. That goal may have had a significant cultic dimension, as it is in the case with Jubilees, for example, where the community that produced this work was clearly concerned (among other things) to make their case for a particular way of viewing the calendrical year. The Dead-Sea community was convinced that the OT prophets spoke ultimately of them and their struggle to create an end-time community over against what they considered to be the questionable practices of the Jerusalem cult at the time.[31] What can be said for these two communities can be said in principle for all Second-Temple interpretive texts: they were written for reasons, and the authors went to lengths to insure that those reasons were not particularly hidden.

The apostles had their own reasons for engaging the OT, their Scripture. How they engaged the OT (interpretive methods) and even their own understanding of certain OT passages (transmission of pre-existing interpretive traditions) were a function of their cultural moment. But why they engaged the OT was driven by their eschatological moment, their belief that Jesus of Nazareth was God with us and that he had been raised from the dead. True to their Second-Temple setting, the apostles did not arrive at the conclusion that Jesus is Lord from a dispassionate, objective reading of the OT. Rather, they began with what they knew to be true—the historical fact of the death and resurrection of the Son of God—and on the basis of that fact re-read their Scripture in a fresh way.[32] There is no question that such

---

30. Speaking of Second-Temple interpreters, Kugel writes, "'pure' exegesis as such does not really exist. The ancient interpreter always had an axe to grind, always had a bit of an ulterior motive . . ." (*Traditions*, 21).

31. See, e.g., 1QpHab 7.1–8.13; 11.2–8. It is partly because of the NT's decidedly eschatological emphasis that considerable hermeneutical overlap is seen between the NT and many Qumran documents. Specifically, a number of scholars have considered apostolic exegesis to have affinities with the pesher method documented in the Dead Sea Scrolls. See Moyise, *Old Testament in the New*, 9–16; Longenecker, *Biblical Exegesis*, 38–45 and throughout.

32. This is one of the central points in McCartney, "New Testament's Use," 101–16.

a thing can be counter-intuitive for a more traditional evangelical doctrine of Scripture. It is precisely a dispassionate, un-biased, objective reading that is normally considered to constitute valid reading. But again, what may be considered valid today cannot be the determining factor for understanding what the apostles did.

For example, it is difficult indeed to read Matt 2:15 as an objective reading of Hos 11:1,[33] likewise, Paul's use of Isa 49:8 in 2 Cor 6:2. Neither Matthew nor Paul arrived at his conclusions *from* reading the OT. Rather, they began with the event from which all else is now to be understood. In other words, it is the death and resurrection of Christ that was central to the apostles' hermeneutical task. As an analogy, it is helpful to think of the process of reading a good novel the first time and the second time. The two readings are not equal. Who of us has not said during that second reading, "I didn't see that the last time," or "So that's how the pieces fit together." The fact that the OT is not a novel should not diminish the value of the analogy: the first reading of the OT leaves you with hints, suggestions, trajectories, etc., of how things will play out in the end, but it is not until you get to the end that you begin to see how the pieces fit together.

Paul did not begin with Isa 49:8, which speaks of Israel's return from Babylon, and conclude grammatical-historically that this speaks of Christ.

It is not the apostles' methods that drove their exegesis but their hermeneutical goal of proclaiming Christ. See also Juel: ". . . the confession of Jesus as the crucified and risen King of the Jews stands at the beginning of Christological reflection and interpretation of the Scriptures" (*Messianic Exegesis*, 171); "The confession of Jesus as Messiah is not a goal toward which scriptural interpretation moves but the presupposition for the interpretive tradition. It is not the solution to some problem generated by earlier exegesis but in large measure the generative problem itself" (ibid., 117); and, concerning Christian interpreters' use of Dan 7 via Ps 110 in relation to their own experiences, "It is to say that what distinguished their exegesis from that of other Jewish sectarian groups was the link with a specific historical figure, Jesus of Nazareth, who was crucified as a royal pretender and vindicated by God at his resurrection. It is still the confession of Jesus as the vindicated King that provides the connection point and controls the shape of the tradition" (ibid., 169). Ellis, contrasting apostolic hermeneutics to rabbinic, speaks of the NT's "eschatological orientation" . . . which centers its use of the OT on "some aspect of Jesus' life and ministry" (*Old Testament in Early Christianity*, 94). Longenecker writes, "The Old Testament contained certain specific messianic predictions, but more than that it was 'messianic prophecy' and 'messianic doctrine' throughout when viewed from its intended and culminating focal point" (*Biblical Exegesis*, 208); "[The earliest Christian interpreters] worked from the same fixed two points: (1) the Messiahship and Lordship of Jesus, as validated by the resurrection and witnessed to by the Spirit; and (2) the revelation of God in the Old Testament as pointing forward to him. Thus, their perspective was avowedly Christocentric and their treatment thoroughly Christological" (ibid., 190).

33. For a recent discussion on Matthew's use of Hosea, see Sailhamer, "Hosea 11:1 and Matthew 2:15," 87–96; McCartney and Enns, "Matthew and Hosea," 97–105.

Rather, it is the reality of the risen Christ that drove Paul to read Isa 49:8 in a new way: "Now that I see how it all ends, I can see how this, too, fits; how it drives us forward." Likewise (if I may speak this way), if Matthew were to be transported back into Hosea's time and tell Hosea that his words would be fulfilled in the boy Jesus and that, furthermore, this Jesus would be crucified and rise for God's people, I am not sure if Hosea would have known what to make of it. But if Hosea were to go forward to Matthew's day, it would be very different for him. There Hosea would be forced, in light of recent events, to see his words, precisely because they are inspired by God, the divine author, in the final eschatological context. It is Matthew who would have shown Hosea how Yahweh's plan for the world, which Hosea had glimpsed in only a partial, proleptic form, had been inaugurated in the death and resurrection of Christ. And so Hosea's words, which in their original historical context (the intention of the human author, Hosea) did not speak of Jesus of Nazareth, now do.

To put it another way, it is the conviction of the apostles that the eschaton had come in Christ that drove them back to see where and how their Scripture spoke of him. And this was not a matter of grammatical-historical exegesis but of a Christ-driven hermeneutic. The term I prefer to use to describe this hermeneutic is "christotelic."[34] I prefer this over "christological" or "christocentric" since these are susceptible to a point of view I am not advocating here, namely, the effort to "see Christ" in every, or nearly every, OT passage.[35] To see Christ as the driving force behind apostolic hermeneutics is not to flatten out what the OT says on its own. Rather, it is to see that, for the church, the OT does not exist on its own, in isolation from the completion of the OT story in the death and resurrection of Christ. The OT is a story that is going somewhere, which is what the apostles are at great pains to show. It is the OT as a whole, particularly in its grand themes, that finds its *telos*, its completion, in Christ. This is not to say that the vibrancy of the OT witness now comes to an end, but that—on the basis of apostolic authority—it finds its proper goal, purpose, *telos*, in that event by which God himself determined to punctuate his covenant: Christ.

---

34. The term "christotelic," as far as I am aware, occurs nowhere else in print. It is derived from Hays's description of Paul's hermeneutic as "ecclesiotelic" (see below), which Hays distinguishes from "ecclesiocentric" (see Hays, "On the Rebound," 77–78). I have been introduced to these terms by my colleagues Professors Doug Green and Steve Taylor.

35. Greidanus speaks of the "danger of Christomonism" in preaching, by which he means a proclamation of Christ apart from the centrality of bringing glory to God, which was the reason for which the Father sent the Son to earth (*Preaching Christ*, 178).

The matter can be put more directly. A grammatical-historical reading of the OT is not only permissible but absolutely vital in that it allows the church the see the varied trajectories set in the pages of the OT itself. It is only by understanding the OT "on its own terms," so to speak, that the church can appreciate the impact that the death and resurrection of Christ and preaching of the gospel had in its first-century setting and still should have today.[36] But a Christian understanding of its Scripture can never simply end with this first reading. What makes it a Christian reading is that it proceeds—and this is precisely what the apostles model for us—to the second reading, the eschatological, christotelic reading.

The coming of Christ is, as the church claims, the central event in the entire human story. The implications of that event included the giving of the Spirit at Pentecost and the formation of a new people of God, the church, where now Jew and Gentile, slave and free, male and female, become one people of God. Whatever racial, class, or gender distinctions might have been operative beforehand now count for nothing. A new world has begun where a Spirit-created people of God are formed into a new humanity, a humanity that lives and worships as one and as such fulfills, at least proleptically, the ideal lost in the garden. In other words, there is not only a christotelic dimension to apostolic hermeneutics but, as Richard Hays argues (see note 34), an ecclesiotelic dimension as well: the apostolic use of the OT does not focus exclusively on the person of Christ, but also the body of Christ, his people. For example, in Gal 3 the church is Abraham's "seed," that is, the people of God are being redefined by faith in Christ, not by some other characteristic (being of Jewish descent). But even here Abraham's seed (Gal 3:29, plural σπέρμα), that is, the new Israel, is properly understood only in its relation to Christ the seed (Gal 3:16, singular σπέρματι): "If you belong to Christ, then you are Abraham's seed, and heirs according to the promise" (Gal 3:29). Paul is not merely "applying" Gen 12:6 to the life of the church. He is saying that the *telos* of Gen 12:6 (assuming he has this text in mind) is realized in the church. More importantly, the ecclesiotelic dimension of Gen 12:6 is an extension of the christotelic starting point. The story of Abraham has its *telos* in the church (we are Abraham's seed) only because Christ completes the story first (he is Abraham's seed).

One can say the same for Rom 15:1-4. Here Paul exhorts the strong to "bear with the failings of the weak." To make his point, he cites Ps 69:9 ("The insults of those who insult you have fallen on me") and continues his argument, "For everything that was written in the past was written to teach

---

36. Moyise speaks of the OT providing "images" to understand Christ, while the NT "redefines" those images in the light of Christ (*Old Testament in the New*, 135).

us. . . ." Although at first blush, this may seem to suggest a direct (moralistic?) application of an OT text to the life of the Christian, it is worth seeing more precisely the manner in which Paul argues his point. Specifically, he does not cite Ps 69:9 with respect to the church primarily, but with respect to Christ and how he *first* fulfills Ps 69:9.

> We should all please our neighbors for their good, to build them up. For even Christ did not please himself but, as it is written: "The insults of those who insult you have fallen on me." For everything that was written in the past was written to teach us, so that through the endurance taught in the Scriptures and the encouragement they provide we might have hope. (Rom 15:2–4)

Hence, the manner in which Ps 69:9 was "written to teach" the church (the ecclesiotelic dimension) was by first seeing Ps 69:9 in its christotelic fullness: it was written to teach us because it is Christ who first brought this text into the life of the church.

I do not hesitate to point out that the christotelic and ecclesiotelic dimensions do not explain absolutely everything the apostles do with the OT. As I mentioned above, there is diversity in how the apostles handled the OT, and I have no desire to gloss over the fact. I will maintain, however, that the shape of apostolic hermeneutics is best explained by bearing in mind the cultural and eschatological factors outlined above. It is far less strained and historically much more justifiable to explain apostolic hermeneutics in its cultural/eschatological context generally and view other uses of the OT within that paradigm than it is to impose a modernist hermeneutic onto the apostles, and then have to contort ourselves to "explain" the other and much more frequent uses of the OT that go against the modernist grain.

Some Implications and Trajectories for the Church's Use of Scripture

It is one thing to observe the phenomenon of apostolic hermeneutics but quite another to suggest what to do with it, specifically how it should affect the church's understanding and use of Scripture for proclamation and teaching. It is precisely this point that will and should remain the topic of vibrant discussion for the church, and so I make no pretense at having arrived at a final solution to the problem; any suggestions toward a solution could be met by very sober counter-reflections. In my view, however, this type of conversation will yield greater clarity. With this in mind, I suggest the following implications for how apostolic hermeneutics affect the contemporary Christian use of the Bible.

How Does Apostolic Hermeneutics Affect Inerrancy?

There is no question that "inerrancy," at least in its earlier formulations, is not a term that is designed to encompass apostolic hermeneutics understood in its Second-Temple context. This is also true for the issues mentioned briefly at the outset of this essay, historicity and extrabiblical data. The evidence with which all biblical scholars work daily was either unknown when evangelicalism was working out this doctrine, or the implications of this evidence had not yet been fully appreciated by a critical mass of theologians. The field of ancient Near East studies (literature, archaeology) was in its infancy in the latter part of the nineteenth century. The Dead Sea Scrolls, which inspired renewed reflection on Second-Temple literature in general, were first discovered in 1947. In view of this evidence, the church must cultivate a culture of vibrant, creative, expectant, and trusting discussion of what the Bible is and, flowing from that, how it is to function in the life of the church.

The purpose of speaking of an inerrant Scripture is not to generate an abstract comment about the church's sacred book, but it is to reflect on our doctrine of God, that is, that God does not err.[37] But such a confession does not determine the manner in which the notion of an inerrant Scripture is articulated. It may well be that the very way in which God "does not err" is by participating in the cultural conventions of the time, in this case, first-century Palestine. The Bible is not inerrant because it conforms to some notion of how we think something worthy of the name "Scripture" should behave. Rather, our doctrine of Scripture flows from, if I may say it, Scripture—or better, Scripture understood in its historical context and not as an a-historical treatise. And the scriptural data include not just texts such as 2 Tim 3:14–17, taken in isolation, that consciously reflect on the nature of the OT. It is just as important to observe how NT authors behave toward the OT. In other words, 2 Tim 3:14–17 is a declarative statement by Paul on his very high view of the OT—it is "God-breathed." But just as interesting to me is to see how Paul puts a principle such as this into practice, to observe how his "doctrine of Scripture," outlined in no uncertain terms in 2 Tim 3:14–17,

---

37. Kevin J. Vanhoozer has articulated an approach to theology that brings doctrine of God and doctrine of Scripture into close conversation (*First Theology*). I cannot help but think that such a proposal will yield very positive results for how the church thinks through its understanding of the nature of Scripture.

plays out in such places as 1 Cor 10:4; 2 Cor 6:2; Gal 3:16, 19, etc. Paul, being a Second-Temple Jew, saw no tension between his high view of Scripture and the hermeneutical practices of his time. If I may speak this way, for God himself, the Second-Temple setting of the apostles is not a problem for modern interpreters to overcome but to understand. The manner in which Paul demonstrates his high view of Scripture is by participating fully in the hermeneutical expectations of his time while also reflecting the inauguration of the eschaton. These factors must be active in any Christian formulation of a doctrine of Scripture.[38]

I am aware that this opens us up to the charge of circularity and subjectivity, but it is no more circular and subjective than adopting any doctrine of Scripture. Any notion of what Scripture is must in the end be in intimate, Spirit-led conversation with what Scripture does. And this is a matter of continual reflection and dialogue among Christians who are so inclined. It is not a matter that is fully worked out by any council or creed but has always a "work-in-progress" dimension. This is not to imply that nothing is settled, but that the church, fully in dialogue with its own past and present, is continually in the process of getting to know better and better the Scripture that God has given us.

The issue, therefore, is not *whether* Scripture is "inerrant" nor certainly whether the God who speaks therein is "inerrant," but the nature of the Scripture that the inerrant God has given us. And this is something the church proclaims to itself and the world by faith. Scripture is not "inerrant" because it can be shown that there really is no "synoptic problem" or that the apostles are doing faithful grammatical-historical exegesis. Ultimately there is no "because" other than "Scripture is inerrant because it comes from God." And the ability to confess this is a gift from God. When the church studies its Scripture, it is not to try to bring the phenomenon of Scripture into conformity with any ready-made doctrine, but to see how an understanding of Scripture in context should define and challenge those

---

38. "We often proclaim our theories about Scripture in the abstract, but the use of the Old Testament by New Testament writers raises questions about our theories" (Snodgrass, "Use of the Old Testament"; cited in Beale, *Right Doctrine*, 31); "It has become all too common in theological circles today to hear assertions as to what God must have done or what must have been the case during the apostolic period of the Church—and to find that such assertions are based principally upon deductions from a given system of theology or supported by contemporary analogy alone . . . Nowhere do we need to guard against our own inclinations and various pressures more carefully than in our understanding of the New Testament writers' use of the Old Testament Traditional views of either the right or the left [cannot] be allowed to stand unscrutinized in light of recent theories" (Longenecker, *Biblical Exegesis*, 185). Longenecker's comments on 185–86 can scarcely be improved upon for relevance and succinctness.

doctrines. Then the church can go about the task of seeing what aspects of these theories are worth keeping near and what should be moved to the side.

Can We Do What the Apostles Did?

I have heard the common objection that the apostles were justified in their "creative" handling of Scripture because their apostolic authority allowed them to do so. This view is seriously problematic. First, I am not sure how appealing to apostolic authority exonerates the apostles. Should not one more readily assume that it is precisely their inspired, authoritative status that would demand they take God-breathed Scripture more seriously? Second, one could just as easily argue that it is precisely because they were the apostles, to whom the inscripturation of the New Testament had been entrusted, that we should follow them. We follow them in their teaching, so why not in their hermeneutic? Otherwise, we might be tempted to impose on Scripture a hermeneutical standard that is essentially foreign to it, which is in fact what has happened. Third, and most importantly, we must remember that the "problematic" ways in which the apostles handled the OT cannot be addressed as a function of the *apostolicity*. In fact, if anything is not a sign of their apostolic authority, it is in how they handled the OT: both their interpretive methods and interpretive traditions are well documented in other Second-Temple texts. To be sure, their christotelic goal is where their apostolic authority should be located, not their interpretive methods.

So, can we do what the apostles did? Responses to this question can be represented by three options: 1) defend the apostles as practicing a hermeneutic that is fundamentally grammatical-historical, which can only be done by dismissing the Second-Temple evidence and ignoring the original OT context of the passages cited; 2) dismiss apostolic hermeneutics as irrelevant to the church's present interpretive task, a position that is more fundamentally problematic for evangelicals than reading their hermeneutic in their Second-Temple context; or 3) acknowledge the Second-Temple setting of apostolic hermeneutics but discern carefully what is and what is not normative for the post-apostolic setting. Richard Longenecker, who has provided the most nuanced answer to this question, adopts the third option and interprets it thus: we may follow the apostles where they treat "the Old Testament in a more literal fashion, following the course of what we speak of today as historico-grammatical exegesis..."[39]

---

39. Longenecker, *Biblical Exegesis*, 217; see also xxxviii. He writes elsewhere, "It is my contention that, unless we are 'reconstructionists' in our attitude toward hermeneutics, Christians today are committed to the apostolic faith and doctrine of the New

I very much appreciate the way in which Longenecker has negotiated this difficult issue in a fresh and creative way. And, in appreciating the force of his argument, one must keep in mind that his audience is not simply evangelicals but also the mainstream of NT scholarship. He wants to guard against the extremes of both liberalism and the Bultmann school, which dismissed apostolic exegesis as "arbitrary" and "ingenious twisting" of the OT, and "Roman Catholic" and "post-Bultmannians," who he feels are too willing to handle the OT in a haphazard fashion.[40]

I agree with Longenecker in employing the third option, but I draw the distinction between what we can and cannot do a bit differently. Longenecker draws the distinction between different types of exegetical methods and argues that those more akin to grammatical-historical exegesis command our attention whereas those more suited to first-century cultural conventions do not. It is hard not to see the common sense in such a proposal. Still, rather than making a distinction between methods on the basis of a modern standard, I would like to suggest that we distinguish between *hermeneutical goal* and *exegetical method*.

The apostles' hermeneutical goal (or agenda), the centrality of the death and resurrection of Christ, must be also ours by virtue of the fact that we share the same eschatological moment. This is why we must follow them precisely with respect to their christotelic hermeneutic. But that means, quite clearly, that we cannot be limited to following them where they treat the OT in a "more literal fashion," as Longenecker proposes, since the literal (first) reading will not lead the reader to the christotelic (second) reading. To limit apostolic authority in the way Longenecker does, it seems to me, amounts to not following the apostles in any meaningful sense. The ultimate standard is still ours, not theirs.

A Christian understanding of the OT should *begin* with what God revealed to the apostles and what they model for us—the centrality of the death and resurrection of Christ for OT interpretation. We, too, are living at the end of the story; we are engaged in the second reading by virtue of our eschatological moment, which is now as it was for the apostles the last days, the inauguration of the eschaton. We bring the death and resurrection of Christ to bear on the OT. Again, this is not a call to flatten out the OT, so that every psalm or proverb speaks directly and explicitly of Jesus. It is, however, to ask oneself, "What difference does the death and resurrection of Christ make for how I understand this proverb?" It is the recognition of

---

Testament, but not necessarily to the apostolic practices as detailed for us in the New Testament" ("Who Is the Prophet Talking About?," 4–8; reprinted in Beale, *Right Doctrine*, 385).

40. Longenecker, *Biblical Exegesis*, 193–96.

our privileged status to be living in the post-resurrection cosmos that must be reflected in our understanding of the OT. Therefore, if what claims to be Christian proclamation of the OT simply remains in the pre-eschatological moment—simply reads the OT "on its own terms"—such is not a Christian proclamation in the apostolic sense.

What then of the exegetical methods employed by the apostles? Here I follow Longenecker to a degree in that we do not share the Second-Temple cultural milieu of the apostles. I have no hesitation in saying that I would feel extremely uncomfortable to see our pastors, exegetes, or Bible Study leaders change, omit, or add words and phrases to make their point, even though this is what NT authors do. One very real danger that we are all aware of is how some play fast and loose with Scripture to support their own agenda.[41] The church instinctively wants to guard against such a misuse of Scripture by saying, "Pay attention to the words in front of you in their original context." What helps prevent (but does not guarantee against) such flights of fancy is grammatical-historical exegesis.

But this does not mean the church should adopt the grammatical-historical method as the default, normative hermeneutic for how it should read the OT today.[42] Why? Because grammatical-historical exegesis simply does not lead to a christotelic (apostolic) hermeneutic. A grammatical-historical exegesis of Hos 11:1, an exegesis that is anchored by Hosea's intention, will lead no one to Matt 2:15. The first (grammatical-historical) reading does not lead to the second reading. This is a dilemma. The way I have presented the dilemma may suggest an impasse, but perhaps one way beyond that impasse is to question what we mean by "method." The word implies, at least to me, a worked out, conscious application of rules and steps to arrive at a proper understanding of a text. But what if "method," so understood, is not as central a concept as we might think? What if biblical interpretation is not guided so much by method but by an intuitive, Spirit-led engagement of Scripture with the anchor being not what the author intended but by how Christ gives the OT its final coherence? As Barnabas Lindars puts it:

> The New Testament writers do not take an Old Testament book or passage and ask, "What does this mean?" They are concerned with the kerygma, which they need to teach and to defend and to understand themselves. Believing that Christ is

41. Of course, the apostles would have a similar problem with this in that the only agenda Scripture is called to support is Christ.

42. The assumption that historical-grammatical hermeneutics is "normal" and transcends cultural and historical boundaries is a common argument among evangelicals. A recent work that propounds this view throughout is Leschert, *Hermeneutical Foundations of Hebrews*. See also Enns, "Review of Dale F. Leschert," 164–68.

the fulfillment of the promises of God, and that they are living in the age to which all the Scriptures refer, they employ the Old Testament in an ad hoc way, making recourse to it just when and how they find it helpful for their purposes. But they do this in a highly creative situation because the Christ-event breaks through conventional expectations and demands new patterns of exegesis for its elucidation.[43]

Lindars makes the point very clearly and picks up on a fundamental truth: what drives apostolic hermeneutics is not adherence to a "method." Rather, the coming of Christ is so climactic as to require "new patterns of exegesis." To speak of the apostles' exegetical "methods" may lead us down the wrong path to begin with.

This is why I have always been attracted to biblical theology, as understood in the trajectory of Geerhardus Vos, as a means of putting some interpretive meat to the christotelic bone. "Biblical theology" is a term that is open to a variety of understandings. I am using the term in the sense in which it was used by Vos, although by no means confined to his use, as the "self-revelation of God" as recorded in the Bible.[44] Inherent in Vos's conception of biblical theology are such notions as the progress of redemption culminating in the person and work of Christ in whom Scripture coheres, while also showing a respect for theological diversity as a function of the historical situatedness of revelation. Both of these dimensions of biblical theology are central to the thoughts I have outlined here. Such an approach to biblical interpretation is not a "method" that assures a stable exegetical result, but a spiritual exercise wherein a Christian looks at Scripture from the point of view of what she/he knows to be true—Christ has died, Christ has risen, Christ will come again—and reads the OT with the expectation that it somehow coheres in that fact.

Perhaps biblical theology is as much about where one starts as it is about where one finishes. From a more explicitly "methodological" point of view, I have tended to focus on such things as links (both on the lexical and larger syntactical levels) between various portions of Scripture as well as larger OT themes that either explicitly or subvocally come to completion in Christ. But these "methods" do not determine the christotelic conclusion. Rather, they are employed with the end result already in mind. This is also true for those portions of the OT that have been resistant (and for good reason) to typology, namely, Wisdom literature. And again, this is why I find

---

43. Lindars, "Place of the Old Testament," 59–66; reprinted in Beale, *Right Doctrine*, 143.

44. Vos, *Biblical Theology*, 5.

the term "christocentric" unhelpful. Christ is not the "center" of Proverbs or Ecclesiastes, but he is the "end." As in-Christ beings participating in the last days, we are obliged to think of how that status impinges upon what a proverb or Ecclesiastes "means." And the "method" by which these horizons are bridged is a creative, intentional, purposeful exploration that moves back and forth between the words on the page and the eschatological context that we share with the apostles but that the OT authors did not.

This leads me to several final suggestions, all of which are interrelated.[45]

Biblical Interpretation, Even That Which Occurs in the Bible Itself, Is Embedded in Culture

The exegetical methods of the apostles were embedded in the cultural expectations of the Second-Temple world. And since we do not advocate a Christian "reconstructionism," as Longenecker puts it (see note 38), the temptation is to dismiss these conventions as irrelevant for contemporary practice. This may be so, but there may be a lesson to be learned here as well.

To understand the contextual nature of even the apostles' interpretive activity should be a healthy reminder to all of us that God gave us the gospel not as an abstract doctrinal formulation, but already contextualized. And if this is true for God, it should remind us that our own interpretations are contextual as well. As "subjective" as this sounds, it is nevertheless inescapable that our own cultural moment plays a significant determining role in how we read and understand Scripture. I would submit that, if this notion is troublesome for us, it is because we have not adequately grappled with the doctrinal implications of the fact that God himself gave us Scripture in context. This fact should motivate us to greater humility about our own interpretive conclusions while at the same time inspiring us to greater depth and profundity as we engage the OT in its christotelic fullness.[46]

---

45. Although these musings are entirely my own, I have benefited from Hays's observation in *Echoes of Scripture*, 178–92. In these pages, which conclude his book, Hays discusses the degree to which Paul's letters can serve as hermeneutical models for today. Interested readers will find there a stimulating discussion that explores some different dimensions of the topic at hand.

46. France puts it well. Speaking of Matthew's use of the OT, he writes, "Our cultural and religious traditions would not allow us to write like this, and do not allow us to read Matthew, initially at least, with the shared understanding which we must assume his original readers, or some of them, would have had. But the inevitable distance which cultural relativity puts between us and Matthew's original readers does not entitle us to write him off as obscurantist or incapable. And when we attempt to read him on his own terms, by putting ourselves in the place of the original readers, we may not only achieve a more respectable appreciation of his literary ability and his skill as a

Biblical Interpretation Is at Least as Much Art as It Is Science

The more I reflect on the nature of biblical interpretation throughout its long history as well as in today's world, the more I am convinced that there must be more to the nature of biblical interpretation than simply uncovering the "meaning of the text," as if it were an objective exercise. Although the OT ultimately coheres in Christ, there are multiple ways of expressing that coherence.[47] In other words, the OT is open to multiple layers of meaning. I may not agree that Moses's raised hands in Exod 17 are a sign of the cross. I may not agree that Rahab's red cord is a type of Christ's blood. But I must remember that there are many in the history of Christ's church who have thought these things. As much as these interpretations may run up against my own hermeneutical sensibilities, I must nevertheless be willing to allow those sensibilities to be open to critique. Moreover, inasmuch as Scripture is the Word of God, I would expect multiple layers of meaning insofar as no one person, school, or tradition can exhaust the depth of God's Word.

So, I do not think Christian proclamation of the OT has taken place where the interpreter remains on the level of grappling with the Hebrew syntax or ancient Near Eastern context. That is merely the first step—an important step, as I mentioned earlier—but still a first step. Christian proclamation must move well beyond the bounds of such "scientific" markers. In the end, what every preacher and interpreter knows instinctively is that the words that actually come out of their mouths are a product of much more than an exegetical exercise. Christian, apostolic proclamation of the OT is a subtle interpenetration of a myriad of factors, both known and unknown, that can rightly be described not as a product of science but as a work of art. It includes such things as creativity, intuition, risk, a profound sense of the meaningfulness of the endeavor, all centered on the commitment to proclaim, "Jesus is Lord."

Biblical Interpretation Is at Least as Much Community Oriented as It Is Individually Oriented

I sometimes speak with younger pastors or students who say, "I worked all weekend on this sermon"; sometimes they even contemplate the passage for

---

communicator, but we may also be in a position to discern those guiding principles of interpretation which need to find as appropriate an expression in our cultural situation as Matthew gave them in his" ("Formula-Quotations," 23–51; reprinted in Beale, *Right Doctrine*, 134).

47. As Greidanus puts it, "Many roads lead from the Old Testament to Christ..." (*Preaching Christ*, 203–25).

as long as a week or two. Others write exegetical papers for my classes that require "research," but such research rarely goes back beyond several recent commentaries or articles. And it is a rarity indeed if they ask their fellow classmates for help (although they do tend to line up outside my door a day or two before the due date).

But biblical interpretation is a true community activity. It is much more than individuals studying a passage for a week or so. It is about individuals who see themselves in a community that has both synchronic and diachronic dimensions. Truly, we are not islands of interpretive wisdom, degrees in hand and off to conquer the Bible. We rely on the witness of the church through time (with the hermeneutical trajectory set by the apostles as a central component), as well as the wisdom of the church in our time—both narrowly considered as a congregation, denomination, or larger tradition, and the church more broadly considered as a global reality. Biblical interpretation is not merely a task that individuals perform, but it is something that grows out of our participation in the family of God in the broadest sense possible.

Biblical Interpretation Is at Least as Much about Progress as It Is Maintenance

At the risk of sounding somewhat simplistic, I think of biblical interpretation more as a path to walk than a fortress to be defended. Of course, there are times when defense is necessary, but the church's task of biblical interpretation should not be defined by such. I see regularly the almost unbearable burden we place on our preachers by expecting them, in a week's time, to read a passage, determine its meaning, and then communicate it effectively. The burden of "getting it right" can sometimes be discouraging and hinder effective ministry. I would rather think of biblical interpretation as a path we walk, a pilgrimage we take, whereby the longer we walk, the longer we take in the surrounding scenes, the more people we stop and converse with along the way, the richer our interpretation will be. Such a journey is not always smooth. At times what is involved is a certain degree of risk and creativity: we may need to leave the main path from time to time to explore less traveled but promising tracks.

To be sure, our job is also to communicate the gospel in all its simplicity, but that does not mean that biblical interpretation is an easy task— the history of the church's interpretive activity should put such notions to rest. Biblical interpretation always requires patience and humility lest we stumble. Such a metaphor helps me remember that I am not required to handle everything that comes my way, and that the gospel will not crumble in the process. But as I attempt to understand Scripture—in the context of the diachronic and synchronic community of which I am a part—I move further along the path. And at the end of the path is not simply the gaining of knowledge of the text, but of God himself who speaks to us therein. The goal toward which the path is leading is that which set us on the path to begin with: our having been claimed by God as co-heirs with the crucified and risen Christ. The reality of the crucified and risen Christ is both the goal and font of Christian biblical interpretation.

A Reformed Postscript

An unspoken principle that has undergirded my thoughts here is my own Reformed conviction concerning the nature of Scripture. To take seriously the historical setting in which Scripture was given—in this case the hermeneutical milieu of first-century Palestine—is to assume that the historical context of Scripture is vital. This principle has been articulated in different ways in the Reformed tradition.[48] For Calvin, it was his frequent appeal in his commentaries and the Institutes to accommodation. For Warfield it was concursus.[49] There are other ways of putting it. I prefer the phrase "incarnational analogy" of Scripture. Whatever the label, what unites these views is that revelation necessarily implies a human context. When God speaks and acts, he does so within the human drama as it is expressed at a certain time and place and with all its concomitant cultural trappings. This makes revelation somewhat "messy," but it does not seem to work any other way. In fact, it would seem that God would not have it any other way. For God to participate in our earthliness in Scripture is analogical to his prime revelation in Christ, who was made in every way like his brothers (Heb 2:17). This is to say that, if to identify Christ himself as a first-century Jew is the great demonstration of the lengths to which God will go to redeem his people, the great manifestation of God's love, is there any reason to shy away from identifying the NT, the written witness to Christ, as likewise defined by its first-century context?

What has motivated my thoughts here is a very conscious attempt to articulate what I see as an important element of a Reformed doctrine of Scripture, that it has pleased God to reveal himself in time and place, and that understanding something about those times and places will help us understand not just what a passage means, but what Scripture is. This

---

48. I am not suggesting that this principle is confined to the Reformed tradition, only that it has been characteristic of a Reformed doctrine of Scripture.

49. Warfield, "Divine and Human in the Bible," 51–58.

is why extrabiblical evidence, which seems to be more plentiful in recent generations than in centuries past, is always a vital "conversation partner" for thinking through what the Bible is. Although the evidence does not determine the outcome, it does affect things, at times even to the extent that new ways are required to think of old problems. In my view, a Reformed doctrine of Scripture will always engage, not reluctantly but with great enthusiasm, the relationship between special and general revelation, with the result being a better understanding of the God who knows us and made himself known to us.

Bibliography

Bauckham, Richard J. *Jude—2 Peter*. Word Bible Commentary 50. Waco, TX: Word, 1983.
Beale, G. K. "Did Jesus and His Followers Preach the Right Doctrine from the Wrong Text?" *Themelios* 14 (1989) 89–96.
———. *The Right Doctrine from the Wrong Text? Essays on the Use of the Old Testament in the New*. Grand Rapids: Baker, 1994.
Bloch, Renée. "Midrash." In *Approaches to Ancient Judaism: Theory and Practice*, Volume 1, edited by W. S. Green and translated by M. H. Callaway, 29–50. Brown Judaic Studies 1. Missoula, MT: Scholars, 1978.
———. "Note méthodologique pour l'étude de la littérature rabbinique." ÄSÄ 43 (1955) 194–227.
Bock, Darreil L. "Use of the Old Testament in the New." In *Foundations for Biblical Interpretation: A Complete Library of Tools and Resources*, edited by D. Dockery et al., 97–114. Nashville: Broadman & Holman, 1994.
Collins, John J. "Sibylline Oracles." In *The Old Testament Pseudepigrapha: Apocalyptic Literature and Testaments, Volume 1*, edited by James H. Charlesworth, 331–32. Garden City, NY: Doubleday, 1983.
Dillard, Raymond B. "Harmonization: A Help and Hindrance." In *Inerrancy and Hermeneutic: A Tradition, A Challenge, A Debate*, edited by Harvie M. Conn, 151–64. Grand Rapids: Baker, 1988.
———. *2 Chronicles*. Word Biblical Commentary 15. Waco, TX: Word, 1987.
Ellis, E. Earle. "A Note on First Corinthians 10:4." *Journal of Biblical Literature* 76 (1957) 53–6.
———. *The Old Testament in Early Christianity: Canon and Interpretation in the Light of Modern Research*. Grand Rapids: Baker, 1991.
———. *Paul's Use of the Old Testament*. 1981. Reprint, Eugene, OR: Wipf & Stock, 2003.
Enns, Peter. *Exodus Retold: Ancient Exegesis of the Departure from Egypt in Wis 10:15–21 and 19:1–9*. Harvard Semitic Monographs 57. Atlanta: Scholars, 1997.
———. "The 'Moveable Well' in 1 Cor 10:4: An Extra-Biblical Tradition in an Apostolic Text." *Bulletin for Biblical Research* 6 (1996) 23–38.
———. "Review of Dale F. Leschert, *Hermeneutical Foundations of Hebrews*." *Westminster Theological Journal* 60 (1998) 164–68.

———. "William Henry Green and the Authorship of the Pentateuch: Some Historical Considerations." *Journal of the Evangelical Theological Society* 45 (2002) 385–403.
Fee, Gordon. *The First Epistle to the Corinthians*. New International Commentary on the New Testament. Grand Rapids: Eerdmans, 1987.
France, R. T. "The Formula-Quotations of Matthew 2 and the Problem of Communication." *New Testament Studies* 27 (1981) 23–51.
Green, William Scott, ed. *Approaches to Ancient Judaism: Theory and Practice*. Brown Judaic Studies 1. 6 vols. Missoula, MT: Scholars, 1978.
Greidanus, Sidney. *Preaching Christ from the Old Testament: A Contemporary Hermeneutical Method*. Grand Rapids: Eerdmans, 1999.
Hays, Richard B. *Echoes of Scripture in the Letters of Paul*. New Haven: Yale University Press, 1989.
———. "On the Rebound: A Response to Critiques of *Echoes of Scripture in the Letters of Paul*." In *Paul and the Scriptures of Israel*, edited by Craig A. Evans and James A. Sanders, 77–8. Journal for the Study of the New Testament Supplements 83. Sheffield: JSOT, 1993.
Hirsch, E. D. Jr. *Validity in Interpretation*. New Haven: Yale University Press, 1967.
Juel, Donald H. *Messianic Exegesis: Christological Interpretation of the Old Testament in Early Christianity*. Philadelphia: Fortress, 1988.
Kaiser, Walter, Jr. *The Uses of the Old Testament in the New*. 1985. Reprint, Eugene, OR: Wipf & Stock, 2001.
Krieger, Leonard. *Ranke: The Meaning of History*. Chicago: University of Chicago Press, 1977.
Kugel, James. *Traditions of the Bible: A Guide to the Bible as It Was at the Start of the Common Era*. Cambridge: Harvard University Press, 1998.
Leschert, Dale F. *Hermeneutical Foundations of Hebrews: A Study in the Validity of the Epistle's Interpretation of Some Core Citations from the Psalms*. National Association of Baptist Professors of Religion Dissertation Series 10. Lewiston, NY: Mellen, 1996.
Lightfoot, John. *A Commentary on the New Testament from the Talmud and Hebraica: Matthew–I Corinthians*. Grand Rapids: Baker, 1979.
Lindars, Barnabas. "The Place of the Old Testament in the Formation of New Testament Theology: Prolegomena." *New Testament Studies* 23 (1976) 59–66.
Longenecker, Richard. *Biblical Exegesis in the Apostolic Period*. 2nd ed. Grand Rapids: Baker, 1999.
———. "Who Is the Prophet Talking About? Some Reflections on the New Testament Use of the Old." *Themelios* 13 (1987) 4–8.
Long, V. Philips. *The Art of Biblical History*. Grand Rapids: Zondervan, 1994.
McCalman Turpie, David. *The Old Testament in the New*. London: Williams & Norgate, 1868.
McCartney, Dan G. "New Testament's Use of the Old Testament." In *Inerrancy and Hermeneutic: A Tradition, a Challenge, a Debate*, edited by Harvie M. Conn. Steubenville, OH: Emmaus, 1993.
McCartney, Dan G., and Peter Enns. "Matthew and Hosea: A Response to John Sailhamer." *Westminster Theological Journal* 63 (2001) 97–105.
McNamara, Martin. *Palestinian Judaism and the New Testament*. Good News Studies 4. Wilmington, DE: Glazier, 1983.

Marshall, I. Howard. "An Assessment of Recent Developments." In *It Is Written: Scripture Citing Scripture, Essays in Honour of Barnabas Lindars, SSF*, edited by D. A. Carson and H. G. M. Williamson, 1–21. Cambridge: Cambridge University Press, 1988.

Moo, Douglas J. "Problem of Sensus Plenior." In *Hermeneutics, Authority, and Canon*, edited by D. A. Carson and John D. Woodbridge, 175–211. Grand Rapids: Zondervan, 1986.

Moyise, Steve. *The Old Testament in the New: An Introduction*. New York: Continuum, 2001.

Neyrey, Jerome H. *2 Peter, Jude: A New Translation with Introduction and Commentary*. Anchor Bible 37C. New York: Doubleday, 1993.

Nicole, Roger. "The New Testament Use of the Old Testament." In *Revelation and the Bible*, edited by Carl F. H. Henry, 135–51. Grand Rapids: Baker, 1958.

Sailhamer, John H. "Hosea 11:1 and Matthew 2:15." *WTJ* 63 (2001) 87–96.

Silva, Moisés. "The New Testament Use of the Old Testament: Text Form and Authority." In *Scripture and Truth*, edited by D. A. Carson and J. D. Woodbridge, 147–65. Grand Rapids: Zondervan, 1983.

———. "Old Testament in Paul." In *Dictionary of Paul and His Letters*, edited by Gerald F. Hawthorne and Ralph P. Martin, 630–34. Downers Grove, IL: InterVarsity, 2009.

Snodgrass, Klyne. "The Use of the Old Testament in the New." In *New Testament Criticism and Interpretation*, edited by David Alan Black and David S. Dockery. Grand Rapids: Zondervan, 1991.

Strack, Hermann L., and Paul Billerbeck. *Kommentar zum Neuen Testamentaus Talmud und Midrash*. Munich: C. H. Beck, 1926.

Taber, Charles R. "Is There One Way to Do Theology?" *Gospel in Context* 1 (1978) 8.

Toy, Crawford Howell. *Quotations in the New Testament*. New York: Charles Scribner's Sons, 1884.

Vanhoozer, Kevin J. *First Theology: God, Scripture & Hermeneutics*. Downers Grove, IL: InterVarsity, 2002.

Van Till, Howard J. "The Fully Gifted Creation." In *Three Views on Creation and Evolution*, edited by J. P. Moreland et al., 159–247. Grand Rapids: Zondervan, 1999.

Vermes, Geza. *Scripture and Tradition in Judaism*. Studia Post-Biblica 4. Leiden: Brill, 1961.

Vos, Geerhardus. *Biblical Theology: Old and New Testaments*. Grand Rapids: Eerdmans, 1948.

Warfield, B. B. "The Divine and Human in the Bible." In *Evolution, Science, and Scripture: Selected Writings*, edited by B. B. Warfield, Mark A. Noll, and David N. Livingstone, 51–58. Grand Rapids: Baker, 2000.

Young, Davis A. "The Antiquity of the Unity of the Human Race Revisited." *Christian Scholar's Review* 24 (1995) 380–96.

———. *The Biblical Flood: A Case Study of the Church's Response to Extrabiblical Evidence*. Grand Rapids: Eerdmans, 1995.

Part II

Reading the World Biblically

6

"Text of Life" and "Text for Life"
The Bible as the Living and Life-Giving Word of God for the Dalits

Peniel Jesudason Rufus Rajkumar

Introduction

Perhaps one word that imaginatively captures the relationship between the Dalit communities and the Bible is "glossolalia" (speaking in many tongues), because the Bible has spoken in multiple tongues *to*, *for* and *through* the Dalit communities. Therefore, on the one hand, we can speak of the Bible as being a "Text of Life" that reflects the struggles, survival stories, and successes of the Dalit communities within the wider framework and prism of a theo-story (God's own story). On the other hand, it can be seen as a "Text for Life," a tool that Dalit communities have creatively and conscientiously appropriated to further the flourishing of their lives at its most fragile moments. Any discerning reader of Dalit theology can attest to its strong biblical underpinnings, which further testify to the fact that the Bible has opened multiple possibilities for Dalit communities to resist oppression, reaffirm identity, and recover possibilities for the flourishing of life in a heteronomous manner.

This two-fold, mutually complementary dimension of the Bible as a "Text of Life" and "Text for Life" reveals an understanding it as both living and life-giving. The Bible is living because Dalits find in its narratives resonances with their own lives. The Bible, through its stories of liberation, offers a surrogate space in which Dalits can see the transformation of their (hi)stories. In Dalit readings of the Bible, there is in many ways a mutual embrace of the world of the Bible and the world of the Dalits—leading to and lending to both worlds the gift of new meanings. The Bible is life-giving for the Dalits because it is discerned as holding in it the promise of life. As has been pointed out, whether as a "dynamic source of energy" for their "corporate and individual attempts at liberation,"[1] or as "the basic faith document that inspires and instills hope and resilience and acts as a shield and a sword in their existential faith journey,"[2] the Bible is pivotal especially for the Christian Dalit struggle for restoration of justice and the reclamation of life.

The Bible as a "Text of Life"

As with different theologies of liberation, the Dalit communities have understood biblical narratives as the story of God's solidarity with them. What makes the Bible a living text for them is the fact that it resonates with their own stories. It is not a record of past events but the unfolding story of God's ongoing relationship with the Dalits. The Bible is a living text because it testifies to the truth as it is embodied in the struggles of the Dalit communities. The Dalits often read their own stories into the text to reaffirm their identity and recover their dignity.

Case 1

The Catholic scholar Jose D. Maliekal recounts the story of how a Dalit named Ebenezer, a village leader belonging to the Madiga community (a Dalit community found in the South Indian state of Andhra Pradesh and usually associated with dead flesh and leather), creatively reinterpreted the biblical narrative of Thomas's post-resurrection meeting with Jesus to reaffirm his own Madiga identity. In this story, based on a real-life experience, Ebenezer boasts that St. Thomas the Apostle belonged to the Madiga community because he dared to place his fingers into the wounded flesh of Jesus. This story is an obvious reference to Jesus's post-resurrection conversation with Thomas in John 20:26–29. It is creatively interpreted with an identity focus, which seeks to make the point that the apostle who is credited with bringing the gospel to India himself "was a Dalit." There is potential in this reinterpretation to dispel the prejudice that exists toward the Madigas because of their occupational dealings with dead flesh. Yet it needs to be noted that nowhere in the biblical narrative is it recorded that Thomas actually touched the wounds of Jesus. According to the biblical text, Jesus

---

1. Jesurathnam, "Towards a Dalit Liberative Re-reading of the Psalms of Lament," 2.
2. Razu, "Bible, a Shield and a Sword," 58.

only invites Thomas to put his fingers into his wounds.³ Maliekal identifies this interpretation as being "the software-chip of a potential Madiga identity theology," whereby Ebenezer was "trying to assert pride in his traditional trade, the identity-marker of his caste, by tracing an aetiology for it and taking off the stigma attached to it."⁴ The strength of the textual appropriation of the Bible by the Dalits lies in such understandings of important biblical characters in interaction with the experiences of the Dalits—in an effort to reconfigure the communal identity of the Dalit communities in an affirmative and identity-enhancing manner.

Case 2

Dalits not only perceive their own lives in the biblical texts but also read the lives of their oppressors through biblical texts in a most profound manner. They use the Bible as a prism through which to reflect on the life of their oppressors. One example of this can be recounted from my own experience. Following the gruesome violence against Dalit and tribal Christians in the Kandhamal district of Orissa in August 2008 (in which about forty people were killed and thousands displaced from their villages following the burning of their homes), I was visiting one of several refugee camps set up for the thousands who had been displaced. I met a group of Dalit Christians who, despite having suffered for embracing the Christian faith, had started a "prayer fellowship" in the refugee camp. Out of curiosity, I asked the man who was the leader of the group what he thought of those people who had burnt his house, killed his relatives, and made him a refugee. Amidst the uncertainty and the miserable conditions of the refugee camp, and in the most sincere manner, he said that he and his family prayed that *the power of the resurrected Christ would touch his persecutors in the same way that it touched Saul in the Bible and converted him into the apostle Paul, an apostle who became even willing to risk his life for the cause of the very people he once wanted completely to annihilate.* His reply left me stunned. What is fascinating is the manner in which he was able to re-imagine his own story in the light of a larger biblical narrative to re-humanize someone who had been most inhumane toward him. In the seamless manner in which he placed these narratives alongside one another, we can see the Bible as being truly the book of life. In their appropriation of the biblical narratives, Dalits have the capacity to foster what Maria Arul Raja calls the spirit of "re-creation," which will enable "both the 're-creation' of the

---

3. See Clarke's interpretation of this story in "Viewing the Bible through the Eyes and Ears of Subalterns."

4. Maliekal, "Identity-Consciousness of the Christian Madigas Story," 25.

Dalit identity from the debris of the battered self and the recreation of any reality into a new reality by Dalit intervention."[5]

Having said this, the way in which Dalits appropriate biblical texts is polyphonic and not monolithic. Different meanings can be derived from one single text. The exodus story of the liberation of the Israelites from the Egyptians and their occupation of the "promised land" is one good example. Some Dalits have understood themselves as the Israelites, the liberated slaves from Egypt for whose sake God was willing to fight and lead to victory. But for others, it has been different and the exodus paradigm has been inadequate. Taking his cue from the unlikely prospect of any radical or large-scale revolutionary structural change to the Dalit situation, Clarke makes a pertinent point about the inadequacy of the exodus paradigm for the Dalit communities:

> . . . the notion of an all-powerful God, who intervenes and completely reconfigures the world for the sake of the oppressed, does not find a dominant place in Dalit thinking and acting. This problematises the grandiose conceptions of God that result from postulating the Exodus paradigm as the heart of liberation theology. In the Indian context it seems that the "mighty acts of God," which deliver God's chosen oppressed ones from the clutches of their oppressors, have either changed their aim or exhausted themselves . . . there has been a winding down of the mighty acts of God! There are no miraculous signs clearly disrupting the hierarchical and unequal social order in India. There is no spectacular parting of the seas; there is no drowning of the violating and violent ones who exploit and destroy the poor and the Dalits. To put it as starkly as possible, the dictum of God's "preferential option for the poor" has remained quite sterile in terms of practical, concrete improvements in the structures of the society for the good of the poor.[6]

As I have described it in a different context, from a Dalit perspective, it often seems as if the ten plagues that God brought upon the Egyptians only affects the Dalits:

> "Because in Dalit experience . . .
>   Only *their* waters are transformed into blood,
>   and more frogs, into their houses flood,
>   gnats infest their grounds;
>   and flies their food and un-sutured wounds.

5. Arul Raja, "Harmony in the Midst of Anarchy."
6. Clarke, "Dalits Overcoming Violation and Violence," 285–86.

> Their . . . *their* livestock alone die of disease
> and it is their bodies that fester with boils.
> thunder and hail target their homes alone;
> as does unfathomable darkness with its pall of gloom.
> Locusts destroy *their* bonded fields,
> making them bonded labourers for life.
> finally, it is not their first born alone . . . but . . .
> their every-born, whom death in its relentless pursuit fells."[7]

The Bible as a Text for Life

The Bible is not just a text that, like a prism, refracts the various dimensions of the life of the Dalits; it is also a text *for* life. It is a tool to further the fullness of life for the Dalits. However, what needs to be taken into account when considering the Bible as a life-giving text is that Dalit appropriation of the Bible is not solely trans-textual. There are several ways in which Dalit communities appropriate the text of the Bible in their struggle for liberation.

When dealing with the Bible as a life-giving word for the Dalits, there is often a tacit inclination for researchers to be overtly text-centered in their focus. However, we need to recognize how, by focusing too much on the textual process, especially in contexts of illiteracy, we quite unintentionally become implicated in the power dynamics implicit in "reading, understanding and interpreting the word." In these contexts, there is need to be open to acquire an awareness of the other non-textual ways in which the Bible may be active in the lives of communities commonly regarded as "inferior."

There is a need for researchers to reorient themselves to the various ways in which the Bible has acted in an empowering manner for different communities and to understand the place of the Bible in the lives of the Dalit communities in creative interaction with such practices. One good example of the way in which the Bible "acts" in the life of the Dalit communities in a non-conventional manner is the case of how the Bible as a book, which can be accessed only through education, proved to be empowering to Dalit women in south India. Historian-theologian James Tanneti helpfully delineates how Telugu Dalit women, who developed a fervor to become Bible women, constructively appropriated the dynamics of the new significance that access to the Bible offered them, in the course of their search "for an alternative religion of the book as a weapon to challenge the ever-absorbing and aggressive Hinduism," which denied the privilege of

---

7. Rajkumar, *Challenges of Transition*, 30.

reading, let alone reading Scriptures, to Dalits and especially Dalit women. According to Tanneti:

> Dalits, who shared oral traditions, would have seen the act of reading and writing as an empowering experience as well as a challenge to Hinduism, which also was a text-based culture. Dalits considered literacy as a political weapon with which they could challenge their Hindu oppressors. . . . According to Hinduism, the very recital of the religious Scriptures and their sounds is sacred and emancipating to one's soul. It was the prerogative of the Brahmins, the "highest" caste in the Hindu hierarchy. In this context, mastering these texts and their sounds is a power claim. Through mastering the sacred texts (the Bible in this case), Telugu women were attempting to create parallel power structures in which they could assert their power. It is evident in the response the women's seminary in Tuni received and in the way Telugu women, especially Dalit women, mastered (memorized) the texts, and rendered them in story forms to their Hindu counterparts.[8]

Thus, for these communities who were not only systematically denied access to traditional Scriptures (Dalits who recited the Scripture had their tongues cut off and molten lead was poured into the ears of Dalits who even inadvertently listened to the reading of the Hindu Scriptures) but were also discriminated against on the basis of the sanctification and justification offered by the same Scriptures, this access to the Bible was subversive as it had the potential "to replace the world view of the Hindu Scriptures and displace the Hindu Vedas."[9] The Bible "not only filled a void but also supplied the Dalits with a framework for knowledge that they did not have to begin with and which they desired."[10]

When understanding the Bible as a life-giving book, it also is necessary to recognize the trans-textual (beyond text-based) and sensory dimensions of the way in which the various subaltern communities appropriate the Bible in an emancipatory manner. The examples cited above show that Dalit communities do not rely solely on the "words within the Bible" for their emancipation. There is need to give space for subaltern reception of the "performative dimension" of the Bible which is crucial to the subaltern understanding of the Bible as being emancipatory. It is appropriate for us to

---

8. Taneti, "Encounter between Protestant and Telugu Women's Paradigms of Scripture," 8–9.
9. Melanchton, "Dalits Bible and Method."
10. Ibid.

turn to the pertinent examples that Kiran Sebastian gives from his pastoral experiences:

> In one case, the family proudly pulled out a steel trunk which was under the rolled-up mattresses in the small house, took out several layers of folded clothing, took out a clean white towel in which a pristine Bible, with many of its pages uncut, lay wrapped; in another, the family pointed to the open Bible which had been placed on a small shelf on the wall, decorated with coloured flashing lights, but when I gingerly took it off the shelf, discovered not only a thick layer of dust, but the remains of a number of flying insects; and in a third case, was given the Bible from among a pile of magazines, only to discover on opening it, that it was serving as a store for the cut-out pictures of film actors and actresses, preserved amongst its pages. The fourth example comes from the time when I was a pastor in the urban Hudson Memorial Kannada congregation in Bangalore, where (among many other things) I had to bless unusual objects, including in this case a machine which converted old paper into pulp and then into egg-trays. The owner told me that he employed a number of "rag-pickers" to bring him paper of suitable quality for this purpose, and discovered that there were a large number of New Testaments and Bibles (most probably those distributed gratis by organizations like the Gideons) in what had been brought in. He told me that at first, he had tried to "rescue" the Bibles from the pile, but then when he realized how many there were, just let them continue the journey of reincarnation into egg-trays.[11]

In a context like this, according to Sebastian "what is interesting and intriguing in the examples is the complex nature of the inter-link between the reality of commitment to a faith-praxis and the instrumentalization of the orienting symbols of that faith."[12]

> The Bible, in these cases, has variously been seen as something so precious that it needs to be carefully stored away out of sight, but unlikely to be out of mind; as something to be illuminated externally, while the "lamp to our feet" idea, in terms of "containing" something illumining, is switched off; as something adding value and providing security to that which offers enrichment to

---

11. Sebastian, "Can We Now Bypass that Truth?," 86–87.
12. Ibid., 87.

one's life; as something whose worth would not be erased, even when the "black marks on white paper" were no longer legible.[13]

These examples point to the unconventional nature of the relationship between the life-giving nature of the Bible and the Dalit communities.

Conclusion

In conclusion, it can be said that the relevance of the Bible for the Dalit communities transcends the spiritual dimension and acquires a much more holistic relevance. In this regard, the Bible becomes the book of life in every sense of the term. As the "living" word of God, it helps the Dalits creatively to negotiate the dialectic between the timelessness and the time-boundedness of biblical experience and Dalit experience; as the "life-giving" word of God, it promises and "produces" empowerment, instills and inspires hope, confirms confidence, and castigates everything that deters Dalits from embracing God's promise of life in all its fullness for all. Therefore, one can claim that the Bible is a book that truly furthers life in all its fullness for the Dalit communities.

Bibliography

Arul Raja, A. Maria. "Harmony in the Midst of Anarchy: The Anatomy of the Spirit of Dalit Liberation." *Vidhyajothi Journal of Theological Reflection* 63 (1999) 416–28.
Clarke, Sathianathan. "Dalits Overcoming Violation and Violence: A Contest Between Overpowering and Empowering Identities in Changing India." *Ecumenical Review* 54.3 (2002) 278–95.
———. "Viewing the Bible through the Eyes and Ears of Subalterns in India." Paper presented at the Ecumenical Enablers' Programme organized by the Christian Conference of Asia (CCA) on "The Quest for New Hermeneutics in Asia," Bangkok, Thailand, March 28 to April 2, 2001. Also published in *Biblical Interpretation* 10.3 (2002) 251–57.
Jesurathnam, K. "Towards a Dalit Liberative Re-reading of the Psalms of Lament." *Bangalore Theological Forum* 34.1 (2002) 1–34.
Maliekal, Jose D. "Identity-Consciousness of the Christian Madigas Story of a People in Emergence." *Jeevadhara: A Journal of Christian Interpretation* 31.181 (2001) 25–36.
Melanchton, Monica Jyotsna. "Dalits Bible and Method." *SBL Forum* (cited Oct 2005) n.p. http://sbl-site.org/Article.aspx?ArticleID=459.
Rajkumar, Peniel Jesudason Rufus. *Challenges of Transition: Religion and Ethics in Changing Contexts.* New Delhi: ISPCK, 2007.

---

13. Ibid.

Razu, I. John Mohan. "The Bible, A Shield and A Sword: From a Perspective of the Subalterns." In *Light on Our Dusty Path: Essays for a Bible Lover,* edited by Israel Selvanayagam, 58–77. Bangalore: South Asia Theological Research Institute and Board of Theological Education Senate of Serampore College, SATHRI/ BTESSC, 2008.

Sebastian, J. Jayakiran. "Can We Now Bypass that Truth?" *Transformation* 25.2–3 (2008), 80–91.

Taneti, James. "Encounter Between Protestant and Telugu Women's Paradigms of Scripture." Paper presented at "Comparative Theology: Engaging Particularities Conference," Boston College, 2007.

7

The Pilgrim Motif in Hebrews
A Biblical Response to the Refugee Problem in Kenya

Emily J. Choge-Kerama

Introduction

The pilgrim motif is central to the Christian life. It plays a key role in the identity and the lives of the people of God in both the Old and the New Testaments. The word "pilgrim" is used in two ways in this study: in the classic meaning of one who makes a journey to a sacred place and also in the general sense that life on earth is a pilgrimage toward some destination. The understanding, therefore, is that life on earth is temporary, but it also has a dimension of purpose. Thus, all strangers, aliens, resident aliens, sojourners, migrants, exiles, or refugees share the element of strangeness or unsettledness, but they are not pilgrims unless there is that added dimension of goal or purpose to their lives. This is what sets a pilgrim apart from an ordinary stranger. This theme is evident throughout much of modern Christian devotional material, whether novels, plays, songs and more recently, movies. Some of the popular Christian songs that incorporate this theme are: "Guide me O thou great Jehovah, Pilgrim through this barren land" and "This world is not my home, I am just a passing through." Novels also employ this theme extensively.

The pioneers of the faith—Abraham, Isaac, Jacob, and their wives—lived as "strangers and pilgrims" even in the land of Canaan, the land of promise. The book of Hebrews tells us that they were looking for the "city that has foundations, whose architect and builder is God" (Heb 11:10).[1] In the Old Testament, the Israelite journey to and from Egypt, and later to exile in Babylon, continues this theme in the life of the people of God. We also

---

1. All biblical citations are from the New Revised Standard Version (NRSV).

note this kind of existence in the life of Jesus as "he set his face to go to Jerusalem," he had "nowhere to lay his head" (Luke 9:51; 9:58). The life of early Christians is also one of movement as depicted by the life of the apostle Paul, who made several missionary journeys to establish churches around the region of the Mediterranean Sea and later in Rome. It is important to note that in both the Old and the New Testament, the emphasis is placed on the practice of hospitality or love for aliens and strangers as an appropriate response to pilgrim existence. The idea is that people who understand what it means to be a stranger should treat strangers better than those who do not. Pohl[2] notes that this was expected of the people of God in the Old Testament, but no less for those in the early church and in the present. She also suggests that these two important motifs are throughout Scripture. She says, "The first is the continuing experience of the people of God as aliens and exiles; being a stranger is normatively central to the Christian identity. The second is the expectation that as strangers themselves, the people of God will welcome strangers and will embody hospitality as a way of life."[3] These two motifs are key to this work, and hospitality will feature as an important practice that should accompany the pilgrim way of life. This essay expands the discussion however, to show how Christians in Kenya should respond to the pressing needs of refugees.

The book of Hebrews focuses on the pilgrim motif and also on the response of hospitality to those experiencing various kinds of trials, especially Christians living in a hostile environment. This essay examines how the author of Hebrews uses the pilgrim motif to speak to the situation of early listeners. Here, I use the word "listeners" rather than "readers," because many scholars argue that the book of Hebrews is more of a sermon than a letter. According to Attridge, Hebrews is "a masterpiece of early Christian rhetorical homiletics or, in its own terms a 'word of exhortation.'"[4] DeSilva also notes that the author of Hebrews uses verbs of speaking when referring to his communication (2:5; 6:9; 8:1; 9:5; 11:32), "he also voices his concern for the addressees' attentive hearing (not reading) of the message"[5] (5:11). The excellent rhetorical features lend themselves more to the ear than the eye. Lane points out that the writer of Hebrews "crafted the written text for the ear, not the eye, to convey a sense of structure and development. By

---

2. Pohl, "Biblical Issues in Mission and Migration," 3–5.
3. Ibid., 5.
4. Attridge, *Epistle to the Hebrews*, 1.
5. DeSilva, *Perseverance in Gratitude*, 36.

appealing to the dynamic relationship of speaking and listening, he is able to establish a sense of presence with his audience."[6]

The key questions will be: *Why does the author use this motif? How does the use of this motif communicate something about the life of the early listeners? What ethical values, principles and practices does the author of Hebrews promote in order for one to persevere in the pilgrimage? Are these values, principles and practices applicable to the church today?* My argument is that the use of the pilgrim motif sets the tone for radical faith and hope in the face of adverse circumstances. That kind of hope should characterize the body of Christ anywhere in the world, but more specifically in Africa where wars, famines, and diseases have caused huge displacements of peoples who live scattered in various lands as refugees, aliens, and strangers. Most importantly, Hebrews provides us with the key principle of pilgrimage, namely, the necessity of entering into God's presence, the true goal of all pilgrimage. Therefore, this is not a theoretical or an abstract reflection, but an urgent call to Christians everywhere to reflect on our true identity as "pilgrims and strangers" and on how this will change the way we live and view the world.

This essay first looks at how the pilgrim motif is portrayed in and lived out in the lives of the people of God in ancient Israel, at the time of Jesus, and in the early church. It also examines what Hebrews says about this theme by showing the centrality of faith and hope in the journey. It then discusses the ethical implications that result from the pilgrim motif with a view to applying them to the church in Africa, more specifically the church in Kenya. In the final analysis, these principles and practices can be carried on by the church worldwide because this calling for Christians to live as "pilgrims and aliens" is for the whole body of Christ, regardless of time and place.

The Pilgrim Motif in Ancient Israel

The central understanding of the people of God both in the old and the new covenant is that of a people always on the move. They are those who have set their eyes on the city "whose maker and founder is God" (Heb 11:10, 16). Here on earth, they have no fixed residence. They live as resident aliens, strangers and foreigners, or pilgrims on a journey to the heavenly city. This identity that embodies movement was brought into place with the calling of the father of faith, Abraham, who was told to move out of the land of the Chaldeans to the land that God would show him. At first, we think that the land he was to inhabit is the land of Canaan, but Hebrews reinterprets this by saying, "By faith he stayed for a time in that land he had been promised,

---

6. Lane, "Standing Before the Moral Claims of God," 204.

as in a foreign land, living in tents, as did Isaac and Jacob, who were heirs with him of the same promise. For he looked for a city that has foundations, whose architect and builder is God" (Heb 11:9–10). This shows that, from the beginning, the heirs of faith were aware that their goal was the eternal or heavenly city, the unshakable realm (Heb 12:22, 26–28).[7]

This pilgrim existence also was embodied by Abraham's descendants, the Israelites, who had been promised that kind of life even before they came to be: "Then the Lord said to Abram, 'know this for certain, that your offspring shall be aliens in a land that is not theirs, and shall be slaves there, and they shall be oppressed for four hundred years'" (Gen 15:13). Even when they had been removed from the bondage of Egypt, the people of God were to embrace their alien and pilgrim existence in the key institutions of their lives in the land, the temple, and the Law. There were several words for strangers in Israel. The word *"Ger"* is translated "sojourner/pilgrim" (KJV), "alien" (NIV), or "resident alien" (NRSV). This is the one who is given full legal rights in Mosaic Law. The word *"toshab"* also is used in much the same way. The Hebrew *"nekar"* or *"ben nekar"* designated a foreigner. It covers anything foreign, regardless of residence. The Hebrew *"zur"* means "stranger" and takes its coloring from the context.

First, we see how their pilgrim existence influenced their relationship to the land. They were clearly instructed not to forget that they were aliens in the land, because the land of Canaan belonged to God. So, they could not treat the land in any way they wanted. Every seven years, the land was to be left fallow so that the poor and the aliens could eat from it. At every harvest, they showed their concern for the aliens by not harvesting to the edges of the field, so that the poor and the alien could glean from those areas (Lev 19:9–10, Deut 14:28–29). The land also was not to be sold in perpetuity. They had to observe the Jubilee principle, which meant that after fifty years the land could be restored to those who had lost it through any means, especially through poverty. Those who fell into hard times were to live among their brothers and sisters as resident aliens until the Jubilee year when they could reclaim their land. The reason is stated here: "The land shall not be sold in perpetuity, for the land is mine; with me you are but aliens and tenants" (Lev 25:23).

We can note the centrality of the pilgrim existence, which also was embodied in their worship lives. They included resident aliens when they worshipped at the tabernacle, during the wilderness experience and also later at the temple in Jerusalem (Deut 16:1ff.). The weekly Sabbath was

---

7. DeSilva, *Perseverance in Gratitude*, 381. Ellingworth, "Jesus and Universe in Hebrews," 587.

meant to be a time of rest for those who were hired servants and aliens (Exod 20:8–10; 23:12). When they offered their annual tithes, they made the confession, "A wandering Aramean was my ancestor; he went down to Egypt and lived there as an alien . . ." (Deut 26:5). Von Rad (1996) argues that these verses contain the earliest digest of Israel's faith. He also suggested that they summarized the core of Israel's salvation history. He further claimed that the outline of events contained in the creed formed the basic historical outline of what came to be called Genesis to Joshua. In his commentary to Deuteronomy, he says that the creed is the most important item in the ceremony offering the first fruits of the land. They were to celebrate the harvest of these first fruits with the Levites and the aliens. Every third year, they had tithes dedicated to aliens and Levites (Deut 14: 28–29; 26:12). One of the annual festivals was the feast of booths (Deut 16:13ff.), in which they re-enacted their pilgrim and wilderness existence. Three times a year also, they set out on a pilgrimage to the house of worship in Jerusalem when the temple was built. Later, when they were scattered in the diaspora, they continued to make these pilgrimages to the temple and also to the city of Jerusalem.

Due to their experience as aliens in the land of Egypt, the Israelites paid special attention to the treatment of aliens, especially as it was stipulated within the law. Van Houten[8] traced the development of Israelite laws with regard to the aliens, showing how they are progressively given an equal status in the community. They recognized that such a sacred responsibility could not be confined to the level of charitable feelings, so it was enshrined within their legislation. The seriousness of violating this legislation can be seen from the consequences that would befall such offenders: "You shall not wrong or oppress a resident alien, for you were aliens in the land of Egypt, You shall not abuse any widow or orphan, If you do abuse them, when they cry to me, I will surely heed their cry and my wrath will burn and I will kill you with the sword, and your wives shall become widows and your children orphans" (Exod 22:21–23). The severity of the punishment is expressed in the fact that the consequences would not just befall individual offenders but the nation as a whole. The prophets view the Israelites' exile in Babylon as a result of not heeding this warning; they did not remember their own alien existence and did not treat the poor, the orphans, the widows, and the aliens well, so they literally became aliens in a foreign land.

In the exile period, the people of God were called to live a pilgrim existence. Yoder[9] offers an important dimension of what the exile meant to the

---

8. Van Houten, *Alien in Israelite Law*, 67, 108, 155–78.
9. Yoder, *For the Nations*, 53–54.

Jews. He argues that the diaspora or *galuth* that had been earlier prefigured in the life in Egypt was a normal part of Jewish existence, and this should also be the case for Christians. He says, "To be scattered is not a hiatus, after which normalcy will resume. From Jeremiah's time on . . . dispersion shall be the calling of the Jewish faith community."[10] He shows further that this was the reason Jeremiah had to write to the exiles in Babylon to "seek the welfare of the city where I have sent you, and to pray to the LORD on its behalf, for in its welfare you will find your welfare. . . . For surely I know the plans I have for you says the LORD, the plans for your welfare and not for harm, to give you a future with hope" (Jer 29:11).

During the time of Jesus and the early church, this motif of living a pilgrim and alien existence was part and parcel of life. Caring for those who were marginalized in this way is clearly continued. Jesus was born while his parents were on a journey because of a census that had been imposed, and there was no room for them in the inn. As a baby, he and his family escaped the wrath of a wicked king by fleeing as refugees into Egypt. This shows, that from the start of Jesus's life, he had to depend on others for his safety and sustenance, and this no doubt shaped his ministry. He welcomed those who were strangers to the community, the sinners, tax collectors, and women. When he sent his disciples on a mission, he also urged them to depend on the hospitality of those to whom they ministered. In one of his key teachings on the final judgment, he shows that our eternal destiny was determined by how we treated strangers. This is evident in his statement, "Come, you that are blessed by my father, inherit the kingdom prepared for you from the foundation of the world; for I was . . . a stranger and you welcomed me . . ." (Matt 25:31ff).

The life of the early Christians was also a life of movement. Due to the persecution that came upon believers in Jerusalem, most of them had to move to places all over the Roman Empire, where they learned to live as aliens and pilgrims. First Peter is especially addressed to such, "to the exiles of Dispersion . . ." They are specifically urged to live an exemplary existence, "Beloved, I urge you as aliens and exiles to abstain from the desires of the flesh that wage war against the soul" (1 Pet 2:11). In his missionary journeys, Paul lived out the pilgrim existence. This is the reason one of the practices the early church emphasized was hospitality (Rom 12:9–13; 15:1; 1 Tim 3:2; Titus 1:2; 2 John 10–12; Heb 13:2).

---

10. Ibid.

The Book of Hebrews

The book of Hebrews has exerted great influence over the Christian church throughout the centuries, despite the fact that much about its authorship[11] and composition are unknown. However, various commentators have speculated about various authors and names that have been proposed, including Apollo, Luke, Silas, Priscilla and Aquila, or Mary the mother of Jesus.[12] Hebrews has appealed to many people for various reasons. For some, the attraction has been the beautiful and artistic literary features the author has used to craft and blend the expository and exhortation parts together. For others, it has been the great themes, such as the completed and superior work of Christ in comparison to the Old-Testament religious systems, the exhortation to follow the heroes of faith by moving toward that eternal home, as well as the call to be faithful even in difficult times. According to Attridge, "The document known as the Epistle to the Hebrews is the most elegant and sophisticated, perhaps the most enigmatic, text of first century Christianity. Its author is unknown, and the circumstances of its composition remain mysterious. Its argumentation is subtle; its language refined; its imagery rich and evocative."[13]

There is no doubt that this book has been a source of inspiration and encouragement to believers for all times. After September 11, 2001, I listened to several sermons from the book of Hebrews to encourage believers in their situation. Though the author is unknown, there are clues from the book that tell us what kind of a person he was. He was not an eyewitness of Jesus (2:3). He was probably in the traveling band with Paul, because he mentions Timothy (13:23).[14] The date of writing is unclear, and the original recipients are not identified. Two dates have been suggested, pre-70 CE and post-70 CE. One of the arguments for the pre-70 CE date is that if the destruction of the temple had already taken place, this would have been his proof to show that the sacrifices in the temple were obsolete. However, this is not considered conclusive, because the author uses language that refers to the tabernacle rather than the temple, so it might have been a theological rather than physical matter. Allison[15] says that the fact the author used "tabernacle" instead of "temple" shows that the author was careful in the choice of words, especially since this was in a very explosive time just before 70 CE.

11. Attridge, *Epistle to the Hebrews*, 1.
12. Ibid.,1–5; Koester, *Hebrews*, 42–46.
13. Attridge, *Epistle to the Hebrews*, 1.
14. See also Attridge, *Epistle to the Hebrews*, 20–21; deSilva, *Perseverance in Gratitude*, 35–71.
15. Allison, *End of the Times Has Come*, 230.

What is clear, however, is that the author, who is well known to his audience, is aware of the fact that they are facing a twofold danger, as Attridge tells us: "external pressure or persecution (10:36–12:13) and a waning commitment to the community's confessed faith"[16] So his response to the first danger is "stern warnings and exhortations to faithful discipleship."[17] For the second danger, he "proposes a renewed and deepened understanding of the community's confession that will inspire covenant fidelity."[18] The author uses the pilgrim motif to call his audience to an awareness of themselves as a covenant people: a reminder that theirs was a pilgrim faith right from the beginning. This would inspire them to persevere through the external trials, while giving them a proper perspective and hope with regard to the eternal treasures that they were to hold on to.

The Importance of Faith along the Journey

The concept of faith is important in the study of Hebrews, seeing that the entire chapter 11 is dedicated to illustrating this key concept. Though there are varied views about what faith looks like, there is agreement that it is related to the overall message of the book. Rhee,[19] who gives it a central place, says that it holds together the various themes such as Christ's Sonship, his high priesthood, and Sabbath rest. In his graphic description, Rhee sees faith as the thread or "string" that holds the precious themes of the book of Hebrews together so that it can shine like a beautiful "necklace made of pearls."[20] Those who affirm the centrality of the pilgrim motif see faith as an important virtue without which those who have embarked on the journey cannot survive.

The word "faith" in Hebrews appears thirty-two times throughout the epistle,[21] out of which twenty-five are in 11:1–12:29. There are also several faith-related words, which show the centrality of faith in the overall message of the epistle. In Rhee's summary of the occurrences of the word "faith" in the New Testament, he says that Michel groups these words into two groups: 1) the *peixomai* group; and 2) the *pistis* group. The total number of *peixomai* uses add up to ninety-four times, while the *pistis* group usage is more

---

16. Attridge, *Epistle to the Hebrews*, 13.
17. Ibid.
18. Ibid.
19. Rhee, *Faith in Hebrews*, xvi.
20. Ibid., 1.
21. Kohlenberger et.al., *Exhaustive Concordance of the Greek New Testament*, 800–807.

frequent. Rhee tells us that the verbal form occurs 242 times ("*pisteuo*" 241 times; "*pisteo*" once), the noun "*pistis*" occurs 243 times, while the adjective "*pistos*" 67 times. The writers of the New Testament also use negative forms to express the negative forms of faith, "*apisteo*," the adjective "*apistos*," and the noun "*apistia*" eleven times. Thus, the total number of the word group "faith" appears 688 times in the New Testament.

It is evident from the references that faith in Hebrews has to do with the finished work of Christ. Although there is no direct reference to faith in Christ, it is clear from the interchange between the doctrinal and the parenetic sections that this faith is understood as having its origin in Christ, that is faith in Christ. Rhee has constructed his argument to prove that Christ is the object of faith in Hebrews. He says that the author employs both doctrine and exhortations to encourage believers to remain in faith.[22] The stylistic alternation between doctrines and parenesis implies that Jesus is to be considered the object of faith as in other books of the New Testament. Though his work is commendable, he has almost belabored the point, although the detailed work he has done is helpful for an in-depth study.

The centrality of Christ as the object of faith can be seen throughout all the major sections of the doctrinal as well as the parenetic sections. After he has given emphasis on the supremacy of Christ in creation and over the angelic hosts (1:1–14), the author gives a call to his listeners to pay attention to this message. Then he offers a warning that, if this salvation is neglected, then there are dire consequences that would befall hearers (2:1–2). When he has shown that Jesus shared in our humanity, he concludes this section by the appeal: "Therefore brothers and sisters, holy partners in the heavenly calling, consider Jesus, the apostle and high priest of our confession" (3:1). After this, he enters into a long discussion of Jesus as the high priest after the order of Melchizedek; his office of everlasting priesthood, and as well as his offering of himself as the perfect sacrifice on the cross, demonstrate the supremacy and completeness of his work. Therefore, he says, "Let us approach with a true heart in full assurance of faith . . . Let us hold fast the confession of our hope" (10:22–23). A serious warning follows immediately that if one persists in sin, there is no more sacrifice for sin, and the punishment will be worse than that which Moses declared (10:26–29). The believers are exhorted to remain steadfast in their suffering as an appeal is made first to their previous exemplary behavior. They proved themselves in the past, and the writer reminds them of this to encourage them to continue in the same behavior (10:35–39). He also lists the Old-Testament saints who stood firm in their faith (11:1–40). At the end of this long narration, he concludes this

---

22. Rhee, *Faith in Hebrews*, 1.

section by presenting Jesus as the *"ton pisteo archon kai telethon"* (12:1). Attridge notes at the conclusion on his excursus on "Faith in Hebrews and Contemporary Literature," "Despite the absence of a Christological referent, Hebrews' understanding of faith is clearly developed within a Christological framework. The faith to which the addresses are here called is both made possible and exemplified by the 'perfecter of faith' (12:2), at whose exaltation hopes have begun to be realized and unseen things proved."[23] Believers are encouraged to look at his sufferings so that they are not discouraged (12:3–4). They also are encouraged to join him outside the city walls: "Let us then go to him outside the camp and bear the abuse he endured" (13:13). This shows that faith in Hebrews is linked to the life and work of Christ.

Faith in Hebrews is not only based in Christ but also it is a key component of the pilgrim's journey. Taking a warning from the wanderings of the people of God in the wilderness, the listeners of Hebrews are alerted that they should not have *apistia* (3:12, 19) lest they should also not enter into the rest that God has promised them. Faith is a necessary response to God for the work that he has done in Christ. It is manifested in trust, obedience, fidelity, and faithfulness to the promise of God. That is why Christ is shown as the supreme example of faithfulness to God. Jesus was faithful (2:1). Moses also was faithful (3:5). The other saints in the hall of faith (11:1–39) demonstrated this element of faithfulness through obedience to God's promises regardless of the price it demanded upon their lives.

Thus, faith in Hebrews also has the element of faithfulness, steadfastness, boldness, endurance, and hope in the midst of suffering. Endurance is necessary on the pilgrim journey because, as is demonstrated in the lives of those on the list of faith (11:1–40), there are difficulties on the journey. It is evident that the community has suffered (10:32–38), although not to the point of losing blood (12:4). A sense of premonition reveals that more persecution is expected, so there is an admonishment to the believers to endure in order to reach the goal of the journey (12:3). Jesus crowns this list as the one who has demonstrated ultimate steadfastness and endurance in his willingness to die shamefully on the cross (12:1–4, 13:12–16). Earlier on, it had been said that although he was a son, he learned obedience through what he suffered (5:8). The implication is that those who have accepted the role of a stranger or pilgrim also have accepted the indignities of being categorized as such. Thus, suffering is the fate of the pilgrim, and that is why endurance, perseverance, and patience are necessary for the journey.

Faith in Hebrews also has a communal component to it. We get this from the negative example of the people of God in the wilderness. A few

---

23. Attridge, *Epistle to the Hebrews*, 314.

individuals disobeyed, but the consequences befell them all. A few of them did not obey, but they all were punished by having to wander in the desert for forty years. Those who left Egypt under Moses were unable to enter the promised rest because of their disobedience. The writer also gives the invitation to approach God in the plural, suggesting that listeners might turn to God together. That is why the writer continually emphasizes the need to "encourage or exhort one another as long as it is called 'today'" (3:14), so that no one would miss entering because of the deceitfulness of sin. He also urges them not to neglect the habit of meeting together so that they "could provoke one another to love and good works" (10:24–25). He commends them for the partnership they had shown in sharing with those who had been persecuted (10:35). They identified with them to the extent that they even visited those who were in prison (10:34). Thus, in order to urge them to be steadfast in this journey he points to the models or exemplars of faith who have gone before them (11:1–39) and to the "cloud of witnesses" who are watching and encouraging them along the way (12:1–2). At the conclusion of the letter, the writer encourages them to continue this mutual love through the practice of hospitality, to remember those who are in prison and to be generous in every good work (13:1–3, 16). Thus, this journey is not undertaken in isolation. They are in exemplary company in the past, the present, and even in the future. As they look forward to the future, they are pointed to a great festive crowd of fellow believers gathered at Mount Zion (12:18–24).

Ethical Implications of the Pilgrim Motif for the Church in Africa

From the above analysis, we note that the main components of the pilgrim motif in Hebrews include: the call to follow Jesus as the pilgrim *par excellence*; the community of faith as pilgrims who rally in support of one another in the journey; and the need to embody the virtues of courage, perseverance, hospitality. and hope in the midst of the vicissitudes of life. I now examine how these is played on in the specific Kenyan situation.

The Kenyan Situation

The conditions in Kenya, and this is true for most of Africa contexts, are paradoxical: the dilapidating social, economic, and political climate has put people in a constant situation of exile, and yet it has resulted in the vibrant and enthusiastic reception to the gospel of Jesus Christ. This second factor has caused some contemporary theologians[24] to claim that Christianity in Africa has become a non-Western religion. The statement is true not only with regard to demographics but also it is the case concerning all other challenges and questions the African situation brings to Christian theology: religious pluralism, theodicy, poverty, response to diseases such as AIDS, multinational corporations, church-state relations, and refugees.

The late Professor Ali Mazrui, a Kenyan historian and political scientist, says that Africa is the most racially humiliated continent in the world.[25] This suffering comes from the time of the slave trade, through colonialism, and presently, neo-colonialism. This does not mean that Africans did not suffer from ravages of war that they inflicted upon themselves, but it is to say that the sufferings Africa has received from outsiders have done untold damage to the continent, the effects of which are still being felt. The recent wave of suffering that comes to the populations and nations of Africa is due to the economic debt that is owed to the West. Due to the structural adjustment programs, countries cannot provide basic social amenities such as water, health, education, and food security to the people.[26] These countries are so busy paying the debt to the World Bank and IMF that they cannot even meet the needs of their citizens. Those who suffer most because of this are the poor, which mainly consists of women and children. To make matters worse in Kenya, the country not only has to bear this burden of its internal problems but also it has to support the refugee populations that have emerged due to the relative stability of the country. Ever since the 1960s, the countries surrounding Kenya—Somalia, Ethiopia, Sudan, Uganda and, more recently, Rwanda, Burundi, and Congo—have suffered due to the ravages of war. Kenya has supported a huge refugee community in the northern part of the country and also in Nairobi. This is not to mention the economic burden and an acute sense of insecurity that has been put on the nation, because some people who declare themselves to be refugees come into the country illegally with firearms, and it is difficult to control them. No doubt, due to these unstable economic and social conditions, the crime rate has escalated, causing the general morale of the country to go down.

However, there is a ray of hope in this situation in that people are responding to the gospel in large numbers, and the church is more vibrant in Africa than anywhere in the world. Due to this phenomenal growth,

---

24. Bediako, *Christianity in Africa*, 3. See also Barrett, "AD 2000: 350 Million Christians in Africa," 39–54 and Walls, "Towards Understanding of Africa's Place in Christian History," 11–13.

25. Mazrui, *African Condition*, 26.

26. Acquah, "African Economic Crisis," 54. See also Olofin, "African Economic Crisis," 78–83.

David Barrett as early as 1970 asserted that Kenya had become a Christian nation.[27] Barrett gave the following statistics to demonstrate this growth: "There were 4.6 million Christians in Kenya in 1962, there are 8.0 million in mid-1972." Following this trend, he predicted that by the year 2000, "there will be 28 million Christians in Kenya, of whom perhaps 15 million will be practicing Christians."[28]

Still, many have been critical of the growth of Christianity and have assessed that the kind of gospel that seems to appeal to the African is the so-called prosperity gospel that seems to promise material wealth because people lack the basic necessities of life. Arowele notes, "Some churches and evangelistic movements in Africa have been accused (not without justification) of materialism and commercialization of the gospel, that they make evangelization an avenue for the exploitation and acquisition of wealth at the expense of poor tithe-payers."[29] This is not the only problem. There also is the problem of false teachers and cults that are proliferating in the environment. Certainly, every wind of doctrine that is passing by may be accepted, because not only are Africans notoriously religious, but also they are in danger of "sacralizing the material."[30] Bediako describes this as the tendency to call upon God in order to obtain material success. When religion is attached so much to the material, then there is the danger of using religious means for personal enrichment. Many Christians who are trying to practice an honest means of livelihood cannot make ends meet because of the poor economic conditions, and it seems that the only reasonable thing they can do is make shortcuts. They participate in cheating the system, so that they can make ends meet. For example, those in the police force receive bribes in order to survive. No simple service is done without asking for or receiving a bribe. If one decides to be honest, it takes a long time for a simple service to be done. If you do not adopt these social norms, you can suffer the consequences, so Christians are forced to live as aliens and exiles even in their own homeland. Hebrews describes their situation aptly: "Here they do not have an abiding city" (13:14). What are some ethical principles and practices that the pilgrim motif in Hebrews prescribes to those on the journey, both the Kenyan Christians and the refugees?

---

27. Barrett, *Kenya Churches Handbook*, 168.
28. Ibid., 177.
29. Arowele, "Pilgrim People of God," 450.
30. Bediako, "Africa in the New World Christian Order."

Christ is the Pilgrim Par Excellence

Hebrews focuses on Christ as the leader of the band. Brown describes him as "the pilgrim *par excellence*, the victorious pioneer (2:10), the trailblazer, the pathfinder, who leads his fellow travelers to their eternal destiny, the forerunner (2:20) who, like a courageous military scout, goes ahead to make sure that the road is safe for all who follow him."[31] He is more superior than the angels. He is a high priest after the example of Melchizedek. It is evident from Hebrews that high Christology is not just demonstrated in the intellectual meditation of Christ for the people; it is directly linked to the adverse conditions of the hearers. As Käsemann puts it:

> Mere paraenesis, as it preponderates in the close of the letter, does not suffice for this. Objective strengthening in hope is needed and is actually offered, first by showing the necessity of discipleship through the example of Christ as the *archon*, then by portraying the certainty of the goal through the vision of the heavenly high priest. Since Christ has broken through the power of death and accomplished the *athetesis,* he is a guarantor of a new covenant and announces it through his unremitting intercession for his own before God. For God's wandering people on earth, this fact contains sufficient reason for *parresia*. Now it can continue and conclude its wandering confidently and certain of its goal.[32]

Therefore, Christ's priesthood and the fact of his actual accomplishment become an encouragement to his suffering brothers and sisters who are experiencing the same suffering. That is why the writer of Hebrews continually points to his readers the example of Jesus Christ who has gone before them. Believers need the assurance that they are with one who has suffered, thus making him able to identify with them. They also know that since he has overcome death, the most formidable enemy, then nothing can conquer them.

The African worldview gives great prominence to exemplary ancestors who have gone before. Jesus as leader and the ancestor *par excellence* would fit very well into African folklore. The fact that he not only lived an exemplary life, but he also offered himself as the perfect sacrifice to cleanse sin, will give him a supreme role in a society that understands what it means to offer sacrifices to cleanse sins. Thus, Jesus will play the role of ancestor, high

---

31. Brown, "Pilgrimage in Faith," 33.
32. Käsemann, *Wandering People of God*, 239.

priest, and the perfect sacrifice for sin. All these roles have reconciling and mediating functions, necessary in a society torn by war, suffering, and strife.

The writer of Hebrews pays attention to other heroes of faith referred to as the "cloud of witness." Believers are exhorted to model these great examples of faith who have gone before us. Our passage (11:13–16) mentions Abraham, Sarah, Isaac, and Jacob. Believers also are reminded of the leaders who spoke the word of God to them, and they are encouraged to imitate their faith and way of life (13:7, 13).

The African church has many examples of people of faith who have fought the good fight and have died doing so. In this group, we have the earlier martyrs who died in Uganda in the 1860s during the days of Kabaka Mutesa. There is a shrine for the martyrs in the Kampala to remind Christians of the work of these young ones during the inception of Christianity. "They did not cling to their lives in the face of death" (Rev 12:11). In more recent times, we are reminded of Archbishop Janani Luwum of the Anglican Church of Uganda, who was killed because he dared to question the activities of the dictator Idi Amin Dada.[33] Similarly in Kenya, there is the Bishop of Eldoret, Alexander Muge, who also died in 1990 because he dared to speak against the injustices the government was committing against his people. As in the African political and social system in which leaders are highly respected, Hebrews values obedience to leaders. This highlights the need to train leaders for the church in Africa who are worthy of integrity and respect.

Community

In all of chapter 11, as well as the entire book of Hebrews, it is evident that this journey of faith is not undertaken individually. The communal element is emphasized in our passage (11:13–16) by the mention of the expression, "all died" (11:13). Recognizing this communal aspect, Koester and deSilva say, "Aware that without support people more easily give way to unbelief, the author urged listeners to exhort each other in order to maintain a high level of commitment to the faith (3:12–13)."[34] Koester also notes that in Hebrews, invitations to approach God are given in the plural (4:16; 10:22).[35] The Hebrews also are encouraged not to forsake the gathering together in order to encourage one another in these days of hardship (3:14; 6:10–12; 10:25; 13:1–2).

33. Ford, *Janani: The Making of a Martyr*.
34. Koester, *Hebrews*, 74; deSilva, *Perseverance in Gratitude*, 68–69, 78.
35. Ibid.

In the face of economic disintegration, the church in Kenya is threatened by the encroachment of individualism and a survival mentality that says, "Everyone for himself and God for us all." In Nairobi especially, insecurity has made people construct houses that are barricaded with barbed wire with signs on the gate, "ultimate security" or "*Mbwa kali.*" This is a Kiswahili word that literally means "fierce dog." It is placed at the gates of the rich residences to show that they are well guarded by dogs, and no stranger—good or ill—should show up at the door. Of course, this goes against the injunction in Hebrews that we should practice hospitality, because in doing so "some have entertained angels" unawares (13:2). The church today needs to recover this ancient practice that is rooted within the Scriptures and also within the traditions of the African peoples. As a result, this communal caring will touch refugees, those who are in prison, and others who are needy (13:3, 16). This will ultimately lead to an ethic of caring for people rather than just material pursuit. As Arowele notes:

> We have noted that according to the NT in general and Heb[sic] in particular freedom from the love of money and wealth pertains to the rule of those on the Christian pilgrimage. Accordingly, inordinate pursuit and acquisition of wealth in the churches is a negation of the true followership [sic] of the One who has nowhere to lay his head (Lk. 9.58), an obstacle to evangelization and contradiction of the heavenly inheritance. Besides the deplorable economies in Africa today call for a less materialistic attitude on the part of the churches, that attitude proper to the exile people of God.... Expensive projects and costly establishments are an oddity in a pilgrim church in poverty-stricken Africa.[36]

There is no more important goal for the church in Africa than to be free from the love of money and to be content with what we have. It is comforting to note that these instructions to care for others are followed by the encouragement that Jesus Christ will neither leave nor forsake us (13:5-6).

Courage

The focus on pilgrim existence shows that the examples of faith in Hebrews were willing to choose a marginal lifestyle for the sake of the promise of God. The author reiterated that they deliberately chose the pilgrim existence instead of going back to the comforts of a settled life in a familiar country. In the face of hardship, they are called to move with courage, perseverance,

---

36. Arowele, *Pilgrim People of God*, 450.

faith, and hope.[37] DeSilva points out that courage was one of the most important virtues in the Greco-Roman world, quoting Aristotle who spoke repeatedly of enduring hardships and terrible experiences because it was honorable to do so and dishonorable not to do so. Courage also was valued, because it set moral obligation above physical safety and comfort. This is a central theme in the book of Hebrews and certainly in chapter 11. In the face of hard times that have fallen and are sure to come, the righteous will live by faith. This reminds me of a letter I received from a friend in Kenya telling me of the Christian response to the difficult times they were facing before the national elections in 2002. She wrote:

> I am sure by now you have probably heard that Kenya faces a grim future. Well in my estimation, we are already in that grim future, but "the righteous (just) shall live by faith." For me as you know it is a case of the Lord drawing me from the miry clay. It is right now very difficult for many families, but the Lord has continued to sustain those who call upon his name. The exciting thing is that right now many are turning to the lord in repentance. Everyone right now realizes that unless we cry out to God and he aids us we are in real trouble.... My steadfast testimony is that the Lord is Lord over Kenya and that he is good even in this apparent gloom.[38]

This kind of positive attitude in the midst of hardship is what we would like to inculcate in all believers. Hebrews calls for the kind of courage that can withstand hardships. As already mentioned, in the African context, there have been those who have shown this courage even to the point of losing their lives; this can encourage Christians today not to give up hope. Those who have lost everything will be encouraged by the words that Jesus will never leave them nor forsake them (Heb 13:6). He is the same yesterday today and forever.

One of the traditional institutions that sought to inculcate courage to the African peoples was the rite of passage that included circumcision. In this ceremony, both men and women were tested in their ability to endure pain and harsh conditions. They underwent a painful operation without the aid of anesthesia, and they were expected to live in tough situations, usually outdoors, for several months. Through this ceremony, young people learned that pain and suffering were a part of human existence. They also were made aware that in order to cope with life, they needed the virtue of courage and perseverance, as well as the support of others. They also were

---

37. DeSilva, *Perseverance in Gratitude*, 430.
38. Chungi, Letter to Emily Choge, 2001.

prepared to accept the responsibilities of adulthood with courage. In the same way, Christians can show that being a disciple of Jesus Christ does not demand less. There is need to demonstrate courage amidst the vicissitudes of life. Christians facing persecutions and trials in various parts of the world would be encouraged if they knew that their perseverance is a source of encouragement to other believers all over the world.

Conclusion

The pilgrim motif ties the parenetic and expository sections of the book of Hebrews together. The writer used this method to encourage Christians experiencing hard times and to highlight certain ethical principles needed for this kind of existence. In exploring the special significance this has for the situation in the continent of Africa, especially for the Kenyan situation, it is clear that certain themes come to bear upon the conditions in Kenya. Christ is the pilgrim *par excellence*, the pioneer and finisher of the faith; thus, the believers can hope in his deliverance and a successful completion of the pilgrim journey. Refugee believers, as well as Kenyan Christians, are assured that they have the support of the community of faith, "the cloud of witnesses," who are encouraging them in this journey. They are reminded that they need to exercise faith, hope, hospitality, courage, and endurance in order to press on toward their destination. The goal of the journey is to reach that eternal city "with foundations" whose architect and maker is God.

Bibliography

Acquah, B. K. "The African Economic Crisis: A Review of the Present State of the African Economy." In *Vision for a Bright Africa: Facing the Challenges of Development*, edited by George Kinoti and Peter Kimuyu. Nairobi: African Institute for Scientific Research and Development, 1997.

Allison, Dale C., Jr. *The End of the Times Has Come: An Interpretation of the Passion and Resurrection of Jesus*. Philadelphia: Fortress, 1985.

Arowele, P. J. "The Pilgrim People of God (An African's Reflection on the Motif of Sojourn in the Epistle to the Hebrews)." *Asia Journal of Theology* 4 (1990) 438–55.

Attridge, Harold W. *The Epistle to the Hebrews: A Commentary on the Epistle to the Hebrews*. Hermeneia. Philadelphia: Fortress, 1989.

Barrett, David B. "AD 2000: 350 Million Christians in Africa." *International Review of Mission* 59 (1970) 39–54.

———, ed. *Kenya Churches Handbook: The Development of Kenyan Christianity 1498–1973*. Kisumu, Kenya: Evangelical House, 1973.

Bediako, Kwame. *Christianity in Africa: The Renewal of a Non-Western Religion.* Edinburgh: Edinburgh University Press, 1995.

———. "Africa in the New World Christian Order." Presented for the Payton Lecture Series at Fuller Theological Seminary, Pasadena, CA, October 2000.

Brown, Raymond E. "Pilgrimage in Faith: The Christian Life in Hebrews." *Southwestern Theological Journal* 28 (1985) 28–35.

deSilva, David A. *Perseverance in Gratitude: A Socio-Rhetorical Commentary on the Epistle to the Hebrews.* Grand Rapids: Eerdmans, 2000.

Ellingworth, Paul. *The Epistle to the Hebrews: A Commentary on the Greek Text.* Grand Rapids: Eerdmans, 1993.

———. "Jesus and the Universe in Hebrews." *Evangelical Quarterly* 58 (1986) 337–50.

Ford, Margaret. *Janani: The Making of a Martyr.* Lakeland 369. London: Morgan and Scott, 1978.

Houten, Christiana van. *The Alien in Israelite Law.* Journal for the Study of the Old Testament Supplements 107. Sheffield: JSOT Press, 1991.

Käsemann, Ernst. *The Wandering People of God: An Investigation of the Letter to the Hebrews.* Translated by Roy A. Harrisville.. Minneapolis.: Augsburg, 1984.

Koester, Craig R. *Hebrews: A New Translation with Introduction and Commentary.* Anchor Bible 36. New York: Doubleday, 2001.

Lane, William L. "Standing Before the Moral Claims of God: Discipleship in Hebrews." In *Patterns of Discipleship in the New Testament,* edited by Richard N. Longenecker. McMaster New Testament Studies. Grand Rapids: Eerdmans, 1996.

Mazrui, Ali A. *The African Condition: A Political Diagnosis.* London: Cambridge University Press, 1980.

Olofin, Sam. "The African Economic Crisis, the Debt Burden and Macroeconomic Mismanagement by Internal and External Managers." In *Vision for a Bright Africa: Facing the Challenges of Development,* edited by George Kinoti and Peter Kimuyu, 74–83. Nairobi: African Institute for Scientific Research and Development, 1997.

Pohl, Christine D. "Biblical Issues in Mission and Migration." *Missiology* 31 (2003) 3, 5.

Rhee, Victor (Sung-Yul). *Faith in Hebrews: Analysis within the Context of Christology, Eschatology and Ethics.* Studies in Biblical Literature 19. New York: Lang, 2001.

Kohlenberger, John R., III et al. *The Exhaustive Concordance of the Greek New Testament.* Grand Rapids: Zondervan, 1995.

Rad, Gerhard von. *The Problem of the Hexateuch and Other Essays.* Translated by E. W. Trueman Dicken. New York: McGraw-Hill, 1966.

Walls, A. F. "Africa and Christian Identity." *Mission Focus* 4 (1978) 11–13.

———. "Towards Understanding Africa's Place in Christian History." In *Religion in a Pluralistic Society: Essays Presented to Professor C. G. Baëta in Celebration of His Retirement from the Service of the University of Ghana,* edited by J. S. Pobee, 180–89. Studies on Religion in Africa 2. Leiden: Brill, 1976.

Yoder, John Howard. *For the Nations: Essays Public and Evangelical.* Grand Rapids: Eerdmans, 1997.

8

Compelling Replication
Genesis 1:26, John 3:16, and Biblical Politics in Fiji

MATT TOMLINSON

" READING THE BIBLE FROM cover to cover can seem like a daunting task. After all, the Bible is a big book that doesn't read like an ordinary book."[1] This soothing observation from the slim volume, *The 100 Most Important Bible Verses*, is followed by a further claim about the Bible's nature, that it is "a love letter from God to the world."[2]

Love letters demand to be read. But how should one read a love letter that is more than three-quarters of a million words long? The anonymous author of *The 100 Most Important Bible Verses* assures readers that they will be introduced to the text "one step at a time," given "a bite-size portion of the Bible" as if the complete work were both a journey and an appetizer, a long walk with short snack breaks.[3] The author's strategy of discursive reduction, of stripping away context to arrive at a core text that can circulate independently of its original setting, is a common one in literalist religious reading practices and modern political "message"-making.[4] In this strategy, certain texts, polished and streamlined, become widely circulated indexes of larger arguments, processes, and identities.

In this essay, I examine the circulation of such a streamlined text, the first part of Gen 1:26 ("And God said, 'Let us make man in our image, after our likeness'"),[5] as I heard it paraphrased by indigenous speakers in rural Kadavu Island, Fiji. In observing how this fragment of Gen 1:26 was used comparatively often, and in different contexts, I demonstrate that many

---

1. *100 Most Important Bible Verses*, 10.
2. Ibid.
3. Ibid., 11.
4. Crapanzano, *Serving the Word*; Silverstein, *Talking Politics*.
5. All biblical citations are from the New King James Version (NKJV).

speakers used it to highlight a gap between divine plans and human actions, both individual and collective. In short, they used it as a lament and a criticism, giving a divine warrant to discourse about decline and loss. As a criticism, it was meant to motivate attempts at transformation.

The essay is divided into three parts. First, I examine interrelated processes of entextualization, dissemination, and replication, and introduce the topic of Bible verses' circulation in markedly political contexts. Next, I discuss theoretical work in the anthropology of Christianity on gaps of various kinds and argue that gaps motivate a shift from dissemination to replication. After briefly describing the use of John 3:16 in US evangelism, I analyze the replication of Gen 1:26 in Kadavu, showing how speakers consistently turned the stilted original version into a memorable poetic paraphrase. Finally, I describe Fiji's tumultuous politics and show how Gen 1:26 confirms indigenous citizens' certainties that the past was an age of greater effectiveness than the present. The verse crystallizes their anxiety about decline and loss of the "*vanua*," a key term in Fijian politics denoting land, people, and chiefly systems, and connoting an always imperiled tradition; it also fosters hope for realignment between indigenous Fiji and God.

Making the Bible Move

In their influential discussion of "entextualization," Bauman and Briggs define it as "the process of rendering discourse extractable, of making a stretch of linguistic production into a unit—a text—that can be lifted out of its interactional setting."[6] In other words, entextualization is the process by which discourse becomes seemingly fixed in form and better able to circulate socially. It is an ongoing process, as the "same" text can be re-entextualized through paraphrase and translation to facilitate its use in different contexts. A focus on entextualization illuminates processes of circulation, revealing how particular stretches of discourse become so widely heard or read that they become common knowledge—whether that commonality is seen as weary cliché or timeless truth. For, as Silverstein and Urban observe, "it is a curious fact that peoples everywhere seem to attempt to reperform or reanimate certain key cultural texts. This alerts us to the fact that not all texts are created equal."[7]

---

6. Bauman and Briggs, "Poetics and Performance," 73. See also Bauman, *World of Others' Words*; Briggs and Bauman, "Genre"; Duranti and Goodwin, *Rethinking Context*; Kuipers, *Power in Performance*; Silverstein and Urban, *Natural Histories of Discourse*.

7. Silverstein and Urban, *Natural History of Discourse*, 12.

The Bible, as a circulating text, is one of the most successful human products of all time. Its textual history is one of ongoing flux, with sources in Hebrew, Aramaic, and Greek molded into later versions that continue to be spun off into ever newer translations. By the end of the twentieth century, full Bible translations had been produced in 371 languages,[8] and the Summer Institute of Linguistics has undertaken a project "to at least start a translation project in every [remaining] language of the world . . . by the year 2025."[9] A key factor in the Bible's mobility as a text is the ideology of its fixed meaning. Christian beliefs that the Bible is the unchanging and unchangeable word of God have motivated evangelical efforts to spread it as widely and in as many languages as possible. (Within the text, too, Jesus demands a project of circulation: e.g., Matt 28:18–20, Mark 16:15.)

Often, people speak of the Bible as if it were a single, discrete entity, but practically they approach it as an uneven terrain of verses, passages, and narratives. Seen in this way, the Bible is not a flat document but a steeply contoured topography, an ever-shifting and multidimensional map of what people consider effective, meaningful, apposite, and so forth.[10] The tension between the Bible's perceived value as a sacred unitary object—a uniform and universal font of meaning—and the different trajectories of particular passages is well illustrated in Vincent Crapanzano's writings on American fundamentalist intellectuals:

> "There are no degrees of [divine] inspiration," a professor told me, "but some passages are more significant than others. If I were left on a desert island, I would rather have John than Ecclesiastes." Others I talked to were reluctant to admit to degrees of significance, so tight was their commitment to the whole, the value of each and every word. They did not deny that they themselves favored certain passages, certain books, but they cautioned against equating what they favored with value. Indeed, there might even be a danger in preferring certain passages to others . . . Still, even those who warned against favoring particular texts, recognized the importance of certain key passages—"chair passages," they called them, from the Latin *sedes doctrinae*—which provide the most extended basis for doctrine.

8. Stine, "Bible Translations," 108.
9. Handman, "Speaking to the Soul," 166 (emphasis deleted).
10. Islamic ideologies of the Qur'an, held to be untranslatable (for ritual purposes) from the original Arabic, stand in contrast to many Christian ideologies of the Bible's translatability. But, like the Bible, the Qur'an circulates effectively through iconic verses: "One finds the same selection of verses singled out as especially powerful in Sumatra, Pakistan, or Egypt as a pan-Muslim tradition about how to use scripture"; Bowen, *Muslims through Discourse*, 96.

Among these are Genesis 1–2 on Creation, Isaiah 53 on atonement, 1 Corinthian[s] 15 on the Resurrection, and Philippians 2:1–11 on incarnation.[11]

As Crapanzano shows, a defining feature of literalist understandings of the Bible is the contention that "certain texts [are] fundamental . . . grounding meaning."[12] But people do not need to be literalists to treat certain parts of the Bible as more significant or forceful than others, as I demonstrate below.

As material tokens, Bible verses, and citations of them, are circulated and reproduced in diverse ways. They are printed on pages, spoken aloud, posted on websites, inscribed on t-shirts, stamped on license plates, and so forth. When tracking circulation, it is crucial to distinguish between "dissemination" and "replication," with dissemination defined as the spread of discourse, the physical movement that gives it access to a public, and replication defined as its uptake and reproduction in new contexts.[13]

The significance of this distinction is seen crisply in a debate published in the journal *The Biblical World* more than a century ago. Participants were asked to respond to the question, "In What Particulars Is the Bible More or Less Familiar Than Fifty Years Ago?"[14] One respondent, William Ingraham Haven of the American Bible Society, wrote confidently that "The Bible is a vastly better-known book than it was fifty years ago," supporting his contention by listing statistics (for example, "The great British and Foreign Bible Society in 1853 issued only 1,168,794 volumes of Scriptures. Its issues last year were 5,067,421").[15] For Haven, the Bible was "better-known" in his day simply because presses had been printing more copies than ever. In short, he focused on the Bible's dissemination, and implied that wide dissemination necessarily made the text more familiar.

In contrast, another participant in the debate paid close attention to the Bible's replication and came to the opposite conclusion. Half a century before the time he wrote, claimed Theophilus Sawin, "it was not an uncommon thing for a child to commit to memory hundreds and even thousands of verses. The language of the Bible thus entered into the common life and common speech of men. . . . [E]ven a conversation between two neighbors was sure to be brightened by some fitly spoken words from the sacred Book."[16] His view seems romantic, but he makes an important point

11. Crapanzano, *Serving the Word*, 62.
12. Ibid., 3.
13. See Urban, "Entextualization"; and Urban, *Metaculture*.
14. Sawin et al., "In What Particulars."
15. Ibid., 266.
16. Ibid., 260–61.

that Haven missed: circulation is not only a matter of the dissemination of objects, but also the ways that those objects are taken up and reproduced by agents in new contexts. Millions of Bibles are printed in hundreds of languages, but the texts remain inert and socially inconsequential until people begin quoting, misquoting, and citing them outside of church services and Sunday-school lessons. Seen in this light, entextualization depends just as strongly on replication as it does on dissemination. This is a counterintuitive argument, as disseminated texts seem to have a stability that is threatened every time people take up texts and reproduce them, introducing variations and inflecting them with new meanings in new contexts. But the key point is that entextualization is an ongoing process. Both clichés and timeless truths must be forged again and again in public discourse.

Tracking the differential circulation of Bible verses through their replication across contexts is an effective way to discover links between Christianity's universalist trajectories and its local appropriations.[17] In Fiji, the Methodist missionary translators who first arrived in 1835 did not march straight through the Bible but proceeded in a particular order, beginning with the gospels (Matthew, Mark, Luke, John), Acts, and Genesis. More than a century later, Alan Tippett reported that, "The whole field of Biblical parable and allegory has been taken over and is in use daily, especially from the Old Testament book of Proverbs and the sayings of Jesus. However the particular sayings used most frequently by Fijians are not those most frequently used by Westerners."[18] He noted the popularity in Fiji of the second half of Eccl 10:8, ". . . whoso breaketh an hedge, a serpent will bite him," but did not offer an explanation for its wide circulation; I suspect that Fijian interest in curses and spiritual punishment played a large part. More recently, Hirokazu Miyazaki has written that during his fieldwork, the people of Suvavou often recited Ps 127:1, "Except the LORD build the house, they labour in vain that build it."[19] At the time, they were trying to construct an office building ("building a house" of sorts), but for them the verse's relevance extended to a "discourse on the importance of prayer in all aspects of Fijian social life."[20] In other words, this verse was taken to mean that human achievement depends ultimately on communication with God. The verse also was used in a newspaper advertisement placed by the Assembly of Christian Churches in Fiji during the 2006 elections, with the

17. See, e.g., Kaplan, "Christianity, People of the Land," 138; Robbins, "God Is Nothing but Talk"; Robbins, *Becoming Sinners*; Schieffelin, "Found in Translating"; Tomlinson and Makihara, "New Paths."
18. Tippett, "Fijian Proverbs," 90.
19. Miyazaki, *Method of Hope*, 111.
20. Ibid., 119.

ACCF using the verse to reinforce its point that "nation building without God is a rewardless labour."[21]

The example of Ps 127:1 highlights the importance of political contexts in shaping verses' comparative significance and potential for circulation. The villagers of Suvavou have long attempted to gain compensation from the government for the alienation of their lands, and the ACCF, like many Christian organizations in Fiji, has been deeply enmeshed in national politics; according to Newland, their newspaper ad was meant to generate support for the ruling SDL party.[22] In a similar vein, Sitiveni Rabuka, the army colonel who carried out two coups in 1987 and then led the nation as prime minister for much of the 1990s, "loved to preach sermons on a text from the Old Testament exilic book of Lamentations (5.2): 'Our inheritance has been turned over to strangers, our homes to aliens.'"[23] The terms "strangers" and "aliens" pointed to Fiji's Indian citizens, descendants of colonial-era plantation laborers who have long served as scapegoats for indigenous Fijians' anxieties about social change. Another prominent verse has been Rom 13:1–2 ("Let every soul be subject unto the higher powers. For there is no power but of God: the powers that be are ordained of God . . ."), which has been used to support the authority of traditional chiefs and the government.[24]

Compelling Replication

In many Christian denominations, the Bible is said to play a crucial mediating role between divinity and humanity: through the Bible, God speaks to humans and reveals the divine plan.[25] Some Christians actively speak

21. Newland, "Role of the Assembly," 300.
22. Ibid., 301.
23. Heinz, "Sabbath in Fiji," 433.
24. See, e.g., ibid., 420; Tuwere, *Vanua*, 101–2.
25. Engelke (*Problem of Presence*) argues that a core paradox of Christianity is its "problem of presence," the ways God is always both present and absent, proximate and distant. Some subjects emphasize empathy; others emphasize incommensurability. At one end of the spectrum is the American evangelist Jonathan Edwards' famous sermon "Sinners in the Hands of an Angry God," preached in 1741, which depicts the relationship as one of alienation tinged with hatred on God's part: "natural Men are held in the Hand of God over the Pit of Hell . . ." he declared, "and God is dreadfully provoked, his Anger is as great toward them as to those that are actually suffering the Executions of the Fierceness of his Wrath in Hell" (Edwards, "Sinners," 13). In Edwards' depiction, humanity is held in God's hand only as a distancing movement of threat and rejection. At the other end of the spectrum are present-day US evangelicals who increasingly seek "remarkably intimate relationships with God," characterizing and treating the

themselves into the Bible, as it were, modelling their actions and identities on biblical characters in order to close the gaps between human stories and characters and divine ones, replicating biblical history as prefigured "types" in always-unfolding narratives.[26] For example, a friend of mine in Kadavu explicitly compared his life to that of St. Paul, as both men had radically changed the courses of their lives to become Christian representatives speaking with divine authority.[27] In Fiji, political leaders are sometimes characterized as biblical types, a point to which I return below.

For the anthropology of Christianity, Susan Harding has offered an influential argument on the ways that narrative gaps compel responses. Jerry Falwell, the late US evangelist, was a narrative cannibal. He gobbled up characters from the Bible, ingesting them figuratively so that he "became" heroes such as Jesus, Jacob, David, and Joshua. As Simon Coleman has observed in a different context, Christians who look for the replication of biblical types in the present believe "that by acting 'as' Jesus, or Moses, or Abraham we can achieve the same results as they, given the constancy of divine power and truth over time."[28] So, for example, in attempting to raise funds to buy lands for his college, Falwell circled the property like Joshua around the walls of Jericho to make the walls of "unsecured indebtedness" fall down.[29] In portraying himself as biblical characters, whether by pointing out parallels in different stories or trying to draw them through his actions, Falwell intended to compel a response from his followers—often, to give him money. While he was quite successful at this, Harding shows that Falwell created another kind of compulsion in his audience as well. She argues, counterintuitively, that Falwell gained his authority not by fitting biblical characters neatly but by fitting them awkwardly. He was a scandalous figure in the late twentieth-century United States, polarizing the public with his aggressive conservatism and highly successful fundraising; locally, he made followers uneasy by attempting to force tithing upon his employees and suggesting his own sexual impropriety.[30] In Harding's view, Falwell was successful with his followers because of the gaps he created between biblical models and his own troubling personality and actions. His supporters worked hard

---

deity as "a buddy, a confidante, the ideal boyfriend"—even "falling in love with Jesus" (Luhrmann, "Metakinesis," 519, 523). One of Luhrmann's subjects "compared her relationship with God 'to a relationship with the man of my dreams'" (ibid., 524), a distinct image from Edwards', in which God is the man of your nightmares.

26. Harding, *Book of Jerry Falwell*.
27. Tomlinson, *In God's Image*, chapter 7.
28. Coleman, *Globalisation of Charismatic Christianity*, 126.
29. Harding, *Book of Jerry Falwell*, 106–8.
30. Ibid., 98–104.

to "harmonize" the dissonant tones, to align characters and actions more closely. In creating this narrative compulsion among his audience, Harding writes, Falwell was able to "bind his people to him by enlisting them in the making of his reputation."[31]

Extending Harding's analysis, I use the term "compulsion" to indicate the ways that actors are motivated to both (1) act authoritatively and (2) displace their agency, at the same time, in projects of replication. This is an inherent paradox in Christian discourse where speakers assert their authority, effectiveness, and responsibility while also claiming that God is omnipotent and interested in human affairs.[32] I am also drawing on Hirokazu Miyazaki's anthropological model of faith and hope, developed in part from his fieldwork in Fiji and inspired by the writings of the philosopher Ernst Bloch.[33] Based on his analysis of Fijian ritual, Miyazaki describes faith as the "capacity to place one's agency in abeyance."[34] In his later writing, he expresses dissatisfaction with the temporal orientation of his previous work, and focuses on hope as "prospective momentum" and "a method of radical temporal reorientation of knowledge," especially self-knowledge.[35] Again examining Fijian ritual, he argues that actors take a forward-looking view whereas analysts take a retrospective one; there is necessarily a "temporal incongruity" between "knowledge and its object."[36] According to Miyazaki, these opposed perspectives cannot be reconciled through misguided attempts at synchronicity; rather, scholars must be motivated by this gap—this difference in temporal perspectives—and reproduce it as a new kind of momentum: "hope as a method does not rest on an impulse to pursue

31. Ibid., 100.

32. Keane, *Christian Moderns*, 208–9 n. 6; Miyazaki, *Method of Hope*, 120.

33. Miyazaki, "Faith and Its Fulfillment"; Miyazaki, *Method of Hope*; and Miyazaki, "From Sugar Cane to 'Swords.'"

34. In formulating this definition of faith, Miyazaki observes that it is different from Kierkegaard's notion of a leap ("Faith and Its Fulfillment," 32). I note, however, that both models depend on the creation of compelling gaps in which agency is both asserted and denied. In the famous opening passage to *Fear and Trembling*, Kierkegaard repeatedly tries to tell the story from Gen 22 of Abraham's sacrifice of his son, Isaac, under God's orders (see also his *Concluding Unscientific Postscript*). He does so in order to show the patriarch's "double-movement": one movement is that of resignation, in which Abraham gives Isaac utterly to God; the other is the movement of faith, in which Abraham knows that he will get Isaac back. The movements constitute a paradoxical assertion and denial or displacement of agency in the same act. In trying to tell the story so that it makes sense, the philosopher fails—and that is part of his point. The story cannot be intellectually convincing, as God's command is horrifying and Abraham's "faithful" acquiescence either loathsome or inexplicable.

35. Miyazaki, *Method of Hope*, 4, 5, 26.

36. Ibid., 23–4.

analytical synchronicity but on an effort to *inherit* and *replicate* that impulse as a spark of hope on another terrain."[37]

The perceived need to cross a gap sparks American evangelical efforts, where preachers target non-believers and urge them to repent and avoid hellfire—to come over to the side of faith, belief, and holiness to ensure their future blessings in heaven. A key text, for many of these evangelists, is John 3:16: "For God so loved the world, that he gave his only begotten Son, that whosoever believeth in him should not perish, but have everlasting life." The verse is described by *The 100 Most Important Bible Verses* as "'the Little Gospel'... it condenses the message Jesus came to share into a single clear-cut sentence."[38] It presents both promise and threat, gesturing expectantly toward heaven while glancing anxiously down at hell in the cautionary three-word phrase "should not perish." The gap it creates, in many evangelicals' understanding, is salvation: one should read this verse in order to gain eternal life. Because of its utility as the Little Gospel, the verse is widely disseminated in evangelical publications and broadcasts, often brought into conjunction with other verses that resonate with it. (The practice of using some verses to prove others is a common evangelical strategy.)[39] In the 1970s and 1980s, it was beamed across millions of American television screens owing to the antics of Rollen Stewart, a schemer who became famous for wearing a rainbow-colored wig and holding up a sign saying "John 3:16" at public venues, especially sporting events.[40]

I did not hear John 3:16 referred to frequently during my fieldwork in Kadavu, however. One reason is that the verse does not serve evangelical purposes in indigenous Fiji the way it does in the United States. Ninety-nine percent of indigenous Fijians are Christians, so in places like Kadavu that have mostly indigenous citizenry, efforts at conversion are largely interdenominational contests. Disputes focus on topics such as infant baptism, or the link between the beverage kava (*yaqona*), and worship of ancestral spirits—not Jesus's role in ensuring salvation, which few would question. The gap between "believers" and "nonbelievers" (in the colloquial sense) hardly exists.[41]

---

37. Ibid., 30 (emphases in original).
38. *100 Most Important Bible Verses*, 106.
39. Crapanzano, *Serving the Word*.
40. Green, "Rainbow Man."
41. It is likely that John 3:16 is used by indigenous Fijians trying to convert citizens who are not Christians, but I do not have any field data on this subject. In this regard, Keane has shown in several publications how missionary encounters create compelling gaps of particular kinds. In the case he examines, Dutch Calvinist missionaries introduced villagers in Sumba, eastern Indonesia, to a new semiotic ideology configuring

Indeed, in my research, I have encountered John 3:16 most memorably in the archive, not in the field. The verse was a favorite of the pioneering Methodist missionary William Cross.[42] On August 16, 1857, another missionary, James Royce, described how he brandished John 3:16 as a weapon in an encounter with a hostile man at a village on Vitilevu, Fiji's largest island:

> . . . [I] met with an impudent fellow, who upon being hailed stated that he was lotu pope [i.e., Roman Catholic], and raising his club said in an air of triumph, this is my book, i[.]e[.] New Test[ament], and taking mine from under my arm I held it up, saying, and this is mine, from which I will read you a verse and then you shall read me one from yours. I turned to John 3.16 and then requested him to give me a portion from his book; the fellow seemed heartily ashamed and soon skulked away.[43]

It is impossible to tell whether the man was really a Catholic, or whether he said this because he knew it would provoke Royce, who, like many Methodist missionaries, distrusted and resented the competition. My point in quoting Royce's description of this event is simply to show how he turned to John 3:16 as the single most useful verse with which to confront an enemy.[44]

"signs and the world they signified" as clearly distinct. This has lessened the risk of failed performance by recasting traditionally effective texts as simple descriptions of an objectified culture, even as it has opened up new gaps between subjects' supposed inner states and their external expressions marked by the index of "sincerity" (see especially the several works of Keane listed in the bibliography). More broadly, Keane ("Spoken House," 106) has observed the ways in which the semiotics of ritual generally create and overcome gaps of various kinds: for example, social ones (such as rules of kin distance for marriageability), political ones (such as divisions between disputants), and ontological ones (such as the living communicating with the dead). He has noted that the reflexivity and formality of ritual speech help constitute attempts to close such gaps, but that other characteristics of such speech—namely, its "[a]mbiguity, allusiveness, and opacity" (ibid., 111)—create gaps of their own, generating a sense of risk in performance and highlighting the possibility of failure.

42. Thornley, *Shaking of the Land*, 434.

43. Royce, "Diary," 135.

44. Engelke (*Problem of Presence*, 47) provides a memorable example of John 3:16 gaining a magical aura in its materiality. The general secretary of Zimbabwe's Bible society, Gaylord Kambarami, tells a story about giving a Bible to a recalcitrant man who insists that he will only take it if Kambarami lets him smoke it, page by page. Kambarami agrees as long as the man is willing to read the pages before he puffs on them. Two years later, he encounters the man again at a tent revival, where the smoker testifies publicly, "So I smoked my way through Matthew. And I smoked the whole of Mark too. Then I smoked Luke. I started smoking John, but when I came to John 3:16 . . . a light shone in my face. And now I am a churchgoing person." See also Young, *Pearls from the Pacific*, 40, 150.

During my research in Kadavu in the 1990s and 2000s, the verse I did encounter notably often was the first part of Gen 1:26 ("And God said, 'Let us make man in our image, after our likeness'"). I heard this verse more often than any other biblical text. An examination of its global journeys would ideally begin with a description of Hebraic myths of creation, continuing onto the entextualization of Gen 1:26 in Scripture by a priestly author from Judah known to literary scholars as "P,"[45] and then onto the translation from Hebrew into the Greek of the Septuagint. I prefer, however, to move directly to the verse's specifically Fijian history, acknowledging but suspending questions posed by theologians about what it means to speak of a pronominally plural God's "image and likeness." As Robert Davidson observes, "Each age has tended to read into the phrase its own highest ideals about man [sic]," whether those ideals concern immortality, rationality, or physical form.[46]

The first translation of Gen 1:26 into a Fijian dialect, by William Cross in 1841, was "*Sa vosa na Kalou, Me datou cakava na tamata me vakai ke datou . . .*"[47] Cross based his translation on the King James Version phrasing because he did not know Hebrew, Greek, or Latin. Unfortunately, he was not expert in Fijian either, as shown by errors such as using "*vosa*" as the verb of speaking rather than "*kaya*" or "*tukuna*," equivalent to saying, "God spoke" rather than "God said." Thirteen years later, the more linguistically adept missionary David Hazlewood changed Cross's version, and in 1864 Hazlewood's version was published in the British and Foreign Bible Society's complete Fijian Bible. Hazlewood rendered Gen 1:26 as "*A sa kaya na Kalou, Me datou cakava na tamata mei tovo vata kei kedatou, ia me ucui kedatou . . .*" (emphasis in original), using a more appropriate verb for speaking and elaborating Cross's vague "*me vakai ke datou*" (to be like us) into a longer phrase meaning "to be like us and to resemble us." A key term that Hazlewood introduced is "*itovo*," meaning "a custom, manner, habit, disposition, quality, character,"[48] which he used for the King James Version of "image." The current standard version of the Fijian Bible, based on Frederick Langham's revised translation of 1902, gives Gen 1:26 as "*A sa kaya na Kalou, Me datou bulia na tamata mei tovo vata kei kedatou, ka me ucui kedatou . . .*" This version substitutes "*bulia*" for Hazlewood's "*cakava*," which can be glossed as replacing "do" with "make," and also changes Hazlewood's choice for "and"—"*ia*"—to the more appropriate "*ka*." These multiple revisions improved the translation. But it is still not fully idiomatic.

45. Friedman, *Who Wrote the Bible?*
46. Davidson, *Genesis 1–11*, 25.
47. Thornley, *Shaking of the Land*, 454.
48. Capell, *New Fijian Dictionary*, 239.

For example, as the linguist Paul Geraghty has noted, "a tediously large proportion of verb phrases in the Bible begin with *a sa*, which is in fact a rarely used pluperfect,"[49] and Gen 1:26 is an example of such phrasing.

Present-day speakers almost never quote the verse verbatim, but instead paraphrase it. In doing so, they make it rhythmic, rhyming, and memorable. In short, they turn it into an eminently mobile text by making it poetic. Changes in the paraphrased version center on the core phrase, "*Me datou bulia na tamata*," "Let us make man." (*Tamata* is gender neutral, so this can be phrased more accurately as "Let us make humanity.") Speakers consistently turn this into "*Tou ia tou bulia na tamata*," a trimeter with stress on the "i" in *ia*, the "li" in *bulia*, and the "ma" in *tamata*. They drop the first "*me*" (let) and insert "*ia*," meaning "to do, to perform, to carry out,"[50] which eliminates "let's" sense of contingency, emphasizes God's power, and rhymes with *bulia*. With "let" dropped, the subjective pronoun is shortened to *tou*,[51] and it is used twice in a rhythmic, internally rhyming construction. This condensed Fijian paraphrase can be translated back into English as "We are making humanity." God is no longer deciding, but doing, and doing so in a stylistically appealing and memorable way.[52]

In using this standard paraphrase, speakers move from dissemination to replication, from published text to uptake and reproduction. This shift to replication is not simply a move from a literate form to an oral one: When reading the preaching notes of Kadavu's superintendent Methodist minister in 2003, I noticed that he used the orally paraphrased version in his written script for May 24, 1998.[53]

Not surprisingly, some of the contexts in which I encountered Gen 1:26 were formal religious performances, specifically speech events during Methodist services. One man used the verse during a prayer, for example. One preacher, Ratu Josaia Veibataki, called attention to the verse in his Christmas sermon at Tavuki's Methodist church in 1998:

---

49. Geraghty, "Language Reform," 387.
50. Capell, *New Fijian Dictionary*, 73.
51. See Dixon, *Grammar of Boumaa Fijian*, 55.
52. For God's verb of speaking in these paraphrased versions, I have recorded speakers using either *kaya* or *tukuna*, both of which mean "say."
53. See Tomlinson, *In God's Image*, 89, 93.

"Sa dana Na Kalou ni sa vicalaji na nodrutu vosa ni vibuli. Ka drutu ma tukuna ke, 'Tou ia tou bulia na tamata me itovo ka ucui kedatou.' Sa nakinaki ke Na Kalou me na dua na gauna me na lokuca me na solia mai ke na luvena e dua bau ga me na mai bula ka vakamurimuria na viere i vinakata Na Kalou me da vadadamuria. . . . Da mai vananuma jiko ina siga nidavu na siga ka sucu mai ke na noda Turaga me mai voli iko vata kei au, ina siga nidavu. Kena ibalebale: na nona sucu mai na Turaga i mini je ere ni vacalaka. I mini vacalakataki na nona lai sucu na Turaga i vale ni manumanu. I mini vacalakataki nona sucu mai na Turaga i vuravura ka baleta ni sa dana Na Kalou sa vicalaji na inaki ni noda bula na tamata. Sa da mini ucuya, sa da mini tovo vata kei kia."	God sees that his word of creation is not being realized. He[*] declared, "We are making humanity in our image and likeness." God intended there to be an appointed time for his only son to be given to live here and make [us] follow the things God wants us to follow . . . Today we are commemorating the day that our Lord was born to buy you and me [i.e., with his sacrifice], today. Its meaning is: the Lord's birth wasn't a mistake. It wasn't a mistake that the Lord went to be born in a stable. It wasn't a mistake that the Lord was born here in this world because God saw the purpose of our human lives was not being realized. We are not in the image, we are not after the likeness of him.

[*] Veibataki used "they" (paucal), not "he," mirroring the paucal tou (We) in God's speech and emphasizing the Christian God's triune nature as Father, Son, and Holy Spirit. Because it sounds awkward to refer to the Christian God as "they" in English, however, I have used "he" instead. This example, and the Fijian-language examples that follow, are discussed separately and for distinct purposes in Tomlinson, *In God's Image*.

Veibataki, a lay preacher, argued explicitly that people were failing to live up to the standard of Gen 1:26. He based his criticism on the original Christmas story: two thousand years ago, God sent his son Jesus to save humanity, but humanity still needs saving. Similarly, the catechist Tomasi Laveasiga delivered a sermon in Tavuki on February 7, 1999, in which he quoted the paraphrased version of Gen 1:26, declaring, "[God] said, 'We are making humanity in our image and after our likeness'" ("*Tukuna jiko, 'Tou ia tou bulia na tamata me itovo vata kei kedatou ka me ucui kedatou'*"), and then added, "We were not made to resemble anything else" ("*Mini da buli me da ucuya e dua tani tale na ere*"), implying that people are now falling short of the divine plan.

Speakers also replicated the verse outside of church. In casual conversation with me, one friend used it to criticize people who often got drunk. Another told me that reading the verse had been a pivotal moment in his life, changing him from a gang member into (he hoped) a future Methodist minister. Similarly, another friend, who narrated his life story to me, alluded to Gen 1:26 as he explained that the path he had been following as a young man—a path of crime, drunkenness, and drug use—was evidently the wrong one.[54] For these men, as for Veibataki and Laveasiga, Gen 1:26 was a model of perfection whose significance was highlighted by the gap between the divine plan and humanity's present situation.

Perhaps the most striking example of the verse's use outside of church was a civil servant's speech at a government-organized workshop in Yawe district, Kadavu, in June 1999. He stated:

"Sa da raica talega mai ni sa vaka vivisau mai na gauna, vivisau mai na bula, o, vivisau talega mai na noda dinata jiko na ijikojiko vakaturaga . . . Na matanitu i taukei se vabauta saka jiko na gauna ra ciqoma kina o ira noda turaga bale na lotu ni sa tadu mai na noda vanua, era ciqoma vata vakakina ni sa dua na jiki ni noda bula vakaitaukei nikua na lotu, ka da vakabauta talega na ivosa ni vibuli ina Nona itekivu kina me buli kina na vuravura. Ni sa kece na vibuli e dua na ka qai eratou kaya na lewe tolu vakalou: 'Tou ia tou bulia na tamata me ucui kedatou, me itovo vata kei kedatou.'"	We also see that the times are changing, life is changing, oh, the ways people look up and recognize chiefs' status have changed . . . The landowners' government believes the time our honorable chiefs accepted Christianity which had arrived in our land, they thus accepted that Christianity is a part of indigenous Fijian life today, and we also believe the word of creation in his beginning to create the world. When the creation was finished, the Holy Trinity said something: "We are making humanity in our image, after our likeness."

The speaker, who was not from Kadavu, was a representative of Fijian Affairs, a division of government overseeing indigenous matters. Although it is not immediately evident, he used the verse in the same critical way as the speakers quoted above. The workshop was a government initiative to foster awareness of "traditional" roles and responsibilities. The premise of the workshop was that tradition was being forgotten and that villagers did not know how to act properly anymore—a premise with which most villagers would agree heartily. Like the speakers mentioned above, the government official was using Gen 1:26 to highlight the past's perfection so that the present's degradation stood out from it.

The meaning of Gen 1:26 is not automatic or stable within Fiji, however. A theologian and former president of the Fijian Methodist Church, Ilaitia Tuwere, gives it a distinct interpretation in which he emphasizes God's humility, arguing that the verse reveals how "God contracts himself. In this contraction, he allows himself to be humiliated. He humiliates himself by cutting himself down to size as it were to be with his earthly creature, the

---

54. See Tomlinson, *In God's Image*, 192–95.

human being, in the process of his coming into being."[55] Tuwere's image of God "cutting himself down to size" inverts the common indigenous Fijian image of a past in which the ancestors were up to God's size, or at least closer to godliness than people at present. Another distinct interpretation is revealed in a recent sociopolitical survey, in which respondents use Gen 1:26 to argue for universal human rights generally and women's rights specifically—neither position being a popular one among conservative Methodists.[56]

Biblical Politics

In the examples described above, speakers in Kadavu used a paraphrased form of Gen 1:26 to highlight their perceptions of a gap between past and present. In the remote past, people lived godly lives, and Jehovah gave the land of Fiji to its indigenous settlers. In the present, by contrast, people are divided and often fail to act as good Christians, and both land and tradition might soon be lost. In the remote past, the ancestors lived lives that resembled those of the ancient Israelites, but in the recent past, non-Christian ancestors resisted European missionaries, and their punitive spirits still curse living villagers. For these reasons, indigenous Fijians declare that the past was a time of "darkness" until Christianity came, but they also express beliefs that their ancestors' conversion to Christianity "did not violate indigenous cultural practice but revealed the inherent Christianity of the Fijian people."[57] Becoming more like God's image and likeness, then, means recapturing the strength, social unity, and moral propriety of an imagined past seen through the lens of the Old Testament.

Fijian politics derives a great deal of nervous energy from the gap between past perfection and present degradation. Within this gap, the central term and concept is *"vanua,"* which, as noted above, denotes both land and people. *Vanua* can be applied generally to landscape, to "people of the land" (i.e., commoners), or specifically to chiefdoms. It strongly connotes "traditional" ways, which include Methodism to a large degree but also include dangerous non-Christian spirits, both ancestral and fantastical. The term carries profound emotional force, as the *vanua* in its broadest sense—land, tradition, chiefly systems—is considered by many indigenous Fijians to be in great peril, in imminent danger of being stolen, lost, or abandoned.

55. Tuwere, *Vanua*, 122.
56. Casimira, *Who Do You Say I Am?*, 134, 141.
57. Toren, "Making the Present," 697; see also Kaplan, *Neither Cargo Nor Cult*; Thomas, *In Oceania*; Toren, *Mind, Materiality, and History*; and Toren, "Becoming a Christian in Fiji."

As both land and people, *vanua* is the most resonant symbol to indigenous Fijians of God's favor and the precariousness of the present age. The islands are considered to be a divine gift to indigenous Fijians. As Robert Norton summarizes a common view, "God made Fiji for the Fijians, just as He had allocated other lands to other 'races.'"[58] Because land is considered a divine inheritance, threats—real or imagined—about the potential loss of land compel political actions. Coups in 1987 and 2000 gained widespread support from indigenous citizens because they were publicly justified with reference to Indian citizens' supposed desires to take over indigenous Fijian lands; recall Rabuka's favorite Bible verse, "Our inheritance has been turned over to strangers, our homes to aliens" (Lam 5:2). Nationally, land is legally secure for indigenous Fijians, as kin groups own the vast majority of it inalienably. Thus, indigenous Fijians are under no actual threat of losing their lands, but the conviction that others might yet take it persistently troubles many of them.[59]

In short, for many indigenous Fijians, visions of divine pasts and sacred, God-given lands do not inspire confidence in the present; quite the opposite, as anxiety about decline and loss buzzes in a profusion of signs that swarm through public discourse. Living people's bodies are imagined to be smaller than ancestors' bodies. Kava is said to be drunk too often by too many people nowadays, in contrast to the chiefly practices of the past. Chiefs are thought to have lost the ability to act effectively. Kinship ties and political titles are said to be forgotten or exercised improperly. These claims gain their aura of incontestable truthfulness by their resonance with each other, somewhat similar to the way that Bible verses are brought into conjunction by evangelicals to prove or support each other. In this regard, the contention that Gen 1:26 supports in Kadavuan discourse—that society is

---

58. Norton, "Reconciling Ethnicity and Nation," 100.

59. In attempting to hold onto the *vanua*, indigenous Fijians perform various rituals that mark sacredness both temporally and spatially. For example, in the late 1980s, indigenous nationalists agitated to make Sunday a legally enforced national day of rest, banning commerce and sports. They were initially successful, although the "Sunday ban" was repealed in 1996 (Srebrnik, "Ethnicity, Religion," 194). "The Sabbath marked Fiji's special election by God, provided for a sanctified Fijian response to God, and kept the people from dangerous assimilations to alien cultures and, perhaps, to modernization" (Heinz, "Sabbath in Fiji," 428; see also Arno, *World of Talk*, 129; Halapua, *Tradition, Lotu and Militarism*, 76–9; Rutz and Balkan, "Never on Sunday"). For a historical analysis of changing Indo-Fijian representations of their position in sacred time focusing on use of the Tulsi Das Ramayan, see Kelly, "From Holi to Diwali." For descriptions and analyses of the sacralization of land in Fiji, see Kaplan, *Neither Cargo Nor Cult*, "Promised Lands," "*Hau* of Other Peoples' Gifts," and "Fijian Water"; Ravuvu, *Vaka i Taukei*; Ryle, "'My God, My Land,'" and Ryle, "Roots of Land and Church"; Tomlinson, *In God's Image*; and Willliksen-Bakker, "Vanua."

suffering decline and loss—sounds obvious and is highly generalized and especially hard to refute. As a result, when I heard speakers refer to Gen 1:26, text and context always seemed to fit together well, and I never heard anyone dispute anyone else's use of the verse.[60]

At times of political turmoil, indigenous Fijian leaders are portrayed as biblical types to show that God's plan is being carried out on behalf of indigenous citizens—that the gap between divine past and disordered present is being closed, that the *vanua* is now being rescued. Rabuka, the leader of Fiji's first two coups in 1987, saw himself as both Stephen the martyr (his namesake) and Jeremiah the prophet,[61] and one evangelical leader compared Rabuka to Moses because he "staged the 1987 military coup[s] to 'liberate' the Fijians (biblical Israelites) from their 'oppressors.'"[62] Once he became prime minister and actually started to govern, however, Rabuka lost support. When he prepared to repeal a "Sunday ban" on commerce in the mid-1990s, angry sabbatarians took to the streets, and "The banners of street marchers . . . proclaimed: 'Rabuka—Judas Escariot!'"[63] In May 2000, Fiji experienced its third coup when the civilian George Speight led a takeover in which members of parliament were held hostage for eight weeks. Unlike Rabuka, Speight did not often describe his actions in terms of divine destiny, but the same speaker who had equated Rabuka with Moses nonetheless announced that Speight was "the Fijian biblical Joshua."[64] Fiji's most recent coup came in December 2006 when military commander Voreqe Bainimarama deposed a government which he denounced as corrupt. If Speight was not as interested in being a biblical type as Rabuka, Bainimarama seemed even less so, and he actively confronted the politically dominant Methodist Church. Yet a chief from the island of Taveuni found a way to tie Bainimarama into the divine plan, declaring that the coup of 2006 had done what God had told the prophet Jeremiah to do: "go out and uproot, destroy, tear apart, and remove."[65]

Biblical figures represent perfect models from the past. By comparing present-day political actors to them, ethno-nationalists suggest that divinely ordained actions can be replicated in the present. In making these comparisons, speakers attempt to overcome the gap between past and present,

60. Cf. Briggs, *Competence in Performance*.
61. Dean and Ritova, *Rabuka*, 162.
62. Ratuva, "God's Will in Paradise," 21.
63. Norton, "Reconciling Ethnicity and Nation," 100.
64. Ratuva, "God's Will in Paradise," 21
65. "2006 Coup Justified."

turning biblical history into Fijian history.⁶⁶ These characterizations of political leaders as biblical figures make sense against the ideological background of compelling gaps between past and present, actual and potential, divinity and humanity: the compelling gaps in which Gen 1:26 gains its effective significance as a micronarrative of loss. Genesis 1:26 emphasizes these gaps, offering a condensed model of radical discontinuity, a vision of time founded on rupture: not the rupture of conversion or eschatalogy, but on a similar principle of consequential difference between past and present.⁶⁷

As shown above, speakers replicate Gen 1:26 across contexts and with different tenors of performance—in conversations, sermons, and speeches, confiding, haranguing, and exhorting. In doing so, they signify discontinuity and motivate attempts at transformation. Recall the speakers who mentioned the verse when explaining how they had altered their lives' trajectories, leaving behind violence and crime. For them, Gen 1:26 called attention to their own behavior and pushed them to begin acting differently. Similarly, the preachers who referred to Gen 1:26 from the pulpit and the government representative speaking at the workshop were not asking their audiences simply to assent to their claims, but to move themselves to act more responsibly, by which they meant more in accord with self-consciously reified tradition, in the manner of the *vanua*.

In this way, the paraphrased version of Gen 1:26 shows a double movement of replication. The verse has long been disseminated throughout Fiji, printed in hundreds of thousands of Bibles. Speakers take up this verse and replicate it in a compact and poetic form, highlighting gaps between what is and what should be. This use of the poetic form of Gen 1:26 is then meant to compel people to bring their actions into line with God's plans. In other words, the first replication comes when the biblical verse is paraphrased, with the second replication intimated in its utterance. By speaking the verse, people are engaged in motivational projects that draw on the perfect past in order to reshape the future: to become, either as oneself or as part of the *vanua*, more like God's image and likeness—morally proper, powerful, indeed dominant, and united in a holy land. These projects are occasionally

---

66. And vice versa; see especially Kaplan, *Neither Cargo nor Cult*.

67. See Robbins, "Continuity Thinking." Michael W. Scott has queried Robbins' claims for Christianity's disruptive cultural force, arguing that Arosi (Solomon Islands) perceive an essential continuity between pre-Christian and Christian practices: in a sense, they were always Christian. However, as Scott acknowledges, "Christian interpretations of Genesis agree that, in the beginning there was an original communion between God and humanity that has been broken by sin. Likewise, because of sin, the original unity and mutual understanding among human beings has been lost, and all human relationships are prone to fragmentation" (*Severed Snake*, 318).

characterized as successful, as when individuals proclaim that they have transformed their lives in godly ways. Often, however, the intimated second replication is not considered successful, and members of the *vanua* monitor decline and loss in a world drawing further away from the divine model.

Conclusion

"No verse in the Bible can stand alone," writes the author of *The 100 Most Important Bible Verses*, even as the book's format undercuts its own claim.[68] In practice, some passages do get treated as if they are singular, timeless truths and become widely circulated texts encountered in multiple contexts. During fieldwork in Kadavu, I repeatedly encountered a paraphrase of the first part of Gen 1:26. It was a poetic oral text, used both within and outside of markedly religious contexts. Speakers used it to highlight a gap between past and present, implying that the future will be strong again if people close the gap to become realigned with the divine plan. Such an interpretation is not universal, but in Kadavu it had the ring of an obvious truth—who could doubt that the world is getting worse?—and one that resonated with other signs of decline to motivate transformative actions from changing the course of one's life to cheering the overthrow of governments. John 3:16, a verse encountered frequently in US evangelical contexts, did not circulate with similar success in Kadavu. One reason is that the gap that makes it compelling to many Americans—the gap between believers and non-believers—does not exist in a place where almost everyone is a Christian, and disputes focus on details of ritual practice.

Genesis 1:26 marks a compelling gap for Methodists in Kadavu. It spurs a movement in which the disseminated text is taken up and replicated in a poetically paraphrased form which has become a new standard. This paraphrased version is meant in turn to motivate transformative actions. In its wide circulation, the Fijian paraphrase of Gen 1:26 is used as an obvious but compelling lament and criticism, pushing speakers and audiences to bring land, people, and God closer together in a project with firm boundaries but no end in sight.

Bibliography

Arno, Andrew. *The World of Talk on a Fijian Island: An Ethnography of Law and Communicative Causation*. Norwood, NJ: Ablex, 1993.

68. *100 Most Important Bible Verses*, 11.

Bauman, Richard. *A World of Others' Words: Cross-Cultural Perspectives on Intertextuality.* Malden, MA: Blackwell, 2004.

Bauman, Richard, and Charles Briggs. "Poetics and Performance as Critical Perspectives on Language and Social Life." *Annual Review of Anthropology* 19 (1990) 59–88.

Bowen, John R. *Muslims through Discourse: Religion and Ritual in Gayo Society.* Princeton: Princeton University Press, 1993.

Briggs, Charles L. *Competence in Performance: The Creativity of Tradition in Mexicano Verbal Art.* Philadelphia: University of Pennsylvania Press, 1988.

Briggs, Charles L., and Richard Bauman. "Genre, Textuality, and Social Power." *Journal of Linguistic Anthropology* 2.2 (1992) 131–72.

Capell, A. *A New Fijian Dictionary.* 3rd ed. Suva, Fiji: Government Printer, 1991.

Casimira, Aisake. *Who Do You Say I Am?: Interaction Between Bible and Culture.* Suva, Fiji: Ecumenical Centre for Research, Education and Advocacy, 2008.

Coleman, Simon. *The Globalisation of Charismatic Christianity: Spreading the Gospel of Prosperity.* Cambridge Studies in Ideology and Religion 12. Cambridge: Cambridge University Press, 2000.

Crapanzano, Vincent. *Serving the Word: Literalism in America from the Pulpit to the Bench.* New York: New Press, 2000.

Davidson, Robert. *Genesis 1–11.* Cambridge Bible Commentary. Cambridge: Cambridge University Press, 1973.

Dean, Eddie, and Stan Ritova. *Rabuka: No Other Way.* Sydney: Doubleday, 1988.

Dixon, R. M. W. *A Grammar of Boumaa Fijian.* Chicago: University of Chicago Press, 1988.

Duranti, Alessandro, and Charles Goodwin, eds. *Rethinking Context: Language as an Interactive Phenomenon.* Cambridge: Cambridge University Press, 1992.

Edwards, Jonathan. "Sinners in the Hands of an Angry God: A Sermon Preached at Enfield, July 8th, 1741." Digital Commons at University of Nebraska—Lincoln, https://digitalcommons.unl.edu/cgi/viewcontent.cgi?article=1053&context=etas.

Engelke, Matthew. *A Problem of Presence: Beyond Scripture in an African Church.* Berkeley: University of California Press, 2007.

Friedman, Richard Elliott. *Who Wrote the Bible?* New York: Harper & Row, 1987.

Geraghty, Paul. "Language Reform: History and Future of Fijian." In *Language Reform: History and Future,* Vol. IV, edited by Istvan Fodor and Claude Hagège, 377–95. Hamburg: Buske, 1989.

Green, Sam. "The Rainbow Man/John 3:16" [documentary film]. San Francisco: Other Cinema DVD, 2005 [1997].

Halapua, Winston. *Tradition, Lotu and Militarism in Fiji.* Lautoka, Fiji: Fiji Institute of Applied Studies, 2003.

Handman, Courtney. "Speaking to the Soul: On Native Language and Authenticity in Papua New Guinea Bible Translation." In *Consequences of Contact: Language Ideologies and Sociocultural Transformations in Pacific Societies,* edited by Miki Makihara and Bambi B. Schieffelin, 166–88. New York: Oxford University Press, 2007.

Harding, Susan Friend. *The Book of Jerry Falwell: Fundamentalist Language and Politics.* Princeton: Princeton University Press, 2000.

Heinz, Donald. "The Sabbath in Fiji as Guerrilla Theatre." *Journal of the American Academy of Religion* 61 (1993) 415–42.

Kaplan, Martha. "Christianity, People of the Land, and Chiefs in Fiji." In *Christianity in Oceania: Ethnographic Perspectives*, edited by J. Barker, 127–47. Lanham, MD: University Press of America, 1990.

———. "Fijian Water in Fiji and New York: Local Politics and a Global Commodity." *Cultural Anthropology* 22 (2007) 685–706.

———. "The *Hau* of Other Peoples' Gifts: Land Owning and Taking in Turn-of-the-Milllennium Fiji." *Ethnohistory* 52 (2005) 29–46.

———. *Neither Cargo nor Cult: Ritual Politics and the Colonial Imagination in Fiji*. Durham, NC: Duke University Press, 1995.

———. "Promised Lands: From Colonial Lawgiving to Postcolonial Takeovers in Fiji." In *Law & Empire in the Pacific: Fiji and Hawai'i*, edited by Sally E. Merry and Donald Brenneis, 153–86. Santa Fe, NM: School of American Research, 2004.

Keane, Webb. "Anxious Transcendence." In *The Anthropology of Christianity*, edited by Fenella Cannell, 308–23. Durham: Duke University Press, 2006.

———. *Christian Moderns: Freedom and Fetish in the Mission Encounter*. Berkeley: University of California Press, 2007.

———. *Signs of Recognition: Powers and Hazards of Representation in an Indonesian Society*. Berkeley: University of California Press, 1997.

———. "Sincerity, 'Modernity,' and the Protestants." *Cultural Anthropology* 17.1 (2002) 65–92.

———. "The Spoken House: Text, Act, and Object in Eastern Indonesia." *American Ethnologist* 22.1 (1995) 102–24.

Kelly, John D. "From Holi to Diwali in Fiji: An Essay on Ritual and History." *Man* (n.s.) 23 (1988) 40–55.

Kierkegaard, Søren. *Concluding Unscientific Postscript to the Philosophical Fragments*. Edited by W. Lowrie; translated by D. F. Swenson and W. Lowrie. Princeton, NJ: Princeton University Press, 1941.

———. *Fear and Trembling: A Dialectical Lyric*. Edited and translated by W. Lowrie. Princeton: Princeton University Press, 1941.

Kuipers, Joel. *Power in Performance: The Creation of Textual Authority in Weyewa Ritual Speech*. Philadelphia: University of Pennsylvania Press, 1990.

Luhrmann, Tanya M. "Metakinesis: How God Becomes Intimate in Contemporary U.S. Christianity." *American Anthropologist* 106 (2004) 518–28.

Miyazaki, Hirokazu. "Faith and Its Fulfillment: Agency, Exchange, and the Fijian Aesthetics of Completion." *American Ethnologist* 27 (2000) 31–51.

———. "From Sugar Cane to 'Swords': Hope and the Extensibility of the Gift in Fiji." *Journal of the Royal Anthropological Institute* 11 (2005) 277–95.

———. *The Method of Hope: Anthropology, Philosophy, and Fijian Knowledge*. Stanford, CA: Stanford University Press, 2004.

Newland, Lynda. "The Role of the Assembly of Christian Churches in Fiji in the 2006 Elections." In *From Election to Coup in Fiji: The 2006 Campaign and Its Aftermath*, edited by J. Fraenkel and S. Firth, 300–314. Canberra, Australia: Asia Pacific Press, 2006.

Norton, Robert. "Reconciling Ethnicity and Nation: Contending Discourses in Fiji's Constitutional Reform." *Contemporary Pacific* 12.1 (2000) 83–122.

100 Most Important Bible Verses. Brentwood, TN: W. Publishing Group, 2005.

Ratuva, Steven. "God's Will in Paradise: The Politics of Ethnicity and Religion in Fiji." *Development Bulletin* 59 (2002) 19–23.

Ravuvu, Asesela D. *Vaka i Taukei: The Fijian Way of Life*. Suva, Fiji: Institute of Pacific Studies, University of the South Pacific, 1983.

Robbins, Joel. *Becoming Sinners: Christianity and Moral Torment in a Papua New Guinea Society*. Berkeley: University of California Press, 2004.

———. "Continuity Thinking and the Problem of Christian Culture: Belief, Time, and the Anthropology of Christianity." *Current Anthropology* 48.1 (2007) 5–17.

———. "God Is Nothing but Talk: Modernity, Language, and Prayer in a Papua New Guinea Society." *American Anthropologist* 103.4 (2001) 901–12.

Royce, James S. H. "Diary: 18 Nov 1855–9 Apr 1862." Microfilm MS499, Alexander Turnbull Library, National Library of New Zealand, Wellington, New Zealand.

Rutz, Henry J., and Erol M. Balkan. "Never on Sunday: Time-Discipline and Fijian Nationalism." In *The Politics of Time*, edited by Henry J. Rutz, 62–85. American Ethnological Society Monograph Series 4. Washington, DC: American Anthropological Association, 1992.

Ryle, Jacqueline. "'My God, My Land': Interwoven Paths of Christianity and Tradition in Fiji." PhD diss., University of London, 2001.

———. "Roots of Land and Church: The Christian State Debate in Fiji." *International Journal for the Study of the Christian Church* 5 (2005) 58–78.

Sawin, Theophilus P., et al. "In What Particulars Is the Bible More or Less Familiar Than Fifty Years Ago? A Symposium." *Biblical World* 21.4 (1903) 260–73.

Schieffelin, Bambi B. "Found in Translating: Reflexive Language Across Time and Texts in Bosavi, Papua New Guinea." In *Consequences of Contact: Language Ideologies and Sociocultural Transformations in Pacific Societies*, edited by Miki Makihara and Bambi B. Schieffelin, 140–65. New York: Oxford University Press, 2007.

Scott, Michael W. *The Severed Snake: Matrilineages, Making Place, and a Melanesian Christianity in Southeast Solomon Islands*. Durham, NC: Carolina Academic, 2007.

Silverstein, Michael. *Talking Politics: The Substance of Style from Abe to "W."* Chicago: Prickly Paradigm, 2003.

Silverstein, Michael, and Greg Urban, eds. *Natural Histories of Discourse*. Chicago: University of Chicago Press, 1996.

———. "The Natural History of Discourse." In *Natural Histories of Discourse*, edited by M. Silverstein and G. Urban, 1–17. Chicago: University of Chicago Press, 1996.

Srebrnik, Henry. "Ethnicity, Religion, and the Issue of Aboriginality in a Small Island State: Why Does Fiji Flounder?" *The Round Table* 364 (2002) 187–210.

Stine, P. C. "Bible Translations, Modern Period." In *Concise Encyclopedia of Language and Religion*, edited by John F. A. Sawyer, J. M. Y. Simpson, and R. E. Asher, 106–15. Amsterdam: Elsevier, 2001.

Thomas, Nicholas. *In Oceania: Visions, Artifacts, Histories*. Durham: Duke University Press, 1997.

Thornley, Andrew. *A Shaking of the Land / Na Yavalati ni Vanua: William Cross and the Origins of Christianity in Fiji / Ko Wiliame Korosi kei na i Tekitekivu ni Lotu Vakarisito e Viti*. Suva, Fiji: Institute of Pacific Studies, University of the South Pacific, 2005.

Tippett, Alan R. "Fijian Proverbs, Metaphoric Idioms and Riddles: An Ethnolinguistic Study." *Transactions and Proceedings of the Fiji Society* 8 (1960) 65–93.

Tomlinson, Matt. *In God's Image: The Metaculture of Fijian Christianity*. Berkeley: University of California Press, 2009.

Tomlinson, Matt, and Miki Makihara. "New Paths in the Linguistic Anthropology of Oceania." *Annual Review of Anthropology* 38 (2009) 17–31.
Toren, Christina. "Becoming a Christian in Fiji: An Ethnographic Study of Ontogeny." *Journal of the Royal Anthropological Institute* 10.1 (2004) 222–40.
———. "Making the Present, Revealing the Past: The Mutability and Continuity of Tradition as Process." *Man* 23 (1988) 696–717.
———. *Mind, Materiality, and History: Explorations in Fijian Ethnography*. London: Routledge, 1999.
Tuwere, Ilaitia S. *Vanua: Towards a Fijian Theology of Place*. Suva and Auckland: Institute of Pacific Studies at the University of the South Pacific and College of St. John the Evangelist, 2002.
"2006 Coup Justified." *Fiji Times*, December 17, 2008.
Urban, Greg. "Entextualization, Replication, and Power." In *Natural Histories of Discourse*, edited by M. Silverstein and G. Urban, 21–44. Chicago: University of Chicago Press, 1996.
———. *Metaculture: How Culture Moves through the World*. Minneapolis: University of Minnesota Press, 2001.
Williksen-Bakker, Solrun. "Vanua—A Symbol with Many Ramifications in Fijian Culture." *Ethnos* 55.3–4 (1990) 232–47.
Young, Florence S. H. *Pearls from the Pacific*. London: Marshall Brothers, 1925.

9

The Samurai Christians
Uchimura, Ebina, and Their Bible

Murayama Yumi

In 1862, Protestantism was introduced to pre-industrial Japan alongside the powerful and progressive Western civilization and was presented as the "religion of the greatest civilization." Protestant missionaries managed to attract young Japanese intellectuals, and those first-generation Christians were mostly from the privileged warrior class. At least initially, they were attracted to Christianity, because their patriotism compelled them to learn from the West in order to make a greater contribution to Japan.

The two theologians introduced here, Ebina Danjō and Uchimura Kanzō, fit this description. They studied in schools run by American scholars and became familiar with the English language and literature, as well as with Western philosophy and theology. Embracing the Western intellectual tradition, they studied the Bible using the historical-critical method. Originally, the Bible was a collection of writings by many authors of different time periods and with differing viewpoints, authors about whom we know nothing for sure. When the Bible was handed down to Japanese intellectuals from Western missionaries, they also inherited the historical-critical method of interpretation, and they began to argue their own theological/political opinions through the reading of the Bible.

In spite of these commonalities, however, Ebina's and Uchimura's theological frameworks came to be very different. Ebina was pastor of a church and a theologian who was open to liberal Protestantism and supportive of the expansion of the Japanese Empire. Uchimura, on the other hand, did not belong to any denomination and was a layperson without a ministerial license who later became an outspoken pacifist. Their different attitudes toward Japan's colonial policy is rooted in the differences in their life stories and their positions within Japanese church and society. It is not only their theological positions and beliefs, then, that led to the different conclusions they reached about Japanese imperialism.

Ebina Danjō (1859–1937)

Ebina Danjō was born in 1859 in Northern Kyushū. He experienced the loss of his mother when he was ten years old as an event that divided his life into two parts, "the earlier happy and innocent, without sorrow or pain, the latter tainted with grief."[1] Once, as he sat with his mother before a brazier, a barefoot man was selling fish outside. His mother asked him, "You are now warm in front of the brazier, and he is selling fish in the cold. Do you know the reason?" Ebina found that he could not answer. His mother continued, "The man does not receive wages from our (feudal) lord, thus he has to work to support his family. Yet, in time of war, he can flee anywhere he wants. You, on the other hand, who are now warm inside, owe it to the lord and the ancestors to stand your ground, ready to die for the lord." This dialogue impressed on his mind the samurai spirit of self-sacrifice.

In 1886, the Meiji government took over and adopted a policy of modernization. Ebina's clan was abolished, and the prince of the clan, a year younger than Ebina, died. This was devastating to Ebina, who had been determined to serve this prince throughout his life. At age sixteen, he left home to pursue his education at Kumamoto Western School, where he learned natural science and history from the American Leroy L. Janes (1838–1909), under whose influence he became a Christian and by whom he was baptized in 1876. Janes taught Ebina that prayer is not asking God to grant what one desires; instead it is a duty of creatures to the creator. This led Ebina to realize that the relationship between God and a human is just like the one between a lord and a vassal.[2]

When he was enrolled in Dōshisha University in Kyoto, Ebina and his colleagues were not content with the theological education they received at the university; they were especially dissatisfied with the Bible and theology course taught by Jerome D. Davis (1838–1910). When students asked questions about miracle stories in the Bible, Davis reacted with an authoritarian emphasis on biblical inerrancy and accused them of impiety.[3] In reaction, Ebina became one of the first to accept Christian liberalism and higher criticism of the Bible.

1. Ebina, "Waga Shinkō no Jinsei II [My Life of Faith II]," 47.
2. Dohi, *Nihon Protesutanto Kirisuto kyōshi* [History of Protestantism in Japan], 173–4.
3. Ouchi, *Kindai Nihon no seisho shisō* [Biblical Thought in Modern Japan], 24.

As an educated son of a samurai, he had come to the conclusion that the "heaven" of Confucianism and the God of Christianity were identical. The brand of Confucianism taught at the school affirmed a personal god who reigns over heaven and earth.[4] Ebina explained his relationship to God by invoking the father-son relationship, one of the five essential relationships in Confucianism.

After graduating from Dōshisha, Ebina became a minister of the Congregational Church in Japan. In 1897, after working in several churches, he moved to the Hongō Church in Tokyo, which he himself had founded in 1886 and from which many prominent scholars and politicians emerged.

Ebina did not consider the Trinity, the bodily resurrection of Christ, or any of the biblical miracles as literal truth. In the 1880s, theologically liberal Protestantism was introduced to Japan by the *Evangelisch-Protestantischer Missionsverein*, whose founders were influenced by the *Religionsgeschichtliche Schule*. Missionaries from the American Unitarian Association also arrived in Japan. Ebina was inspired by theological liberalism to promote independence from the missionaries not only financially and politically but also doctrinally.[5]

For Ebina, it is not the Bible that is important, but the *logos*, which is the immanent God apprehended in the creation, in the Bible, and most prominently in the person of Christ—and also in Japanese nature, history, and literature. When the *logos* is actualized among the people of Japan, a new Scripture should emerge from them. Ebina argued that even if the Bible disappeared, something similar to it would emerge in Western society, because the *logos* or the living spirit of God cannot be confined within one book:

> Therefore, we must expect the emergence of something superior to the Bible. In reading from the Bible, I do not value the whole Bible equally. We have to select from the Scriptures what seems to be given by God to us today. We should fill the spirit in the world of literature to produce a new Bible through the prompting of the heavenly inspiration.[6]

---

4. Dohi, *Nihon Protesutanto Kirisuto kyōshi*, 173; Takeda, "Ebina Danjo Den. [Biography of Ebina Danjo]," 1960.

5. Ebina, "Kirisuto kyōkai dokuritsu shugi [Principle of Independence of the Christian Church]," 6–9.

6. Ebina, "Sachiwau kotodama [Blessed Logos]," 6.

Uchimura Kanzō (1861–1930)

Uchimura Kanzō, founder of the *Mukyōkai* (non-church) movement, was also a son of a samurai. He encountered Christianity when he entered Sapporo Agricultural School in 1877. The school was founded by the government to educate those who would work for the government project to exploit Hokkaido, where Japanese sovereignty was not yet established. The headmaster William S. Clark returned to the United States.

Uchimura worked in the civil service for colonial policy in Hokkaido until he left for the United States in 1884. He then found a job as a nurse at the Pennsylvania Training School, and after seven months, moved to Amherst College as a part-time student. Upon obtaining a Bachelor of Science degree, he entered Hartford Theological Seminary in Boston. However, Uchimura did not find the study of theology there stimulating, and with the decline of his health, had no option but to return to Japan in December 1888.

When one talks about Uchimura's life, it is not possible to avoid mentioning the "Imperial Rescript" incident that occurred when he was a high-school teacher in Tokyo. After adopting the ideas and institutions of Western origin, the Meiji government promoted strong conservatism to secure its power and social order. The Imperial Rescript on Education was a product of this conservatism and creation of a rigid national orthodoxy. It was an ordinance issued in the name of the Meiji emperor, reinforcing the eternal lineage and to which the Japanese are subject. It taught subjects to sacrifice their lives in the case of national crisis based on the moral conduct of Japanese people following Confucianism. The ordinance was distributed to all schools throughout Japan.

This incident, which made clear the tension between the government's policy and Christian religion, happened soon after the promulgation of the constitution and the Rescript on Education. In 1891, Uchimura, who was teaching at one of the imperial high schools, did not bow deeply enough to the Imperial Rescript of Education during the ceremony for its dedication at the First High School of Tokyo. Both teachers and students were expected to bow to show their respect to the Rescript that carried the emperor's sacred signature. Uchimura was not sure if the bow signified respect to the emperor or religious veneration of the deified emperor. Being uncertain, he made only a slight bow, which offended his colleagues, students, and the public. The criticism was so strong that Uchimura became ill with pneumonia and, in the same year, his wife died due to the stress of public criticism and of taking care of her sick husband. He also lost his position in the high school and even in the church.

Uchimura's resentment of the criticism from within the church was so intense that he "almost committed spiritual suicide" by renouncing his faith.[7] His later writing on the book of Job reflects this experience:

> Let Job be a Christian today. He was perfect in his faith and deeds, admired as a model Christian among the other members of the church, and he was also quite wealthy. The church members considered his fortune as a result of his strong faith. However, Job lost everything overnight, became like a beggar, and his body was diseased. None of the church members understood what had happened, and all the church meetings were diverted by gossip and criticisms about Job. Some said it was evidence that God does not exist, since such a man of faith was now experiencing such misfortunes. Others said that God may exist yet may not be the God of love. However, the majority agreed with the old pastor who said that it was because Job sinned in darkness that the misfortunes were given to him by God. Now the congregation decided that representatives from the church should visit Job to make him confess his sin while consoling his pain so that he could come back to the grace of God. The representatives are the old pastor Eliphaz, a theologian in the prime of his life, Bildad, and an able youth, Zophar.[8]

Amidst disappointment and anger, however, Uchimura found "God" through "the Bible." This moment is crucial to understanding Uchimura and his theology: he encountered God in his hardship through reading the Bible *alone, apart from* the church and theologians.

> Yet, God, my savior, you saved me from this peril. When the opponents lay blame on me using the Bible, the armor to protect me was the Bible. The Church and theologians rejected me, yet the very fact that I did not discard the Bible was the assurance that you did not forsake me.[9]

Thus, for Uchimura, the Bible was "the shield of the lonely, fortress of the weak, the resting place of the misunderstood. With the Bible, I shall be able to stand against the Pope, Archbishop, or Doctors of Theology."[10] Uchimura clung to the Bible as his authority and the way to God, but unlike others he remained a loner. No matter how many disciples followed him, he did not attempt to create an alternative institution. In fact, he was against

---

7. Ibid., 32.
8. Uchimura, "Yobuki no kenkyū' [Study of the Book of Job]," 674–5.
9. Uchimura, *Kirisuto shinto no nagusame* [Consolation of a Christian], 33.
10. Ibid.

the very idea of an "institution" as a way to God. This idea of the Bible as one's only companion is the foundation of Uchimura's theology and the guiding conviction of the Non-Church movement.

In 1900, he published the first issue of *Bible Study*, which became his life work. This monthly journal devoted most of its space to commentaries or lectures on the Bible or other issues of faith, but often included Uchimura's view on public and political issues. In the first issue, Uchimura presented his view on the Bible:

> It is the one and only book in the world, the only authority to save the peoples, with beauty as literature, with value as a philosophy of life.... A civilized person who is not familiar with the Bible is just like a Chinese person who is ignorant of the Analects of Confucius, or a Japanese person who has not memorized the Imperial Rescript on Education. If one does not know the Bible, how can one possibly appreciate the world's literature?[11]

Footnotes and bibliographies are largely lacking in his biblical commentaries, partly because he saw lengthy bibliographies as "showing off one's credibility to the readers."[12] Still, it is obvious that he owed much to British or American scholars: in his commentary on Romans, for example, he names F. H. Scrivener, John D. Davis, Barnes, Hodge, and Lightfoot.[13] However, *Bible Study* was not merely a copy or synopsis of Western biblical scholars' work. Its aim was to explain the Bible to the Japanese people and discuss the current affairs of the country. Some readers and subscribers belonged to different faith communities, yet they came to respect Uchimura's faith and personality. The Non-Church movement is a Bible-study movement centered on this periodical. Through this publication, Uchimura believed, the Japanese would come to know true Christianity founded on the Bible, which would change individuals and society. Thus, he proclaimed introducing Christianity to the Japanese to be "my work of social reform."[14]

The Russo-Japanese War (1904–1905)

Japan had secured its position in Korea after the Sino-Japanese War, and its next obstacle was Russia, which had occupied Manchuria in 1901. In 1904,

---

11. Uchimura, "Seisho no Hanashi [Story of the Bible]," 26.
12. Uchimura, "Pauro no Kirisutokan [Paul's Christology]," 31.
13. Ibid.
14. Uchimura, "Yo no jyūjishitsutsu [Social Reform I Undertake]," 114.

the Japanese government attacked the Russian Fleet at Port Arthur, which was followed by the declaration of war.[15]

About six months before the declaration, Uchimura wrote an article, "Abrogation of War" (1903), in the *Chō-hō-sha* newspaper. This was his first essay to argue against war on pacifist grounds. He denounced his previous essay, "Justification for the Korean War," which was written during the Sino-Japanese War (1894–1895), in which he argued that China was not promoting the adaptation of the "new" civilization (namely, Western civilization), and was hindering Korea's progress; Japan's "calling" was to be the "mediator" between the East and the West, the "Warrior of Progress in the East."[16]

In "Abrogation of War," he states that after the Sino-Japanese war, the independence of Korea failed, China was in crisis and was being divided up by the Western powers, financial burdens came upon the Japanese people, moral decay permeated Japanese society, and the whole of East Asia was in trouble.[17] Also, in *Bible Study*, he rejected the possibility of using the Old Testament to justify a war. He believed the Bible to be God's progressive self-revelation, which does not reveal God's absolute will as transcending time and space. God did not allow the heroes in the Old Testament to wage war because God approves of a war; it was "because of the hardness of their heart" that God overlooked it until they learned it was sinful. Matthew 5:38–42 states that with the advent of Christ, retaliation and war are absolutely rejected. One may learn from Joshua or Gideon about faith and obedience, not about war. Christians, by virtue of knowing Christ, stand above Abraham or David in viewing war as absolutely evil.[18]

Ebina, however, disapproved of Uchimura's pacifism and encouraged Christians to "fight with Christ to build the kingdom of God, by shedding one's blood, breaking one's body, and undergoing every hardship."[19] Responding to Uchimura, Ebina wrote an article entitled "A Biblical Perspective on War" (1904). He emphasized that the Torah and most of the Old Testament is a history of war and that, nowhere in the Bible, not even in the New Testament, is war prohibited. Even John the Baptist or Jesus did not tell the Roman soldiers to abandon their profession. In Acts 10, a soldier, Cornelius, was baptized.

---

15. Iriye, "Japan's Drive to Great-Power Status," 776.

16. Uchimura, "Nihonkoku no tenshoku [Calling of Japan]," 170–173; Uchimura, "Sekai rekishi ni shirushite [Thesis on the Relationship]," 213–21.

17. Uchimura, "Sensō haishi ron [Abrogation of War]," 296–7.

18. Uchimura, "Heiwa no Fukuin [Gospel of Peace]," 404–9.

19. Ebina, "Kami no kuni no hatten [Advance of the Kingdom]," 13.

Ebina argues that a war is inevitable when a nation is thriving. Until the kingdom was established, Israel not only waged war for the sake of defense but also attacked neighboring peoples in Palestine. When the two kingdoms were sacked, the Jews clung to their religious values and teachings. When Jesus was born, there was no hope of independence, and that was not his purpose; his movement was to establish a spiritual, not a political community, and he attempted to achieve this in a non-violent way. However, in the Roman Empire, there was no reason for a soldier to renounce his arms since the empire was thriving; thus, Jesus did not command them to do so. Then Ebina concluded, "If one should oppose war because it is brutal, what about Jesus's cross? Even the spiritual battle for love was not nice and neat."[20] Christ even said, "Do not think that I have come to bring peace to the earth; I have not come to bring peace, but a sword" (Matt 10:34).[21]

In "The words of Christ cited by warmongers" (1904), Uchimura denounced Ebina's use of Matt 10:35. He argues that the sword in this passage is the sword of persecution, held by enemies of Christians, not by Christians themselves. He may have misunderstood Ebina, who did not use this passage simply to say, "Christians can take up the sword," but often cited it as showing that the way of Christ is not for the weak: Ebina's samurai Christian spirit is summed up in this saying of Jesus. Another passage Uchimura deals with is Luke 22:36, in which Jesus says: "The one who has no sword must sell his cloak and buy one." Since Jesus heals the slave of the high priest stricken by his disciple later in the same chapter, he cannot have meant that his disciples should literally obtain swords. In any case, if they needed actual swords, only two for twelve disciples would hardly be "enough." He concludes, "One cannot read the Bible with fidelity and piety and justify a war based on these sayings of Jesus"; it is in fact absurd to think that an international war is promoted based on two statements uttered by Jesus 2,000 years ago.

Ebina then wrote another article, "The Beauty of War," in which he claimed that there is "beauty" in human suffering, as can be discerned in the book of Job when one hears Job's cry from his soul. There is outstanding beauty in the cross of Christ. In the same way, there is beauty in war:

> If we see the Russo-Japanese War from this perspective, we can discern some nobility and beauty. Of course it is unbearable to see human bodies exploding, bloodshed, bones broken, and men and horses collapsing with screams. . . . Nonetheless, my friends, there is something greater than flesh, namely spirit. Where the spirit is vigorous with utmost faithfulness, it is

20. Ibid., 10.

21. All biblical citations are from the New Revised Standard Version (NRSV).

beautiful beyond description. When the soldiers sacrifice their lives, having left families behind, dart into the rain of bullets, crawling over corpses, and fighting with their sword against the enemy; at that moment, the spirit's vigor is nothing less than amazing . . . This is where the beauty of life evolves.[22]

The most horrifying scene takes on the utmost beauty for Ebina. This is a rhetorical technique Ebina frequently employed: he deconstructs the common meaning of a word or concept and reconstructs the meaning that fits his purpose. For example, "meekness" in the sermon on the mount (Matt 5:5), for Ebina, means "meekness to God," and to be meek to God, one has to be healthy, wise, knowledgeable, generous, and strong-willed. So what Jesus meant was, "blessed are the healthy, wise, knowledgeable, generous, and strong-willed: they will inherit the earth!"[23]

Throughout the Russo-Japanese War, Ebina and Uchimura held firm to their positions. History, in the short term, seemed to be on the side of Ebina. Even though Japan accrued huge debts from this war, patriotism, militarism, and imperialism were reaffirmed.

Ebina and Uchimura on Japan and Japanese Imperialism

Both Ebina and Uchimura held the Japanese emperor to be their "father," to whom their absolute loyalty was due. Both used Rom 13 to affirm the basic function of the Japanese government.[24] They admired the "patriotism of the Jewish people," which they saw in Ps 137.[25] However, their patriotism took two different expressions, and their interpretation of Christianity also developed into very different forms after the Russo-Japanese War.

The Bible, for Uchimura, gradually became a tool with which he critiqued Japan and its policy. He was convinced that to believe and propagate Christianity was the way to save the nation. Japan was full of corruption among politicians, educators, and religious leaders, swindling, bribery, fornication, theft, robbery, murder, syphilis, discord, deception, betrayal. Uchimura took Isa 1:4–6 as the description of Japan: "Ah, sinful nation, people laden with iniquity . . ."[26] Jeremiah was his favorite prophet and a close friend, because Jeremiah, like Uchimura, was a layperson without

---

22. Ebina, "Sensō no bi [Beauty of War]," 20.

23. Ebina, "Chi wo uketsugu no nyūwa [Meekness that Inherits the Earth]," 12–14.

24. Ebina, "Romansho [Romans]," 32; Uchimura, "Yudayajin no aikokuka [Patriotic Song]," 145.

25. Ebina, "Marukoden [Mark]," 55.

26. Ibid., 232.

any supporters as he prophesied against kings, politicians, military men, religious leaders, and his own people.²⁷

Christianity for Uchimura was not the religion of the West any longer; Britain, Germany, France, Russia, and the United States were none of them "Christian" in Uchimura's eyes. Europe's warmongering is compared to the deluge in the Old Testament: "If the Western civilization is what witnesses Christianity, Christianity is an evil teaching that generates wars, and not the gospel of the prince of peace."²⁸ To be saved by Christ, in this context, means to hold firm to the principle of non-violence. "I, with Jesus, am free from the poison of war: I do not hate the enemy; I do not support a war; I shall make every effort to restore peace."²⁹ Thus, the war in Europe was God's punishment to those who immerse themselves in materialism in pursuit of fleshly desires.³⁰

Uchimura's skepticism toward Western "Christian" countries became unalterable when the US Congress passed the so-called Asian Exclusion Act in 1924, which restricted Japanese immigration. Many Japanese went to California as immigrants, especially after the Russo-Japanese War, and the United States saw this as Japan's expansionism, claiming that those Japanese immigrants were not interested in naturalization. Britain, Japan's ally, sided with the United States.³¹ Uchimura was enraged on hearing about this, and saw it as an "insult" to Japan. The May to October 1924 issues of *Bible Study* were full of columns criticizing the United States and its missionaries. Uchimura came to the conclusion that the racist Western countries and civilization had nothing to do with "true" Christianity. He denounced the church, its missionaries, and Western nations, and stood on his own with the Bible. He sought Christ alone and found hope in Job 19:25: "For I know that my Redeemer lives, and that at the last he will stand upon the earth." Uchimura was Job, who discovered the hope of redemption, in absolute solitude.³²

In 1910, when Japan annexed Korea, Ebina published *Discipline of the New Citizens*, in which he considered ways of assimilating the "new citizens"—namely the Korean people—to the Japanese. According to Ebina, Japan originally consisted of several different tribes, including the Ainu, the Malay, the Koreans, and the Chinese. To unite all these peoples, the rulers

27. Uchimura, "Eremiyaki Kansō [Notes on the Book of Jeremiah]," 493–94.
28. Uchimura, "Noa no kōzui wo omou [Contemplation on the Deluge]," 475.
29. Ibid., 476.
30. Ibid., 478.
31. Iriye, "Japan's Drive to Great-Power Status," 779.
32. Tomioka, *Uchimura Kanzo*, 152–53.

contextualized Buddhism, Confucianism, and Shinto in the Japanese milieu to create a tribal myth: "The Japanese people enslaved Buddhism or Confucianism to form a unified national identity."[33] However, it would not be reasonable to force the traditional Japanese identity onto the Korean people; to assimilate them to the Japanese, they should be treated equally as brothers and sisters with equal rights. Christianity should become the tool to evoke the *Weltgeist* so as to unite them in Japan as one nation. Confucianism and Shinto are too narrowly tribal to serve this cause, and Buddhism, although in its original form was a world religion, has become indigenized in Japan and has lost its universal spirit.[34]

Ebina is not encouraging the entire population of Japan and Korea to be converted to Christianity. What he is promoting is the spirit of tolerance, human rights, and individual conscience. He argues that Christianity is a spiritual imperialism. Christ often taught about the kingdom of God. Christianity is an exclusive and invasive authority submissive to Christ's religious consciousness. This does not mean, however, that it destroys other religions and enslaves the people of other faiths—because every religion, whether it is from heaven or from humanity, contains a grain of truth. When it encounters Christianity, the religion obtains its fulfillment, and the process is the voluntary subjection to the truth, not enslavement. Therefore, the imperialism of Christianity is not destructive, but constructive. It is the kingdom where the sovereign, "came not to be served but to serve, and to give his life a ransom for many" (Matt 20:28).[35]

For this purpose, the Japanese people need to realize the honorable character in themselves. Ebina called this character the "new person," by which he meant a strong conscience and the will to obey it.[36] In *National Morality and Christianity*, he argues that to be a truly civilized nation, Japan must adopt Christianity, which had been nourishing the Western people. If National Shinto is not a religion but a way to show respect to the emperor, the ancestors, and the Japanese tradition, it should be able to co-exist with Christianity. Shinto is originally an animistic religion, yet the modern Japanese people cannot possibly bow to primitive superstitions such as animism, totemism, or fetishism. As the Korean people welcome Christianity, the Japanese government must change its critical view of Christianity and promote it for the purpose of assimilation. Especially the teaching "Love

---

33. Ebina, *Shin Kokumin no Shūyō*. [Discipline of the New Citizens], 4.
34. Ibid., 1–15.
35. Ibid., 79–83.
36. Ebina, "Shin dōtoku no kisō' [Foundation of the New Morality]," 8–12.

your enemy" will encourage Koreans not to hold a grudge against the Japanese and to cooperate for the greater cause.[37]

To construct his argument, Ebina approached the Bible selectively. Commenting on Rom 13, he says:

> Christianity affirms that the Great Japanese Empire with its two thousand year history has its foundation in God's providence and protection. The establishment of the nation is God's will. Therefore, to revere its quality and serve for its prosperity is a duty for those Japanese who honour God. Hence to neglect this duty is insolence to God.[38]

However, he completely rejected the view of the book of Revelation:

> Some Protestant Christians believe in Jesus of Nazareth not as Christ but as if he was an earthly ruler. The New Testament in fact praises him as a prince on earth. Such a Christ inevitably clashes with the emperor. Christ in Revelation was in conflict with the emperor of Rome, and the Messiah in Daniel with the King of Assyria. A Christianity like this cannot avoid a conflict with the fundamental character of Japan. Therefore Christians in the Japanese Empire must reject the political Christ and adopt the Logos Christology.[39]

For Ebina, the Bible is not the greatest revelation of God, but God reveals himself to humans through their conscience.[40] The Bible is always secondary to human experience.

Samurai Colonialists: Ebina and Uchimura in History

As we have seen so far, Ebina and Uchimura, Christian converts who came from samurai families, reached different conclusions about Japan and its imperialism. Bushidō, the way of the samurai, was originally an art of fighting and killing. When Japan was unified, and the society became stabilized, bushidō became more of a philosophy of life for warriors, yet the interpretations varied since there were no specific sources to define exactly what this philosophy was. Ebina and Uchimura agreed that Christianity and bushidō were compatible. However, for Uchimura, a samurai was a person who

37. Ebina, *Kokumin dōtoku to Kirisutokyō* [Morality of the People and Christianity], 146.
38. Ebina, "Romansho [Romans]," 33.
39. Ebina, *Kokumin dōtoku to Kirisutokyō*, 70.
40. Ebina, "Religion of Conscience," 17.

abides by justice: he is honest, genuine, and sincere. A samurai Christian, for Uchimura, endures any hardship for the sake of justice, unswayed by the opinions of others. Thus, Uchimura persisted in the principle of non-violence, which was for him the way of justice and truth.[41] For Ebina, a samurai is anyone, regardless of their gender and social status, who is of strong will, ready to fight, and willing to undertake self-sacrifice for a larger cause. The most crucial element in bushidō for Ebina was loyalty, that is, loyalty to the nation—which is patriotism. Christian patriotism, then, is the love for one's compatriots.[42] Even though their interpretations of bushidō diverged, for both of them, the model of the true samurai was Jesus Christ.

Coming from the ruling class of feudal Japan, their Christian view of society is often marked by an elitist attitude, and it attracted many of their own kind. For example, Uchimura was critical of universal suffrage. He compares this democratic movement away from a centralization of power with the great statue of Nebuchadnezzar's dream (Dan 2), and augurs that it will bring Japan to the stage of being "partly of clay and partly of iron."[43] The Christianity of these first-generation Japanese Christians was a religion of Western civilization, and a religion of the elite.

Ebina learned from and embraced the Western colonial discourse, and the role that Christianity and the Bible played in it. The way he argued that Christianity should be the tool for Japan's overseas expansion and ruling policy is reminiscent of the colonial West. The liberal theology that flourished in Germany and influenced Ebina had failed to critique the state and its projects of colonial expansion.

Contrary to one's image of religious conservatism today, it was the theologically liberal Ebina who became an advocate of Japan's imperialism, while the theologically more conservative Uchimura became a critic. Uchimura experienced Western society first-hand when he studied in the United States. He was rejected by (or he himself rejected) Japanese society and the church in the Imperial Rescript incident. His concept of Non-Church met severe criticism from foreign missionaries. All these experiences led him to grow critical of Western society and the church, and the fact that he did not belong to either a powerful social group or the institutional church allowed him to maintain his opinions. Ebina, on the other hand, was an authoritative figure in a church denomination, and cooperated with foreign mission societies. His church was a gathering place for the elite, and he held a high opinion of Western civilization until the end.

41. Uchimura, "Bushidō to Kirisutokyō' [Bushido and Christianity]," 292–97.
42. Ebina, "Shin Bushidō [Neo-Bushido]," 10–14.
43. Uchimura, *Danierusho no kenkyū* [Study of the Book of Daniel], 608.

The Japanese government did not take up Ebina's proposal to use Christianity to control both the colonies and the homeland, yet it did fully apply the colonial discourse, an appropriation of that of the West. Uchimura, who died in 1930, did not see his nation join another world war like those Western nations he criticized during the First World War. Ebina, who died in 1937, also did not see the full implications of Japan's imperialist policy, which he strongly supported during his lifetime.

Bibliography

Dohi, Akio. *Nihon Protesutanto Kirisuto kyōshi* [History of Protestantism in Japan]. 5th ed. Tokyo: Shinkyo shuppan, 2004.
Ebina, Danjō. "Chi wo uketsugu no nyūwa [The Meekness that Inherits the Earth]." *Shinjin* 5.6 (1904).
———. "Fukuin Shinpō kisha ni atauru no sho [A Letter to the Author of *Fukuin Shinpō*]." *Shinjin* 2.3 (1901).
———. "Kami no kuni no hatten [The Advance of the Kingdom of God]." *Shinjin* 5.1 (1904).
———. "Kirisuto kyōkai dokuritsu shugi [Principle of Independence of the Christian Church]." *Shinjin* 1.3 (1900).
———. *Kirisutokyō no hongi* [The Essence of Christianity]. Tokyo: Hidaka Yurindo. 1903.
———. *Kokumin dōtoku to Kirisutokyō* [Morality of the People and Christianity]. Tokyo: Hokubunkan, 1912.
———. "Makoto no pan [The Bread of Truth]." *Shinjin* 4.4 (1903).
———. "Marukoden [Mark]." *Shinjin* 12.6 (1911).
———. "Religion of Conscience." *Shinjin* 18.12 (1917).
———. "Romansho [Romans]." *Shinjin* 6.5 (1905).
———. "Sachiwau kotodama [Blessed Logos]." *Shinjin* 7.12 (1906).
———. "Seisho no sensō shugi [A Biblical Perspective on War]." *Shinjin* 5.4 (1904).
———. "Sensō no bi [The Beauty of War]." *Shinjin* 5.8 (1904).
———. "Shin Bushidō [Neo-Bushido]." *Shinjin* 2.10 (1902).
———. "Shin dōtoku no kisō" [The Foundation of the New Morality]." *Shinjin* 12.7 (1911).
———. *Shin Kokumin no Shūyō*. [Discipline of the New Citizens]. Tokyo: Jitsugyo no Nihonsha. 1910.
———. "Shohihyō wo yonde futatabi yo ga Kirisutokyōkan wo akirakanisu [Clarifying my Christology after Having Read the Criticisms]." *Shinjin* 2.9 (1902).
———. "Uemura shi no tōsho wo yomu [Reading Mr. Uemura's Reply]." *Shinjin* 2.4 (1901).
———. "Waga Shinkō no Jinsei II [My Life of Faith II]." *Shinjin* 25. 2 (1924).
———. "Waga Shinkō no Jinsei IV [My Life of Faith IV]." *Shinjin* 25. 4 (1924).
Furuya, Yasuo, ed. *A History of Japanese Theology*. Grand Rapids: Eerdmans, 1997.
Hirakawa, Sukehiro. "Japan's Turn to the West." In *The Cambridge History of Japan, Volume 5—The Nineteenth Century*, edited by Marius B. Jansen, 432-98. Cambridge: Cambridge University Press, 1989.

Iriye, Akira. "Japan's Drive to Great-Power Status." In *The Cambridge History of Japan, Volume 5—The Nineteenth Century*, edited by Marius B. Jansen, 721–82. Cambridge: Cambridge University Press, 1989.

Kim, Mungil, *Kindai Nihon Kirisutokyo to Chōsen* [Christianity in Modern Japan and Korea]. Tokyo: Akashi shoten, 1998.

Ouchi, Saburo, *Kindai Nihon no seisho shisō* [Biblical Thought in Modern Japan]. Tokyo: Nihon Kirisutokyodan shuppan, 1959.

Sawa, Masahiko, *Nihon Kirisuto kyōshi* [History of Christianity in Japan]. Tokyo: Sofukan, 2004.

Suzuki, Torisho et al., eds. *Uchimura Kanzō zenshū*. Tokyo: Iwanami, 1980–84.

Takeda, Kiyoko. "Ebina Danjō Den. [Biography of Ebina Danjō]." *Shinjin no Souzō* [Creation of a New Person]. Tokyo: Kyobunkan, 1960.

Tomioka, Koichirō. *Uchimura Kanzō*. Tokyo: Satsuki Shobo, 2001.

Uchimura, Kanzō. "Bushidō to Kirisutokyō [Bushido and Christianity]." *Seisho no kenkyū* 339 (1928).

———. "Chōsenkoku to Nihonkoku [Korea and Japan]." *Seisho no kenkyū* 115 (1909).

———. *Danierusho no kenkyū*. [A Study of the Book of Daniel]. Tokyo: Seisho Kenkyū sha, 1922.

———. "Eremiyaki Kansō [Notes on the Book of Jeremiah]." *Seisho no kenkyū* 74 (1906).

———. "Foreign Policy of Japan Historically Considered." *The Japan Weekly Chronicle* (1904).

———. "Heiwa no Fukuin [The Gospel of Peace]." *Seisho no kenkyū* 44 (1903).

———. "Heiwa no jitsueki [Profit of Peace]." *Yorozu chōhō* (1903).

———. *Kirisuto shinto no nagusame* [The Consolation of a Christian]. Tokyo: Keiseisha, 1893.

———. "Long Live the Emperor!" *Yorozu chōhō* (1897).

———. "Miscellaneous Notes." *Yorozu chōhō* (1897).

———. "Mokuteki no shinpo [Progress Toward my Goal]." *Seisho no kenkyū* (1913).

———. "Nihonkoku no tenshoku [The Calling of Japan]." *Rikugō zasshi* 146 (1892).

———. "Nisshin sensō no gi wo ronzu [Justification for the Korean War]." *Kokumin no tomo* 234 (1894).

———. "Noa no kōzui wo omou [Contemplation on the Deluge]." *Seisho no kenkyū* 185 (1915).

———. "Nōfu Amosu no kotoba [The Words of Amos the Farmer]." *Kokumin no tomo* 253 (1895).

———. "Pauro no Kirisutokan [Paul's Christology]." *Seisho no kenkyū* 8 (1901).

———. "Seisho no Hanashi [The Story of the Bible]." *Seisho no kenkyū* 1 (1900).

———. "Sekai no heiwa wa ikanishite kuruka [How Can Peace be Achieved?]." *Seisho no kenkyū* 134 (1911).

———. "Sekai rekishi ni shirushite Nisshi no kankei wo ronzu [Thesis on the Relationship between Japan and China in World History]." *Kokumin shinbun* (1894).

———. "Sensō haishi ron [Abrogation of War]." *Yorozu chōhō* (1903).

———. "Sensō no yamu toki [When War is No More]." *Seisho no kenkyū* 174 (1915).

———. "Shitsubō to kibō [Despair and Hope]." *Seisho no kenkyū* 34 (1903).

———. "Shusenronsha ni yotte inyō seraruru Kirisuto no kotoba [The Words of Christ cited by Warmongers]." *Seisho no kenkyū* 51 (1904).

---. "Sōseiki 1 sho–8 sho [Genesis Chapters 1–8]." *Seisho no kenkyū* 1–31 (1900–1903).

---. "Waga shinkō no hyōhaku [Statement of My Faith]." *Rikugō zasshi* 131 (1891).

---. "Yobuki no kenkyū" [Study of the Book of Job]." *Seisho no kenkyū* 181 (1915).

---. "Yo ga hisenronsha ni narishi riyu [The Reasons I Became a Pacifist]." *Seisho no kenkyū* 56 (1904).

---. "Yo no jyūjishitsutsu aru shakai kairyō jigyō [The Social Reform I Undertake]." *Yorozu chōhō* (1901).

---. "Yudayajin no aikokuka [A Patriotic Song of the Jew]." *Seisho no kenkyū* 11 (1901).

Uemura, Masahisa. "Fukuin dōmei to taikyo dendō [Evangelical Alliance and Mass Evangelism]." *Fukuin shinpō* 234 (1901).

Wataze, Tsuneyoshi. *Ebina Danjō Sensei*. Tokyo: Ryuginsha, 1938.

10

Homeless Voices
Self and Other

DAVID NIXON

I'm glad you're doing it, I'm glad somebody's doing something, that and I'm glad somebody's interested in it, because it will help, it does help as well.
(Caroline)[1]

THE CONTEXTUAL BIBLE STUDY that Susannah Cornwall and I facilitated with a group of homeless people focused on three themes: home and place, judgment and stigmatization, and Jesus. Home was seen, unsurprisingly, as a contested term, as much about people as place: "I haven't found *somewhere*, I've found *someone*."[2] The discussion of jobs that were seen to carry stigma (traffic wardens and politicians, for example) led to an exchange about the way in which homeless people are seen by others. Interpretations of Jesus's character and actions covered a range of ideas from traditional to unexpected. Indeed, the notion of counter-interpretations formed another section, along with an expression of our own concerns about ethical imbalances of power. We concluded that "homeless participants' liminal, insider-outsider relationship to the rest of society is a significant factor in their ability to query and subvert established discourses, providing flashes of imagery which might be deemed prophetic."[3]

1. Nixon, *Stories from the Street*, 102.
2. Cornwall and Nixon, "Readings from the Road," 14.
3. Ibid., 17. This same research data also was used in a chapter in Nixon, *Stories*

This chapter revisits the same material from another perspective in several different ways. First, I wanted to re-emphasise the importance of vernacular contextual readings of "liberation theology with a twist." Second, I was interested in teasing out participants' perceptions of self and perceptions of other, the latter category certainly including ideas about the Otherness of God and/or Jesus. Finally, I wished to juxtapose more of the biblical verses with participants' comments, so that present readers might have more of a sense of the experience of hearing these homeless voices.

In the original (British-Academy-funded) research project, we engaged a group of homeless men and women attending a "soup kitchen" in a small city, where the lead researcher, Susannah Cornwall, was known already to the organizers and to some of the participants. After a meal (some people left at this point) and an icebreaker, we read aloud four passages from Luke: 1) the temptation of Jesus and the start of his public ministry/4:1–24; 2) calling disciples, several healings, and a banquet with outsiders/5:1–32; 3) sharing a meal with Simon and a sinful woman forgiven/7:36–50; and 4) story of the prodigal son and his brother/15:11–32. In a guided discussion, we talked about the passages and heard various reactions; these were audio recorded and transcribed. Thirteen different people took part in the study, and eleven participants agreed to us using their comments. Names and identifying details have been changed, the pseudonyms used in the original article and book chapter have been maintained and, following our agreement with participants on the use of data, no quotations have been used that are not already in the public domain.[4]

The broader context for the study, at least in the UK, was the re-emergence in 2017/18 of housing and homelessness as a public issue. Perhaps this issue has come to the forefront again as a way to mark the ten-year anniversary of the economic crisis of 2008 (often seen as originating in the US housing market), perhaps it results from changes in the payment of welfare benefits, or perhaps it is receiving renewed attention because of the inability of even employed millennials to afford to buy property in much of the UK. Current statistics suggest an increase of 134 percent in rough sleepers since 2011; in addition, the average life expectancy for homeless men is 47 years and for women is 43 years, compared to the national average of 79 and 83 years respectively.[5] These statistics prompt an urgency for a theological response, and have given a critical edge to such an undertaking.

---

from the Street.

4. These interviews were conducted by Susannah Cornwall and David J. Nixon at a soup kitchen in southwest England on June 8, June 15, June 29, and July 6, 2010.

5. Mackenzie, "Vendor Tragedy."

Theoretical Overview

An outline of Contextual Bible Study (CBS) is given in the original article.[6] The emphasis here is to understand CBS as an attempt to knit together theologies of place and space with theologies of liberation, so that it matters where the Bible is read and with whom. In her own exploration of CBS, Lawrence comments:

> . . . it is only in the collision of various contextual readings that liberatory narratives have been constructed; master narratives couched in patriarchy, slavery and racism have been exposed as oppressive by those counter stories from below.[7]

In the context of South Africa and black theology, Moore makes the same point more stridently:

> What is the meaning of the Gospel for those living not with their white bums in the butter but with their black backs to the wall?[8]

In the shift from universal to contextual, Segundo writes about "an epistemological premise for an interpretation of the word of God," and Witvliet refers to the "epistemological break" that allows the inclusion of previously silenced voices.[9]

Vernacular or "everyday theologies" is the phrase used by the Church of England Report, *Faithful Cities: A Call for Celebration, Vision and Justice*.[10] In developing the concept of "faithful capital" based on the notion of social capital, the report also drew on an inductive liberation theology to analyse the experience of those living in English cities at that time. The report drew primarily on the biblical text, as well as doctrines of incarnation and cross, to picture Christ in the city, oppressed, and rejected. These images spoke to and derived from the experiences of those who participated. Elaine Graham, one of the report's commissioners, summarizes this in a later article:

> *Faithful Cities* therefore talks of "theology in the vernacular," adopting the "everyday" or popular speech; of listening to those

---

6. Cornwall and Nixon, "Readings from the Road."
7. Lawrence, *Word in Place*, 126.
8. Moore, *Black Theology*, x.
9. Segundo and Hennelly, *Signs of the Times*, 122; Witvliet, *Place in the Sun*.
10. *Faithful Cities*, #2.63.

at the grass-roots and of paying testimony to the vitality of expressions of faith to be found at the margins.[11]

Graham also examines a "theology in the vernacular" or a "local theology" as one of the methods of theological reflection she considers, adding the location in time to that of culture and geography. She goes as far as saying that the gospel cannot exist independently of a particular embodied expression, citing examples in the documents of the Second Vatican Council (*Lumen Gentium*) and *Christianity Rediscovered*.[12] The question of language also is present when Morisy describes "apt liturgy," which reflects the speech patterns and objects of ordinary living. Davey calls for "a theology prepared to be on the streets, in estate communities, in the slums and favelas" so that others may be brought into the conversation about how the divine is realized in urban areas.[13]

The reason for "liberation theology with a twist" is that developments in postmodern theologies place some of those easy liberation ideas under a more critical spotlight. There is a tendency to homogenize and see unitary groups, expressed normally with the definite article: the poor, the homeless, the disabled, and so on. Not only does this do a disservice to the range of background and experience of poor, homeless, or disabled people, but also it fails to recognize differential discrimination. What Youdell refers to as "constellations" of identity helps us understand why, for example, the experience of gay men differs from that of gay women.[14] A focus on the operation of power (following Foucault) is also the gift of postmodern thinking, so with biblical interpretation in mind Aichele writes:

> . . . to read the Bible in the traditional scholarly manner has all too often meant reading it, whether deliberately or not, in ways that reify and ratify the status quo—providing warrant for the subjugation of women (whether in the church, the academy or society at large), justifying colonialism and enslavement, rationalising homophobia, or otherwise legitimating the power of hegemonic classes of people.[15]

Nevertheless, with these caveats in mind, CBS remains a valuable tool in opening up potentially new meanings of the biblical text.

---

11. Graham, "What Makes a Good City?," 21.

12. Graham, Walton, and Ward, *Theological Reflection*; Donovan, *Christianity Rediscovered*.

13. Morisy *Beyond the Good Samaritan*; Davey, "Better Place," 35.

14. Youdell, "Sex-Gender-Sexuality," 268.

15. Aichele, *Postmodern Bible*, 4.

Repeated readings of the CBS transcripts indicate a complex of movements, circling around self and other/Other, finding a relationship between the biblical passage and personal experience, and then projecting this outward to find external connections, sometimes in the person of Jesus—and all of this in the presence of other participants, where voices may be overlaid, or where one voice attempts to dominate. It is this movement toward self and other/Other placed next to the relevant biblical text that forms the central part of this analysis.

Homeless Voices: Self

The following verbatim comments illustrate some of the ways in which participants relate to and make sense of the stories told by and about Jesus.

"When Jesus came to Nazareth where he'd been brought up he went to the synagogue on the Sabbath day as was his custom . . . [22] *They said, 'Isn't this Joseph's son?'* [23] *He said to them, 'Doubtless you will quote to me this proverb "doctor cure yourself" and you will say "do here also in your home town the things that we've heard you did at Capernaum."'* [24] *And he said, 'Truly I tell you no prophet is accepted in the prophet's home town.'"* Luke 4:16, 22–24*	"I've seen the benefits of staying put. Maybe not in exactly in the same place but in the near vicinity, you know. People get used to you, they know what you're capable of . . . It's like before I left Scotland . . . I could walk into building work, I could walk into landscaping, tree surgeon, chef, anything I wanted, you know, mechanics, anything I wanted. Because I knew people that was involved in that. Coming into a new environment I know nobody involved in anything . . . (Danny)

* All biblical citations are from the New Revised Standard Version (NRSV).

"Then Levi gave a great banquet for Jesus in his house. And there was a large crowd of tax collectors and others sitting at the table with them. [30] The Pharisees and their scribes were complaining to his disciples saying, 'Why do you eat and drink with tax collectors and sinners?' [31] Jesus answered, 'Those who are well have no need of a doctor but those who are sick. I have come to call not the righteous but sinners for repentance.'" Luke 5:29–31	"Homeless people. They're unpopular with people. I used to hear comments by people. I don't know what it is, but I've had some cruel words, I suppose. Vindictiveness." (James) "You do get some horrible . . . and most people I've met, I mean, we've both had full-time jobs, but there's a lot of mental illness out there. And I've met so many people that have been, you know, like upstanding citizens and they've just fallen. It's not their fault, you know. And that's what angers me. But you do get some horrible comments, don't you? You just get, 'Get a job,' 'Scum,' 'Drug addict'—and you just think, 'you don't know me.' Do you know what I mean? . . . yeah, trying to. Exactly. We wouldn't be here if we . . . It's like I say it's not through choice, you know. We don't choose to, you know, 'I think I'll just go and live in a tent for the summer.' It's not . . . it can happen to anyone." (Fiona)
"'A certain creditor had two debtors; one owed five hundred denarii,* and the other fifty. [42] When they could not pay, he cancelled the debts for both of them. Now which of them will love him more?' [43] Simon answered, 'I suppose the one for whom he cancelled the greater debt.' And Jesus* said to him, 'You have judged rightly.'" Luke 7:41–43	"Say if John has borrowed ten grand off you and I borrowed . . . five hundred quid. We're the same. But I was ashamed of asking you for five hundred quid because . . . I thought I can't be asking her that kind of thing. As it is I was supposed to go to see my kids last week and I asked somebody to borrow fifty quid and I were let down . . . I wouldn't ask somebody for something if it wasn't necessary . . . But he didn't mind asking you for ten grand just to fritter on whatever . . . If that person was . . . forced to ask because . . . it was life or death time or whatever, then they'd feel more obliged than what he would just putting it on the horses or whatever kind of thing. (Al)

"Then Jesus* said, 'There was a man who had two sons. ¹² The younger of them said to his father, "Father, give me the share of the property that will belong to me." So, he divided his property between them. ¹³ A few days later the younger son gathered all he had and travelled to a distant country, and there he squandered his property in dissolute living.'" Luke 15:11–13	"Well, a similar thing happened with me and with my brother . . . while he was away, he was fighting in Japan at the time, but when he came back, he thought he should rule the roost kind of thing. And I'd been working all the time he'd been away, even though I was very young, and supporting me mother. And yet when he came back he thought he should take over, which I thought was wrong." (Ray) "I did. On my 18th birthday I inherited £13,500 but it was too easy, and I spent it in two weeks on crap. I haven't got one thing to show for it." (Michael)

These extracts provide examples of participants relating the stories told by and about Jesus to their own lives and particularly to their understandings of self. Reading the biblical passages aloud may have helped group members to picture the scene, and with very little prompting, see their relationship to it, or even see themselves as part of it. Danny contrasts the good things about being at home, where you are known, with the problems of finding casual work as a stranger; several members of the group reflect what it is like being homeless with the knowledge that they are also part of a group which is stigmatized. Al questions the traditional interpretation of the verses about debt and forgiveness based on the notion of shame and his own experience of borrowing in an emergency. The sum of money is less important than the shame attached to having to ask. The story of the prodigal son evokes two reactions from young men who have spent out an inheritance too quickly (one quoted here) and reminds one participant very clearly of his own family, but with the older brother returning home and demanding his place.

Readings and interpretations tended to be literal, but nonetheless there is an immediacy and freshness here that implies a real engagement with the text. Particularly striking are participants' comments about themselves as homeless people, but the robustness and tone of the responses, which partly emerge in the written text, do not at all imply that they see themselves as victims.

Homeless Voices: Other

"And Jesus said, 'Truly I tell you no prophet is accepted in the prophet's home town.'" Luke 4:24	"So, for her to go back home is not happening, do you know? She's never, wherever she's been, it's like, I've met her in a few different places and she's never at home wherever she is. If she went back to where her parents and her family are from, do you know, there is no comfort there. She's looking for that comfort. But she's got never comfort with a companion either because she's learned to distrust people." (Danny)
"Then the devil led Jesus up and showed him in an instant all the kingdoms of the world. ⁶ And the devil said to him, 'To you I will give their glory and all this authority for it has been given over to me and I will give it to anyone I please. ⁷ I you then will worship me, it will all be yours.'" Luke 4:5–7	"You are not going be the same as everybody else, you're going to be above everybody else. And that's what the system basically tells everybody to be." (Niall).
"And a woman in the city, who was a sinner, having learned that he was eating in the Pharisee's house, brought an alabaster jar of ointment. ³⁸ She stood behind him at his feet, weeping, and began to bathe his feet with her tears and to dry them with her hair." Luke 7:37–38	"She was a working lady and she doesn't want to be like that anymore." (Fiona)

"When [the younger son] came to himself he said, 'How many of my father's hired hands have bread enough and to spare, but here I am dying of hunger! [18] I will get up and go to my father, and I will say to him, "Father, I have sinned against heaven and before you; [19] I am no longer worthy to be called your son; treat me like one of your hired hands."' [20] So he set off and went to his father." Luke 15:17–20	"The younger son. I don't think he would gone home in the first place. He would have been too proud, he would have known he'd messed up. And if he had have gone home, the father would have been like, 'What the fuck are you doing here?,' and the older brother would have been, like, 'Really good to see you.' He would have probably been the most accommodating . . . yeah. Well, yeah, otherwise you wouldn't have the story. But the younger son would realize he'd screwed up and would take it upon himself to then correct his mistake, to get back on his feet and then go home, maybe with the same amount as or a little bit more money." (Glenn)

These examples illustrate participants' adeptness at relating the biblical stories and images to situations faced by other people. Danny describes a young woman suffering sexual abuse, which means a return home is made very problematic, and indeed because of a wider distrust, the whole concept of being at home is thrown into doubt. Niall has a clear notion of how to interpret Jesus's temptations in respect to early twenty-first century capitalism, with reference elsewhere to the economic crisis of 2008 and Tony Blair's part in the Iraq War. There is a sense of two women making a sympathetic connection as Fiona uses the phrase "a working lady" to describe the woman who washes Jesus's feet with her hair and tears, imagining that what she really wants is love, comfort, and respect. The group also is not so intimidated by the text that they cannot offer an alternative view; so Glenn reverses the roles of father and older son, making the father the one who might reject the repentant boy and the brother much more welcoming. There is a sense here too of psychological realism or "getting inside the characters' heads." Glenn, for example, thinks it more likely that the younger son would not return until he had something to show for his absence.

Homeless Voices: Other as Jesus/God

"Once while Jesus was standing by the lake of Gennesaret and the crowd was pressing in on him to hear the word of God, ² he saw two boats there at the shore of the lake. The fishermen had gone out of them and were washing their nets. ³ He got into one of the boats, the one belonging to Simon, and asked him to put out a little way from the shore." Luke 5:1–3	"I get a picture that Jesus, because he calls him *Master*, and people ask him to do so many things, but he wants to go away sometimes and withdraw, doesn't he, and just be on his own for a bit. Because you know, everyone is asking him and asking him and asking him. He needs his space as well, doesn't he? That's what I like about it, that's what's so human about him." (Fiona)

"Then Jesus said to Simon, 'Do not be afraid, from now on you will be catching people.'" Luke 5:10	"Well, the fishing, when they're fishing they're fishing for food, aren't they? So, I mean, they could assume that, they could think this guy is a bit of a cannibal . . . like Ripley's Believe It or Not! You know, have you seen them in Blackpool, one of them ones? 'Come and see a man who catches men, not fish!'" (James)

The second reading—fishing with Jesus and for others—proved to be the most fruitful in terms of reflections on the person of Jesus. Fiona's rather traditional picture of Jesus withdrawing for a period of recovery is strong in its humanity, and in her recognition that this is what is attractive. By contrast, James pushes the literalness of the image of "fishing for people" to its limits: food, therefore cannibalism and, by extension, Jesus is like an act in a circus, a freak show. I wonder here how seriously to take James's comment, and how seriously he takes it himself. My impression was not that he was trying to shock or bait the researchers or other group members; rather this was a playful, surreal, imaginative exploration of an odd phrase in a strange story. He almost needed to voice it aloud to see if it worked.

A Theology in the Vernacular?

I should like to re-phrase Moore's question about black theology to read: *What is the meaning of the Gospel for those who sleep not in houses and homes but with the hassle and horror and hardness of the street?* The conversations witnessed here in a group of homeless people responding to four passages from Luke point not only to the value of Contextual Bible Study but also to the beginnings of what might be called a "theology in the vernacular." Clearly, this encompasses the language of the participants—not necessarily polished or conceptual, but still reflective and often fresh and surprising. This genre echoes Milbank, whose desire is to "articulate Christian difference in such a fashion as to make it strange."[16] The style of such contributions jolts readers out of potential lethargy and comfort, reminding them of the newness and originality of the story of Jesus and Jesus's stories. The quality of such input does rely on the ability of the facilitator, not least to allow space for participants to contribute—and space here also means not encouraging, however covertly, the standard pseudo-canonical interpretations. There is sufficient evidence here and elsewhere to suggest that real engagement at all levels, moving personal stories and new insights, can all be expected.

However, these are not worked-up arguments or carefully thought out positions; they are rather what Forrester calls "fragments" of theology, or a theological bricolage, which with other similar explorations move toward something more substantial.[17] In other words, these images and ideas are a snapshot of a particular group in a particular context at a particular time. And for the reasons adduced earlier, they carry some weight as manifesting a desire for theology to move away from the abstract toward the personal and individual—as Gorringe phrases it, away from the "great tradition" toward the "little tradition." It is this tradition that values the insights of the "little people" of the world as having a special place in God's economy.[18]

The ethical imperative that derives from this is less comfortable, especially given the urgency of the statistics around homelessness. If homeless people and others in similar situations are helping us, the comfortably housed and well-paid, to develop and enliven our faith, there is a strong risk of another loss imposed on an already marginal population. Caroline, whose words from another study are quoted at the start of this chapter, underlined that she wanted her story of homelessness told. This was the kind of unspoken moral bargain struck between participant and researcher. Here, this theology in the vernacular needs to work through not only how to value the words and insights of homeless people—how to involve them more in the production of mainstream theology—but also how to ensure that they know just how valuable and valued they are. If not, then the vernacular is

---

16. Milbank, *Theology and Social Theory*, 381.
17. Forrester, "Theology in Fragments."
18. Gorringe, *Theology of the Built Environment*, 9.

just another specimen for the disinterested academic to dissect and discard, a visit to a theological zoo with a new population of inmates.

Bibliography

Aichele, George, ed. *The Postmodern Bible*. New Haven: Yale University Press, 1995.

Cornwall, Susannah, and David Nixon. "Readings from the Road: Contextual Bible Study with a Group of Homeless and Vulnerably-Housed People." *Expository Times* 123/1 (2011) 12–19.

Davey, Andrew P "Better Place: Performing the Urbanisms of Hope." *International Journal of Public Theology* 2/1 (2008) 27–46.

Donovan, Vincent J. *Christianity Rediscovered*. London: SCM, 1982.

Faithful Cities: A Call for Celebration, Vision and Justice. The Report of the Commission of Urban Life and Faith. London: Church House and Methodist Publishing House, 2006.

Forrester, D. B. "Theology in Fragments: Practical Theology and the Challenge of Post-Modernity." In *Globalisation and Difference: Practical Theology in a World Context*, edited by Paul Ballard and Pamela Couture, 129–33. Cardiff: Cardiff Academic, 1999.

Gorringe, T. J. *A Theology of the Built Environment: Justice, Empowerment, Redemption*. Cambridge: Cambridge University Press, 2002.

Graham, Elaine L. "What Makes a Good City? Reflections on Urban Life and Faith." *International Journal of Public Theology* 2/1 (2008) 7–26.

Graham, Elaine L., Heather Walton, and Frances Ward. *Theological Reflection: Methods*. London: SCM, 2005.

Lawrence, Louise J. *The Word in Place: Reading the New Testament in Contemporary Contexts*. London: SCM, 2009.

Mackenzie, Steven. "A Vendor Tragedy: Five Years On, We Remember Ian and Wayne." *The Big Issue* 129 (January 2018) 8–14.

Milbank, John. *Theology and Social Theory: Beyond Secular Reason*. Signposts in Theology. Oxford: Blackwell, 1990.

Moore, Basil, ed. *Black Theology: The South African Voice*. London: Hurst, 1973.

Morisy, Ann. *Beyond the Good Samaritan, Community Ministry and Mission*. London: Mowbray, 1997.

Nixon, David. *Stories from the Street: A Theology of Homelessness*. Farnham, UK: Ashgate, 2013.

Segundo, Juan Luis, and Alfred T. Hennelly. *Signs of the Times: Theological Reflection*. Translated by Robert R. Barr. Maryknoll, NY: Orbis, 1993.

Witvliet, Theo. *A Place in the Sun: Liberation Theology in the Third World*. London: SCM, 1985.

Youdell, Deborah. "Sex-Gender-Sexuality: How Sex, Gender and Sexuality Constellations are Constituted in Secondary Schools." *Gender and Education* 17 (2005) 249–70.

11

Offending, Restoration, and the Law-Abiding Community
Restorative Justice in the New Testament and in the New Zealand Experience

Christopher D. Marshall

From humble, experimental beginnings in the early 1970s, restorative justice has grown into one of the most vigorous and successful justice-reform movements in the world. It has had an impact on criminal-justice policy and practice in many countries, perhaps most notably in New Zealand. But what is "restorative justice"? What has the New Testament got to do with it? And how has it come to occupy an important place in the New Zealand justice system? In my ongoing research, I have sought to bring New Testament teaching on crime and punishment into dialogue with restorative-justice theory and practice. My goal is partly to allow restorative-justice insights to cast new light on early Christian texts that involve justice and punishment, and partly to furnish a biblical and theological basis for Christian involvement in criminal-justice reform in a restorative direction. I have found that bringing a restorative-justice lens to the task of New Testament interpretation has been enormously productive. It has afforded me, for example, a fresh way of thinking about the great Pauline doctrine of justification by faith, the logic of which, I think, makes far more sense when conceptualized within a restorative rather than a retributive-justice frame of reference.

The Character of Restorative Justice

Restorative justice is known by a variety of names and takes many different forms. Some call it "transformative justice"; others "relational justice"; still others prefer "community justice," "collaborative justice," "reparative justice," or simply "real justice." Whatever it is called, advocates of restorative justice insist that it is not simply a minor variation on the current justice system, a way of helping the existing system become more effective or more humane. It is, rather, an *alternative* way of doing justice, a "third way" between the retributive and rehabilitative models that have dominated penal philosophy, a distinctive way of thinking about crime and punishment, a different "paradigm," to use Howard Zehr's term, to conceptualize justice and its demands.[1]

For some, the distinctiveness of the restorative paradigm lies in its processes or practices. Restorative justice is characterized as a particular process in which all those affected by an incident of wrongdoing—victims, offenders, and their supporters—come together, in a safe and controlled environment, with trained facilitators, to *name* the wrong done, to describe how they have been personally *affected* by it, to speak about the material and emotional *needs* it has created, and to resolve together how best to *repair* the harm and prevent recurrence. On this understanding, the heart and genius of restorative justice lies in its use of face-to-face meetings between affected parties, and its concern to empower those present, and especially victims, to deal with the harm in a way that best addresses their needs.

For others, the distinctiveness of restorative justice lies in its *core values or its moral commitments*. Restorative justice is distinguished by the priority it gives to the values of healing and respect, democratic participation, accountability, truth-telling, empathy, mutual care, reconciliation, and peacemaking. Guided by such values, restorative justice seeks to deal with the full moral, spiritual, relational, and emotional consequences of offending, not simply its legal description and punitive implications.

Of course, there is no need to set these "process-" and "values-" conceptions against each other. Both must be held together in order to appreciate the special character of restorative justice, for it is the values that determine the process, and the process that makes visible the values.[2] If restorative justice privileges the values of respect and truth, for example, it is crucially important that the practices followed in a restorative-justice setting exhibit equal respect for all parties and give ample opportunity for everyone present to speak their truth freely. On the other hand, as long as

---

1. Zehr, *Changing Lenses*. See also Zehr, *Little Book*.

2. Strang and Braithwaite rightly insist that a combination of values and process conceptions should be seen as a "normative ideal" for restorative justice, *Restorative Justice*, 13.

these values are honored, there is room for a diversity of processes, a flexibility of practice, and a variety of cultural expressions.[3]

So restorative justice is *both* a distinctive process *and* a distinctive set of values, with each requiring the other. Having said that, what is most important, I believe, to the success and the future of restorative justice, especially as it becomes more professionalized and institutionalized, is that restorative *values* are nurtured and affirmed by its practitioners. Of course, as every ethicist knows, values do not exist in a vacuum; they are held by flesh-and-blood people who belong to particular historical communities. If it is to flourish, then, restorative justice must be anchored in alternative "communities of value," that is, in communities of people who accord the highest importance to the values of mutual care and moral accountability, honesty and compassion, confession, forgiveness, and reconciliation.

One such community in which this ought to be the case is the Christian church. After all, Christians boast a religion that centers on repentance, forgiveness, and new life, convictions that also lie at the heart of restorative justice. One would therefore expect Christians to be vigorous supporters of judicial and penal reform in a restorative direction. Sadly, this has not been the case historically (with some notable exceptions), and it is not always the case today (again with notable exceptions). Perhaps part of the mission of the restorative-justice movement, which is itself now hugely diverse and extensive, is to remind the Christian church of what it supposedly believes and ought to practice more consistently.[4]

Restorative Justice in New Zealand

Restorative justice in New Zealand arose in the 1980s out of dissatisfaction in the Maori community with the way its young people were being treated by the criminal-justice system. The basic social unit in Maori society is the *whanau* or extended family, and Maori had become increasingly troubled at the way the justice system functioned to remove young offenders from any positive influence from their *whanau* by dumping them into prisons or other punitive facilities. After a lengthy consultation process, the government undertook to overhaul the entire juvenile-justice system. At the center of the new system that emerged lay the concept of a "Family Group Conference," which all first-time young offenders are required to attend.

---

3. On this, see Boyack, Bowen, and Marshall, "How Does Restorative Justice," 265–76.

4. For a superb, up-to-date review of restorative justice theory and practice, see Johnstone and van Ness, *Handbook*.

Such conferences bring together the offender with his family and friends, police officers, youth-justice workers and, if in agreement, the victims of the offence to discuss what happened and why, and to determine appropriate sanctions and reparation plans.[5] This new mechanism quickly led to a massive reduction in custodial sentences for juvenile offenders, with some 55 percent of those attending FGCs not going on to reoffend in the future.[6]

Despite such positive outcomes, little interest was shown by government in extending similar provisions into the adult system, even though many community-based groups had already developed models for doing so and were actively employing them. But after a groundswell of popular agitation, in 2001 the government commissioned a four-year long restorative-justice pilot scheme for serious adult offenders in four district courts in the land, with a view to evaluating its potential. But by now a head of steam had built up, and even before the evaluation process had been completed, four major pieces of legislation had been passed by Parliament which served, *inter alia*, to embed restorative practices permanently into our adult justice system. The Sentencing Act 2002, the Parole Act 2002, the Victims' Rights Act 2002, and the Corrections Act 2004 all make explicit provisions for restorative justice and impose a duty on all members of the judicial system to encourage meetings between offenders and their victims, at the victim's discretion.

In some respects, then, New Zealand has made a progressive and principled commitment to the integration of restorative-justice options into its national justice system. But don't be too impressed! For there is still a dark side to our corrections system, which has witnessed, for example, an enormous increase in rates of imprisonment over the past 10 years and a continuing pattern of racial and socio-economic bias, which sees 60 percent of the prison muster drawn from the 20 percent of the population with brown skins. Yet, arguably it is this over-representation of indigenous peoples in criminal-justice statistics that underscores the importance of continuing to cultivate restorative-justice alternatives. For, as many authors have observed, restorative processes resemble the traditional mechanisms used in many indigenous societies for dealing with wrongdoing and restoring well-being.

One recurring feature of such traditional mechanisms is the overt place they give to the *realm of the spirit and spirituality*. Among indigenous peoples, there seems to be an instinctive recognition that doing justice in

---

5. See, for example, Zehr and Macrae, *Little Book*.

6. Fifteen thousand family group conferences were held in NZ in 2005. Research shows that 55 percent of those who attend FGCs do not go on to re-offend. See further Beacroft, "Towards a Restorative Society."

the face of harm is a deeply *spiritual* undertaking.⁷ It is not simply a matter of assessing facts, determining blame, and allocating penalties. It is also about addressing the loss of what Maori call *"mana"* or spiritual dignity caused by the offence, lifting the shame inflicted on the victim and incurred by the offender and shared by their wider kinship groups, repairing the rupture done to the fabric of the community, and restoring order and balance to the spiritual domain, which interconnects all things.

Behind this approach lies a realization, I think, that justice is fundamentally to do with persons and with relationships, and with the right ordering of relationships, both in community and on a broader spiritual plane. For that reason, justice can never be wholly reduced to abstract notions of just deserts or the application of legal rulings, but also must attend to the moral, emotional, and relational integrity of the persons affected, and it is this that gives justice a spiritual dimension.

Such an understanding of justice, it seems to me, is similar to what we find in the biblical text. There too, justice has to do with the right ordering of the universe, with things being as God intends them to be, and with the restoring of harmony or shalom when things go wrong. In my ongoing work, I have traced how this integrated understanding of justice emerges in the New Testament, particularly in Paul's extensive reflections on the saving justice of God disclosed in the life, death, and resurrection of Christ. It is this larger biblical apprehension of God's redeeming justice at work in the world, I believe, that furnished the horizons for early Christian thinking about how justice should operate within the human community. Human justice-making is to be a response to divine justice-making.

This is not to suggest that we can look to the New Testament for a ready-made set of criminal-justice policies that can be transposed directly into our society. That is *not* what the New Testament offers us. What it *does* offer, however, is a vision of what human life and human relationships ought to be like—and *can* be like—in consequence of the revelation of God's redeeming justice in Christ to put the world to rights, and it invites us to imagine forms of social policy that bear witness, however imperfectly, to that reality. The New Testament does not prescribe a set of criminal-justice norms, but it does point us in a direction. And that direction is a decidedly *restorative* direction.

Allow me now to offer one extended illustration of this. Recently, I have been pondering what is perhaps the best known and most-loved of all of Jesus's parables, the Parable of the Prodigal Son (Luke 15:11–32). In

---

7. On the indigenous contribution to restorative justice, see Consedine, *Restorative Justice*, 81–89. See also Church Council, *Satisfying Justice*.

many ways, this parable captures perfectly both the restorative impulse of God's justice and what it might mean for us to enact this kind of justice in the world. I would like to offer a few reflections on this parable, as a kind of case study of restorative justice in action—or at least of *certain aspects* of restorative justice (of course, not everything important about restorative justice can be located in one story).

A New Testament Illustration

The Parable of the Prodigal Son tells the story of a young man who demands his share of the family inheritance in advance, squanders it in wild living in a distant land, then comes to his senses and returns home deeply chastened, where he is joyfully reconciled with his father and profoundly resented by his older brother. The impact of this parable on Christian thought and practice, and on Western cultural formation in general, has been incalculable. It is the parable most frequently represented in European art, and it has furnished the subject matter for numerous works of music, choreography, drama, literature, and philosophy.[8]

At over 390 words, it is also the longest and the most elaborate of Jesus's extant parables. It has a substantial *dramatis personae* and is full of vivid background detail, features which have invited extensive allegorization at the hands of Christian interpreters down through the centuries.[9] Classical allegorism is now rightly repudiated as an interpretive procedure for expounding Jesus's parables. Yet the texture of this parable is so richly evocative that it invites legitimate interpretation at multiple levels and from different perspectives. As Kenneth Bailey, who has spent the best part of his academic career pondering this parable, observes: "Nearly everyone who wrestles seriously with this pericope ends up with a sense of awe at its inexhaustible content."[10]

---

8. Cf. Fitzmyer, *Luke*, 2:1083. Parallels of the story have been uncovered in Babylonian and Canaanite texts, in the Lotus Sutra and in Greek papyri. "Yet none of the parallels or the retellings can measure up to or compare with the moving force of this story put on the lips of Jesus in this Gospel" (1084). The story is rich in intertextual echoes from the Old Testament, with the cycle of the Joseph stories in Gen 37–50 affording several reminiscences. The parable also evokes the host of other biblical stories involving older and younger brothers, in which the younger ones are often rebels and the older ones niggardly and rigid (see Derrett, *Law*, 116–21). For a comprehensive discussion of Greco-Roman parallels, comparisons and analogies, see Holgate, *Prodigality*.

9. See Tissot, "Patristic Allegories."

10. Bailey, *Poet and Peasant*, 158.

The reasons this exquisite parable has exerted such a powerful influence on the Western imagination are not hard to find. In purely *literary terms*, it is a masterpiece of storytelling, lauded by one literary critic as "an absolutely flawless piece of work."[11] The characters are true-to-life, utterly believable at one level, yet shockingly unconventional at another. The plot is realistic and straightforward, moving in a simple linear sequence, yet involving ironic reversals and concluding on a strikingly open-ended note.[12] Hearers are left dangling in suspense, not knowing whether the angry elder son relented of his indignation and joined the family festivities, or whether he stood his ground on a self-evident matter of principle. Listeners are required to finish the story for themselves, and in so doing to ponder deeply where their own sympathies in the whole affair lay.[13]

Another reason the parable has been so highly prized is for its penetrating insights into human psychology. The story deals with universal human themes of freedom and responsibility, leaving and returning, offending and forgiveness, estrangement and reconciliation, shame and honor, generosity and ingratitude, justice, jealousy, and joy. In particular, it explores the anatomy of moral change: what spawns it, what it requires in practice, what it achieves, and how it may sometimes be greeted with sullen resistance on the part of more respectable onlookers.

But beyond its literary qualities and it psychological acuity, the parable has been cherished most of all for its theological value. The parable is unsurpassed in the biblical tradition in its depiction of the love and forgiveness of God. It has frequently been dubbed an *evangelium in Evangelio*, a gospel within the Gospel.[14] Some balk at this label since the parable contains little Christology and no atonement theology, no indication of the objective basis

---

11. Robert Bridges, quoted by A.M. Hunter, *Interpreting*, 61.

12. Crossan terms it a "parable of reversal," noting the ironical reversal involved in the picture of "a vagabond and wastrel son being feted by his father and a dutiful and obedient son left outside in the cold," *In Parables*, 74. Via proposes that its movement from wellbeing through fall and back to wellbeing gives the parable the structure of a comedy, *Parables*, 165–6, 174–75.

13. Kelber (*Oral and the Written Gospel*) describes Jesus' parables as "hermeneutically unfinished stories," 62. For a helpful analysis of how and why the parables are polyvalent or plurisignificant, see Wittig, "Theory," 75–103. Wittig argues that the rhetorical purpose of parables is not to create one particular meaning but to create the conditions under which individual readers or hearers may create and define meaning for themselves, and who through doing so come to a clearer understanding of their expectations and preconceptions. In other words, parables do not have a meaning, but are semantically constructed so as to create a multiplicity of meanings and a variety of significations.

14. For example, Plummer, *St Luke*, 371 (citing Grotius); Farrer, *St Luke*, 254; Lenski, *Interpretation*, 807.

on which sins are forgiven and sinners restored. Yet there is an important sense in which the parable goes beyond or behind any mechanics of atonement to accentuate the fundamental driving force behind the good news of salvation proclaimed by Jesus in the gospel tradition: the yearning love and renewing power of the reign of God.

It is for these three reasons, then, that the Parable of the Prodigal Son has lodged itself so deeply in the Western mind—its superb literary qualities, its emotional intensity and psychological insight, and its theological depth. The parable not only has furnished the subject matter of great literature, art, music, drama and theological reflection, but also it has surfaced in discussions of moral and ethical issues, including, from time to time, discussions of crime and punishment. It is mentioned briefly, for example, in the November 2000 statement by US Council of Catholic bishops on criminal justice, where it is used to encourage acceptance of offenders who are contrite and change their way of life.[15] More drastically, Thomas Shaffer uses the parable to commend what he calls a "jurisprudence of forgiveness," which will inevitably destabilize and subvert "the legal order that serves the politics of coercive power."[16]

Yet there is still more blessing to be wrested from this parable, if we read it from a restorative-justice point of view. There are two reasons I think this is a legitimate thing to do. The first is that the main characters in the story occupy the roles of the three main parties to every incident of criminal wrongdoing—those of offender, victim, and the wider law-abiding community. The younger son is portrayed as a serious and serial offender. The father is the primary victim of his offending, as well as being a cipher for the divine judge of human sin, while the older brother is expressly depicted as a diligent and law-abiding member of the wider household community who is outraged at the judicial leniency extended to his offending sibling.

This is the second reason it is profitable to read the parable from a criminal-justice angle—the older brother's reaction centers directly on the contestable *justice* of his father's actions:

> Listen! For all these years I have been working like a slave for you, and I have never disobeyed your command; yet you have never given me even a young goat so that I might celebrate with my friends. But when this son of yours came back, who has

---

15. United States Council of Catholic Bishops, "Responsibility."
16. Shaffer, "Radical Reformation," 321–40 (quote at 324). For a critique, see Murphy, "Christianity." Murphy thinks Shaffer's analysis of forgiveness is "fundamentally mistaken," and that he is wrong to see forgiveness and punishment as mutually exclusive (267).

devoured your property with prostitutes, you killed the fatted calf for him! (vv. 29–30)[17]

Plainly it is the *idea* of justice that drives this final scene of the narrative, even if the word itself is not used, just as the ideas of repentance, love, forgiveness, and mercy drive earlier scenes in the story, without the actual terminology being employed. The parable reaches its climax, then, in a dispute about whether the father, in restoring his offending son to community, has acted justly or unjustly.

So, for these two reasons it is appropriate to read the parable in a jurisprudential light. This is not to suggest, of course, that the parable provides normative guidelines for how we should go about constructing a Christian ethics of justice. It is, after all, just a parable, not a moral or legal treatise. But it is precisely as a parable that it is relevant to Christian reflection on justice issues. For the leading purpose of Jesus's parables is to break open existing frames of reference, to challenge or overturn taken-for-granted ways of understanding the world and its notions of justice, and to offer a different way of conceiving reality, a way that is conditioned by the inbreaking of God's eschatological kingdom of justice and peace. Surely if there is anything that makes Christian ethics distinctively "Christian," it is its attempt to formulate ethical truth in a way that is informed not only by the downward drag of normal human behavior but also by the radical possibilities for human transformation opened up by the manifestation of God's saving power in Jesus Christ.

What insights, then, does this parable have to offer that may be germane to Christian reflection on criminal justice? Perhaps the first thing it offers is an emphasis on the *relational impact of human offending*. It underscores the restorative-justice principle that what that makes criminal behavior so harmful is that it violates *relationships*, the relationships that bind us together in community and that constitute our very humanity.

Offending as Relational Rupture

The parable involves three main characters. Interpreters have long debated which of the three is the intended focus of attention, with persuasive arguments being available for each.[18] But to insist on one central protagonist is

---

17. All biblical citations are from the New Revised Standard Version (NRSV).

18. The parable's traditional title (which is found as a marginal note in sixteenth-century English Bibles and derived from the Vulgate's *De filio prodigo*; the traditional German title is *Der verlorene Sohn*) suggests that the story is principally about the prodigal son. There are still scholars who defend this view. According to Via, it is the

to miss the important narrative clue given at the very outset in the story. The parable's pointed introduction—"a certain man had two sons" (v. 11)—functions to direct attention away from any one individual performer and on to the *relational* bonds between them. The parable is all about interpersonal relationships. Even in the description of the prodigal's degraded lifestyle in the second scene of the story (vv. 13-19), fully half the text is occupied by a soliloquy in which the estranged boy reflects on his relationship with "my father" (vv. 17-19). The older son too is detached from his father, though in a different way, and speaks contemptuously of his brother as "this so-called son of yours" (v. 30). It is the dysfunctional, triangular relationship between family members that is the real subject matter of the story, with the spotlight falling on what is needed to bring about reconciliation.

The first part of the parable is devoted to the offending of the younger son (who is probably around 17 years of age, since he is old enough to leave home but is not yet married).[19] It is ironic that, whereas the boy himself comes to interpret his behavior in the gravest of terms as a case of "sinning against heaven and against his father" (vv. 18, 21), modern readers often struggle to see wherein his sin actually lay. True, he was a spendthrift who squandered his possessions in an intemperate lifestyle.[20] That was cer-

---

younger son's actions that drive the entire plot and "the main interest of the story as a whole is seen to be the redemption of the prodigal" (*Parables*, 164, cf. 167; also cf. Jülicher, *Gleichnisreden Jesu*, 420). Also cf. Green, *Luke*, 578. More commonly, however, it is the *father* who is viewed as the main character, since he is mentioned in most scenes of the story (the word πατήρ occurs almost a dozen times in the text), and the account concludes with his words of celebration. Both structurally and didactically, it is the father's actions and values that are most critical to the meaning of the story (so Holgate, *Prodigality*, 53-54, 67). Jeremias (*Parables*, 128) and Fitzmyer (*Luke*, 1084) think the account would therefore be better titled, "the parable of the forgiving father" or "the parable of the father's love." Yet a case also can be made for seeing the *elder son* as the focal point of the narrative (e.g., D. Buzy, cited by Bovon, "Parable," 49), especially since it is his sullen response to his father's forgiveness of his brother that gives the parable its sharply polemical edge (15:1-3, cf. Hunter, *Parables*, 61, who describes the parable as "polemic at its finest"). The story reaches its climax in the only two-way conversation that occurs in the parable, in which the father replies to the stinging criticisms of his first-born son.

Some scholars suggest that both sons have equal attention. Manson calls it "the parable of the two sons" (*Sayings*, 284), Fuchs "the parable of the prodigal sons" (*Studies*, 60-62), and Beasley-Murray the "parable of the two lost sons" (*Jesus*, 113).

19. So Jeremias, *Parables*, 129; Marshall, *Luke*, 607. Derrett notes that if the boy had been married, his sinfulness in leaving and behaving as he did would have been magnified out of all proportion (*Law*, 106 n.1).

20. According to Via, the younger son's sin was his wasteful mode of life. "He became an unworthy son through the wanton irresponsibility with which he dissipated his father's living, which had been freely given to him" (*Parables*, 170). Derrett cites Deut 20:19 as an indication that a waste of assets was considered sinful (*Law*, 111 n.1),

tainly a foolish thing to do, but to modern sensibilities it scarcely counts as dreadfully *sinful* (except perhaps to tight-fisted capitalists!), and it is not clear why the boy's wastefulness of his own possessions constituted a grievous sin against his father. In any event, living like there's no tomorrow is fairly typical teenage behavior, and at least this lad ends up getting a job to support himself—which actually makes him quite a good role model for contemporary youth!

Later in the story, his older brother accuses him of having spent his money on prostitutes (v. 30). This does perhaps up the sin-stakes a little further.[21] But the narrative description of the prodigal's behavior does *not* include him visiting brothels, and the accusation that he did so could simply be prurient speculation on the part of his uptight brother.[22] As for his initial act of asking for his slice of the inheritance in advance, several commentators can see no objection whatsoever in this request, and some even consider it a commendable sign of industriousness on the part of an ambitious young entrepreneur.[23]

---

but the context is far removed from our parable. For an impressive demonstration of how prodigality was generally considered to be a vice in Greco-Roman moral thought, see Holgate, *Prodigality*, 90–130. It is still doubtful, to my mind, that this is the sole locus of the boy's sin.

21. Both Jewish and Hellenistic moralists disapproved of prostitution (see Holgate, *Prodigality*, 144 nn. 50, 51 for references). But Derrett suggests that given the boy was unmarried, it is unlikely that contemporary Jews would have viewed his consorting with harlots to be as sinful as disobeying parents (*Law*, 112).

22. As Caird observes, the older son "had no more evidence for the harlots than his imagination and bad temper could supply" (*Saint Luke*, 183). So too Johnson (*Luke*, 238) who notes the similarity with accusations against Jesus for keeping bad company (Luke 7:34, 39); cf. Holgate, *Prodigality*, 144 n.49. The decadence of his lifestyle is conveyed by the adverb ἀσώτως (literally "unsaving" or "non-salutary") in v. 13, which suggests wildness and wastefulness, but not necessarily sexual license, though that was seen as a closely related vice (see Foerster "Ἀσώτως"; Plummer, *St Luke*, 373; Manson, *Sayings*, 287). Bailey (*Poet and Peasant*, 170) notes that neither the Greek text nor the various oriental versions indicate that the boy was guilty of sexual immorality, although Holgate notes the common link between covetousness and immorality in Jewish, Greco-Roman, and early Christian literature, *Prodigality*, 142–8. This is the only occurrence of the adverb ἀσώτως in the New Testament, although the noun ἀσωτία occurs in Eph 5:18, Titus 1:6, 1 Peter 4:4; cf. Prov 28:7 and 2 Macc 6:4.

23. According to Harvey, "The younger son's request was quite normal: the main part of the property would in any case go to his elder brother, and he could expect to do better by turning his share into cash and setting himself up in business among the Jews of the Dispersion in some foreign city, than by trying to live on a small-holding in the over-populated farmland of Palestine." (*New English Bible Companion*, 266). So too Linnemann, who thinks "emigration was the order of the day" at the time, and that Palestinian hearers would not have imagined it to be an act of rebellion, (*Parables*, 75). Gnilka also sees the boy's actions as "certainly legally proper." He views him as minor

But what appears to modern Western readers to be relatively innocent teenage behavior would have surely struck Jesus's first-century Palestinian audience, and many indigenous hearers today, as utterly repugnant and wholly blameworthy. They would have been appalled at the younger son's actions, which breached prevailing social and legal custom in a succession of ways, so that his offending actually compounds as the story advances. The boy's behavior is not merely irregular; it is offensive to such a severe degree that he almost certainly stood in breach of the fifth commandment to honor one's parents,[24] and could well have been viewed as a candidate for the category of the "stubborn and rebellious son" in Deut 21:21 who is adjudged worthy of execution.

His rebellion comprised of a thoroughgoing rejection of his relational connection with, and responsibilities toward, his father, his brother, and his local community. He exhibited profound disrespect for his father in demanding a share of his estate in advance of his death.[25] He then proceeded to act as though his father were *already* dead, and with no further moral or legal claims upon him, by cashing up his inheritance and emigrating, leaving no provision behind him for the support of his father in his declining years. He also abandoned his brother and spurned his village community,[26] which would have been horrified at how glibly he discarded his family patrimony

---

who, on reaching the age of responsibility, leaves home to establish an independent household (*Jesus of Nazareth*, 99). See also Via, *Parables*, 170.

24. Exodus 20:12; Lev 19:3; Deut 6:13; Prov 3:9. The biblical command to honor one's parents was not merely an ethical rule but an economic responsibility. Nor was this responsibility in any way diminished by any discourtesy, unfairness or favoritism on the part of the parent. See Derrett, *Law*, 109–11.

25. This is disputed, since some exegetes see nothing irregular in this detail (Linnemann, *Parables*, 74–75; Bovon "Parable," 53). But according to Bailey, it is totally unprecedented for a Jewish son to insist on a division by his father while he is still alive; "to my knowledge, in all of Middle Eastern literature (aside from this parable), from ancient times to the present, there is no case of any son, older or younger, asking for his inheritance from a father who is still in good health" (*Poet and Peasant*, 164). Such a request would have been considered to be "an extraordinary insult to the father" since it was tantamount to wishing the father dead (163). It is one thing for an old man to anticipate the property implications of his own eventual death; it is quite another for a child to let his father know how eagerly he awaits his demise because of the financial benefits that might accrue! One who honors his father does not covet his father's property; one who covets his father's property dishonors his father (cf. Derrett, *Law*, 110). So too Young, *Jesus*, 145–46; Green, *Luke*, 580–81.

26. Through his selfishness, the younger son had knowingly deprived his own father of his rightful due. He also had disrepected his older brother, for his actions precluded any chance of "dwelling together" with him in unity on the family estate after their father's passing, which was the biblical ideal (Ps 133:1).

(ὁ νεώτερος υἱὸς ἀπεδήμησεν εἰς χώραν μακρὰν καὶ ἐκεῖ διεσκόρπισεν τὴν οὐσίαν αὐτοῦ, v. 13).

Once resident in foreign territory, he shows total disdain for the value of what he had received, scattering it to the four winds in hedonistic excess.[27] But then he experiences what Farrer terms "retributive anguish," as the intrinsic consequences of his actions come home to roost.[28] He is reduced to rags. But instead of returning home or seeking help from fellow Jews, he glues (ἐκολλήθη, v. 15) himself to a Gentile patron, being prepared even to wallow among unclean animals, and to accept the religious compromises and ritual pollution that came from doing so.[29] He is portrayed, in other words, as a serious and repeat offender, who has so thoroughly covered himself in sin and shame that no place remained for him in regular society. He is utterly unclean, in every sense of the word.

But then something shifts in him, and his long journey back to right standing in society commences—which brings us to a second lesson the parable teaches about the nature of justice: *the obligation it confers on offenders*.

The Obligation on Offenders

According to restorative-justice thinking, the first crucial step in restoration is for an offender to accept responsibility for his or her actions and freely undertake to make amends. The theological word for this is "repentance," and in both Jewish and Christian understandings, repentance is neither cheap nor painless. It requires contrition, confession, correction of life, and

---

27. His disregard for the intrinsic value of what his father had freely given him is captured in the verb "squander" (διασκορπίζω), which suggests throwing something into the air to be scattered by the wind. He threw away all that his father had entrusted to him. His reckless waste of possessions was in itself reprehensible according to the moral and cultural codes of the time. But what made his prodigality especially despicable was that it thwarted his obligations to his father. Any inkling that he might have reserved some of his money to send home to his father in his dotage is now gone forever.

28. Farrer, *St Luke*, 257. Early pagan, Jewish, and Christian moralists differed on whether famines could be attributed to providence (as a form of divine punishment) or were simply an inescapable part of life (Holgate, *Prodigality* 148–53). Here the retribution is not the famine, but the boy's inability to cope with it due to his choices.

29. Jeremias points out, working for a foreigner in constant contact with unclean animals would have precluded him from observing the Sabbath and would have "practically forced [him] to renounce the regular practice of his religion" (Jeremias, *Parables*, 129; Linnemann, *Parables*, 76; also Forbes, "Repentance," 216.) Holgate notes that a number of Greco-Roman moralists also saw pigs as a symbol of moral degradation, *Prodigality*, 157.

atonement.³⁰ Almost all these elements are present in the description of the prodigal's transformation in the middle section of the parable (vv. 17-21).

On the edge of starvation, the boy's downward spiral finally bottoms out. In a lengthy soliloquy, he compares his own destitution with the circumstances of his father's hired hands, who not only have bread to eat in place of pigswill, but also have it in abundance (v. 17). He therefore hatches a plan to return home and throw himself on his father's mercy. Although his decision could be construed as self-centered expediency, there are several textual clues that genuine contrition is being signaled.

To begin with, the entire soliloquy is predicated on the boy having "come to himself" (εἰς ἑαυτὸν δὲ ἐλθών, v. 17), an idiom found in several languages to denote a thoroughgoing change of heart.³¹ While this change of heart is triggered by hunger pangs, what the boy *actually* laments is the forfeited relationship with his father. It is the recollection of his father, and of his father's generosity, as much as his own physical need, that evokes remorse.³² Twice in the monologue he uses the phrase "my father" (v. 17), and later he addresses him with the vocative "father." The verbal confession he rehearses in his head also centers on his father—on the wrong he has done to him and on his unworthiness to be called his son (v. 19). When the boy finally puts his plan into action, the parable touchingly says that "he went to his father"—not to his house or to his village, but to "his very own father" (τὸν πατέρα ἑαυτοῦ, v. 20).³³ The boy's contrition, in other words,

---

30. In rabbinic Judaism, "Repentance entails confession of the sin before God and formulation of a resolve not to commit the same sin again. In the case of a sin against another person, repentance is possible only after full restitution or correction of the wrong deed has been made and a pardon from the other person has been obtained. In Scripture's system, repentance is followed by an expiatory offering. After the destruction of the temple and the cessation of the sacrificial cult, the rabbis found a replacement for this offering in charitable deeds. Rabbinic authorities viewed repentance and charity together as a person's greatest advocates before God (B. Shabbat 32a), Neusner and Green, *Dictionary*, 524. See also Moore, *Judaism*, II:507-45.

31. Jeremias (*Parables*, 130) and Marshall (*Luke*, 609) deem it to be a Semitic phrase for repentance, while Manson notes that the same construction is found in Greek, Latin, and Hebrew (*Sayings*. 288). Holgate reviews its usage in the Greco-Roman philosophical tradition and concludes that Luke's readers would have understood its usage here to designate either a sudden or gradual conversion resulting from some form of moral self-analysis stimulated by adverse circumstances (*Prodigality*, 198-206).

32. Bornkamm, *Jesus* 126-27; Via, *Parables*, 168. Holgate writes, "The father functions as a moral example to both his sons. It is the recollection of his behavior as an employer which encourages the younger son to return home," (*Prodigality*, 174, cf. 172).

33. Plummer sees ἑαυτοῦ as emphatic (*Luke*, 375), although other exegetes doubt this. In any event, Bailey is wrong to propose that he plans "to go back to his village but not to his home. Planning to work as a servant and live in the village, he intends to save himself" (*Poet and Peasant*, 205-6), since the text quite clearly has him returning to his

was evinced by, and focused upon, a realization of the relational damage his behavior had caused—something restorative justice also seeks to place center-stage in its response to crime.

Contrition, if it is genuine, will lead to confession and apology, which, as restorative justice strongly emphasizes, plays an important role in vindicating the victim and promoting healing. What is remarkable about the boy's confession or apology in the parable is the way is crystallizes so succinctly what it means for an offender to assume moral responsibility.

The first thing it requires is an *acceptance of moral blame:* "Father," the boy admits, "I have sinned." No mitigation is offered. No attempt is made to minimize his offending as a mistake, or as a lapse of judgment. He accepts full culpability. He also accepts, secondly, that *his actions have injured others:* "Father, I have sinned *against heaven and against you.*"[34] The phrase "against heaven" underscores the fact that when a wrong is committed against another human being, a *spiritual* as well as a material harm is done: a sin is committed against God.[35] This is not just because God's law is broken (in this case the fifth commandment), but because, in the biblical tradition, God so identifies with innocent victims that when they are abused, God too is personally offended. To injure another person *is* to sin against God; they are not two separate offences.[36]

A third element in the boy's confession is recognition that his wrongful actions have *changed the nature of his relationship with the victim.* Once he stood in a relation of filial duty and respect. But having betrayed his father's trust, he concedes that: "I am no longer worthy to be called your son; treat me like one of your hired hands." Their relationship has changed. Interestingly, a number of scholars detect in this request to become a hired hand an intention by the boy to earn sufficient income from his labors to pay *restitution* to his father, something prescribed in biblical law and strongly emphasized in restorative-justice theory.[37]

---

father, not his village.

34. The two prepositions probably both have the same force of "against," with "before you" being a verbal variation of "against."

35. Cf. Num 5:6–7; Lev 6:1–7; Exod 10:16; Psa 32:5; 51:4.

36 Luke's two other uses of the verb ἁμαρτάνω also focus on offences against other human beings or institutions (Luke 17:3–4; Acts 25:8). The thought, then, is that the prodigal's offence against his father has a religious dimension, not that an offence against God has a social dimension (Holgate *Prodigality,* 208–10).

37. So Bailey, *Poet and Peasant,* 177–80; Derrett, *Law,* 110–16; Young, *Jesus,* 150; cf. Forbes, "Repentance," 219; Holgate, *Prodigality,* 193–97.

As much as I would like to believe otherwise, this reading seems improbable to me.[38] I doubt that the penitent boy is thinking of monetary restitution at this point; rather he is openly acknowledging that his offending has destroyed the relationship of mutuality and trust he once enjoyed with his victim, and he has no right to expect otherwise. Simple justice dictates that he relinquish his status as a son and adopt a more formal, distant relationship. The most he can hope for is that enough mercy will prevail that he is not banished forever from contact with his father but can find a place on his estate as a μίσθιος, a humble day-laborer.

But what the boy now encounters transcends all recognizable notions of justice or mercy. For what he experiences is the *justice of grace*, a justice in which his father restores him fully to the position of sonship he had so casually renounced.

The Challenge to Forgiveness

The father's role in the parable is double-sided, since at the story-level he represents the human victim of wrongdoing, while at the discourse-level he signifies the divine judge to whom sinners are accountable. But at both levels, the father's response to his returning son is nothing short of breathtaking. It is so out of character for a wronged Palestinian *paterfamilias* to act as he does, and so unjustified by the circumstances of the offence, that he will later be accused of behaving unjustly (vv. 29-30). But according to the father's scale of values, no injustice is entailed by allowing new life to trump former death, or recovery of the lost to cancel out their alienation and separation (v. 32, cf. v. 24). To favor restorative forgiveness over punitive exclusion permits a *better* justice to emerge, a justice that is satisfied,

---

38. Day laborers (μίσθιοι) were the lowest of the three classes of workers and were not considered part of the extended household (cf. Bock, *Luke,* 1313). Bovon notes that the condition of a μίσθιος was not necessarily the most miserable, but was the most despised ("Parable," 55). In asking to be ranked among them the prodigal was, rather than presuming on his legal status of sonship, expressing his readiness to accept the most menial role available in order to be near to his father again and to render him service. It was not just a means to some other laudable end, as Bailey (*Poet and Peasant*) implies, for the boy does not ask to be *made* a hired servant but to be made *as* a hired servant (ποίησόν με ὡς ἕνα τῶν μισθίων σου, v. 19). That is, to be treated as someone of equivalent status and position as a hired hand. It is also worth noting that day laborers usually lived at a mere subsistence level, since casual work was not always available. It is hard to believe that the prodigal, who himself had wasted away as a laborer on a pig farm, imagined that by becoming a μίσθιος of his father's he could generate enough surplus income to repay all his debts, even if, to be fair, he does note that his father's μίσθιοι "have bread enough and to spare" (v. 17). If restitution is in view, it is a restitution of service more than a restitution of money.

not by retribution, but by the reconciliation of aggrieved parties and the reintegration of the offender into healthy community.

There are several features of the father's behavior that are hugely instructive in this connection, such as the respect he shows for his son's moral agency and autonomy; the way he refuses, over many years,[39] to give up hope for his son's ultimate return; and the profound empathy he feels for the boy's derelict condition, as he is "filled with compassion" at the mere sight of him. But what is most striking is the father's utter *self-abnegation in the interests of reconciliation*. He does not stand on ceremony, which would dictate that he wait at a dignified distance until his son approached and bowed before him. Instead, the parable says, "he ran and put his arms around him and kissed him" (v. 20).

There is an interesting parallel in the apocryphal book of Tobit, in which Tobias's mother is waiting for her son's return, looking intently down the road on which he would travel. When she sees him, she tells her blind husband of the boy's approach, then runs to embrace him with tears of joy (11:5–15). In our story, it is the *father* who runs down the road to greet the traveler.[40] As commentators invariably point out, it was extremely undignified for a great man or the head of the household to hike up his robes, expose his legs, and run in public. No ordinary Oriental father would humiliate himself in this way. But the father of the prodigal sprints toward his lost boy and falls on his neck, kissing him repeatedly (κατεφίλησεν αὐτόν, v. 20).[41]

Yet for all his eagerness to welcome him, he still makes space for *moral accountability*, as the boy confesses his wrongdoing and his unworthiness to be counted as a son (v. 21). But no sooner is the confession out than the father quickly (ταχὺ, v. 22) sets about restoring the sinner to a place of honor and dignity in the local community.[42] He orders the slaves to fetch clothing

---

39. We are not told how long his younger son had been gone from home, but it could have been for several years. The older brother's complaint about having worked as a slave for "all these years" (τοσαῦτα ἔτη, v. 29) could refer to the period following the division of the inheritance, which would underscore his virtue of continuing to work like a slave though now the legal proprietor of the estate. In any event, the boy clearly saw his own departure as permanent. His selling up lock, stock, and barrel indicated that he had no intention of ever returning, so that for all intents and purposes his father considered him as good as dead (vv. 24, 32).

40. Via suggests that, from a Jungian point of view, this could be sees as "an instance of the 'the forgotten feminine in the Gospels,' an occasion of eros, the principle of relatedness, expressed by a man," "Prodigal Son," 21–43 (quote at 37).

41. The compound κατεφίλησεν αὐτόν either means "kissed him fervently or affectionately" (Plummer *Luke*, 375; cf. 211) or, more likely, "kissed him again and again" (Bailey, *Poet and Peasant*, 182).

42. The boy's actual confession (v. 21) is an abbreviated version of the one he rehearses ahead of time (v. 18), although some MSS render them identical. Most

and dress the boy, just as they would the master of the house, an action that would serve to re-establish an appropriate relationship between the servants and the restored son, as well as to draw attention to the moral transformation in the boy that had made this restoration possible (new garments are a common biblical metaphor for a change of moral character).

In the ancient world, clothing was a crucial indicator of social standing. The impoverished majority of the population wore short, unbleached tunics of poor quality, and slaves went about barefooted. Those of higher rank wore richly colored garments, with the length, fullness, quality of fabric, and degree of ornamentation being visible markers of social location.[43] The prodigal expected to be relegated to class of manual laborer. Instead he is clothed in his father's finest robe, his calloused feet are shod with sandals, and a signet ring of authority is placed upon his finger. It is impossible to miss the message here: the father does not merely supply the boy's bare physical necessities, he confers upon him the full dignity of sonship, notwithstanding his past offences.

The father caps off these restorative gestures by *going public* and throwing a lavish party. Forgiveness may be a personal transaction between individuals, but it has significant social or political ramifications. Feasts were not a common occurrence in village life, and few could afford to eat meat. So, when the father assembles musicians and dancers (v. 25) and orders the slaughtering of the fatted calf, he is announcing to the whole village society the great esteem his son now enjoyed.[44] The young lad had disowned his father by selling up and leaving forever. But the father refused to disown his son. For all his spiteful actions, when he came back, his father embraced him as "this son of mine" (v. 24, cf. 30). He refused to exclude him from belonging and would not to let others exclude him either (v. 32). All this

---

commentators suggest that the father interrupted his son's apology because he was so eager to forgive. Some commentators however think that the boy revised his confession once he experienced his father's reception, realizing that his offer to serve as a hired hand would do nothing to heal the broken relationship.

43. Resseguie, *Spiritual Landscape*, 89–100.

44. There are several indications that the feast was for the whole village. A fattened calf would feed hundreds, and the presence of an orchestra and dancers at the ceremony (συμφωνίας καὶ χορῶν, v. 25) points to a community-wide gathering. Holgate suggests that the shift from the second-person plural imperative θύσατε to the first-person plural of φαγόντες εὐφρανθῶμεν (v. 23) shifts the reader's attention from the slaves to the celebration of the whole community (*Prodigality*, 178 n.52). The wider context of Luke 15 also points in this direction. Just as the shepherd who found his lost sheep and the woman who found the lost coin summoned their friends and neighbors to rejoice with them at their good fortune (vv. 6, 9), so the father invites his friends and relations in the village to "celebrate and rejoice" (v. 32) with him.

stands in stark contrast to what usually prevails with ex-offenders today. A former prison inmate in New Zealand recently made this comment:

> In the eyes of society, I am condemned forever to the underclass, to sub-citizenship. I will carry the stigma of a convicted career criminal for the rest of my life—never to be accepted by society as a person worthy of any meaningful degree of respect or dignity. The weight of shame and guilt is too great a burden to carry with me forever. Slowly the depth of my punishment became clear to me and I realized that certain elements of my punishment and stigmatization will follow me back into society and remain in place as long as I live. There will be no forgiveness.[45]

Not so with the prodigal son. Of course, the sheer magnanimity of the father's response to him in the parable is intended to depict the nature of God, a God who, as Ps 103 observes, is also "filled with compassion" at the distressed state of his children and delights to heal, forgive, and restore them. But it is clear from the placement of the parable in Luke 15 that Jesus is doing more than speaking about God in the abstract. He is using God as a viable model for how his hearers are to treat those who victimize them, and those whom the community judges to be treacherous offenders worthy only of exclusion, or even execution. They are to emulate the restoring love of God for them—which means inviting their repentance, receiving their confession without objection, and restoring them to full participation in community. To do this is to imitate the love of God; but it is equally to imitate the *justice* of God, for, in the final scene of the parable, the father must defend himself from harsh accusations of having perpetrated an injustice.

The Challenge to the Law-Abiding Community

The response of the older brother brings a note of stark realism to the episode. He is portrayed as a hard-working and law-abiding individual who recoils in disgust at the sheer unfairness of showing grace to a serious and repeat offender.[46] "All these years I have slaved for you," he complains, "and

---

45. Cahill, "Victimisation," 2.

46. Many commentators take this reference to law keeping as an unmistakable allusion to the Pharisees (cf. Luke 18:11–12), who criticized Jesus for his intimacy with sinners and outcasts (15:1–3). Plummer says his claim to have never transgressed a single commandment is a clear indication that the elder brother represents "the blind self-complacency of the Pharisee, trusting in his scrupulous observance of the letter of the Law . . . rather than the Jewish nation as a whole, which could hardly be supposed to make so demonstrably false a claim" (Plummer, *Luke*, 378). Scott, however, denies that the identification of the elder brother with the Pharisees is adequate to understanding

I have never disobeyed your command (οὐδέποτε ἐντολήν σου παρῆλθον). Yet you have never given me even a young goat so that I might celebrate with my friends" (v. 29). As one commentator observes, the older boy is clearly "jealous, and regards his father as utterly weak in his treatment of the prodigal; but what specially moves him is *the injustice of it all*. His own unflagging service and propriety have never been recognized in any way, while the spendthrift has only to show himself in order to receive a handsome recognition."[47]

It is not hard to feel sympathy for the older son. On the face of it, he has a valid complaint. But the instant rage (ὠργίσθη, v. 28)[48] he experiences at news of his father's actions suggests that behind the facade of a conscientious, law-abiding individual who wants simple justice to prevail lies a range of attitudes and attributes that blind him to justness of his father's actions. These attitudes and attributes are present in all of us to some degree. But they are magnified out of all proportion in the psyche of *collective* society, which so often greets efforts to rehabilitate or reintegrate offenders with indignation and disgust.

One such attribute in the older son is his tendency toward *haughty judgmentalism*. The parable makes it clear that he is "in the field" when his brother returns and has no idea why music and dancing are emanating from the house (v. 25). When told by a servant of his brother's return and his father's joy, he explodes in anger. He does not inquire into his brother's moral condition or attitude; he does not contemplate the possibility of him having changed. He simply recalls his past identity as someone who had defrauded his father and consorted with prostitutes, someone beyond the pale who ought to be excluded from communal gatherings, not fed the fatted calf!

Such exclusionary judgmentalism is paired with an *exaggerated sense of his own virtue*. "For all these years I have slaved for you, and I have never disobeyed your command" (v. 29). There are two tragic ironies here. The first is that he views himself as a *slave* when in fact he is the first-born son. His work on the estate is performed from a cold sense of duty, not out of loving devotion to his father.[49] His virtue is only skin deep, an exterior con-

---

the parable (Scott, "Prodigal Son," 45–73).

47. Plummer, *Luke*, 378 (emphasis added). Holgate agrees: "The son's complaint focuses on the injustice of his father's treatment of him" (*Prodigality*, 185).

48. Holgate observes that "Not only does he lack his father's liberal virtues of compassion and generosity, he also lacks his prodigal brother's attractive qualities of initiative, decisiveness, readiness to act, generosity, self-assessment, repentance, and desire for good relationships with his family and friends . . . The parable ascribes to him only one active emotion, anger" (*Prodigality*, 228).

49. Not all exegetes agree on this. Bovon observes that δουλεύω does not necessarily

formity to rules and regulations rather than an inner fidelity to what is true. The second irony is that at the very point of appealing to his unstinting obedience to his father, he actually is standing in defiance of him. Custom required that he should be present at family banquets, where he would serve as joint-host with the master. Yet despite his father's repeated pleading (παρεκάλει, v. 28), he refuses to join the feast, launching instead a bitter and insulting tirade against his father's integrity.[50]

It is because the older son exaggerates his own virtue and magnifies his brother's vice that he fails to see their common kinship. He considers himself to be more virtuous than his brother, but in fact he resembles him in many ways. Both boys are fully prepared to dishonor their father for personal ends, one by selling off his livelihood, the other by refusing to join him as village host. Both are preoccupied with money and pleasure.[51] The younger son asks for his inheritance so that he can live the high life now; the older son complains his father has never given him anything to allow him to celebrate with his friends.[52] Both sons are lost to their father. But whereas the prodigal comes to acknowledge his sin and confess his unworthiness, his older brother cannot see beyond his own meticulous morality.

Structures of exclusion and stigmatization—of which the fantastically misnamed "Corrections System" is the most hideous and violent example—are invariably sustained by such refusal on the part of the "righteous" to admit their common, flawed humanity with those they deem to be intractable sinners and criminals. Because "we" are not like "them," they can be treated in ways that we would never consider appropriate for ourselves.

A third attribute that precludes the law-abiding son from accepting his father's actions is his *acute sense of victimhood*. On the one hand, he

---

designate a servile attitude but may describe filial piety, "Parable," 60. So too Linnemann, *Parables*, 79; Julicher, *Gleichnisreden* II:355. However, the force of "slaving" does fit the characterization of the older son well.

50. Custom required that he should be present at family banquets, where he would serve as joint-host with his father, greeting important guests and ensuring that they were properly provided for. His continued refusal to participate in the feast (οὐκ ἤθελεν εἰσελθεῖν), despite his father's repeated pleading (παρεκάλει), together with the bitter tirade he launches at his father ('Ἰδοὺ /, "listen to me!") would have counted culturally as "profoundly deep public insults against the father" (Bailey, *Poet and Peasant*, 196). Most oriental patriarchs would have reacted with violent fury to such insolence. But this father goes out (ἐξελθὼν) from the banquet to seek out his son in order to reason with him and reassure him (v. 28). For the second time in the story, the father publicly lays aside his own dignity and pride to move benevolently toward his disobedient children, and for the second time he expresses no recrimination at the wrongs they have inflicted on him.

51. Holgate, *Prodigality* 153–54.

52. Note the parallel between δός μοι in v. 12 and ἐμοὶ οὐδέποτε ἔδωκας in v. 29.

encourages his father to dwell on his own victimization at the hands of his villainous offspring, who "devoured *your* property with prostitutes" (v. 30). On the other hand, he casts himself as a victim of his father's cold-hearted neglect in the past and blatant favoritism in the present: "You have never given me even a young goat so that I might celebrate with my friends; but when this son of yours came back . . . you killed the fatted calf for him!" (vv. 29–30). His sense of victimhood runs so deep that he assumes the celebration thrown for his brother somehow detracts from his own superior virtue or devalues his standing in his father's eyes.

This entrenched sense of personal victimhood explains yet another attribute observable in the older brother—his instinctive *distrust of judicial leniency*. He is angered by his father's apparent indulgence of his brother's wrongdoing and contests the justice of throwing a party for someone so unworthy. The father repudiates this charge of injustice in two ways. First, he rejects the implication that love is a *limited commodity*, that love shown to the delinquent son must first be deducted from the love available for his other son. "Dear child (τέκνον)," the father says with great tenderness, "you are always with me, and all that is mine is yours" (v. 31).[53] He loses nothing from the love displayed to his brother; his standing is in no way diminished. If anything, it is *enhanced*, for the offender's return to right relationship only serves to vindicate his brother's choice to remain always with his father. True virtue should need no other reward than to see vice freely relinquished by the penitent.

The second defense the father offers is more significant. The older son assumed that the banquet in full-swing was simply a celebration of his brother's homecoming, for all he had been told by a passing servant was that "your brother has come" (v. 27). Such merriment he judged to be totally unjustified, given his brother's disgraceful behavior. But for the father, the feast is a celebration, not of his son's return, but of his *transformation*. "We had (ἔδει) to celebrate and rejoice," he explains, "*because* (ὅτι) this brother of yours was dead and has come to life; he was lost and has been found" (v. 32).[54] As David Holgate observes:

---

53. Τέκνον is more intimate than υἱός, and the addition of the grammatically unnecessary pronoun σύ underscores the intimacy intended.

54. The impersonal verb "must" (ἔδει) lacks a stated subject. Most modern translations supply a plural subject ("we must celebrate") but given the predominance of singular pronouns in the immediate context it is equally possible to read singular subject ("you must celebrate"). The law-abiding brother has a bound duty to celebrate, along with the father, because *his* brother has been transformed and restored. It is also important to note that δεῖ is one of Luke's favorite ways of speaking of divine necessity (e.g., 2:49; 4:43; 9:22; 11:42; 15:7,10; etc.).

The father's words express a recognition that the son has gone through a life-changing experience. What is celebrated is not the son's restoration to his former state (which was one of moral death leading to physical death, v. 17c), but a celebration of his new state, which is one of moral life. There is also the implication that part of this recovery of life is a recovery of relationship.[55]

That is why no injustice has occurred. What made the feast entirely just and equitable was that it marked the prodigal's renewed commitment to right living, in parallel with his brother's alleged commitment. The essential "justice" of restorative justice, in other words, depends on *factoring in repentance*. For genuine repentance induces a transformation of identity, so that the contrite sinner becomes, in a real sense, a different person than he was before, and therefore a candidate, not merely for an amnesty, but for a new beginning. No injustice transpires when the lost are recovered, when the dead are restored to life, when sinners are forgiven. Justice is vindicated in such transformations, for things are returned to how they ought to be, and righteousness prevails once more.

Conclusion

The father's final words to his older son contain a double challenge. Would he recognize the forgiven offender as "this brother of yours," someone to whom he owes fraternal love as "flesh of his flesh," as a fellow, flawed human being, or would he continue to despise him as an outcast? And would he join the celebration of his restoration and eat his share of the fatted calf, or would he keep his distance on the strict principle of retributive justice?

One last point needs making, though it is rarely noticed. For the older son to relinquish his objections and join in the feast of forgiveness would be costly for him, for it could require of him a willingness to share his goods with his penniless brother. The prodigal had lost everything through his reckless living, and while his father could confer on him the symbols of forgiveness and familial esteem, he could not give him any more land, for what remained had already been gifted to his other son (vv. 12, 31). The prodigal's inheritance had gone for good—*unless* his upright brother should graciously choose to give him a stake in what he possessed.

This, then, is the final challenge of this parable of restorative justice to the law-abiding community—a challenge to contemplate, not only the restoration and reintegration of offenders, as an outworking of the Christian

---

55. Holgate, *Prodigality*, 167.

discipline of forgiveness, but also to display toward them an open-handed hospitality, a readiness to share with them what the parable calls our "living" (βίον) and "substance" (οὐσία), so that they may again participate as equals in the social and economic life of society. Nothing less than this qualifies, finally, as restorative justice. Nothing less accords with the graciousness of God, who "makes his sun to rise on the evil and on the good and sends rain on the righteous and on the unrighteous" (Matt 5:45). If all this leaves us shaking our heads and thinking "it couldn't possibly work," then perhaps we have yet to "hear" this parable in all its offensive glory.

Bibliography

Bailey, Kenneth E. *Poet and Peasant and through Peasant Eyes: A Literary-Cultural Approach to the Parables in Luke*. Grand Rapids: Eerdmans, 1983.
Beacroft, A. "Towards a Restorative Society." http://www.vuw.ac.nz/ips/completed-activities/Becroft.Paper%20October%202005.pdf.
Beasley-Murray, George R. *Jesus and the Kingdom of God*. Grand Rapids: Eerdmans, 1986.
Bock, Darrell L. *Luke Vol 2: 9:51–24:53. Baker Exegetical Commentary of the New Testament*. Grand Rapids: Baker, 1997.
Bornkamm, Günther. *Jesus of Nazareth*. Translated by Irene and Fraser McLuckey with James M. Robinson. New York: Harper, 1960.
Bovon, François. "The Parable of the Prodigal Son, Luke 15:11–32, First Reading." In *Exegesis: Problems of Method and Exercises in Reading (Genesis 22 and Luke 15)*, edited by François Bovon and Grégoire Rouiller, 43–74. Translated by Donald G. Miller. Pittsburgh Theological Monograph Series 21. Pittsburgh: Pickwick Publications, 1978.
Boyack, James, H. Bowen, and C. Marshall, "How Does Restorative Justice Ensure Good Practice? A Values-Based Approach." In *Critical Issues in Restorative Justice*, edited by Howard Zehr, and Barb Toews, 265–76. Monsey, NY: Criminal Justice, 2004.
Cahill, Dan. "Victimisation." *Movement for Alternatives to Prison* 98 (2006) 2–3.
Caird, G. B. *Saint Luke*. Pelican Commentaries. Harmondsworth, UK: Penguin, 1963.
Church Council on Justice and Corrections. *Satisfying Justice: A Compendium on Initiatives, Programs and Legislative Measures*. Ottawa: Church Council on Justice and Corrections, 1996.
Consedine, Jim. *Restorative Justice: Healing the Effects of Crime*. Lyttelton, New Zealand: Ploughshares, 1995.
Crossan, John Dominic. *In Parables: The Challenge of the Historical Jesus*. 1985. Reprint, Sonoma, CA: Polebridge, 1992.
Derrett, J. Duncan M. *Law in the New Testament*. 1970. Reprint, Eugene, OR: Wipf & Stock, 2005.
Farrer, F. W. *The Gospel according to St Luke*. Cambridge Bible for Schools and Colleges. Cambridge: Cambridge University Press, 1905.
Fitzmyer, Joseph A. *The Gospel according to Luke*. 2 vols. Anchor Bible 28, 28A. Garden City, NY: Doubleday, 1981, 1985.

Foerster, Werner. "Ἀσώτως, ἀσωτία" in *Theological Dictionary of the New Testament*, edited by Gerhard Kittel, 1:506–7. Translated by Geoffrey W. Bromley. Grand Rapids: Eerdmans, 1964.

Forbes, Greg. "Repentance and Conflict in the Parable of the Lost Son (Luke 15:11–32)." *Journal of the Evangelical Theological Society* 42.2 (1999) 211–29.

Fuchs, Ernst. *Studies of the Historical Jesus*. Translated by Andrew Scobie. Studies in Biblical Theology 1/ London: SCM, 1964.

Gnilka, Joachim. *Jesus of Nazareth: Message and History*. Translated by Siegfried S. Schatzmann. Peabody, MA: Hendrickson, 1997.

Green, Joel B. *The Gospel of Luke*, New International Commentary on the New Testament. Grand Rapids: Eerdmans, 1997.

Green, Joel B., and Max Turner. *Jesus of Nazareth Lord and Christ: Essays on the Historical Jesus and New Testament Christology*. Grand Rapids: Eerdmans, 1994.

Harvey, A. E. *The New English Bible Companion to the New Testament*. Cambridge: Cambridge University Press, and Oxford: Oxford University Press, 1970.

Holgate, David A. *Prodigality, Liberality and Meanness: The Prodigal Son in Greco-Roman Perspective*. Journal for the Study of the New Testament Supplements 187. Sheffield: Sheffield Academic, 1999.

Hunter, A. M. *Interpreting the Parables*. London: SCM, 1964.

Jeremias, Joachim. *The Parables of Jesus*. Rev. ed. Translated by S. H. Hooke. London: SCM, 1972.

Johnson, Luke Timothy. *The Gospel of Luke*. Sacra Pagina 3. Collegeville, MN: Glazier, 1991.

Johnstone, Gerry, and Daniel van Ness, eds. *Handbook on Restorative Justice*. Cullompton, UK: Willan, 2007.

Jülicher, A. von. *Die Gleichnisreden Jesu*. Vol. 2, *Auslegung Der Gleichnisreden der Drei Ersten Evanelien*. Freiburg: Mohr/Siebeck, 1899.

Kelber, Werner H. *The Oral and the Written Gospel: The Hermeneutics of Speaking and Writing in the Synoptic Tradition: Mark, Paul, and Q*. Philadelphia: Fortress, 1983.

Lenski, R. H. C. *The Interpretation of St Luke's Gospel*. Minneapolis: Augsburg, 1946.

Linnemann, Eta. *Parables of Jesus: Introduction and Exposition*. Translated by John Sturdy. London: SPCK, 1966.

Manson, T. W. *The Sayings of Jesus: As Recorded in the Gospels according to St. Matthew and St. Luke*. London: SCM, 1957.

Marshall, Christopher D. *Compassionate Justice: An Interdisciplinary Dialogue with Two Gospel Parables on Law, Crime, and Restorative Justice*. Eugene, OR: Cascade/Wipf and Stock, 2012.

Marshall, I. Howard. *The Gospel of Luke: A Commentary on the Greek Text*. New International Greek Testament Commentary. Grand Rapids: Eerdmans, 1978.

Moore, George Foot. *Judaism in the First Centuries of the Christian Era: The Age of the Tannaim*. 3 vols. 1927–1930. Reprint. Peabody, MA: Hendrickson, 1960.

Murphy, Jeffrie G. "Christianity and Criminal Punishment." *Punishment and Society* 5 (2003) 261–77.

Neusner, Jacob, and William Scott Green, eds. *Dictionary of Judaism in the Biblical Period: 450 B.C.E. to 600 C.E.* 2 vols. 1996. Reprint, Peabody, MA: Hendrickson, 1999.

Plummer, Alfred. *The Gospel According to St Luke*, ICC. Edinburgh: T. & T. Clark, 1901.

Resseguie, James L. *Spiritual Landscape: Images of the Spiritual Life in the Gospel of Luke.* Peabody, MA: Hendrickson, 2004.

Scott, Bernard Brandon. "The Prodigal Son: A Structuralist Interpretation." *Semeia* 9 (1977) 45–73.

Shaffer, Thomas L. "The Radical Reformation and the Jurisprudence of Forgiveness." In *Christian Perspectives on Legal Thought*, edited by Robert F. Chochran Jr., et al., 321–40. New Haven: Yale University Press, 2001.

Strang, Heather, and John Braithwaite, eds. *Restorative Justice and Civil Society.* Cambridge: Cambridge University Press, 2001.

Tissot, Yves. "Patristic Allegories of the Lukan Parable of the Two Sons." In *Exegesis: Problems of Method and Exercises in Reading*, edited by François Bovon and Grégoire Rouiller, 362–409. Translated by Donald G. Miller. Pittsburgh Theological Monograph Series 21. Pittsburgh: Pickwick, 1978.

United States Council of Catholic Bishops. "Responsibility, Rehabilitation, and Restoration: A Catholic Perspective on Crime and Criminal Justice." *A Statement of the Catholic Bishops of the United States* (November 15, 2000). http://www/nccbuscc.org/sdwp/criminal.htm.

Via, Dan O., Jr. *The Parables: Their Literary and Existential Dimension.* 1967. Reprint, Eugene, OR: Wipf & Stock, 2007.

———. "The Prodigal Son: A Jungian Reading." *Semeia* 9 (1977) 21–43.

Wittig, Susan. "A Theory of Multiple Meanings." *Semeia* 9 (1977) 75–103.

Young, Brad H. *Jesus the Jewish Theologian.* Peabody, MA: Hendrickson, 1995.

Zehr, Howard. *Changing Lenses: A New Focus for Crime and Justice.* 3rd ed. Scottdale, PA: Herald, 2005.

———. *The Little Book of Restorative Justice.* Intercourse, PA: Good Books, 2002.

Zehr, Howard, and Alan Macrae. *The Little Book on Family Group Conferences: New Zealand Style.* Intercourse, PA: Good Books, 2003.

Zehr, Howard, and Barb Toews. *Critical Issues in Restorative Justice.* Monsey, NY: Criminal Justice Press, 2004.

12

"Discover Your Destiny"
Sensation, Time, and Bible Reading among Nigerian Pentecostals

JESSE DAVIE-KESSLER

"**B**E THE WORD OF GOD!" The pastor's injunction to the congregation caught me short. Since beginning my fieldwork with Pentecostal Christians in the southwest Nigerian town of Ile-Ife in 2010, I had heard about reading the Word, preaching the Word, and doing the Word. Now, I was told to *be* the Word. I gathered that the Word, "*oro*" in Yoruba, was related to the Bible. However, my non-Christian upbringing in the United States did not prepare me to know the significance of this term to members of my institutional base, the Redeemed Christian Church of God (RCCG).[1]

Redeemers, as RCCG members called themselves, approached the Word as the sensual event of interpreting Scripture. This method of interpretation was tied to Pentecostalism's central feature: felt experiences of the Holy Spirit, which believers worldwide define as God's earthly manifestation.[2] Redeemers' biblical interpretation, or hermeneutics, involved the feeling of feathery pages, the visual encounter with lines of black text, and finally, the bodily reception of the Holy Spirit in visions, voices, and ineffable feelings. Participant-observation, interviews, and media analysis

---

1. I capitalize "Word" to help readers distinguish the Nigerian Pentecostal concept from other denotations of "word." In their own writing, Redeemers sometimes capitalized "Word" and sometimes did not.

2. Social scientists often use the term "charismatic" interchangeably with "Pentecostal" to denote born-again Christian churches claiming that "God, acting through the Holy Spirit ... play[s] a direct, active role in everyday life." (Pew, "Global Christianity"). For the sake of simplicity, I use the term "Pentecostal" to refer to non-mainline churches in which Nigerian congregants claimed to experience the Holy Spirit, even if they identified more closely with the labels "holiness," "Spirit-filled," "charismatic," or simply—like many Redeemers—"Christian."

reveal that Redeemers used scriptural interpretations to relate their lived experiences to a God-given personal destiny.

The Redeemed Christian Church of God—and by implication, Redeemers' hermeneutic approach—was widespread in Ile-Ife. By the time I left Nigeria following 12 months of research, Ile-Ife held more than thirty RCCG branches. The RCCG's popularity in Ile-Ife reflected its popularity in the rest of Nigeria: the RCCG is the largest Pentecostal church in a country that attracts the world's second largest Pentecostal population.[3] RCCG church buildings speckled Ile-Ife's streets, competing for members with mosques, mainline churches,[4] and a variety of Pentecostal churches in the town's thriving "religious marketplace."[5] Roughly 50 percent of Ile-Ife's population identified as Christian, 50 percent identified as Muslim, and a small number identified as African "traditionalists" who worshipped Yoruba spirits and gods. Christians included Baptists, Methodists, Anglicans, and Catholics, but these groups were far outnumbered by various Pentecostal congregations affiliated with a church rather than a denomination. There were more than twenty Pentecostal ministries in the town, including the pervasive RCCG.

Just as striking as the number of RCCG churches in Ile-Ife was the ubiquity of English and Yoruba scriptural passages. The sight and sound of biblical language seemed to surround me on the street: church speakers blasted sermons citing Scripture; Bible passages decorated buses and roadside posters; strangers sang verses fashioned into hymns. Central to Redeemers' oral, visual, and bodily engagement with biblical language was the practice of reading. "One week without the Bible makes one weak!" went a familiar adage. In church and at home, Redeemers bent over English- and Yoruba-language Bibles in efforts to "be the Word of God." As they read, Redeemers said, they merged the felt presence of the Holy Spirit with scriptural text, forming through the Word a bodily relationship to the divine. Readers sensed God's presence in Scripture and also made sense of that Spirit-filled text with respect to their day-to-day lives. Put differently, Redeemers used ongoing experience as both the means and the context for interpreting scriptural messages.

Redeemers interpreted these messages as signs of individualized destiny. "If you want to discover your destiny, then search the Bible," a Sunday school teacher exhorted students. Pentecostal Redeemers' approach to

---

3. Pew, "Global Christianity."

4. I use the term "mainline" to describe traditional Protestant denominations. In Ile-Ife, Baptist and Methodist churches predominated among the mainline churches.

5. Hackett, "Appropriation," 1.

Scripture aligns with that of non-Pentecostal evangelicals who frame the Bible literally, "as a constitutive text, establishing the cosmos, the social world, its customs, and its laws."[6] From Redeemers' evangelical standpoint, Scripture both reflected and encompassed a God-given history for all humankind.[7] But while Redeemers approached Scripture as a singular history, they also accepted that many biblical histories existed—one for every born-again reader.

My research on Redeemers' embodied interpretations of destiny frames Christian sensation in temporal terms. In the context of Pentecostalism's global expansion in recent decades, anthropologists have taken into consideration the tactile and affective dimensions of Pentecostal and also non-Pentecostal Christians' lives.[8] Research focused on Christian sensation uses a spatial frame to understand subjects' physical interactions with the social and material world. However, when Redeemers sensed material Scripture, they also operated within a temporal frame, constructing a distinct relationship to the future. Simon Coleman's notion of "historiopraxy" is relevant here; Redeemers "attempt[ed] to 'perform' the relationship between the past and the present (and the future) in a productive sense, not only through narrative accounts but also through embodied forms of worship and mission."[9] With other evangelicals, Redeemers hoped to rupture the Christian present with a non-Christian past,[10] but their sensual hermeneutics emphasized the continuity between an always-unfolding embodied present and a God-given near future.

Redeemers' scriptural interpretations of time exemplified what Birgit Meyer calls a "sensational form," a culturally and historically specific style of contacting the divine learned through religious practice.[11] Meyer's concept contributes to efforts by anthropologists of Christianity, and religion more broadly, to develop "more adequate conceptual tools for grasping religious bodily sensations ... [and] to avoid the pitfall of taking the feeling body for

---

6. Crapanzano, *Serving the Word*, 38. See also Harding, *Jerry Falwell*, 2000.

7. The similarity between Pentecostal and evangelical hermeneutics is unsurprising given the historical continuity of these religious forms; Pentecostalism emerged as a distinctive evangelical strand in the early twentieth century. I follow Joel Robbins in approaching evangelical Christianity as a religious form distinguished by an emphasis on conversion—the conscious choice to become "born again" and to convince others to become "born again"—and by a view of the Bible "as a text possessed of the highest religious authority." See Robbins, "Globalization," 120.

8. See Keane, *Christian Moderns*; Meyer; "Complete Break"; and Engelke, *Problem of Presence*.

9. Coleman, "Historiopraxy," 434.

10. See Meyer, "Complete Break"; and Robbins, "Continuity Thinking."

11. Meyer, *Aesthetic Formations*.

granted as a prime phenomenological reality."[12] I complement these efforts methodologically, tracking the steps through which Redeemers' hermeneutic learning process culminated in the sensational form of Bible reading. The temporality *of* reading as well as the temporality *produced by* reading constituted Redeemers' hermeneutics. My approach draws on the work of Tanya Luhrmann, who explores how converts train over time to think, feel, and act as Christians.[13] When Redeemers were new church members, they learned to conceptualize Scripture as doctrine applicable to all readers. Slowly, with the sedimentation of reading experience, Redeemers developed a Bible-reading aesthetic in which they embodied God, the revealer of destiny. With each stage, Redeemers generated cosmological conceptions and a sense of Christian subjectivity. Redeemers' sociocultural worlds, then, followed from and also helped to advance Redeemers' hermeneutic learning process.

After situating Redeemers' Word in intersecting regional and global Christian histories, I explore how new church members' verbal and bodily techniques shaped their approach to the Bible and a process of Christian world- and self-making. Ultimately, Redeemers' Bible reading, world, and self came together in the Word, a triadic combination of text, God, and reader. While reading the Word, Redeemers uncovered, narrated, and felt what they saw as personal, Bible-based destinies.

The RCCG and the Word

I carried out the bulk of my fieldwork in a heterogeneous RCCG branch in Ile-Ife, Nigeria that I call Grace Sanctuary.[14] The 500–member branch attracted university faculty and also tradespeople. Grace Sanctuary's congregation also varied in age, gender, and religious background. Congregation members were moderately proficient in English and Yoruba, and most people spoke Yoruba at home. Apart from a small group of "elders" over the age of sixty, though, people owned and read English Bibles. Most members used the King James Version, but the New King James Version, the New International Version, and the Good News Translation also appeared on Sunday mornings.

Redeemers used Bibles translated into a Western language, but their hermeneutic method was grounded in a unique regional history. I trace this

12. Klaver and van de Kamp, "Embodied Temporalities," 421.
13. Lurhmann, "Metakinesis."
14. I use pseudonyms for RCCG churches and members throughout to protect the anonymity of my informants.

history from the encounter between Yoruba people and the Church Missionary Society (CMS), a powerful social, political, and economic force in southwest Nigeria in the mid and late 1800s.[15] Bible reading among Yoruba Christians has followed a distinctive trend over the last 150 years: believers have sometimes treated the Bible as a guide to salvation in the next world, and sometimes as a direct, "this-worldly" portal to the supernatural. Intriguingly, contemporary Redeemers spoke about the English-language Bible as both a means of immediate contact with God and a means of self-improvement for salvation.

Local converts to Christianity in the colonial era saw the "Book people," as they called British and indigenous CMS missionaries, as conveyers of *awo*, spiritual secrets.[16] Some new converts viewed Bible reading as a replacement for Yoruba divination tools like the kola nut, which diviners used to invoke Yoruba spirits. Meanwhile, European missionaries urged against such a perspective. In one exchange, a local political leader affiliated with the CMS told a diviner, "[O]ur book never changes. Open the same place a hundred times and you will find the same thing."[17] This view found traction among independent Christian churches in the early twentieth century. These "Aladura" churches—literally, "one who prays"—taught local members to read the Bible as "ethically oriented, fixed, [and] universal in application."[18] Meanwhile, the churches sought direct connection with God by means of other than Bible reading, including spoken prayer and the recording of dreams and visions.[19]

Aladura churches' view of Scripture as a fixed body of knowledge extended into postcolonial Nigeria's dynamic born-again Christian movement. A universalized approach to Scripture is evident in the history of the RCCG, founded in 1952 when Josiah Akindayomi broke away from a prominent Aladura church. Seeking to distance himself from certain "traditional" Yoruba practices in his church like incense burning and dealings with ancestral spirits, Akindayomi aligned himself with a Pentecostal movement influenced by American and British missionaries.[20] In the 1970s, the RCCG incorporated a "holiness" doctrine centered on moral purity,

---

15. The CMS intervened in local political structures, established Anglican churches and mission schools, and taught converts to read, sometimes in English and sometimes in a newly developed Yoruba language. See Ajayi, *Christian Missions*.

16. Peel, *Religious Encounter*, 223.

17. Ibid., 225.

18. Ibid.

19. Probst, "Letter and Spirit."

20. Ukah, *Paradigm*.

anti-materialism, and the promises of salvation.[21] Like Aladura practitioners, people in holiness churches treated Scripture as a set of static truths that were equally applicable to all readers. Through Bible reading, they sought to learn about and avoid sinful and "disobedient" actions such as drinking, smoking, fornication, or stealing.[22]

In the 1980s and 1990s, popular Pentecostal churches developed a "this-worldly" focus on prosperity in which they continued to read the Bible but renewed a commitment to prayer. This period of Nigerian Pentecostalism was shaped by a "new wave" of Pentecostalism that began in the United States and spread to Latin America and Africa.[23] Nigerian prosperity churches used prayer as a means to immediate spiritual and material blessings, contextualizing earlier Aladura churches' use of prayer in a period of financial crisis and political upheaval. A popular moniker for the prosperity doctrine in Nigeria—"name it and take it"—highlights the prosperity gospel's emphasis on the spoken word as a tool of self-care, and even self-preservation.

The RCCG certainly stressed professional success and upward mobility while I was in Nigeria from 2010 to 2011. Pastors pushed members to pray and read the Bible in English because, as Pastor Ajayi told the congregation, "English is the language of the future." English is Nigeria's national language, and many middle- and upper-class jobs in southwest Nigeria require an intermediary knowledge of the language. So did active participation in Grace Sanctuary, which conducted most of its nightly and weekend meetings in English.

English was entangled for contemporary Pentecostal Redeemers with promises of spiritual and economic power. Following the RCCG's founder, Redeemers tended to associate Yoruba language and cultural practices with a sinful past, and English with a blessing-filled future. Contemporary Redeemers' desire to "break with the past" echoes the narratives of evangelicals in a number of other contexts.[24] But even as Redeemers attempted to achieve well-being by breaking with local "tradition," they worried about creating a public image that was too closely associated with the materialistic greed of "this world." One pastor confided to me that he did not want people to see the RCCG's version of Christianity as a "get-rich-quick plan." Like other Nigerian Pentecostal churches, the RCCG struggled to situate itself in

21. Ojo, "Contextual Significance."
22. Marshall, *Political Spiritualities*, 71.
23. Marshall-Fratani, *Babel and Pentecost* and Gifford, Rose, and Brouwer, *Exporting*.
24. Meyer, "Complete Break"; see also Robbins, "Continuity Thinking"; and Engelke, "Discontinuity."

a "middle ground" on a "spectrum of 'holiness-prosperity.'"[25] Perhaps for this reason, during my fieldwork I noticed that pastors actively promoted Bible reading as a way to become more obedient to God. Pastors at Grace Sanctuary lectured the congregation to come to weekly Bible studies, where they would learn about "righteous," or holy, habits.

However, Bible study in Grace Sanctuary only partially resembled a holiness approach to Scripture. Redeemers read the Bible to inhabit righteousness, but their biblical hermeneutics combined an accent on holiness with an accent on divine contact. The latter dimension of Bible reading signaled continuity with the "this-worldly" dimension of the RCCG's history. Redeemers' two uses of Scripture—one as a guide for moral purity and the other as a conduit for the divine—manifested in readers' learning experiences.

Learning the Word: A Temporal Map

When Grace Sanctuary members saw me around Ile-Ife, they sometimes encouraged my fieldwork: "*Eku ise*, Sister Jesse": "greetings on your work." At least, I *thought* my acquaintances were recognizing my research. One month after I began my fieldwork, I realized that people referred to Bible reading as *ise*, work. I had recently arrived at Grace Sanctuary, and people categorized me as a convert who was assimilating to the RCCG's method of Bible reading. I don't blame them, since as a non-Christian agnostic, I was indeed experiencing the Bible as a beginner. Redeemers saw the Word as "a complex process, and above all else, a learning process," and one that took time and work for a new reader to understand.[26]

Unlike me, most newcomers to Grace Sanctuary had previously converted to Christianity in other Pentecostal churches along the "holiness-prosperity" spectrum. Others had previously attended mainline churches and Islamic mosques.[27] Regardless of religious background or expertise, the RCCG treated all newcomers as if they were "making a fresh start in Christ." People who joined the church were required to undergo a "second baptism" by a pastor from the RCCG even if they had already been baptized.

New church members were exposed to the RCCG's doctrine and practices in required classes for new members. The weekly, one-hour classes typically attracted about fifteen teenagers and adults. They began with Bible

---

25. Marshall, *Political Spiritualities*, 85.
26. Lurhmann, "Metakinesis," 519.
27. Everyone I met in Grace Sanctuary was affiliated with some sort of religious institution before joining RCCG.

reading, prayer, and sung praise, and then a teacher lectured on spiritual disciplines like prayer and fasting or social mores like courtship etiquette and marriage. In contrast to these other topics, the Word was rarely explicitly addressed. Instead, new members encountered the Word in a piece-meal fashion, in Bible study sessions, church services, all-night vigils, evangelizing missions, and conversations with long-time Redeemers. During roughly the first year of membership, Redeemers moved from a "beginning" stage of Bible reading to an "advanced" stage of Bible reading.[28]

At first, I did not view scriptural interpretation in terms of learning stages. Instead, I saw a puzzling disjuncture between two ways of reading. In one interpretive stance, the Bible was a story of God's "plan" for humanity, and central to this plan was a set of rules for righteous living. In the second interpretive stance, the Bible was a medium for felt contact with God and his revelations of personal destiny. The generic and sensual interpretive stances initially seemed antithetical to one another, but I found they facilitated, respectively, Redeemers' beginning and advanced interpretive stages.[29] The mastery of these frames in sequential order helped members create a cosmology, a set of categories that encompassed the universe as a whole.[30] Learning the Word was at once a form of subject-making and a form of world-making, the construction of collective and also personal narratives of the past, present, and future.

Beginners, or new converts, learned to speak about the Bible and God as cosmological entities distinct from lived experience. In so doing, beginning readers expressed into existence the difference between the Christian person, on one hand, and God and the Bible, on the other hand. Church leaders in Grace Sanctuary told newcomers that Scripture was unchanging and fundamentally true; the Bible taught a fixed set of actions and attitudes that together constituted a "Christian lifestyle," habits that accorded with holiness doctrine and ruptured with the unholy practices of a non-Christian past. Leaders found guidance on Christian lifestyle primarily in the New Testament. New Redeemers learned, among other lessons, to give

---

28. For clarity, I draw on Michael Lambek's adoption of Alfred Schutz's notion of the "ideal type" to distinguish groups of people with different levels of religious knowledge. While the religious practitioners Lambek studies on the island of Mayotte are fixed in categories of expertise like "expert" and "man on the path," I show that any Redeemers could move from a "beginning" level of hermeneutics to an "advanced" stage. See Lambek, *Knowledge and Practice*, 3; and Schutz, *Collected Papers*.

29. One might frame Redeemers' stances as part of a two-stage "textual ideology," a term coined by James Bielo to denote the socially negotiated and always embodied assumptions guiding the reading of particular texts. See Bielo, "Textual Ideology," 160–61.

30. Tambiah, *Culture*.

freely (Luke 6:38),[31] tell the truth (Prov 12:19), cleanse the mind of sinful thoughts, (Rom 12:2) and, above all, love and follow God (2 Cor 10:5; Gal 1:10).

New RCCG members were taught that a Bible-based Christian lifestyle would eventually purify them of sin and make them worthy of feeling the Holy Spirit while they read the Bible. Mr. Udoh, a Sunday-school teacher, shared a personal experience of purification during a Sunday-school class themed "Sanctified Vessels": "Before, I wouldn't tell my wife if I had money. But now, I find it difficult to lie . . . We are talking about spiritual heart surgery here! Through God, all bad things in our body are flushed out." Later in the class, Mr. Udoh spoke about the effect of a pure heart on the Holy Spirit's presence in a believer. "Are you obedient to God's will? That is the litmus test." Once Redeemers were cleansed of "bad things" through a Christian lifestyle, new church members learned, they would have the potential to experience the Holy Spirit through Scripture.

Advanced readers claimed to do just that. They continued to read the Bible as a guide to life as a Christian, naming the difference between two dyads: Christians and God, and Christians and Scripture. At the same time, after at least one year of RCCG membership, Redeemers fused the human "spirit" with the Holy Spirit during the act of reading. Redeemers explained that the spirit, a point of connection with God, was held within the heart or soul, a moral space of decision-making in the born-again Christian. The spirit shaped the heart's direction of the body, the third and outermost part of the person. Speaking about the layers of the Christian person, Pastor Ajayi told Grace Sanctuary's congregation, "The man has a body, a soul, and a spirit. The real you is within—the spirit. He is the inward man." Advanced readers aimed to embody God in a (masculinized) human spirit so that their daily desires and actions would adhere ever more fully to the holy lifestyle outlined in the Bible.

Advanced readers' inward, spiritual encounters with the Word were not constrained to the act of reading. Redeemers used the term "*oro*" to denote speech as well as text, and my acquaintances reported hearing and also seeing biblical verses and spoken revelations from God. In this respect, they mirrored the experiences of Pentecostal groups elsewhere. For instance, Simon Coleman writes of a Pentecostal congregation in Sweden, "Powerfully charged language is read, spoken, written, memorized, prophesied, translated . . . and, so it is believed, embodied not only in the flesh Christ, but also in that of his followers."[32] I follow RCCG members' emphasis on

---

31. All biblical citations are from the New King James Version (NKJV).
32. Coleman, *Spreading the Gospel*, 117.

the read Word, tracing Redeemers' shifting encounters with the "powerfully charged" text of Scripture.

If Redeemers' knowledge of the written Word eventually involved feelings of the Holy Spirit, mine merely involved explanations and performances of these feelings. Toward the end of my fieldwork, I did experience occasional and quickly fading sensations of vibrancy while I read my travel-sized King James travel Bible. My heart would quicken after reading a passage, and I would read the passage again, mentally sorting through its implications for my life. My Bible held a sense of possibility for me; part of me dearly wanted to know "the Word." However, my training as a social scientist kept me from embracing a view of Scripture as God's message or a conduit for the Holy Spirit. Without a commitment to Pentecostal doctrine, I was still "finding my way," as Redeemers put it; I was not yet born as a Christian person.

Beginning Bible Reading

"New believers are like infants in Christ," Pastor Ajayi liked to say at the end of Sunday services at Grace Sanctuary. Going on, he sometimes exclaimed, "The Bible is like milk. You need to read it every day to grow strong as a Christian." Church leaders blended the metaphor of bodily growth with a globally popular Pentecostal metaphor of spiritual warfare.[33] New members were told that as "infants in Christ," their hearts were susceptible to the sinful force of the Devil. Prayer was one method through which members could win the fight over their spirits and hearts: "Spiritual battle calls for what? Prayer to God," an assistant pastor of Grace Sanctuary urged. Reading the Bible was a second way Redeemers strengthened the born-again heart. Church leaders encouraged new RCCG members to imbibe the spiritual nourishment of Scripture by themselves and in collective Bible studies.

In Bible studies, new church members learned to utter into existence a three-part relationship between readers, God, and the Bible. That is, Redeemers who took part in Bible studies talked about the difference between their experiences as earthly humans and the transcendent God described in the page of their Bibles. Much of this cosmological category-making took form in didactic discussions about Christian lifestyle, and new members presumably applied this reading style to their solitary study. The beginner's Bible—like the Aladura Bible—was universal; its prescriptive narrative applied to all human life.

---

33. Robbins, "Globalization," 122.

One of the first Bible studies I attended at Grace Sanctuary showcased beginners' pronouncements of the person-Bible-God relationship. The day's topic was "Seek the Lord." An older woman standing at the front of the church read a passage out loud:

> Seek ye the Lord while he may be found, call ye upon him while he is near. Let the wicked forsake his way, and the unrighteous man his thoughts, and let him return unto the Lord, and he will have mercy upon him; and to our God, for he will abundantly pardon. (Isa 55:6–7)

The woman paraphrased the quote from Isaiah: "We must seek Him continuously, with all our hearts. This is what the Bible tells us." Next, the Bible study leader asked a question. "Who is God?" A few church members raised their hands. "He is the creator," 40-year-old Mr. Rotimi said. "God is love," another man offered. Next, young Mrs. Alejo took to her feet: "God is the I am that I am." The leader agreed, adding, "He is not past, present, or future, but ongoing. He is omnipresent."

Redeemers clearly viewed appreciation of God's greatness as a requisite attitude for a proper Christian lifestyle. Perhaps the Bible study was a space for practicing the felt aptitude of spiritual awe. Long-time members also may have experienced an intimate, felt connection to God as we discussed Isa 55; advanced readers did not limit their embodied interpretations of the Word to solitary reading. Still, in addition to embodying awe and even God in this and other collective Bible studies, Redeemers were focused on the work of creating cosmological categories. In repeated statements about God's greatness, Redeemers uttered into being God's existence, and by implication, his difference from humans. Redeemers' emphasis on the cultural and religious project of cosmology building, together with the wide range of biblical translations they used, may have contributed to a marked lack of disagreement in Grace Sanctuary about the significance of specific Bible verses.

The purpose of collective Bible study in the RCCG differs from the group Bible readings in Thomas Kirsch's ethnographic study of Pentecostal literacy in Zambia, in which he argues that people who were not intimate with the Holy Spirit required "spiritualized social intermediation" from church leaders.[34] Kirsch notes that Bibles were sparse in the Zambian context, and suggests the scarcity of personal Bibles lent significance to the "spirit-led" performances of leaders.[35] In contrast, new RCCG members—

---

34. Kirsch, *Spirits and Letters*.
35. Ibid., 137.

all of whom owned their own Bibles—used guided reading to shape their conceptualization of a God-centered world.

However, Redeemers were doing something even more complex in Bible studies than learning a Christian lifestyle and differentiating Christian persons and God. In group Bible readings, beginning readers also established a second cosmological difference, this one between the person and Scripture itself. During Bible studies, members developed generic explanations of biblical text that implicitly distinguished the person's feelings from the universal language of Scripture. In the lesson above, for instance, we discussed God's omnipresence and the mandate to "become like" God. These interpretations applied to everyone in the room, and in the context of our conversation had little to do with personal experiences and circumstances.

If beginning readers clearly distinguished between themselves, on the one hand, and God and the Bible, on the other hand, the third relationship constituting this cosmological formation—the relationship between God and text—was more ambiguous. Given Redeemers' insistence on God's greatness during collective Bible reading, did they think he loomed above Scripture or—alternatively—that God infused the text?

Advanced Bible Reading

In Bible-study classes and prayer sessions, evangelism trips and all-night vigils, I found that the answer to this question depended on a church members' adherence to the Christian lifestyle outlined in Scripture. The RCCG's Bible was an entity that filled with the presence of the Holy Spirit *if*—and only if—the reader's spirit was cleansed of sin. New RCCG members learned that when an unconverted person read the Bible, it would appear no different than any other sort of writing. However, when a purified Christian "close" to God read the Bible, the Holy Spirit jumped like a spark from the reader to the book, infusing the text with divine presence. As far as I could tell, the Word, *oro*, was like a finely crafted instrument that responded to the touch of a maestro.

Redeemers entered an advanced Bible reading stage when they began to feel, see, and hear God while reading Scripture. Deji, a friend and a pastor-in-training, described the Word from the perspective of an advanced reader while we sat on the stoop of his tailoring shop. Deji spent his spare time studying a stack of Nigerian- and American-published Christian books piled next to his bed, and between his pastoral training and independent reading, he was more familiar with Christian terminology than most advanced readers. "When you are talking of the Word, there is something we call '*logos*' that is the written Word of God, and then there is something we call '*rhema*.'" He paused and flipped through a Bible in his lap. "*Rhema* is the voice of God giving an understanding of his Word. If you have Christ, the Holy Spirit will be telling you a lot of things about that one verse."

Deji distinguished between two much-debated theological forms of Christian knowledge: *logos*, which Redeemers often referred to as "dead text," and *rhema*, which Redeemers sometimes called the Holy Spirit, the voice of God. Without the presence of the Holy Spirit, Redeemers insisted, Scripture was lifeless. As Pastor Ajayi sometimes repeated in reference to what he called the misuse of biblical text by non-Christians, ". . . for the letter killeth, but the spirit giveth life." (2 Cor 3:6) Without inspiration from God channeled by the Holy Spirit into the born-again reader, claimed Redeemers, the Bible was meaningless.

Deji went on to explain the theological formation of *rhema*, which all started with the departure of Christ from earth:

> When Christ was leaving, he said, 'I'm going, o', but I'm going to send unto you a Comforter. He will reveal everything you are reading here. Now you are going to have the revelation of this Word through the Holy Spirit.' When you have Christ, you will discover that even when God created the earth, everything was spoken into existence by the Holy Spirit. When you read it, for instance, you will see, 'God said let there be light,' and there was light. And when Jesus had performed what he wants to do here, he now said he was going to give us that Spirit again. . . . If you don't have the Spirit of Christ in you, you will just be reading the Bible as if you are reading a novel. In the moment you are reading the Bible, you can read only one verse and the Holy Spirit will be telling you a lot of things about that one verse.

Deji suggested that whereas the Holy Spirit was originally immanent in God's creative act of speech—"when God created the earth, everything was spoken into existence by the Holy Spirit"—the Spirit of God was now absent from the written form of the Bible when read by unbelievers.

For advanced readers like Deji, the contemporary Bible was like straw, drained of the divine life that had once given it freshness and vitality. But Deji did not see the Holy Spirit as altogether absent from the biblical text. Upon Jesus's departure, he explained, the son of God relocated the Holy Spirit from the biblical text to the born-again person. Like other Christians, Redeemers balanced their distance from Jesus with a corresponding proximity,[36] and they found this proximity in their direct experiences of the

---

36. Engelke, *Problem of Presence*, 16.

Holy Spirit. In turn, Deji implied, the born-again person brought the Holy Spirit with her to an encounter with the biblical text. "In the moment you are reading the Bible . . . the Holy Spirit will be telling a lot of things about that one verse." In other words, in the act of reading the Bible, the born-again person restored the Holy Spirit to the biblical text, resurrecting what Deji called the "living Word."

Over time, advanced readers complicated a view of Scripture as a static set of signifiers that held the same significance for everyone. Advanced readers continued reading practices that distinguish God and the Bible from the self, creating the categories constituting their Christian cosmology. However, these distinction-making practices unfolded alongside the work of feeling God and the Bible. In the convergence of three elements—text (*logos*), the voice of the Holy Spirit (*rhema*), and the embodied reader—Redeemers found the Word: a sensual, interpretive event.

The work, *ise*, of becoming a Bible reader in the Nigerian RCCG exemplifies Tanya Luhrmann's learning-centered approach to Christian subjectivity.[37] Similar to the American evangelical Christians studied by Luhrmann, Redeemers who experienced the Word mastered "techniques of identifying the presence of God through the body's responses" and used spoken categories to organize these sensations "into a new understanding of their bodies and the world."[38] Luhrmann brings a psychological slant to her research through an emphasis on cognitive and syntactical learning, and I refocus her lens on the production of embodied social discourse. Luhrmann's approach illuminates Redeemers' gradual accumulation of assumptions, spoken categories, and habits surrounding Scripture—a slowly built cultural assemblage that constituted the sensational form of the Word.

Redeemers recognized that biblical uses and significance shifted as "infants in Christ" matured, but they also acknowledged the variation of scriptural interpretations across long-time church members. When advanced readers vivified the Word's significance in lived experience, they highlighted how many interpretations—and destinies—one congregation could hold.

Finding the Future

Advanced readers in the RCCG sometimes experienced the Word during collective church events like Sunday services or Bible studies. Just as often, they "got in touch" with God through solitary Bible reading, or "meditation."

37. Luhrmann, "Metakinesis" and *God Talks Back*.
38. Luhrmann, "Metakinesis," 522.

While beginning readers tried to make a habit of reading the Bible once a day, advanced readers bragged about filling their spare moments with prayer and Bible reading. I cannot ascertain the accuracy of claims of frequent Bible reading, but I often noticed long-time church members looking at Bibles when I happened upon them during the day. During a three-month homestay with a devout Redeemer, moreover, I became used to reading the Bible with my host while we waited for rice to boil or for the electricity to return.

I also took part in meditation when my friend Kemi invited me to study the Bible with her over the course of several weeks. Kemi had converted to Christianity from Islam four years prior and had passed through several RCCG training programs on discipleship and religious leadership. She now managed the bookshop at the RCCG Headquarters in Ile-Ife, so she spent her days surrounded by Christian readers, films, and Bibles of various translations. An analysis of Kemi's meditation complements my interpretation of Redeemers' gradual mastery of the Word with an interpretation of the Word itself: a performance of scriptural significance that varied according to the reader's experiences and constructed his or her relationship to time. Scholars have examined both Pentecostal and non-Pentecostal evangelical groups that deploy the "common practice of radical recontexualization of Scripture,"[39] but Spirit-centered Pentecostal Redeemers like Kemi brought a distinctively embodied lens to the personalization of the biblical story.

Before my series of meditations with Kemi, I saw Redeemers' Word as similar to the Zambian Pentecostal concept of reading Scripture, which Thomas Kirsch describes as a "triad of texts, readers, and Spirit."[40] Both Pentecostal groups viewed the work of the Holy Spirit as instrumental to the reader's selection and interpretation of biblical passages. After my meditation sessions with Kemi, I modified my notion of the Word by adding a temporal dimension. Advanced Bible readers carried out a process of historiopraxy; they performed the text-reader-Spirit triad as a cosmological entity that extended into a lived present and constantly moved toward the future.

My understanding of the Word shifted most radically over the course of a single afternoon with Kemi. She placed her Bible on its spine and let it fall open, asked the Holy Spirit to guide our reading, and began to read aloud. "These things command and teach. Let no man despise thy youth; but be thou an example of the believers, in Word, in conversation, in charity, in spirit, in faith, in purity." (1 Tim 4:11–12) She stopped. "See? We are youth! 'Let no man despise thy youth.' We are young, but we cannot stop spreading

---

39. Bialecki, "Dialogue and Dissemination," 145.
40. Kirsch, *Spirits and Letters*, 127.

the Word of God. Praise the Lord," she added, and I supplied the expected response: "Hallelujah." Kemi used the term "youth" to refer to the relatively few years we had lived—both Kemi and I were in our mid-twenties—and to our shared status as unmarried adults. At 25, Kemi was running out of time to find a husband by Yoruba standards.

Kemi claimed to draw on the silent, interior voice of the Holy Spirit while she meditated on Scripture. It is possible that Kemi invoked the voice of the Holy Spirit because she had a stake in exhibiting her Christian zeal. Since the RCCG Headquarters only employed born-again Christians, Kemi's income depended on her reputation as a devout practitioner. Kemi may have reasoned that I held some administrative sway. However, Kemi's account of the Holy Spirit's voice was similar to other Redeemers' reports of encounters with the divine. Sometimes, Redeemers claimed they heard an audible voice from the Holy Spirit. More often, they described the voice as interiorized. Likewise, my research assistant and a long-time RCCG member, told me that the Holy Spirit's voice was like "intuition." "It is something deep inside you," she explained. "It touches you and talks to you."

Back in the bookstore, Kemi continued to read the first book of Timothy aloud: "Till I come, give attendance to reading, to exhortation, to doctrine. Neglect not the gift that is in thee, which was given thee by prophecy, with the laying on of the hands of the presbytery. Meditate upon these things—." (1 Tim 4:13–15) She interrupted herself. "The Holy Spirit is telling me another message. That one was for both of us, but this is just for you. The Holy Spirit is telling me that you were destined to preach the Word of God to others. That is what I am being directed to say. God intends for you to go out and preach the Word." Noticing my shocked expression, Kemi added, "When you get home, read this passage, and see what God tells you."

I did read the passage again that evening. Whatever aliveness Kemi found in the text eluded me. More palpable was my surprise at being included in Kemi's Bible-centered cosmology. Kemi's immediate surroundings—and her lived past and hopes for the future—shaped the Word's significance in the moment of meditation. Even as Kemi employed felt experience to *perform* the Spirit-filled Word, she drew on experience to *contextualize* that performative act. Kemi, like other Redeemers, used experience as a way to sense and to make sense of Scripture.

Inasmuch as Redeemers performed relationships to Scripture and God, they invoked the phenomenological bent of some anthropologists of religious experience who explore "modalities of human existence within ever-shifting horizons of temporality."[41] Redeemers articulated a hermeneutic

---

41. Desjarlais and Throop, "Phenomenological Approaches," 88. See also Desjarlais,

phenomenology that, from their perspective, momentarily broke down the boundaries between self and other, heaven and earth, Christian experience and Christian language. Still, Redeemers stressed that God was impossible to fully fathom. Again and again, I heard about how God was "omniscient, omnipresent, and omnipotent." Redeemers constantly referenced the ungraspable greatness of "the alpha and the omega": God encompassed human experience, but humans came nowhere close to encompassing God.

And yet advanced readers like Kemi did incorporate the "living Word" into a horizon of lived experience, weaving biblical text into a personalized, God-given story. This story unfolded toward the future: Redeemers claimed to uncover hidden messages about personal destiny in the Spirit-filled Word. Brother Abraham told a Sunday-school class one morning, "Our God is a revealer of deep secrets. He shows our destiny to us by the Holy Spirit so that we will not be a failure." He held a Bible above his head. "Our destiny is embedded in this Bible. If you want to discover your destiny, then search the Bible." In the act of reading, Redeemers established a Spirit-led present that would continue after that act was complete.

As discussed earlier, Redeemers shared with other evangelicals an emphasis on personal and historical rupture from a non-Christian past. Yet, their Scripture-based historiopraxy was less focused on breaking with a sinful past than with creating lived continuity with a holy future. In his study of Swedish charismatics, Coleman notes that historiopraxy ruptures with the past "even as it needs to work with the material of other aspects of past action."[42] Meanwhile, Redeemers show the extent to which the material of *present* action shapes evangelical constructions of time. Redeemers invoked unadulterated feelings of God to purify the present and perceive a realistic—though not yet real—near future.

Redeemers' biblical interpretations were informed by, and also framed within, overlapping geographical scales. RCCG members sometimes spoke about destiny on the global scale. They cited earthquakes in Latin America and tsunamis in Asia as signs of the apocalypse, the return of Christ. At other points, they situated destiny in national terms: as the 2011 presidential election approached, members of Grace Sanctuary gathered nightly to read the Bible and thank God for "taking Nigeria's future into [His] hands." Redeemers' interpretations of large-scale events were akin to those of Baptists in the American south, who understand lived events in terms of an

---

Body and Emotion; Jackson, *Relatedness*; and Csordas, *Sacred Self*.

42. Coleman, "Historiopraxy," 435.

overarching biblical narrative that begins with genesis and ends with the apocalypse.[43]

More often, though, Redeemers divined destinies that involved smaller-scale and more intimate concerns like relationships, grades, and the spiritual well-being of non-Christian friends. This is not to say that Redeemers did not experience Nigerian politics or global events in personal ways. Rather, the point is that Redeemers placed as much emphasis on readers' mundane near-futures as humankind's ultimate future, and even saw personal histories as constitutive of the Bible's collective history. For this reason, narratives of individualized and collective Bible-based destinies did not come into tension in the eyes of Redeemers. *Open Heavens* likened the expansiveness of pre-ordained destiny to a play: "Unlike human playwrights, His scripts are so all-embracing that one way or another, every human being finds himself or herself fitting into one of the roles or characters."[44] When each Christian plays their "role," they together form a collective future: "The greatest destiny anyone can have is to fit like a jigsaw puzzle into the Maker's plan for his or her life."[45] Through the Word, Redeemers lent significance to the Bible and to the "script" of everyday life.

Conclusion

Against a background of national precarity—Christian-Muslim riots in northern Nigeria; oil-related violence in southern Nigeria; uncertain flows of electricity, goods, and money throughout the country[46]—Redeemers' Bible reading took on particular resolve. As the electricity flickered off one morning, Kemi sighed in frustration and patted the Bible she held in her lap. "You just read every day! I ask God to give me the grace to let the Holy Spirit plan my days." Members of the Redeemed Christian Church of God in southwest Nigeria learned to "be the Word": to enliven Scripture through the bodily act of reading, and in turn, to frame "the Maker's plan" in terms of everyday experience. Nigerian Pentecostal Redeemers performed that God-given plan day after day, week after week, through repeated readings of the Bible.

Time figures into my examination of Redeemers' sensual hermeneutics as a perceptual experience and an objective measure of practice. As a perceptual experience, time was entangled with the physical; Redeemers'

43. Harding, *Jerry Falwell*.
44. Adeboye, *Open Heavens*.
45. Ibid.
46. Guyer, *Marginal Gains*.

embodied readings of destiny strained toward the future. Redeemers' future-oriented historiopraxy mirrors that of other evangelicals and Pentecostals who strive to rupture connections to a local past. Redeemers share striking resonances with Coleman's Swedish charismatic interlocutors, who make history by "taking time by the scruff of its temporal neck" and leading it forward.[47] However, while the Swedish Christians in Coleman's research guide time toward the apocalypse, Redeemers were equally concerned with the foreseeable future.

Moreover, if Coleman's notion of historiopraxy emphasizes Christians' attempts to divide the past and the present, Redeemers' experience-centered hermeneutics aimed to connect the present with the future. The embodiment of a desirable, Christian present was just as relevant for Redeemers' historiopraxy as an undesirable, non-Christian past. Further research might explore how bodily sensation figures into Christian constructions of time across varied historical and cultural contexts, particularly with respect to debates about continuity and rupture.[48] More specifically, studies might examine the relationship between sensation, time, and the use of Bibles, building on a growing comparative literature on the socially situated ideas and practices surrounding Scripture.[49]

My stage-based approach could be of use in these studies of Christian sensation and in studies of ineffable religious experience more broadly. Anthropologists who research religious experience have largely given up "attempt[s] to name-call into existence a phenomenon that refuses to be verbalized."[50] They turn their attention instead to the way "historically distinctive disciplines and forces" shape religious life.[51] In this vein, I borrow Tanya Luhrmann's process-oriented method to unpack the sequential relationships between, and the sociocultural effects of, the shifting practices and concepts that helped Redeemers learn the sensual Word. Redeemers created cosmological categories and a sense of religious subjectivity by reading Scripture first as a set of guidelines for holiness, and later as a felt manifestation of God-given destiny. A stage-based analysis illuminates the complexity and cultural reach of Redeemers' hermeneutic learning: the process of learning to read Scripture helped produce Redeemers' relationships

---

47. Coleman, "Historiopraxy," 433. See also Guyer, "Prophecy" and Scherz, "Ethics."

48. Robbins, "Continuity Thinking" and Engelke, "Discontinuity."

49. Bielo, "Textual Ideology"; Engelke, "Reading and Time"; and Harding, *Jerry Falwell*.

50. Van de Port, "Spirit Possession Ceremonies," 152.

51. Asad, *Genealogies*.

to the Christian cosmos and Christian self, which in turn authorized experiences of the "living Word."

My stage-based approach also opens the way for showing the ethnographer's shifting understandings of cultural practice. I have noted the dynamism of the Pentecostal Bible for me, the ethnographer, as well as for my interlocutors, in order to help readers evaluate my conclusions for themselves. Together with Redeemers' reading practices, my embodied interpretations co-construct what I represent as the Word. My fieldwork—and therefore my temporal frame—was limited to one year; a longer period of time might have revealed an even more complex and socioculturally generative process of learning to read the Bible. With more time in the field, I might even have joined my interlocutors in experiencing, or at least seeking, God through Scripture. Even if I do not "spread the Word" as Kemi predicted, though, I trace the edges of the Word's pulsing aliveness for Redeemers: its dynamic significance across and within the lives of church members, its hard-earned materialization in the act of reading, and its charged opening onto the not quite known.

Bibliography

Adeboye, E. A. *Open Heavens: Volume 11.* Lagos, Nigeria: Tie Communications, 2011.

Ajayi, J. F. Ade. *Christian Missions in Nigeria, 1841–1891: The Making of a New Elite.* Ibadan History Series. Evanston, IL: Northwestern University Press, 1965.

Asad, Talal. *Genealogies of Religion: Discipline and Reasons of Power in Christianity and Islam.* Baltimore: Johns Hopkins University Press, 1993.

Bialecki, Jon. "The Bones Restored to Life: Dialogue and Dissemination in the Vineyard's Dialectic of Text and Presence." In *The Social Life of Scriptures: Cross-Cultural Perspectives on Biblicism,* edited by James Bielo, 136–56. New Brunswick, NJ: Rutgers University Press, 2006.

Bielo, Jon. "Textual Ideology, Textual Practice: Evangelical Bible Reading in Group Study." In *The Social Life of Scriptures: Cross-Cultural Perspectives on Biblicism,* edited by James Bielo, pp. 157–75. Signifying (on) Scriptures. New Brunswick, NJ: Rutgers University Press, 2006.

Brouwer, Steve, Paul Gifford, and Susan D. Rose. *Exporting the American Gospel: Global Christian Fundamentalism.* New York: Routledge, 1996.

Coleman, Simon. *The Globalization of Charismatic Christianity: Spreading the Gospel of Prosperity.* Cambridge: Cambridge University Press, 2000.

———. "'Right Now!': Historiopraxy and the Embodiment of Charismatic Temporalities." *Ethnos* 76 (2011) 426–47.

Crapanzano, Vincent. *Serving the Word: Literalism in America from the Pulpit to the Bench.* New York: New Press, 2000.

Csordas, Thomas. *The Sacred Self: A Cultural Phenomenology of Charismatic Healing.* Berkeley: University of California Press, 1997.

Desjarlais, Robert. *Body and Emotion: The Aesthetic of Healing in the Nepal Himalayas*. Philadelphia: University of Pennsylvania Press, 1992.

Desjarlais, Robert, and C. Jason Throop. "Phenomenological Approaches in Anthropology." *Annual Review of Anthropology* 40 (2011) 87–102.

Engelke, Matthew. "Discontinuity and the Discourse of Conversion." *Journal of Religion in Africa* 34 (2004) 82–109.

———. *A Problem of Presence: Beyond Scripture in An African Church*. Berkeley: University of California Press, 2007.

———. "Reading and Time: Two Approaches to the Materiality of Scripture." *Ethnos* 74.2 (2009) 151–74.

Guyer, Jane. *Marginal Gains: Monetary Transactions in Atlantic Africa*. Chicago: University of Chicago Press, 2004.

———. "Prophecy and the Near Future: Thoughts on Macroeconomic, Evangelical, and Punctuated Time." *American Ethnologist* 34.3 (2007) 409–21.

Hackett, Rosalind. "Charismatic/Pentecostal Appropriation of Media Technologies in Nigeria and Ghana." *Journal of Religion in Africa* 28.2 (1998) 258–77.

Harding, Susan Friend. *The Book of Jerry Falwell: Fundamentalist Language and Politics*. Princeton: Princeton University Press, 2000.

Jackson, Michael. *The Palm at the End of the Mind: Relatedness, Religiosity, and the Real*. Durham: Duke University Press, 2009.

Keane, Webb. *Christian Moderns: Freedom and Fetish in the Mission Encounter*. Berkeley: University of California Press, 2007.

Kirsch, Thomas G. "Performance and the Negotiation of Charismatic Authority in an African Indigenous Church in Zambia." *Paideuma* 48 (2002) 57–76.

———. *Spirits and Letters: Reading, Writing, and Charisma in African Christianity*. New York: Berghahn, 2008.

Klaver, Miranda, and Linda van de Kamp. "Embodied Temporalities in Global Pentecostal Conversion." *Ethnos* 76.4 (2011) 421–25.

Lambek, Michael. *Knowledge and Practice in Mayotte: Local Discourses of Islam, Sorcery, and Spirit Possession*. Toronto: University of Toronto Press, 1993.

Luhrmann, T. M. "Metakinesis: How God Becomes Intimate in Contemporary U.S. Christianity." *American Anthropologist* 106.3 (2004) 518–28.

Luhrmann, T. M. *When God Talks Back: Understanding the American Evangelical Relationship with God*. New York: Vintage, 2012.

Marshall, Ruth. *Political Spiritualities: The Pentecostal Revolution in Nigeria*. Chicago: University of Chicago Press, 2009.

Marshall-Fratani, Ruth, and Andre Corten. *Between Babel and Pentecost: Transnational Pentecostalism in Africa and Latin America*. London: C. Hurst, 2002.

Meyer, Birgit. "'Make a Complete Break with the Past': Memory and Post-Colonial Modernity in Ghanaian Pentecostalist Discourse." *Journal of Religion in Africa* 28.3 (1998) 316–49.

———. *Aesthetic Formations: Media, Religion, and the Senses*. New York: Palgrave Macmillan, 2009.

Ojo, Matthews. "The Contextual Significance of the Charismatic Movements in Independent Nigeria." *Africa* 58 (1988) 175–92.

Peel, J. D. Y. *Religious Encounter and the Making of the Yoruba*. Bloomington: Indiana University Press, 2000.

Pew Research Center. *Global Christianity: A Report on the Size and Distribution of the World's Christian Population*. Washington DC: Pew Research Center, 2011.

Probst, Peter. "The Letter and the Spirit: Literacy and Religious Authority in the History of the Aladura Movement in Western Nigeria." *Africa* 59.4 (1989) 478–95.

Robbins, Joel. "The Globalization of Pentecostal and Charismatic Christianity." *Annual Review of Anthropology* 33 (2004) 117–43.

———. "Continuity Thinking and the Problem of Christian Culture: Belief, Time, and the Anthropology of Christianity." *Current Anthropology* 48.1 (2007) 5–17.

Scherz, China. "Let us Make God Our Banker: Ethics, Temporality, and Agency in a Ugandan Charity Home." *American Ethnologist* 40.4 (2013) 624–36.

Schutz, Alfred. *Collected Papers II: Studies in Social Theory*. Edited by Arvid Brodersen. The Hague: Nijhoff, 1964.

Tambiah, Stanley. *Culture, Thought, and Social Action: An Anthropological Perspective*. Cambridge: Harvard University Press, 1985.

Ukah, Asonzeh. *A New Paradigm of Pentecostal Power: A Study of the Redeemed Christian Church of God*. Trenton, NJ: Africa World, 2008.

Van de Port, Mattijs. "Circling Around the Really Real: Spirit Possession Ceremonies and the Search for Authenticity in Bahian Candomblé." *Ethos* 33.2 (2005) 149–79.

Subject Index

Africa, 4, 5, 11, 13, 15, 17, 19, 27, 29, 32–35, 37–41, 44, 46, 132, 140–48, 168, 190, 199, 227, 231, 246–47
alien, 5, 49, 130–35, 139, 142, 145, 148, 154, 164, 194, 227
alienation, 39, 41, 154, 215
Anabaptists, 49–57, 59–62
apostles, xi, 4–5, 12, 18–19, 22, 24, 27–29, 86–95, 97–113, 115–17
apostolic hermeneutics, v, xi, 86–93, 95, 97–105, 107, 109–11, 113, 115, 129
appropriation, 28, 34, 36, 39–40, 42–45, 56, 123, 125, 185, 227, 246
assimilation, 164, 182
authority, 19, 21, 23, 25, 28, 40, 53–54, 63, 65, 82–83, 102, 107–8, 117, 154–56, 169, 176–77, 182, 184, 195, 217, 228, 246, 247

Babylon, 32, 36, 39, 45, 101, 130, 134–35, 205
baptism, 18, 24–25, 55, 157, 232
believing community, 12, 16, 18, 27, 49, 63, 65, 67
biblical theology, 1, 85, 110, 117, 224
black theology, 40, 45–46, 190, 197, 199
born-again, vii, 226, 230, 234–35, 238–39, 241
Buddhism, 182, 186

Calvinist, 52–53, 56, 61, 68, 114, 157
Canaan, 33–35, 43, 130, 132–33
canon, 31, 55–56, 115, 117

Caribbean, viii, xi, 4, 31–37, 39–42, 44–47
Catholicism, 33, 55, 56
center (and margin), 78, 80–81
christocentrism, 16, 51, 56, 101–2, 111
Christology, 60, 143, 148, 177, 183, 185–86, 206, 224
circumcision, 81–82, 146
colonial discourse, 184–85
colonialism, 6, 32, 36–37, 46, 154, 169, 172, 175, 184–85, 230, 246
community of the Spirit, 4, 50, 52, 58, 62
confession, 17, 21, 101, 134, 137–38, 202, 212–14, 216–18
Confucianism, 174–75, 182
conquest, 35, 46–47
contextual Bible study, 5, 188, 190, 198–99
contextual hermeneutics/theology, 1, 3, 4, 38, 43
contrapuntal reading, 2
cosmology, 229, 233, 235–37, 239–41, 244
criminal-justice reform, 200
crucifixion, 80–82, 85
cultural negation, 36

Dalits, viii, xi, 5, 121–26, 128
"de-churched" society, 70, 72, 74
destiny, vi, xii, 6, 39, 135, 143, 165, 226–29, 233, 239, 242–44
discipleship, 137, 143, 148, 240
dissemination, 5, 150, 152–53, 160, 240, 245
domination, 55, 64–65

ecclesiocentric, 102
ecclesiotelic, 102–4
ekklesia, 75, 77
emancipation, 4, 32, 37, 126
embodied reading, 228–29, 236, 239, 244–45
empire criticism, 74
enlightenment, 12, 23, 86, 92
entextualization, 150, 152–53, 159, 171
epistemology, 59
eschatology, 88, 100, 108, 109, 148
ethics, vii, xii, 34, 60, 128, 148, 208, 244–47
evangelical, xi, 23, 26, 30, 78, 86–89, 91–93, 95, 98, 101, 105, 116, 142, 145, 147–48, 150–51, 157, 165, 167, 187, 224, 228, 237, 239–40, 242, 245–46
exegesis, 17, 29, 76, 89, 91–94, 98–102, 106–10, 115–16, 223, 225
exile, 5, 32, 37–39, 45, 130–31, 134–35, 140, 142, 145
exodus, xi, 4, 31–36, 38–40, 42–47, 97–98, 115, 124
exploitation, 1, 35, 41, 142

faith, ii, vii, 3–6, 13–6, 19–21, 23–25, 27–28, 35, 49–51, 56, 61–63, 76, 82, 84, 90, 103, 106–7, 122–23, 127, 130, 132–40, 143–48, 156–57, 169, 173, 176–79, 182, 185, 187, 190–91, 198–200, 240
fides divina, 21
fides humana, 21
Fiji, 149–50, 153–58, 162–66, 168–71
forgiveness, 16, 194, 202, 206–9, 215, 217–18, 222–23, 225
form criticism, 13
fundamentalism, 52, 54, 245
fusion of horizons, 13–14, 59

globalization, 2, 66, 228, 235, 245, 247
glorification, 79–80
glossolalia, 15, 21, 121
Greco-Roman world, 75, 146

Hagar, 40–43

hermeneutical circle, 13, 52, 92
historical context, 92–93, 99, 102, 114
historical-critical method, 26, 92–94, 102–3, 106–9, 172
historiography, 88
historiopraxy, 228, 240, 242, 244–45
"holiness," 230–32
homelessness, viii, 41, 188–89, 193–94, 197–99
hospitality, vii, 131, 135, 140, 145, 147, 223

identity, 1, 5, 19, 32, 36–39, 58, 67, 75, 121–24, 128, 130–32, 148, 182, 191, 219, 222
idolatry, 53
indigenous peoples, 5, 35, 43, 149–150, 154, 157, 162–65, 203, 211
inerrancy, 57, 105–6, 115–16, 173
interpretive methods/process, 14, 23, 91, 93–94, 100, 107
interpretive traditions, 91, 94–98, 100, 107
Israelites, 32, 35–36, 38–39, 42–43, 97, 124, 133–34, 163, 165

Jamaica, viii, 32, 37, 39, 46–47
Japan, viii, xi, xiii, 5, 172–75, 177–86, 194
Japanese imperialism, 5, 173, 180
Jesus, 4, 6, 14, 16–20, 28, 40, 51–52, 54–58, 60–64, 66–67, 76, 78–79, 82, 85, 89, 93–94, 100–102, 108, 112, 115, 122, 131–33, 135–36, 138–40, 143, 145–48, 151, 153, 155, 157, 161, 178–81, 183–84, 188–89, 192–95, 197–98, 205–11, 213–14, 218, 223–25, 238
Jewish community, 76
Judaism, 76, 89, 91, 98, 115–17, 213, 224
justice, viii, xiii, 6, 17, 31, 36, 45, 122, 144, 184, 190, 199–208, 212, 214–15, 218–19, 221–25
justification, 51, 56, 126, 142, 178, 186, 200

Kenya, vii, 130–32, 140–42, 144–47

SUBJECT INDEX 251

kerygma, 56, 109
Korea, 177–78, 181–83, 186

liberalism, 53–54, 65, 108, 173–74
liberation theology, 1, 12, 34–35, 40, 45, 47, 75, 122, 124, 189–91, 199
literal interpretation, 25, 108, 194
logos, 27, 174, 183, 185, 238–39
LXX, 78, 90, 96

magisterial reformers, 51, 55
marginalization, viii, 2, 4, 40, 70–77, 80–83, 95, 135, 145, 198, 208, 243, 246
meta-narrative, 24
methodology, 13–15, 24, 28, 44, 46, 100, 108–11, 116, 126, 128, 147, 153, 156, 169, 172, 223, 22526, 229, 232, 235, 244
missionaries, 26, 29, 70, 131, 135, 153, 157–59, 163, 172, 174, 181, 184, 230
modernism, v, xi, 5, 17, 27, 58, 86–89, 104

narrative tradition, 24–26
Netherlands Bible Society, 72, 73, 85
new birth/creation, 41, 52, 54
Nigeria, 6, 227, 229–31, 243, 245–46

oppression, 5, 35, 44, 59, 67, 81, 121
orthodoxy, 17, 175
Other, vi, 33, 188–89, 192, 242
outsider, 6, 41–43, 188

Palestinian, 37, 42, 91, 116, 210–11, 215
Pentecostal hermeneutic, 11, 12, 16–20, 22, 24–28
Pentecostalism, v, vii, viii, 4, 6, 11–30, 226–28, 230–32, 234–36, 240, 243, 245–47
pilgrim motif, vii, 5, 130–32, 137, 140, 142, 147
pilgrimage, 5, 39, 113, 130–33, 137, 139–140, 143, 145, 147–48
postcolonial biblical interpretation, 1
post-modernism, 57–58

poverty, 37, 41, 74, 141, 145
power, 2, 6, 15, 18, 21–22, 29, 35, 46, 66–67, 77, 80, 82, 93–94, 123, 125–26, 143, 150, 154–55, 160, 168–69, 171, 175, 178, 181, 184, 188, 191, 207–8, 231, 245, 247
praxis, vii, 16, 26
preferential option for the poor, 74, 124
pre-understanding, 12–13, 20, 24
promised land, 32–33, 37, 124
promise-fulfillment, 92
prophecy, 15, 22–23, 28, 97, 101, 241, 244, 246
Protestantism, 17, 52–57, 169, 172–74, 185

Rastas/Rastafarians, 36–39, 40, 44, 46
reading from the margin, 34
reception, 6, 31, 33, 35, 126, 140, 217, 226
reconciliation, 201–2, 206, 209, 216
reconstructionism, 111
redaction criticism, 13
Redeemed Christian Church of God/ RCCG, 6, 226–27, 229–32, 234–37, 239–43, 247
Reformation, 50–52, 54–55, 207, 225
Reformed doctrine of Scripture, 114–15
refugees, vii, 5, 123, 130–32, 135, 141–42, 145, 147
relativism, 58, 60
repatriation, 37, 39
repentance, 146, 193, 202, 208, 212–14, 218–19, 222
replication, 5, 149–50, 152–56, 160, 166–67, 171
restoration, vi, xii, 6, 72, 122, 200, 212, 217, 222, 225
restorative justice, vi, vii, viii, xii, 6, 200–5, 207–9, 212, 214, 222–25
revelation, 16, 22, 87–88, 101, 110, 114–15, 117–18, 183, 204, 238
Roman Empire, 76, 135, 179

salvation, 20–21, 23, 26, 39, 51, 53–54, 57, 61, 76, 134, 138, 157, 207, 230–31
samurai, xi, 5, 172–75, 179, 183–84
second naiveté, 57
Second-Temple period, 5, 88, 91, 93–96, 100, 106–7, 109, 111
Self, vi, 33, 188–89, 192, 242
Shinto, 176, 182, 186
slavery, 33, 35–36, 39–41, 43, 78, 80, 103, 141, 179, 190, 207, 216, 219
social location, 46, 217
sojourner, 130, 133
source criticism, 13
Spirit/Holy Spirit, 4, 6, 12–30, 50, 52–55, 58, 61, 62, 66, 76, 79, 81, 89, 101, 103, 106, 109, 123, 128, 161, 173–74, 179, 182, 203, 226–27, 230, 234–44, 246–47
subaltern, 123, 126, 128, 129
subjectivism, 21–22, 106, 111, 160
synoptic gospels, 24, 87, 106

text criticism, 13

theological education, xi, 4, 48–49, 61–63, 68, 129, 173
theological reflection, 32 44, 46–47, 128, 191, 199, 207
theology in the vernacular, 190–91, 197–98
Torah, 36, 178
tradition criticism, 13
transforming texts, 3, 4
translation, 48–49, 85, 90, 96, 117, 148, 150–51, 159, 168, 170, 221, 229, 236, 240
triumphalist interpretations, 4, 34

vernacular hermeneutics, 1, 2, 3, 7

word of God, 16, 20, 22, 23, 29, 44–45, 54, 112, 121, 128, 144, 151, 168, 190, 197, 226–27, 238, 241

Yahweh, 35–36, 43, 78

Zion, 37, 45, 140

Name Index

Acquah, B. K., 141n26, 147
Adeboye, E. A., 243n44, 245
Agosto, Efraín, 76n19, 84
Aichele, George, 191, 199
Ajayi, J. F. Ade, 230n15, 231, 234, 235, 238, 245
Allison, Dale C., 136, 147
Althouse, Peter, 22n82, 27
Anderson, Allan, 15n38, 25n98, 27
Archer, Kenneth J., 12n8, 19, 24n90, 25n96, 26n102, 27
Armitage, David J, 74n14, 84
Arno, Andrew, 164n59, 167
Arowele, P. J., 142, 145, 147
Arrington, F. L., 16n39, 27
Arul Raja, A. Maria, 123, 124n5, 128
Asad, Talal, 244n51, 245
Assmann, Aleida, 83n32, 84
Attridge, Harold W., 131, 136, 137, 139, 147
Autry, Arden C., 19n65, 27

Balkan, Erol M., 164n59, 170
Bailey, Kenneth E., 205, 210n22, 211n25, 213n33, 214n37, 215n38, 216n41, 220n50, 223
Barrett, David B., 141n24, 142, 147
Bauckham, Richard J., 97n24, 115
Bauman, Richard, 150, 168
Beacroft, A., 203n6, 223
Beale, G. K., 90n10, 92n13, 93n14, 106n38, 108n39, 110n43, 112n46, 115
Beasley-Murray, George R., 209n18, 223
Becker, Eve-Marie, 79n25, 84
Bediako, Kwame, 141n24, 142, 148

Beekers, Daan, 75n16, 84
Bernts, A. P. J., 71n3, 84
Bialecki, Jon, 240n39, 245
Bielo, Jon, 233n29, 244n49, 245
Billerbeck, Paul, 97n26, 117
Bloch, Renée, 98n27, 115
Bock, Darrell L., 93n14, 115, 215n38, 223
Bornkamm, Günther, 213n32, 223
Bovon, François, 209n18, 211n25, 215n38, 219n49, 223, 225
Bowen, H., 202n3, 223
Bowen, John R., 151, 168
Boyack, James, 202n3, 223
Braithwaite, John, 201n2, 225
Briggs, Charles, 150, 165n60, 168
Brouwer, Steve, 231n23, 245
Brown, Raymond E., 143n31, 148
Bryant, Joseph M., 74n13, 84
Burger, Isak, 19n60, 27

Cahill, Dan, 218n45, 223
Caird, G. B., 210n22, 223
Capell, A., 159n48, 160n50, 168
Caputo, John D., 60n22, 68
Cargal, T. B., 17n47, 27
Carr, David M., 75n15, 84
Casimira, Aisake, 163n56, 168
Castells, Manuel, 67n27, 68
Choge-Kerama, Emily J., vii, 5, 130
Clark, M. S., 17n46, 19n63, 27
Clark, Mathew, 22n84, 25n97, 27
Clarke, Sathianathan, 123n3, 124, 128
Clements, E. Anne, 75n15, 84
Coleman, Simon, 155, 168, 228, 234, 242, 244, 245
Collins, John J., 97n23, 115

NAME INDEX

Consedine, Jim, 204n7, 223
Cornwall, Susannah, 188, 189, 190n6, 199
Corten, Andre, 246
Crapanzano, Vincent, 149n4, 151, 152, 157n39, 168, 228n6, 245
Crossan, John Dominic, 206n12, 223
Csordas, Thomas, 242n41, 245

Dam, Peter van, 73n12, 84
Daniels, W. H., 16n44, 27
Davey, Andrew P., 191, 199
Davidson, Robert, 159, 168
Davie-Kessler, Jesse, vii, xii, 6, 226
De Beer, F. J., 18n59, 27
de Kamp, Linda van, 229n12, 246
de Wit, Hans, 57n17, 68
Dean, Eddie, 165n61, 168
Denk, H., 51, 52, 59n20, 68
Derrett, J. Duncan M., 205, 209n19, 210n21, 211n24, 214n37, 223
deSilva, David A., 131, 133n7, 136n14, 144, 146, 148
Desjarlais, Robert, 241n41, 246
Dillard, Raymond B., 87n4, 115
Dixon, R. M. W., 160n51, 168
Dohi, Akio, 173n2, 174n4, 185
Donovan, Vincent J., 191n12, 199
Driver, John, 57n16, 68
Du Plessis, David, 18n54, 27
Duranti, Alessandro, 150n6, 168

Ebina, Danjō, Xi, 172, 173, 174, 178–187
Edwards, Jonathan, 154, 155, 168
Ellington, Scott A., 21n79, 23, 28n86
Ellingworth, Paul, 133n7, 148
Elliott, John H., 76n17, 84
Ellis, E. Earle, 90n9, 91n11, 92n13, 93n14, 97n26, 101n32, 115
Engelke, Matthew, 154n25, 158n44, 168, 228n8, 231n24, 244n48, 246, 250n36
Enns, Peter, vii, xi, 4–5, 86, 87n2, 97n26, 98n27, 101n33, 109n42, 115, 116
Ervin, Howard M, 13n22, 28

Fackre, Gabriel J., 24n93, 28
Farrer, F. W., 206n14, 212, 223
Fee, Gordon, 97n26, 116
Fernández, Antonio González, vii, 4, 48
Fish, Stanley, 26n101, 28
Fitzmyer, Joseph A., 205n8, 209n18, 223
Foerster, Werner, 210n22, 224
Fogarty, Stephen, 17n50, 22n84, 26n104, 28
Forbes, Greg, 212, 214, 224
Ford, Margaret, 144n33, 148
Forrester, D. B., 198, 199
France, R. T., 111n46, 116
Friedman, Richard Elliott, 159n45, 168
Friedmann, Robert, 55n12, 68
Fuchs, Ernst, 209n18, 224
Furuya, Yasuo, 185

Gadamer, Hans-Georg, 12n10, 13n12, 14, 15n31, 28, 29, 58n18, 59n21, 69
Gee, Donald, 14n24, 28
Geraghty, Paul, 160, 168
Gifford, Paul, 231n23, 245
Gnilka, Joachim, 28, 210n23, 224
Goodwin, Charles, 150n6, 168
Gorringe, T. J., 198, 199
Gräbe, P. J., 12n7, 13, 14n23, 15n35, 18n53, 28, 29
Graham, Elaine L., 190, 191, 199
Green, Doug, 102
Green, Joel B., 209n18, 211n25, 224
Green, Sam, 157n40, 168
Green, William Scott, 98n27, 115, 116, 224
Greidanus, Sidney, 92, 102n35, 112n47, 116
Guyer, Jane, 243n46, 244n47, 246

Hackett, Rosalind, 227n5, 246
Halapua, Winston, 164n59, 168
Handman, Courtney, 151n9, 168
Harding, Susan Friend, 155, 156, 168, 228, 243, 244, 246
Harper, Michael, 16n44, 28

NAME INDEX

Harrison, James R., 75n16, 77n19, 84
Hart, Trevor A., 25n99–n100, 28
Harvey, A. E., 210n23, 224
Hawk, L. Daniel, 25, 28
Hawthorne, Gerald F., 76n19, 84, 117
Hays, Richard B., 102n34, 103, 111n45, 116
Heinz, Donald, 154n23, 164n59, 168
Hennelly, Alfred T., 190n9, 199
Hirakawa, Sukehiro, 185
Hirsch, E. D. Jr., 99n29, 116
Holgate, David A., 205n8, 209n18, 210n20, 212n28, 213n31, 214n36, 217n44, 219n47–n48, 220n51, 221, 222n55, 224
Hollenweger, Walter J., 24n95, 28
Holloway, Paul A., 77n19, 84
Houten, Christiana van, 134, 148
Hubmaier, Balthasar, 69
Huckle, John S., 23, 28
Hunter, A. M., 206n11, 209n18, 224

Iriye, Akira, 178n15, 181n31, 186

Jackson, Michael, 242n41, 246
James, Leslie R., 31, 32n3, 46
Jeanrond, W. G., 13n16, 14n27, 15n32, 28
Jeremias, Joachim, 209n18–n19, 212n29, 213n31, 224
Jesurathnam, K., 122n1, 128
Johns, Cheryl Bridges, 20n71, 28
Johnson, Luke Timothy, 210n22, 224
Johnstone, Gerry, 202n4, 224
Juel, Donald H., 98n27, 101n32, 116
Jülicher, A. von, 209n18, 220n49, 224

Kaiser, Walter C. Jr., 11n4, 12n6, 14n30, 15n31, 15n35, 28, 94n17, 99n28, 116
Kaplan, Martha, 153n17, 163n57, 164n59, 166n66, 169
Käsemann, Ernst, 143, 148
Kasper, W., 13n19, 28
Keane, Webb, 156n32, 157–58n41, 169, 228n8, 246
Kelber, Werner H., 206n13, 224
Kelly, John D., 164n59, 169

Kennedy, James, 73n12, 85
Kennedy, Philip, 11n2, 28
Kierkegaard, Soren, 156n34, 169
Kim, Mungil, 186
Kirsch, Thomas G., 236, 240, 246
Klaus, B. D., 17, 18n51, 29
Klaver, Miranda, 229n12, 246
Koester, Craig R., 136n12, 144, 148
Kohlenberger, John R., 137n21, 148
Krieger, Leonard, 87n3, 116
Kugel, James, 95n19, 97n24, 100n30, 116
Kuipers, Joel, 150n6, 169

Lambek, Michael, 233n28, 246
Lane, William L., 131, 132n6, 148
Lategan, B. C., 11n1, 12, 13n15, 13n17, 24n91, 29
Lawrence, Louise J., 190, 199
Lederle, H. I., 17n46, 19n63, 27
Lenski, R. H. C., 206n14, 224
Leschert, Dale F., 109n42, 115, 116
Lightfoot, John, 91n11, 116, 177
Lindars, Barnabas, 109, 110, 116, 117
Linnemann, Eta, 210n23, 211n25, 212n29, 220n49, 224
Lochmann, Jan Milič, 29
Long, V. Philips, 116
Longenecker, Bruce W., 78n23, 85
Longenecker, Richard, 91n11, 92n13, 100n31, 101n32, 106n38, 107, 108, 109, 111, 116, 148
Lowe-Ching, Theresa, 34, 44, 46
Luhrmann, Tanya M., 155n25, 169, 229, 239, 244, 246

Ma, Wonsuk, 16n42, 29
Mackenzie, Steven, 189n5, 199
Macrae, Alan, 203n5, 225
Maliekal, Jose D., 122, 123, 128
Manson, T. W., 209n18, 210n22, 213n31, 224
Marchal, Joseph A., 77n19, 84
Marshall, Christopher D., vii, xii, 6, 200, 202n3, 223, 224
Marshall, I. Howard, 92n13, 117, 209n19, 213n31, 224
Marshall, Ruth, 231n22, 232n25, 246

Martin, Ralph P., 76n19, 84, 117
Mazrui, Ali A., 141, 148
McCalman Turpie, David, 89, 116
McCartney, Dan G., 92n12, 93n14, 100n32, 101n33, 116
McClung, L. Grant, 19n61, 29
McNamara, Martin, 91n11, 116
McQueen, Larry R., 20, 21, 24, 29
Meeks, Wayne A., 74n13, 85
Melanchton, Monica Jyotsna, 126n9, 128
Menzies, Robert, 26n103, 29
Meyer, Birgit, 228, 231n24, 246
Miki, Makihara, 168, 170, 171
Mikkers, Tom, 71n5, 85
Mittelstadt, Martin W., 24n94, 29
Miyazaki, Hirokazu, 153, 156, 169
Möller, François Petrus, 16, 17n45, 20n67, 21, 22n80, 28, 29
Moo, Douglas J., 92n13, 93n14, 94n17, 117
Moore, Basil, 190, 197, 199
Moore, George Foot, 213n30, 224
Moore, Richie D., 20, 29
Morisy, Ann., 191, 199
Mosala, Itumeleng J., 44, 45, 46
Moyise, Steve, 91n11, 93n15, 100n31, 103n36, 117
Murphy, Jeffrie G., 207n16, 224
Murrell, Nathaniel Samuel, 34n9, 36, 37, 46

Nel, Marius, viii, 4, 11, 19n60, 27
Nelson, Alissa Jones, 2, 6
Nelson, P. C., 20n68, 24n93, 29
Ness, Daniel van, 202n4, 224
Neusner, Jacob, 213n30, 224
Newland, Lynda, 154, 169
Neyrey, Jerome H., 97n24, 117
Nicole, Roger, 92n13, 117
Nixon, David, viii, 5–6, 188, 189n4, 190n6, 199
Norton, Robert, 164, 165n63, 169

O'Brien, Peter T., 76n19, 85
Ojo, Matthews, 231n21, 246
Olofin, Sam, 141n26, 148
Ouchi, Saburo, 173n3, 186

Owens, Joseph, 38, 39n21, 46

Paas, Stefan, 72n8, 85
Palmer, Richard E., 11, 29
Paul, Herman, 71n4, 85
Peel, J. D. Y., 230n16, 246
Penney, John Michael, 25, 26n103, 29
Perkins, Anna Kasafi, viii, xi, 4, 31, 42n26, 46
Pinnock, Clark H., 23, 29
Plaisier, Arjan, 72n7, 85
Plummer, Alfred, 206n14, 210n22, 213n33, 216n41, 218n46, 219n47, 224
Pohl, Christine D., 131, 148
Probst, Peter, 230n19, 247

Rad, Gerhard von, 134, 148
Rajkumar, Peniel Jesudason Rufus, viii, xi, 5, 121, 125n7, 128
Rance, DeLonn L., 12n9, 14n26, 22n83, 29
Ratuva, Steven, 165n62, 169
Ravuvu, Asesela D., 164n59, 170
Razu, I. John Mohan, 122n2, 129
Resseguie, James L., 217n43, 225
Reumann, John, 76n19, 85
Rhee, Victor (Sung-Yul), 137, 138, 148
Ricoeur, Paul, 14, 15n34, 29, 57, 69
Ritova, Stan, 165n61, 168
Robbins, Joel, 153n17, 166n67, 170, 228n7, 231n24, 235n33, 244n48, 247
Rooy, Sidney, 61n25, 69
Rose, Susan D., 231n23, 245
Royce, James S. H., 158, 170
Rutz, Henry J., 164n59, 170
Ryle, Jacqueline, 164n59, 170

Said, Edward W., 2, 3n6, 6, 42, 43n30, 47
Sailhamer, John H., 101n33, 116, 117
Sandford, Michael J., 74n14, 85
Sawa, Masahiko, 186
Sawin, Theophilus P., 152, 170
Schafroth, V., 18n55, 30
Scherz, China, 244n47, 247

NAME INDEX 257

Schieffelin, Bambi B., 153n17, 168, 170
Schinkel, Dirk, 82n31, 85
Schmeets, Hans, 71n2, 85
Schnackenburg, Rudolf, 15n36, 30
Schutz, Alfred, 233n28, 247
Schütz, Christian, 13n21, 30
Scott, Bernard Brandon, 218n46, 219, 225
Scott, Michael W., 166n67, 170
Sebastian, J. Jayakiran, 127, 129
Segundo, Juan Luis, 190, 199
Shaffer, Thomas L., 207, 225
Shaner, Katherine A., 77n22, 85
Silva, Moisés, 11n4, 12n6, 14n30, 15n31, 28, 90n9, 117
Silverstein, Michael, 149n4, 150, 170, 171
Smit, Peter-Ben, ix, 4, 70, 77n21, 79n26, 80n27, 81n28, 82n30, 85
Smith, Ashley, 33n7, 34, 47
Snel, Jan Dirk, 72n6, 85
Snodgrass, Klyne, 90n10, 106n38, 117
Srebrnik, Henry, 164n59, 170
Stadler, Ulrich, 54, 69
Stark, Rodney, 74n13, 85
Stine, P. C., 151n8, 170
Strack, Hermann L., 97n26, 117
Strang, Heather, 201n2, 225
Stronstad, Roger, 17, 19n64, 26, 30
Stuhlmacher, Peter, 15n33, 30
Sugirtharajah, R. S., 1, 2, 3n7, 6, 84
Suzuki, Torisho, 186

Taber, Charles R., 94n17, 117
Takeda, Kiyoko, 174n4, 186
Tambiah, Stanley, 233n30, 247
Taneti, James, 126n8, 129
Taylor, Steve, 102
Thiselton, Anthony C., 3, 7, 12, 13n13, 30
Thomas, G. C. H., 47
Thomas, John Christopher, 30
Thomas, Nicholas, 163n57, 170
Thompson, James W., 78n23, 85
Thornley, Andrew, 158n42, 159n47, 170
Throop, C. Jason, 241n41, 246

Tippett, Alan R., 153, 170
Tissot, Yves, 205n9, 225
Toews, Barb, 223, 225
Tomioka, Koichirō, 181n32, 186
Tomlinson, Matt, ix, xi, 5, 149, 153n17, 155n27, 160n53, 161, 162n54, 164n59, 170, 171
Toren, Christina, 163n57, 171
Toy, Crawford Howell, 88n6, 117
Turnage, Marc, 17n48, 30
Turner, Bryan S., 84
Turner, Max, 224
Tuwere, Ilaitia S., 154n24, 162, 163, 171

Uchimura, Kanzō, Xi, 172, 175–181, 183–186
Uemura, Masahisa, 185, 187
Ukah, Asonzeh, 230n20, 247
Urban, Greg, 150, 152n13, 170, 171
Urk, Eva van, ix, 4, 70

Van de Port, Mattijs, 244n50, 247
Van der Walt, S. P., 22n81, 30
Vanhoozer, Kevin J., 105n37, 117
Van Till, Howard J., 88n5, 117
Vattimo, Gianni, 58n18, 69
Veenhof, Jan, 18n52, 30
Vermes, Geza, 95n19, 117
Via, Dan O., Jr., 206n12, 208n18, 209n20, 211n23, 213n32, 216n40, 225
Vos, Geerhardus, 110, 117

Walls, A. F., 141n24, 148
Walton, Heather, 191n12, 199
Walzer, Michael, 42, 43, 47
Wansink, Craig S., 77n20, 85
Ward, Frances, 191n12, 199
Warfield, B. B., 114, 117
Warrior, Robert Allan, 35, 43, 47
Wataze, Tsuneyoshi, 187
Wawire, Pius, 20n68, 24n93, 29
Wielenga, Friso, 73n12, 85
Williams, Delores S., 40, 43, 44, 47
Williams, George Huntston, 50n4, 60n24, 69
Williams, J. Rodman, 16n43, 30

Williksen-Bakker, Solrun, 164n59, 171
Wittgenstein, Ludwig, 58n19, 69
Wittig, Susan, 206n13, 225
Witvliet, Theo, 190, 199

Yoder, John Howard, 64n26, 68, 69, 134, 148

Youdell, Deborah, 191, 199
Young, Brad H., 211n25, 214n37, 225
Young, Davis A., 88n5, 117
Young, Florence S. H., 158n44, 171
Yumi, Murayama, viii, xi, 5, 172

Zehr, Howard, 201, 203n5, 223, 225

Scripture Index

Hebrew Bible/Old Testament

Genesis

1–2	152
1:26	5, 149, 150, 159–167
12:6	103
15:13	133
16:1–16	41
21:9–21	41

Exodus

1:15	97
3:6	93, 94
6:8	35
10:16	214
17	95, 96, 112
17:11	95
20:8–10	134
22:21–23	134
23:12	134

Leviticus

6:1–7	214
19:9–10	133
25:23	133

Numbers

5:6–7	214
21:16–20	97

Deuteronomy

14: 28–29	133, 134
16:1	133, 134
16:13	134
26:5	134
26:12	134
33:2–3	96

Job

19:25	181
30:30	30

Psalms

32:5	214
51:4	214
69:9	103, 104
119:83	38
127:1	153
137	180

Proverbs

12:19	234

Ecclesiastes

10:8	153

Song of Songs

3:1–5	60

Isaiah

1:4–6	180
2:3	20
44	18
49:8	101, 102
53	152
55:6–7	236

Jeremiah

14:2	38
29:11	135

Lamentations

4:8	38
5:2	154, 164
5:10	38

Ezekiel

37	18

Daniel

2	184
9:2	20

Hosea

1:1	20

Joel

2	18
2:8	38
3	18

Micah

3:9–10	45

Habakkuk

2:10	38

New Testament

Matthew

2:15	101, 107, 109
5:5	180
5:38–42	178
5:45	223
10:34	179
10:35	179
18:3	50
20:28	182
22:23–33	87
22:29	93
22:33	94
23:7–10	64
23:11–12	64

Mark

12:18–27	87
16:15	151

Luke

2	189
2:49	221
3	189
4	189
4:1–24	189
4:5–7	195
4:16	192
4:22–24	192
4:24	195
4:43	221
5:1–32	189
5:1–3	197
5:10	197
5:29–31	193
6:38	234
7:36–50	189
7:37–38	195
7:41–43	193
9:22	221
9:51	131
9:58	131
11:42	221
15:1–3	218
15:7	221

15:10	221	7:22	97
15:11–32	189, 204	7:53	96
15:11–13	194	10	178
15:11	209	15	22
15:12	222	25:8	214
15:13–19	209		

Romans

15:13	210
15:15	212
15:17–20	196
15:17–19	209
15:17–21	213
15:17	213, 215, 222
15:18	209, 216
15:19	213
15:20	213
15:21	209, 216
15:22	216

12:2	234
12:9–13	135
13:1–2	154
13	180, 183
15:1	103, 135
15:1–4	103
15:2–4	104

1 Corinthians

15:24	215, 216, 217
15:25	217
15:27	221, 222
15:28	219
15:29–30	208, 215, 221
15:29	208, 215, 216, 219, 220, 221
15:30	209, 210

2:4–5	21
10:4	97, 106, 115
15	152

2 Corinthians

15:31	221
15:32	215, 216
17:3–4	214
18:11–12	218
20:27–40	87
20:37	93
20:39–40	94
22:36	179

3:6	238
6:2	101, 106
10:5	234

Galatians

1:10	234
3:16	103, 106
3:19	96, 106
3:29	103
4:21—5:21	41

John

3:16	xi, 149, 150, 157, 158, 167, 168
14:24	20
16:13	18
17:14	20
17:17	20
20:26–29	122

Philippians

1	77, 80, 83
1:12–18	78
1:19–24	79
1:29–30	80
2	77, 79, 80, 82
2:1–11	152
2:5–11	78, 80, 82
2:7	78
2:9	80
2:9–11	81
3	77, 83

Acts

1:5, 8	16
2	25
7	96
7:2–53	95

Philippians (continued)

3:2	81
3:3	81
3:14	82
3:17	82
3:19	82
3:20–21	82
4:10–20	80
4:11–12	79

1 Thessalonians

4:15	20

1 Timothy

3:2	135
4:11–12	240
4:13–15	241
3:8	97
3:14–17	105

Titus

1:2	135

Hebrews

1:1–14	138
2:1–2	138
2:1	139
2:2	96
2:3	136
2:5	131
2:10	143
2:17	114
2:20	143
3:1	138
3:5	139
3:12–13	144
3:12, 19	139
3:14	140, 144
4:16	144
5:8	139
5:11	131
6:9	131
6:10–12	144
8:1	131
9:5	131
10:22–23	138
10:22	144
10:25	144
10:24–25	140
10:26–29	138
10:32–38	139
10:34	140
10:35–39	138
10:35	140
10:36–12:13	137
11:1–12:29	137
11	96, 146
11:1–39	138, 139, 140
11:3–31	95
11:9–10	133
11:10	130, 132
11:13–16	144
11:16	132
11:32	131
12:1	139
12:1–2	140
12:1–4	139
12:2	139
12:3–4	139
12:3	139
12:4	139
12:18–24	140
12:22	133
13:1–3	140
13:1–2	144
13:2	135, 145
13:3	145
13:5	145
13:6	145, 146
13:7	144
13:12–16	139
13:13	139, 144
13:14	142
13:16	145
13:23	136
16	140
26–28	133

1 Peter

2:11	135

2 Peter

2:5 97

Jude

9 97
14–15 97

Revelation

1:14 38
12:11 144

Apocryphal/Deuterocanonical Books

1 Enoch

1:9 97

Tobit

11:5–15 216

Pseudepigrapha

Jubilees

1:27–29 96
2:1 96

www.ingramcontent.com/pod-product-compliance
Lightning Source LLC
Chambersburg PA
CBHW071247230426
43668CB00011B/1628